CROSSING CULTURAL BOUNDARIES

CHANDLER PUBLICATIONS IN ANTHROPOLOGY AND SOCIOLOGY
Leonard Broom, *General Editor*

ANTHROPOLOGY
L. L. Langness, *Editor*

CROSSING
CULTURAL
BOUNDARIES

The Anthropological Experience

Edited by

SOLON T. KIMBALL *University of Florida*

AND

JAMES B. WATSON *University of Washington*

CHANDLER PUBLISHING COMPANY
An Intext Publisher
SAN FRANCISCO • SCRANTON • LONDON • TORONTO

Library of Congress Cataloging in Publication Data

Kimball, Solon Toothaker.
    Crossing cultural boundaries.

    (Chandler publications in anthropology and sociology)
    Bibliography: p.
    1. Anthropology—Field work.   2. Anthropology as
a profession.   I. Watson, James Bennett, 1918–
joint author.   II. Tilde.
GN33.K5   301.2   71–169580
ISBN 0–8102–0434–7

To all who, feeling the bond of brotherhood, yet find
wondrous the diversity of man

Contents

Illustrations

MAPS

PHOTOGRAPHS

Acknowledgments

To all those who help to bring a book into being the debt is usually great and one's ability to convey thanks is limited. The present book is no exception.

If the individual selections and the book as a whole convey to interested readers, to our colleagues, and in particular to the oncoming generation of anthropologists some sense of becoming and being an anthropologist; then we believe that we can say for all who have helped to produce this book that their efforts have been properly rewarded.

As editors, we wish to express our sincere appreciation to each of the contributing authors. In a special sense this book is theirs because it was through their efforts that a goal has been achieved.

Notes on Contributors

JAN VAN BAAL is Professor of Cultural Anthropology at the State University of Utrecht. He was Director of the Department of Anthropology of the Royal Tropical Institute at Amsterdam and was associated with the University of Utrecht as an Extraordinary Professor, teaching theory of religion and theory of acculturation. His early career was in the administrative service of the then Netherlands East Indies, and he became Governor (1953–1959) of Netherlands New Guinea. He did field work in Lombok (Indonesia) and New Guinea, the latter being his choice for regional specialization. His studies of the Marind-anim culture, initiated by his doctoral dissertation, culminated in the publication of *Dema*. He has also written *Over Wegen en Drijfveren der Religie* and *Mensen in Verandering*, and he expects to publish in English a comprehensive study of the theory of religion. He has in recent years concentrated on problems of structure in culture.

HOMER G. BARNETT is Professor of Anthropology at the University of Oregon. He was with the Bureau of American Ethnology (1944–1946) and for a decade after World War II was involved in anthropological studies and administration in the Pacific. He was a member of the National Research Council's Coordinated Investigation of Micronesian Anthropology, a staff anthropologist for the Trust Territory of the Pacific Islands, and a member of the Research Council of the South Pacific Commission. He was also Adviser on Native Affairs to the Netherlands government of New Guinea, during which time the episode described in this book occurred. He has held summer visiting professorships at Harvard University, Columbia University, the University of Hawaii, and the University of British Columbia. He was a Senior Research Fellow of the National Science Foundation, a Fellow at the Center for Advanced Study in the Behavioral Sciences, and is a past president of the Society for Applied Anthropology. His books include *Palaun Society, Being a Palaun, Innovation: The Basis of Cultural Change, Indian Shakers*, and *Anthropology in Administration*.

PAUL BOHANNAN is Professor of Anthropology and Education and Stanley G. Harris Professor of Social Science at Northwestern University. He holds a doctorate from Oxford University, and has taught at Oxford and Princeton. He has done field work in Nigeria, Kenya, and among middle-class American divorcées in the Bay Area of California. He has been a Fellow at the Center for Advanced Study in the Behavioral Sciences and a Senior Postdoctoral Fellow of the National Science Foundation. He won the August Vollmer Award for *African Homicide and Suicide* and the Herskovits Award for *Tiv Economy*. His other books include *Justice and Judgment among the Tiv, Africa and Africans, Social Anthropology,* and *Divorce and After.* He is, with Laura Bohannan, co-editor of the *American Anthropologist* (beginning in 1970).

WILLIAM E. CARTER is Director of the Center for Latin American Studies and Professor of Anthropology at the University of Florida. He has also taught at the University of Washington, Brooklyn College, and the National School of Social Work in La Paz, Bolivia. Earlier he taught in an Aymara boys' school —an experience which led him to graduate study in anthropology at Columbia University, where he received his doctoral degree, and to several years of research among the Aymara in the Bolivian Highlands. He is the author of *Aymara Communities and the Bolivian Agrarian Reform, New Lands and Old Traditions, The First Book of Bolivia,* and *The First Book of South America.*

GEORGES CONDOMINAS is Director of Studies at the Ecole Pratique des Hautes Etudes. A Eurasian, he was born in North Vietnam. He received his secondary education in Paris and his law degree in Hanoi. Mobilized in Indochina (1940–1946), he saw service in the navy and spent six months in a Japanese prisoner-of-war camp. Upon returning to Paris, he studied for a *licence ès lettres* while undertaking his professional training at the Centre de Formation aux Recherches Ethnologiques of the Musée de l'Homme. As an ethnologist with the Office of Overseas Scientific and Technological Research seconded to the Ecole Française d'Extrême-Orient, he went to Vietnam (1947–1950)—a mission which formed the subject of *L'Exotique est quotidien.* Awarded the Diploma of the Ecole Pratique des Hautes Etudes for his book *Nous avons mangé la forêt de la Pierre-Génie Gôo,* he subsequently undertook missions to Togo, Madagascar, and Thailand (including a brief visit to Săr Lŭk, Vietnam). He has worked for UNESCO in Laos, Cambodia, Taiwan, the Philippines, and Indonesia. He has held visiting professorships at Columbia University and Yale University. He has also written *Fok'onolona et collectivités nirales en Imerina.*

WILLIAM N. FENTON is Research Professor of Anthropology at the State University of New York in Albany. He received his training at Yale University and began field work among the Seneca in 1933, at Six Nations Reserve in

1939. In 1950 he studied factionalism at Taos, New Mexico; Klamath, Oregon; and among the Blackfeet in Montana. He was United States Indian Service Community Worker among the Iroquois (1935–1937), taught at St. Lawrence University (1937–1938), and was with the Bureau of American Ethnology (1939–1951). He was the first Executive Secretary for Anthropology and Psychology at the National Academy of Sciences–National Research Council (1952–1954) before becoming Assistant Commissioner for the New York State Museum and Science Service (1954–1967). He holds the Cornplanter Medal for Iroquois Research and the Peter Doctor Award of the Seneca Nation. A past president of the American Folklore Society and the American Ethnological Society, he has also served on the executive board of the American Anthropological Association. Since 1952, he has been on the Permanent Council of the International Union of Anthropological and Ethnological Sciences. Besides editing *Parker on the Iroquois,* he has written *American Indian and White Relations to 1830* and *Contacts between Iroquois Herbalism and Colonial Medicine.*

ROSEMARY FIRTH is Lecturer in Health Education at the Institute of Education of the University of London, where she concentrates on the family and social services, illness and deviant behavior. Her particular interest is in developing theoretical insights in the applied fields of teaching, social work, and public health. She was graduated from the University of Edinburgh in economics in 1935. The following year she married Raymond Firth and accompanied him to Malaya (1939–1940)—a field trip which provided the basis for her contribution to this book. During World War II she worked for the Board of Trade, gathering information about shortages of household goods, and afterwards retired for about ten years of maternal domesticity. In 1956 she took up voluntary social work with the London County Council's school health service and received a diploma in social science and administration from the London School of Economics, after which she taught for five years in a college of education. In 1963 she revisited Malaya briefly and subsequently published a revised second edition of *Housekeeping among Malay Peasants.* Recently she has turned her attention to women's problems in the Western world.

ANTHONY FORGE is Senior Lecturer in Social Anthropology at the London School of Economics. His formal training in anthropology was received at Cambridge University. His research interests and field study include primitive art in New Guinea and kinship in London. His first trip to New Guinea, which lasted about two years, was financed by the Horniman Fund, and during his second trip (1962–1963) he was a Fellow of the Bollingen Foundation. He has also been involved in a cooperative study of kinship in a middle-class sector of London. Since 1964 he has been Managing Editor of the London School of Economics Monographs on Social Anthropology. During the fall term of 1969 he was Visiting Professor of Anthropology at Yale University. With Raymond Clausen he edited *Three Regions of Melanesian Art, New Guinea and the New Hebrides.*

SYLVIA GRONEWOLD is a student of social anthropology at the University of Washington. Her earlier training, at the University of Chicago, was in English and history. After teaching for a time, she became interested in social work and criminology, both of which were specialties of her husband, David Gronewold, who teaches in the School of Social Work at the University of Washington. Her graduate study in anthropology at the University of Washington and at the London School of Economics was supplemented by a period of field work at an institution for girls. Her master's thesis, "The Fantasy Family in a State Training School," was based on this field work. Her training in history attracted her to a study of early American anthropologists—of the motivations which led these men of diverse background and training to the anthropological field. Among the most colorful of the anthropologists of the late nineteenth century was the almost legendary figure of Frank Hamilton Cushing—the subject of her contribution to this book.

A. IRVING HALLOWELL is Professor Emeritus of Anthropology at the University of Pennsylvania. He received his education at the University of Pennsylvania and with the exception of several years at Northwestern University and visiting appointments at a number of other universities has been associated with his alma mater for his entire professional life. His field work with the St. Francis Abenaki, first published in 1928, inaugurated a lifelong study of the Algonkian-speaking peoples—in later years, particularly the Ojibwa and Salteaux. He is a past president of the American Anthropological Association and the American Folklore Society, a recipient of the Viking Medal, and a member of the National Academy of Sciences and the American Philosophical Society. Though best-known for his work in culture and personality, notably on the use of projective techniques, his writing and his erudition are of much greater breadth. The largest collection of his writings is *Culture and Experience.*

SOLON T. KIMBALL is Graduate Research Professor in the department of anthropology at the University of Florida. He has also held academic appointments at Columbia University's Teachers College, the University of Alabama, and Michigan State University. He has been Visiting Professor at the University of Chicago, the University of Puerto Rico, the University of California at Berkeley, the University of Oklahoma, and the Princeton Theological Seminary. Immediately before World War II he worked for the United States Departments of Agriculture and Interior on the Navajo reservation and later with the War Relocation Authority. He was a UNESCO consultant to the Brazilian Center for Educational Research and was the campus coordinator for an AID project with the Peruvian Ministry of Education (1963–1964). He is a past president of the Society for Applied Anthropology and of the American Ethnological Society, and has been a Faculty Research Fellow of the Social Science Research Council and a Guggenheim Fellow. He is co-author of *Family and Community in Ireland, The Talladega Story, Education and the New America,* and *Culture and Community.*

NANCY OESTREICH LURIE is Professor of Anthropology at the University of Wisconsin at Milwaukee and has served as department chairman (1967–1970). Her major interest is in American Indian studies, with particular reference to culture-contact adaptations and the contemporary scene, the foci of extensive field work among the Winnebago in Wisconsin and Nebraska and the Dogrib of northern Canada. She has served frequently as a consultant and expert witness for attorneys representing tribal clients before the United States Indian Claims Commission, and in 1961 was Assistant Coordinator to Sol Tax of the American Indian Chicago Conference. *The American Indian Today,* which she edited with Stuart Levine and to which she contributed two articles, won the Anisfield-Wolf Award in 1968 as the best scholarly book in intergroup relations. Her other publications include *Mountain Wolf Woman: Sister of Crashing Thunder,* the annotated translation of the autobiography of a Winnebago Indian.

MARGARET MEAD is Curator Emeritus of Ethnology at the American Museum of Natural History, Adjunct Professor of Anthropology at Columbia University, Visiting Professor in the School of Psychiatry at the University of Cincinnati, and Chairman of the Social Sciences Division and Professor of Anthropology at Fordham University's Liberal Arts College (Lincoln Center Campus). She has conducted research among nonliterate peoples of the Pacific and among literate peoples of the Western world. She has been active in many interdisciplinary projects, including those concerned with child care and rearing, hunger and nutrition, mental health, and the urban environment. She is a past president of the American Anthropological Association and the World Federation for Mental Health. Among her well-known writings are *Coming of Age in Samoa, Growing Up in New Guinea, Keep Your Powder Dry, An Anthropologist at Work: Writings of Ruth Benedict,* and *New Lives for Old.* Her most recent work is *Culture and Commitment: A Study of the Generation Gap.*

THERON A. NUNEZ is Associate Professor of Anthropology and Assistant Dean of the Graduate School at the University of Florida, where he has taught since receiving his doctorate from the University of California at Berkeley in 1963. His current research interests include peasant society and culture, middle America, and the anthropology of death. Although he bears a Spanish surname, he acquired his knowledge of the language and culture of Mexico as an adult, for his antecedents were Protestants from the state of Georgia. He has published several articles based on his research in Cajititlan, Mexico, and served as consultant for an educational film portraying traditional life in that village.

KALERVO OBERG is Professor of Anthropology at Oregon State University. He has also taught at Cornell University and the University of Southern California. He retired from federal-government service in 1963. His twenty-five years of government work included the Department of Agriculture in the Southwest and teaching and field-work training of students in Brazil as a member of the Institute of Social Anthropology of the Smithsonian Institution. He has contributed field research in applied anthropology to various foreign-aid programs in Ecuador, Peru, Brazil, and Surinam. His early field work was in Alaska and Uganda. In addition to two monographs on the tribes of Mato Grosso, Brazil, he has contributed to anthropological journals in the United States and England, but much of his work consists of unpublished government reports. He thinks of himself as a field worker of the "old school" and likes to mention that, besides his field research, he has mushed dogs in Alaska, hunted big game in East Africa, paddled canoes on the Amazon, and ridden horses on the plains of southern Brazil. More than that of anyone else, his writing has given currency to the term and concept of "culture shock."

MARTIN G. SILVERMAN is Associate Professor and Chairman of the Department of Anthropology at Princeton University, where he has taught since 1966. He attended Harvard University (B.A. 1960) and the University of Chicago (M.A. 1964, Ph.D. 1966) and was a Fulbright Scholar at the Australian National University (1960–1961). His book *Meaning and Struggle in a Resettled Pacific Community* is a study of a century of symbolic and social transformations in the Banaban community, both in their original homeland (Ocean Island, Gilbert and Ellice Islands Colony) and on Rambi Island (Fiji), to which the Banabans moved in 1945.

NORMAN STOKLE is Assistant Professor of Romance Languages at the University of Washington. Born in England and educated there, in Canada, and in the United States, he has degrees from Durham University (B.A.), the University of British Columbia (M.A.), and Syracuse University (Ph.D.). He has annotated and published translations from the French of both dramatic works and literary criticism. He is particularly interested in the avant-garde theater of France, a country he has visited often and where he feels quite at home. His translation of Georges Condominas' chapter for this book is his first effort in the literature of anthropology.

ANTHONY F. C. WALLACE is Professor and Chairman of the Department of Anthropology at the University of Pennsylvania. He is also associated with the Eastern Pennsylvania Psychiatric Institute as a Medical Research Scientist. He has served as a consultant to or member of a variety of groups or committees, including the Research Advisory Committee of the Commonwealth Mental Health Research Foundation, the Fellowship Review Panel for Behavioral Sciences of the National Institute of Mental Health, the National Research Council of the United States Office of Education, and the Social Science Advisory Committee of the National Science Foundation; he was president of the American Anthropological Association in 1971–1972. He has carried on research among the Tuscarora and Seneca Indians and in the field of mental health. He has been awarded research grants by the American Philosophical Society and the National Institute of Mental Health. He has been a Faculty Research Fellow of the Social Science Research Council. He is the author of *Culture and Personality, Religion: An Anthropological View, King of the Delawares: Teedyuscung, 1700–1763,* and *The Death and Rebirth of the Seneca.*

JAMES B. WATSON is Professor of Anthropology at the University of Washington. Since 1959 he has been Principal Investigator for the New Guinea Microevolution Project. He was educated at the University of Chicago (A.B. 1941, A.M. 1945, Ph.D. 1948). He has also taught at Washington University, St. Louis (1947–1955). He was Associate Editor of the *American Anthropologist* (1963–1966) and is a past president of the Central States Anthropological Society and a former Senior Specialist of the East-West Center. He has also been a consultant to the United Nations' Fund for the Development of West Irian. His principal field work has been in the Eastern Highlands District of Australian Papua–New Guinea (1953–1955 and 1963–1964). In addition to numerous articles in journals, he has contributed chapters to several books and has edited *New Guinea: The Central Highlands.*

MARTIN M. C. YANG is Emeritus Professor of Rural Sociology, former Chairman of the Department of Agricultural Extension, and Director of the Graduate Institute of Extension Education at National Taiwan University. He has been Visiting Professor of Sociology at Cornell University, Stanford University, and Hartford Seminary Foundation. He did research on Chinese social structure at the University of Washington. Prior to the Communist occupation of mainland China, he was Professor of Sociology and Chairman of the Department of History and Sociology and then Dean of the College of Liberal Arts at Cheeloo University. He received his postgraduate training in sociology and cultural anthropology at Yenching University and Cornell University. His published works include *A Chinese Village,* which was the product of research at Columbia University under the direction of the late Ralph Linton; *Chinese Social Structure* (published in Taipei); and *Socio-Economic Results of Land Reform in Taiwan,* prepared while he was a Senior Specialist at the East-West Center.

CROSSING CULTURAL BOUNDARIES

INTRODUCTION

More than a decade ago, the editors of this book found themselves of an evening at an after-hours gathering, one of those informal sessions that spring largely from the collegiality of common expatriation. "Anthropological shop-talk" only roughly describes such proceedings. Perhaps that particular evening was more lively than others we had known. Certainly the anecdotes—a majority of them in essence interethnic encounters—came forth almost end-lessly, each evoking another. Whatever the reason, the thought struck us both: here was a genre of experience of considerable intrinsic interest—the accounts as entertaining or dramatic as one had learned to expect. It not only provided a code in which one could tell his peers he is an anthropologist and hear the same from others, but also had in fact much to say about what anthropology is—above all, much that is not readily accessible. "Someone ought to write some of these things down," one of us commented. We agreed they would make a fine book.

The hard core of such conversations is usually "the field"—as well it might be, for there is no other subject or setting more distinctive of what anthropolo-gists do, none more indelible for the doers. It does not matter fundamentally whether the field is a hunting band of desert Bushmen in Africa or a commu-nity of tribal horticulturalists in the New Guinea Highlands; a peasant village of India or a symbiotic town-and-country situation of the American Midwest; a hundred fishermen on a mile-square atoll or scattered thousands of steppe pastoralists or a ghetto. The field is for many an anthropologist—in theory for all who are concerned with the living varieties of man—both apprenticeship and initiation into a guild. It is frequently the testing ground for his skills, his quality as a craftsman. Its day-to-day challenges and encounters may some-times be his personal trial. In the midst of an act so deliberate and unsolicited, there must be few who have not asked themselves: What am I doing here? Why —or how—do these people accept me? What do I owe them that they do accept me? And few, surely, have failed to answer these questions in some fashion, imaginative or mundane.

1

There is sometimes the hint of an almost mystical "field," a romantic Grail attainable only by the gifted of mind, the sensitive, the dedicated. Except in a formal study of field work, a lengthy consideration of this view would be out of place. It was at any rate no part of our impulse to confirm, much less extend, the image of the anthropologist's data-gathering mission as sacred or ineffable! Whatever remains obscure about the endeavor probably arises in part from the remoteness and intangibility of the field for all but those who have been there. Romanticism has to some degree battened upon the combination of a transient oral lore and a paucity of self-critical writing. The field *has* been elusive, its life almost limited to after-hours conversations and quasi-private classroom reminiscences. That is, its *authentic* life has had such limits, for the situation of the anthropologist-in-the-field has enjoyed a surprisingly large and public pseudolife in the form of innumerable jokes and cartoons—a genre of humor that surrounds what is on the one hand a bizarre but fascinating notion, on the other a business scarcely known. (There is also the Hollywood caricature, the jungle heroine's scientist father, equally absurd but quite humorless.) It is usually possible to know with what facts or formal theories a man entered the field, with what ideas he returned. Rarely, however, could one see much of what happened in between. Surely it could not all have been so straightforward as presented in the formal report. But what *had* it been? From this perennially unanswered question comes the aura: the personal field as something one would have to know on his own or never know, the field mission as the solitary quest.

As for reasons that can explain the lack of writing, the most extreme claim is that the profounder incidents of field work are incommunicable but for mere externality. Less romantic and more immediate is the tradition—almost a code —of the third person: the anthropologist does not go to the field to discover or write of himself but to write of the subjects of his research. He does so, moreover, in a manner that as far as possible ignores his own presence among them. This is deliberate. Not only is the field trip not a personal odyssey and not reportable as such, but its purpose is to provide a profile of the group "as they really are"—*au naturel.* Since few groups, except in jokes, come regularly equipped with a resident anthropologist, that means a profile drawn as of before the observer's arrival or at least one drawn apart from him. (There is furthermore the ethical injunction that the observer be in fact as unobtrusive as possible in the life of his hosts.) Still other reasons have doubtless contributed to making the field unrecorded and little known. One of them is the intellectual and academic emphasis on what is rational and matter of fact, even prosaic. This bias militates, surely, against dealing with the subjective improvisations and ambiguities of one's own existence in the field. If these are not trivial, they may be embarrassing. They are not usually compatible with the published findings. Furthermore, it may be thought profitless or *infra dig* to review the intellectual false starts, impasses, and errors that afflict the observer in his observation and understanding of the study people. So the finished report typically projects a smoothness of fit that quite belies whatever doubting and brainwracking may underlie its composition or qualify its orderliness. Finally, in anthropology as in other walks of life, perhaps including that of the professional writer, few indeed are insightful and gifted enough to write engagingly of their calling or their personal experience of it. For the many it is only the singular incident, the lively anecdote that is sufficiently obvious or compelling to overcome a lack of facility and style. The subtler aspects of living and studying among strange, perhaps unlovable hosts are sacrificed for the merely curious, for bits of humor or excitement.

Though scarcely well formulated, thoughts like these probably account for the abruptness of our agreement on the evening in question. The idea then was a fairly simple one: to record and document, to make a book of some of the unwritten material that first prompted us. We would gather a sample of the things anthropologists could but seldom did say about themselves or their work. We might even think especially of persons who had had unusual experiences or who were known for their skill as raconteurs. There might also be ancedotes, some of the "good stories" of the fraternity. Even by itself a collection of heretofore off-the-record tales would reflect a neglected dimension of anthropology that is real enough and also important.

As so often happens with sudden inspirations, however, we did not for some time go beyond the mutual conviction that what had occurred to us would be something worth doing. It was several years—actually, since we live at opposite ends of the country, several meetings—later that we decided as partners to attempt a book of the sort we had imagined. In November 1966 we agreed to go ahead with the project by turning first to colleagues for their advice and suggestions. By then each of us had given the book further reflection and we were resolved not to stress the purely anecdotal and often ephemeral incident for its sheer entertainment. Primarily we hoped to show, whether through anecdote or otherwise, some of the intimate aspects of the practice of anthropology.

Thus in the spring of 1967 we wrote to some three dozen anthropologists informing them of the objectives of the book we planned and requesting their comments. We enclosed a descriptive statement entitled *On Becoming and Being an Anthropologist: A proposal to assemble for publication as a book a variety of experiences of anthropologists which have relevance for professional development.* Much of the original statement, written in April 1967, still seems to us to be valid for expressing the purpose and function of the book as it now exists. Some passages, in fact, serve as well to preface the selections that comprise this book as anything we might write anew. In addition, the statement will give the reader an indication of the terms in which we invited our contributors to join us in the present venture.

"Anthropologists in the course of graduate training or later professional activity often undergo experiences which significantly affect their understanding and interests. Or the events of a career—cumulatively—lead them toward singular scientific, ethical, or aesthetic perspectives not captured or fully expressed in the typical professional writing of the field. Some experiences are intimately related to the direction or success of their work. Most of them reveal something about what anthropologists are like or what it is like to be an anthropologist. If nothing more, they indicate the surprises, the excitement, the charm, or the disappointments of the field. Sometimes, however, the experience has a marked effect upon research, upon relationships with other people, upon personal or professional outlook.

"Particular experiences, if colorful, may be related as anecdotes among friends or at professional gatherings. Their greatest use, however, rarely exceeds enlivening a conversation or classroom lecture. The anecdotes are but infrequently recorded in serious writing. The longer developments that shape or orient the professional anthropologist are left for biographies, more often than not never written. To the extent that it is public at all, this segment of anthropological experience—in contrast to the reporting of formal findings—constitutes a largely oral tradition, the significance of which could be expanded and made explicit.

"The anthropological posture is characteristically ethnographic: to write about other people, not about oneself, except perhaps about the logic of one's inferences or conclusions. Data are detached from professional experience. The possible contribution of much of this experience to the field at large is thus limited, precarious, or in due course simply lost.

"Yet in sum these experiences are important. As a body of lore they reflect anthropology and anthropologists. Oftentimes they contain important truths about the conduct of field work or about the intellectual and professional orientation of members of the profession. They reflect the anthropologist's self-image or the image and expectations that he discovers others have of him. They measure the viability of the ideas and ideals with which he tries to work or the insights he has in matters of rapport. The experiences challenge or define his ethics, sharpen his purpose in becoming an anthropologist—or sometimes defeat him. Even the incident that seems merely colorful can suggest the curious juxtapositions of motive and relationship to which one may be brought in pursuit of anthropological objectives.

"We are convinced that this body of experience is rich and that it should be moved from the verbal realm of anthropological literature to some more permanent and generally available record. Our goal is not alone to preserve representative and interesting items of professional experience—though that in itself would be worthwhile. It is also to call attention to the implications of some of the unrecorded incidents and developments of anthropological careers. We believe the material is intrinsically valuable, for example, in the preparation of students for the field and the profession. It should also be valuable to an ever-larger professional group in which the personal reminiscence and the professional anecdote can no longer be shared as it once was in the small and intimate anthropological circle of yesteryear. Such material, it seems to us, is far more significant of the practice and purpose of anthropology than its present, largely haphazard status suggests. We believe that a representative variety of such experiences should be recorded and analyzed to show the professional development of the individual, and their relevance to anthropology.

"Various settings can be imagined in which significant experiences have occurred. One naturally tends to think first of field work with its often fascinating incidents. Here is the anthropologist at work in his own shop, the shop which affords him—and, vicariously, others—the intellectual and emotional (and perhaps the physical) adventure uniquely identified with the discipline. Unquestionably, field-work settings should be well represented in the book we propose. There are other settings, however, which have conditioned the careers of anthropologists. These might be the setting in which an individual was deflected from another career into choosing anthropology; they might include his graduate training, highlighted perhaps by the influence of a great book or a great teacher, or an association with an insightful layman, colleague, or student, an engagement as a consultant, a membership in a large, multidisciplinary enterprise or organization. Even a difficult encounter with suspicious and sensitive officialdom, of which one published account exists, could be germane. In a word, we believe that a wide range of situation exists in which experience relevant to the theme of the proposed book has occurred.

"It is unlikely that we as editors could imagine in advance all possible topics and aspects of the general theme, what it is to be an anthropologist, or the difference that particular conditions of professional practice have in a given case made, either to anthropology or to the individual anthropologist. Each contribution will reveal something about becoming or being an anthropologist. It will illustrate conditions which an anthropologist may encounter and which some anthropologist has encountered. It will reflect the impact of some experience upon the individual's knowledge of himself as a professional anthropologist, his understanding of the place of anthropology in the culture of which it is part, or the reasons for what are to him the most feasible, urgent, or rewarding tasks or emphases of the anthropological field.

"We would hope for some indication of what brings men and women into anthropology, and the kinds of men and women. What particular purpose? What dedication? How realized, how modified, how frustrated by the professional experience? If anthropology is for some a 'spirit quest,' what are the forms it takes, what its satisfactions? What are the varieties of sublimated idealism: the anthropologist as spokesman for those with no voice of their own; as the sole recorder of an endangered tradition; the cultural conservator; as the apologist for practices that may but for judicious exposition be defamed, sensationalized, obscenely rendered; as the domesticator of the exotic; as the adversary of parochialism; as the professional estranged; as the unsentimental materialist; as the unromantic scientist; and so on.

"The list suggests the variety of purposes and dedications held by various anthropologists. We would want at least one valid instance of radical identification of anthropologist with the studied group—'going native.' There is the sometimes critical problem of departure from one's group and subsequent reentry to the academic environment. We equally want to document the abandonment of cherished ideas, the disappointment of expectations, perhaps those fostered by one's very choice of a career or inculcated by respected masters.

"We propose to canvass some of our colleagues for their ideas of the kinds of experiences the book should contain, and if possible their suggestions to anthropologists—themselves or others—with such experience to report. With as broad a view as we can obtain through our own knowledge and the help of colleagues, we propose to invite a number of anthropologists to contribute to the book. Each contributor would write of experience he regards as significant for his own career. In a few cases, we hope to ask those sufficiently informed to describe the unique experience of some individual now deceased.

"The organization of the accounts may be broadly similar, though the substance will vary greatly. Each contribution would describe setting, actors, precipitating act or cumulative development, and consequences. The consequences, together with the writer's reflections, would provide the methodological and theoretical richness of the piece.

"Our goal is to produce a book in which the student or reader can see the field with some of the intimacy of those within it, and perhaps even with greater intimacy than some of those within it now see it."

These words are sufficient to recount the birth of an idea and to trace its formulation. In the chapters which follow, each of the anthropologists describes some encounter with the lives of other human beings which had special meaning for him. The chapters are divided into three groups but only very loosely. All reflective writing must be in some sense retrospective, so that one cannot characterize any chapter simply as "historical." What the chapters of Part I share is a perspective of the larger career of an individual, a relatively long and continuous interplay between the person and his hopes and experiences as anthropologist. Most of the chapters of Part II, on the other hand, deal with particular problems or situations, brief but eventful periods or episodes—sometimes crises—that occurred in the course of field work; how the writer then coped or how, with the power of hindsight, he now wishes he had coped; and how event and outcome on reflection relate more generally to the anthropological experience. "Field method" is much too didactic a subheading for a book like the present one, but some of the chapters of Part II are at least close to that concern. The chapters of Part III are the most resistant to labeling. To call them "personal" might suggest that the preceding sections were dedicated to detached description and analysis. Say, rather, that the chapters of Part III depict singular experience or singular response to experience, their primary emphasis being the pure affect of unusual events which could not easily be replicated and which could thus be taken only in a general way as representing something larger.

It is no small irony that in a field where personal involvement is both deep and inevitable the literature is largely committed to the third person. This must also be no small part of the reason that the experiential field has remained indeterminate. Only two of the chapters in this book—on Cushing and Malinowski—are written in the third person, and each concerns an ethnographer whose self was especially prominent in his record and his writing. In the rest of the book there is neither an intermediary writer nor a fictional anonymity. Because it consists almost entirely of anthropologists writing of themselves we believe this volume will add measurably to limning the anthropological experience.

Part I / ANTHROPOLOGY
AS CAREER

1 / From Wife to Anthropologist

ROSEMARY FIRTH

A FORMAL VIEW OF FIELD EXPERIENCE

Most people embark on field work because they want to become professional anthropologists. With me it was the other way round. I was drawn into the situation when I accompanied Raymond Firth to Malaya in 1939 for a year's study of the economics of the fishing industry. I found it a fascinating experience, as others have done, and it ultimately led me to attempt theoretical study, which of course would ordinarily precede field study.

I suppose I have always remained on the edge of the profession, looking on at the involvement of others in analysing alien societies and tentatively applying some of the insights gained in this way for my own personal satisfaction, mostly in trying to understand what is involved in teaching and in social work.

Just because my involvement was at first that of an amateur, perhaps I had more time to reflect on the situation of the observer, as well as on the many experiences marginal to the actual collection of field data. I have always been intrigued by the two-way interaction which must go on in any field situation; this aspect is only just beginning to be looked at professionally.

Field work can be seen as an attempt to understand, by close and direct contact, how a living community works and what the beliefs, norms, and values by which it lives are. The close and direct contact between the anthropologist and the society he investigates is a personal and unique experience which can never be literally duplicated. Other workers in adjacent areas, or later workers in the same area, may try to check, expand, or reinterpret material previously collected; but not even the worker himself can repeat exactly his original experience in any particular field. It is a necessary result of studying human material, using the human personality of the investigator as one of his most powerful tools. While the training of the anthropologist aims to help him use his personality to best advantage, it does not aim to make him a nonhuman or automatic collector of information. Hortense Powdermaker has written:

he will be expected to behave according to some status assigned him by the local people. If not overtly viewed as a potential enemy, at least he is likely to be seen as some kind of official, missionary, or teacher, according to the previous experience which the local people have of educated Europeans. Before he can do work of any real value, he has to extinguish the image of this status and create for himself a new one. This will be accompanied by what Meyer Fortes (1962, p. 72) has called "the imposition of distinctive imperatives of apparel, speech, conduct, and behaviour."

ENTRY INTO A PROFESSIONAL WORLD

It may be that this rather formal way of considering the impact of field experience was forced upon me, owing to the fact that my marriage precipi-tated me, as a young girl, into the small, well-integrated group of anthropolo-gists centred mainly round Bronio Malinowski and the London School of Economics department in the 1930's. I was, at this time, a very young and very inexperienced new graduate from Edinburgh. There, under the guise of some-thing called "political economy" I had studied Durkheim and Maine, Adam Smith and Alfred Marshall, and I intended to use my training to become a social worker, not then as common a goal for young women graduates as it is now. Raymond, however, nearly twelve years older than I and already an experienced worker with *We, the Tikopia* almost ready for publication, had no intention of letting that happen. He wanted at that time to study the social economy of peasant farming somewhere in Southeast Asia, and nothing seemed more natural than that I should go along with him, to help in a general way. It also seemed appropriate that I should attend some of the lectures and seminars which were going on at the school at that time.

The initial shock of being precipitated into this group of experienced people was considerable. I had never before been among those who, so it seemed to me, brought their professional interests so consistently into their social life. I well remember my wondering amazement at a luncheon party in 1935 in Great Ormond Street when I was introduced to Lucy Mair and Audrey Richards, and it seemed to me as if the conversation was conducted entirely in a code which I could not understand. References to "affines," "joking relationships," "reciprocity," "food exchange," and "kula partnerships" cropped up at men-tion of every subject on which conversation was likely to be interesting, and I seriously began to wonder whether I should ever be able to get used to this curious way of conducting social interchange. The obvious thing to do seemed to be to learn the language and habits of the group into which I was marrying, and I think that this is how I saw my abashed entry to Malinowski's famous seminars at that time.

I came as a special guest, as an observer strictly, not as a participator. That is, I was not expected to contribute a paper, nor did I—as far as I remember —take any part in discussion. Bronio was well known for his "interaction"

A quite new development, not yet strong enough to be called a trend, is
that the field-worker is himself an inherent part of the situation studie
personal as well as scientific reactions, are an important part of the r
(Powdermaker, 1968, p. 422).

The more I think about it, the more clear it becomes to me th
such thing as *the* typical field experience which might be describe
or laymen, but only individual experiences resulting from conta
individual and his field at one time. Valuable insights, which
develop and evaluate the field skills of the anthropologist, m
considering the unique experiences of others. But since the skills
craft skills, each must practise them in his own way. By observ
his craft, one may perfect and refine one's own skills. It should b
to add that the value of the finished result depends at least as
theoretical problems posed as on the methods used to elucidat
I am going to talk about here is field method in its effects on t
I am concerned only indirectly with its effect on the theoret
studied.

We have very little descriptive material, particularly on early
such as were used by the anthropologists of a generation ago.
them were too busy in theoretical consideration of their mate
methodology, perhaps someone like myself, marginal to anth
provide some data on the conditions and difficulties of field activi
years ago.

In an illuminating study of his own field methods, John Beat
the criticisms of those who allege that

social anthropologists are so obsessed by field work for its own sake tha
for them a kind of mystique, and has become a sort of indispensable
for the aspiring professional ... essentially a ritual that must be perform
before he can become one of the elect (Beattie, 1965, p. 57).

In my opinion, the view that field work provides an experie
to a rite of passage for the social anthropologist is no romantic
one which can be argued on strictly analytic grounds. In orde
collect his material, the anthropologist must temporarily detacl
the accepted behaviour and point of view of his own society a
of an alien group. It is not fantastic to conceive this process as
tion, transition, and *incorporation*—in the classical terms used I
Gennep. Although this may not be seen, in the culture he aspir
a ritual performed by the novice, it can, I think, usefully be tl
ritual which he has to undergo and which, moreover, he will
undergo most easily if he understands it in these terms.

When the anthropologist comes into the field he is to study

method of teaching; he engaged his students from the first and provoked them to think and argue, rather than laying out lines of theoretical thinking for them and inviting them to follow.

I was pretty much out of my depth, and used to marvel at the ingenious theoretical arguments which he developed out of seemingly unrelated material —as a conjuror produces rabbits out of a hat. I do not think, however, that my bewilderment arose just from stupidity. There was something very special about the group at that time, but in particular all of them had been in the field, and their intellectual efforts were squarely concentrated on bringing theoretical order into empirical material which they knew at first hand. I, on the contrary, had no first-hand experience of an alien culture, but I learnt something about teaching general sociology to beginners, which is perhaps of even more relevance today than it was then.

Theories are attempts to understand and to coordinate observed facts, whether these facts are shapes seen under the microscope, or regularities or irregularities in human behaviour. One of Malinowski's favourite sayings in these seminars was that one cannot begin to collect facts without some theory, nor can one develop a theory excepting one based on a few facts. The first necessity in learning a new discipline is to understand what kinds of fact it examines as well as what kind of theory it deals with. In the new behavioural sciences, every student has to make his own discovery that what he is to be trained to observe are facts visible only in their effects, not directly. The concepts of marriage, family, chieftainship, law, and religion are all symbolic ideas which press people in a society to conform to certain patterns of behaviour. But the student has to learn that these social facts are differently perceived in different cultures, and to do this he has first to get rid of some preconceptions about them from his own culture. The reason I was out of my depth in this seminar is the same reason that many young students today assimilate the "jargon" of sociology or social anthropology without ever realising how the terminology relates to social reality. They may learn to speak the language of science, without having anything to say, because they have never really "seen" the raw material.

Just as I could not at first understand the constant references at that first lunch party to "joking behaviour," "avoidance," and so on, because I could not see that there was anything to explain, so students need to be taught to "see" the social material before them in order to understand what it is their theories attempt to explain. If one has not been in the field, this is much more difficult than many teachers believe. Much early learning, as a result, is just so much verbiage, absorbed without any conception of the reality to which it corresponds.

Field work quickly shows one how differently other people conceive of what they do, as well as how differently they actually do similar things, so that theoretical discussion about differences in behaviour takes on new meaning after one has experienced it. Just as there are levels of experience, so there can be levels of comprehension, which extend knowledge at different levels. These second-level flashes of comprehension have been described by field workers, forced to compare the new cultural experience they were learning with the one they had learnt from birth. Examples of such intuitive revelations have been given, for instance, by Audrey Richards (1956) when she described how, greeted one morning by the freshly initiated girls after the *chisunga* rituals, she understood anew the meaning of "rites of transition." Laura Bohannan (Bowen, 1954) has described the personal experience of fear in the cross-barrage of witchcraft accusations in West Africa, and Bronio Malinowski (1962) how he was struck by similarities between the Roman Catholic and the Melanesian attitudes and rituals surrounding death.

SEPARATION FROM ONE'S OWN CULTURE

The modern student has plenty of material to read which informs him about the different ways of life cultures not his own. But in the 1930's there was very much less of this material available than there is today. And it referred to distant communities, far away and self-contained, hard to reach and taking a long time to return from. There were fewer who had already been there, and I think for this reason "culture shock" was more of a reality than it is today, when there is such an abundance of field monographs to study and both students and their professors may dash off to the field by air and back again within weeks.

By contrast, not only was it traditional to have a farewell dinner given by the London seminar to celebrate departure, but also people even came to see one off on a field trip in those days. When Raymond and I eventually left for a year of work in Malaya, quite a large group gathered at Paddington Station to see us off on the boat train to Southampton.

Of course, there had been intellectual preparation for the Malayan field trip in the way of meeting people in England who knew Malaya, mostly civil servants and people in the then Colonial Office who had worked out there. We also took lessons in the language at the School of Oriental Languages, where Sir Richard Winstedt lectured. We bought grammars and little textbooks and studied and tried to practise speaking. We also collected a lot of personal introductions to help us on our arrival overseas, and in general perhaps made more fuss about our going than does the modern worker, who may just hop off with some letters to the anthropology department of the nearest university.

But we were hoping to do something rather different than Audrey Richards, remote among the Bemba of Northern Rhodesia, Malinowski in the Tro-briands, or Evans-Pritchard among the little-known Azande, and certainly different from Raymond Firth's previous trip to Tikopia, where he lived in isolation from Europeans for more than twelve months. We were to study a peasant community living not far from civilised urban European life in a country with a long tradition of civilisation well known to the West, which was at that time a novel thing to do. One encountered different obstacles, the obstacles of distrust and misunderstanding which result from wishing to examine something which many people believed was already quite familiar and did not need investigation.

The research grant from the Leverhulme Trustees was given us to examine the economics of the fishing industry somewhere on the east coast of Malaya, at that time administered by the Colonial Office. The subject was expected to have some practical application, so that when we set out in July 1939, we had letters of introduction from private, business, and government circles which brought out quite an embarrassing display of "red carpet" on our eventual arrival in Singapore, after a sea journey of nearly five weeks.

The sea journey was, for me, the beginning of that process of separation from my own culture which had to precede the long process of transition to another, which was yet to come. I kept a diary, which was meant to be a consecutive personal record of events which should act as an outline map of time against which our notebook records of collected information could be checked. As well as providing that outline, it became for me a sort of lifeline, or checking point to measure changes in myself. I believe Raymond Firth kept a mainly chronological-record type of diary when he was in Tikopia, and Malinowski the more personal sort when he was in the Trobriands. Mine was used as an emotional outlet for an individual subjected to disorientating changes in his personal and social world. Perhaps ideally, both kinds should be kept: first the bare facts, the news summary as it were; then the personal reactions. But since notes have to be taken on what is observed and discussed every day, this only highlights the enormous amount of actual writing which has to be done in the field and which is usually felt as a regular burden of work pressing for attention, particularly at the end of every day.

The station farewell made no dramatic break in my mind, for it seemed like the prelude to a holiday. But during the early days on shipboard, in trying to prepare for an entirely new experience, I felt reserved, closed up, and not myself. My diary records: "I have lost my standards of measurement, either to be pleased or unhappy, but feel as if a hundred new photographs were being taken in my mind, but none yet developed, so there is no material yet to react on." Some withdrawal seems a natural accompaniment to new experience for me; it is as if I were sorting the cards dealt me in my mind, and until this is done, I cannot take an interest in the game, much less say whether it is a good game or not.

When two people go into the field together, sensitivity to small signs of strain and the ability quickly to interpret the feelings of the other are obviously important. In the loneliness of the field situation, the presence of another can be a real source of comfort. But the obligation to give support to another may also be a serious additional burden on a field worker to begin with. I am not surprised then at the anthropologist who wishes to break ground before he brings his wife or family. The need to adapt to internal stresses as well as to those of a small group in a strange situation may also account for the relatively poor success which anthropologists have had in group research with other disciplines.

I reacted to our arrival in Singapore with uninhibited criticism, which perhaps also illustrates certain difficulties the anthropologist meets in areas where he is not yet in the field proper—and therefore not yet consciously using his techniques of detachment, tact, and withholding of judgement to an understanding of the new way of life—nor on familiar ground either.

I wrote home to my father:

Our impressions of Singapore have been distinctly mixed—on the whole I don't think we've much enjoyed ourselves, and I look forward to getting up country the day after tomorrow. I suppose one is always a bit maladjusted when one gets on land after a long sea voyage, and the heat made us feel very limp and lackadaisical, disinclined to get on with ordering our stores and so on. It is quite a strain being continually with utter strangers, and we have hardly had a minute to ourselves. The life that is led here seems a strange and artificial one to us.

When we got to the east coast, we felt the same antagonism to the social life of the European community, in spite of their great hospitality to us. I suppose that we did seem rude and strange creatures to them; prewar tensions were beginning to build up and there was much local misunderstanding of our intentions. The hard-working expatriate European population had perhaps some reason for regarding us at the time as clumsy amateurs in a field which they believed they had cultivated, through administration, over many years. We were often aware of the unspoken comment: What did these strangers expect to find out in ten months that we do not know who have given as many years to the service of this country?

Our dependence on the goodwill and help which local people could give us before we were settled was considerable; yet it irked us to have to use it. We had to be careful with our money, and were grateful for such help as the offer of free railway passes for both of us for six months on the Federated Malay States Railways, as well as for personal hospitality. When we left Singapore on what was then affectionately called the Sakai express, it took us from ten o'clock in the morning till four o'clock next afternoon to reach the east coast, now a few hours' flight by air. The slower travel of those days emphasised the distance between us and home, and perhaps also made us more apprehensive of our lost contacts, more critical of the local Europeans with their insistence on maintaining home standards, and more defensive about our work than might be the case today, when flying visits from overseas visitors are so commonplace as to be almost a nuisance. In 1939 it took us six weeks even to reach the field, whereas in 1963, six weeks allowed us to fly there and back and to do a short spell of research.

Rosemary Firth and Minoh, in whose house the Firths lived and who cooked for them in Kelantan, 1963.

TRANSITION TO THE STUDY CULTURE

We were feeling our way into the field, meeting government officers concerned with fisheries, marketing, boat registration, and so on; talking about

Malay-Chinese relationships, education, art, religion, and social affairs; inves-
tigating the possibilities of employing servants; estimating the probable ex-
penses of wages, housebuilding, food stores, transport, furnishing our house;
and the like. There is even today no real way to discover what is and what is
not possible until one is on the spot, able to assess the obstacles of official
hindrance as well as the best use of official and private offers of help, tangible
and intangible.

For instance, not until we were actually in the east-coast state of Kelantan
did we decide to stay in the fishing village of Perupok, near Kota Bharu,
because we found that there was a lively fishing industry there allied to some
rice cultivation inland—a village not too scattered or remote from urban
settlement nor too primitive to seem a possible neighbourhood for me as well
as for Raymond and, last but not least, with a friendly and cooperative District
Officer who understood our needs and was anxious to help us in getting settled
comfortably.

While we were deciding on the exact spot to live, we were fortunate to be
able to borrow the bungalow of the British Advisor, who lent it to us complete
with Chinese boy. The fact that the coast was beautiful and the local food good
was a bonus, but one for which I was particularly grateful.

I wrote a letter home to my father describing in glowing terms the physical
beauty of the coast. The long beach of white sand bordered by palm trees, the
clusters of thatched houses with nets and fishing gear laid out before them, the
boats with their brightly coloured sails and decorated prows, which put out
in a silent flock every morning at dawn and returned in a straggle in the late
afternoon—all seemed idyllic to me, ideal as a place either for work or for a
holiday. We could stroll along the beach to watch an old man spinning twine
with a hand loom from coconut fibre, and when we were hot and thirsty, a
small boy would oblige us by shinning up a tree to bring us down a couple of
green coconuts, from which we drank the milk of the unripe fruit. There were
no Europeans in this village, twenty miles from the nearest town, except at
weekends, when they sometimes came down to the clubhouse for a bathe and
a drink.

The aura of romantic Eastern beauty and quiet was enhanced by uncertain-
ties over our future, due to the outbreak of war in Europe, but after we had
gathered that our funds would not cease from London for six months at least,
we decided to start work seriously. "We have ordered a house to be built for
us, a little apart from the other houses in the village, but quite near the sea;
it will be bamboo and thatch and will cost us £12–15. We expect it to be ready
in ten days or a fortnight." Alas for my optimistic letter home! Perhaps due
to the machinations of a local spirit, whose acquaintance we made later, as well
as to more mundane matters, six weeks passed and we were still dependent on
local hospitality. However, our perceptions of the growing exasperation with
what must have seemed, to busy civil servants, to have been our aimless life

of idleness and tiresome curiosity had led us to take up residence in the local guest house.

Eventually we arrived in our village with a lorry containing eight large packing cases of food, a sack of rice, two army sacks with our camp beds, eight trunks with clothing, medicine, and notebooks, four chairs and a table, a bath, a crate of kitchen equipment, several braziers, and a roll of mats, besides the luggage of our two servants. We found a house with only half a roof on, no doors, windows, kitchen, or bathing accommodation, but a swarm of local villagers, men and boys summoned in last-minute urgency, all working like mad to finish it. I suspect our actual appearance with so much luggage was essential for the final burst of activity. At any rate, very much depressed ourselves, and regarded with the most incredulous scorn by our Malay boy and his wife for even considering life in conditions so unusual and unsuitable for Europeans, we deposited our luggage within the protection of that half of the roof which was finished, left Marmat and his wife to camp out there as best they could to guard our possessions, and retired down the beach to the club bungalow for the night.

Next morning, finding at least the roof finished, we firmly announced our intention of sleeping there, and that the house should be finished around us.

We put up our beds and hung the mosquito curtains, got a table covered in sand, a few bricks and some iron bars laid across them on which to make a cooking fire, unpacked our tinned food, began to lay out mats on the floor and to arrange our furniture for settling in. We also demanded the digging of a privy, and shortly afterwards had a superior brickfloored bathroom made for us. An enormous jar of cold water, with a coconut scoop on a long handle stood there, from which one poured water over oneself, so that it ran down onto the sloping floor and out of an open pipe into the sandy waste around. This is one of the simplest and most delightful ways of bathing in the tropics which I have yet discovered.

Our house was built by local people in the local fashion, with some minor modifications for our literacy needs. It was of woven bamboo tied in with strakes to bamboo poles and covered with a thatch of palm leaves. It had one large room divided by a half partition, behind which were our camp beds draped in mosquito curtaining. A cabin trunk served as cupboard and dressing chest, and we hung our clothes on string runners. For drying things in the monsoon, we had a curious contraption like a hen coop woven for us which we then placed over a charcoal fire and laid our damp clothes upon it. Bamboo stretchers, such as are used by Indian watchmen at night, were placed around the walls, and on these we spread our books and papers. It was far from being a burglar-proof house and, as well as air, cats, chickens, and the curious glances of children could all make their way through the spaces in the walls. Also, it was only partly weatherproof, and in the monsoon season a great wind brake was erected between us and the sea, and a kind of "hair net" put over the roof to prevent the thatch from blowing up on end. But it was a marvel-lously cool and airy place to live, with a balcony running along the whole of one side of the house, facing the sea, so that we could watch all that went on.

Faced with the urgent necessity for meals without time to teach Marmat's wife English cooking, we opted for Malay food "to begin with." We discovered that we had in her a superb cook, and the idea of lessons in English cooking was abandoned forthwith. Every evening we ate a variety of several delectable fishes straight from the sea, cooked in coconut milk and spiced sauces, with local vegetables and a big bowl of rice. The daily cost was a few cents a day, and for their wages of three pounds ten a week (under ten American dollars) our water was carried from the well, boiled and filtered or stored for bathing, and our shopping, cooking, and cleaning was all done for us by Marmat and his wife. In addition, they acted as intermediaries, at first ambivalent, between us and the local Malays. They turned into very efficient and eventually very loyal and loving servants. Having come to the conclusion that we were crazy to want to live in such conditions, they decided to manage our affairs for us, in an attempt to protect us from the worst evils of our singular situation!

It was unheard of for Europeans to live without car, refrigerator, or alcohol, to keep open house to the whole village, to eat local food, to walk about on the beach, talking to all and sundry and endeavouring to learn not just the language but, worst of all to Marmat, the strong local dialect of the fishermen. It is the doing of just these things which differentiates the anthropologist from other students of social behaviour, however, and most anthropologists do enjoy the local way of life when they have adapted to it. But the process is not without difficulty and pain, which are perhaps deliberately forgotten after-wards. To begin with, one's feelings are bound to be ambivalent. Although delighted at the prospect of settling down at last in a rural area with the chance of getting on with the real job, both of us spent uncomfortable periods of depression as the ties with our European friends and Western style of living were slowly broken.

While we were waiting to settle into village life, we had become increasingly conscious of the social gap which began to widen between the local European population and ourselves. It was a relief, therefore, to have at last our own house with our own boy and his wife and to stop worrying about whether we should dine or drink with so-and-so or continue to attempt explanations of the projected nature of Raymond's work. No critical, sceptical European scrutiny of our odd way of living need bother us any more; since we had no car, no refrigerator, and no alcohol, the wherewithal for normal entertaining was absent. It was not long before we used to eye occasional visitors to the club-house a mile or two down the beach with a certain amount of dismay and to hope that they would ignore us—which, of course, most of them did. This made it easier to forge social links with the villagers, which was what we next proceeded to do.

INCORPORATION INTO THE NEW SOCIETY

Raymond had spent those weeks waiting for our house in collecting a great deal of paper information, a necessary prelude to the empirical examination of the working of the economic system. For instance, he had studied boat registration, records of fishing equipment and rice lands owned locally, and details of various other activities, such as tile making, weaving, and so on. Before him lay the much more demanding job of collecting a mass of empirical information on the day-to-day fishing. But first of all, this required a much improved knowledge of the language, so that he could follow the quick interchange of conversation in bargaining by the boats and note what was said as well as done at the time. Asking about it all afterwards, he found that the leisurely explanations and later discussion could never be a substitute for the first-hand observation of market relations. To start with, of course, they were. Before he understood the whole system, each individual beach transaction had no proper significance; but only by looking at each of these transactions *as if* they had significance on their own could the significance of the whole be ultimately understood. General fluency in language must be acquired first, then the technical terms for specific operations, then the use of technical terms to explore and test his own understanding of the system. I think the use of certain local-dialect phrases referring to the marketing of fish on the beach, which Raymond used in Trengganu later in the year when we went down the coast on a comparative tour, made the most immediate impact on otherwise shy or hostile fishmen and became an instrument for very rapid rapport with men willing to give more information to one who already seemed to them to have so much.

There is a sort of paradox here in the anthropologist's techniques, since both his ignorance and his special knowledge when used together seem to be the key which elicits further information. There are analogies, I think, in the general teaching situation; knowledge and ignorance complement each other in the pursuit of further knowledge and the clarification of new areas of ignorance. More experienced than I, Raymond leapt into the fray, going down to the beach each morning with notebook and pencil and endlessly asking questions of all sorts. Then he would come home and go over his notes every evening, making lists of new words, of the names of people he had talked to, of what he thought he had made out of the system so far, and of what he had still to check.

At the start of any field-work project, one is bound to be working under two frustrating disabilities: first, that of not being able to talk or understand talk without much strain; and second, that of not being able to understand the system you need to talk about. As one painfully makes one's way through these two complementary confusions, a great deal of useless, mistaken, or misplaced information is bound to be collected. Much of what is written down and learnt in the early field-work days may have to be later corrected, rejected, and unlearnt. This is one of the reasons for depression after early elation in the apparent mastering of language, which I think is probably a classic field experience. It is then that there may come the flood of doubts.

The realisation that, after all, you seem to know very little, have misunderstood a great deal, hardly have an idea left in your head, even may begin to hate the people, or perhaps feel a personal failure probably comes to all anthropologists at some period in their work. I think it is important to clarify this for the inexperienced. The feeling may come at the time when the local people have decided that the game of being hospitable and protective to this odd, ignorant intruder has gone on long enough and time now suggests he cease his queries and go home. It is part of that process of detachment from one's own culture but before any real acceptance into the new has taken place. It is the time of transition after separation and before incorporation, in the terms of the patterns of initiation of which I spoke earlier.

The necessity to cut ties with one's own background and throw oneself onto the social mercies of the local people is that which epitomizes for me the nature of the anthropologist's task. In doing so, he demonstrates once for all, and in personal terms, the interdependence of man in society, his imperative need for social contact and a certain measure of approval, his inability to suffer more than a certain amount of isolation and social disapproval.

I was myself a long way yet from learning these lessons. I was still at the stage of fantasy when all I contemplated doing was to learn to live amicably with the wives and children of our neighbours, the local fishermen, and to enjoy the release from European social restraints. The Europeans had rejected us, so it seemed, because not unnaturally they did not understand or approve of what we were trying to do. The local fishermen made a polite show of accepting us, because perhaps no others had yet shown quite the same interest or persistence in enquiring about their affairs. That this was yet only a superficial acceptance I did not guess, although Raymond knew by experience that this would prove to be so.

He encouraged me to go and sit outside our house, somewhere near a path where people passed up and down, and this experience, which was painful to me at first because I was dreadfully shy and self-conscious, was my way of enlightenment and the beginning of social acceptance. In sitting thus and listening mainly, I was doing more than accustoming my ears to the strange sounds—an essential prerequisite to imitating them—I created a situation in which the social initiative passed to the Malay villagers. For a stranger who just comes and sits among you without evident reason excites curiosity, and curiosity leads to some attempts at solving the problem of the stranger's identity.

Even if the uppermost reaction is hostility—and there is no absolute reason why it should be—this will be expressed in questions: "What does she want? Where does she come from?" and perhaps as importantly, "When is she going away?" Sooner or later, dissatisfied by attempts to answer these questions among themselves, one among them, either more friendly or more bold than the others, will directly address you. Your halting attempt to reply may be the first step to genuine social acceptance because you will be giving the alien group something they have asked for, rather than asking of them, as in your initial attempts at communication you may have had to do.

It is vitally important for building up the participant observation situation for the anthropologist to be seen as soon as possible as someone who has something to give as well as something to get. Participation is a two-way relationship, but the group will not for a long time be able to comprehend exactly what the anthropologist wants, and many of the things he will want they will initially be very unwilling to offer. But in order to establish that the relationship envisaged is to be two-way, they must see him as wanting something which they can give without danger.

The need for social relationship for its own sake is one which is easily grasped. If one can show that one wants to understand the way of life and how quite simple everyday things are done, perhaps pointing out ways in which our own habits differ, this creates a situation of potential equality between the field worker and the group because it shows up the weakness of the worker. The feeling of helplessness, which may make the field worker miserable, can elicit the help he needs. "Here is a person," they may be supposed to think, "far from his friends and family. He cannot fish or grow rice or find his way about or even speak properly. We must help him learn these things." Thus the informant is led to see his role as offering what he has no fear of losing, knowledge of the language and general social skills. Help with speaking a language is a potent neutral link between two strangers. Anxiety will not be raised about the use to which the knowledge is to be put, as it may be about certain kinds of factual information, for instance, census material or opinions on economic or religious matters. It may even be that from the psychological point of view the field worker's need to speak places him in the role of child and the local group in the parental role, and thereby encourages interdependence on both sides.

But, for an adult, the dependence inseparable from the need to learn local patterns of social life is often galling. One of the simplest humiliations—so it often seemed to me—was to be constantly followed about by a chattering and inquisitive mob of children. There were times when I came near admitting a wish to throw stones at them, as one might at a pack of yelping dogs at one's heel! Worse still was lack of privacy, especially at night. The visit of an intelligent potential informant with material to offer was something naturally to be expected and therefore to be endured, even if at the particular moment one was not feeling very sociable. Collection of information is like any other routine job and must be done when work is to hand, not just when one is in the mood for it. What I did not at first see was why a host of hangers-on should be permitted to congregate round the open door and to stare and listen whenever they could. But of course, if you obtrude yourself, as an anthropologist, into the private affairs of others at your own convenience, why should not the local people have similar rights?

In the acquisition of greater fluency in language, it usually seems to happen that a few individuals will present themselves as willing and able to be the worker's main teachers. These teachers will often constitute themselves as protectors and defenders of the field worker towards the outside world, interpreting his needs to their group as well as the other way round.

One can rarely choose such invaluable allies; the job of nurse-protector will be spontaneously taken up. It will not be quite the same job as that of the servant or interpreter chosen by oneself. What one has to look out for is to avoid being dominated throughout by such a person. A partial "weaning" is usually necessary from the original informant at some later stage, if the anthropologist is not to have access to some parts of the society blocked in this way. The informant's esteem and pride are often involved in his new role; and sometimes a tricky situation can develop when an open quarrel threatens as to which of two informants is to arrange a visit, make a new introduction, or act as guide in some expedition. The anthropologist is also likely at some stage to resent the implication that he "belongs" to his erstwhile teacher; yet open revolt will probably not be appropriate or to his long-term interest. Jealousies also arose in our case between our boy Marmat and a most respected but "bossy" old fisherman, Pa Che Mat, who made great play with the idea that he was our guard, against physical as well as spirit dangers. Marmat was bursting with indignation one evening because Pa Che Mat actually entered our hourse while we were away. Raymond had to mediate and lay down a law, thereafter scrupulously observed, that Marmat's domain lay within the house, where he was king, and Pa Che Mat's province was on the beach and in the village, where he was held in respect.

If my interpretation that the very social vulnerability of the anthropologist before he is able to speak disarms hostile feelings, the reverse may also be true; and one who comes already knowing the language may appear potentially more hostile, because a stranger, and thereby arouse anxiety. In respect of learning the language, having a spouse present may be at some points a hindrance because one is not driven by the desperation of loneliness to make outside contact. Perhaps this is also a reason why teamwork, combining medical, agricultural, economic, or demographic experts in the field together, is not always easy or successful. The anthropologist is then seen by the people he wishes to know as one of a group with its own social cohesion, and the usual in-group, out-group mechanisms of defence may operate, leaving the anthropologist unacceptable to both groups.

On the other hand, some possibility of being able to talk over the early feelings of confusion and failure is an important safety valve. In the absence of a partner on the spot, a nearby colleague, a visiting tutor, or in the last resort a friend at home able and willing both to receive and answer letters may provide the indispensable lifeline. If one has been through this crisis, with luck one may also have acquired a valuable teaching skill. One may be able to recall the despair which often assails a student when he is mastering a new discipline, to discover that the little he manages to learn seems only to highlight the relative amount of his ignorance. This swing of mood between feelings of mastery and of incompetence must be common to other fields of scientific enquiry. What makes it unusual in the field situation is that there may be little apparent escape from the "laboratory," where the observer is both guinea pig and technician. It does not usually happen that the physical scientist is dependent on his laboratory subjects for his recreational and social needs at the same time. Sometimes the field worker may need to drop the attitude of recorder, leave his notebooks at home for a rare holiday, and just go out to enjoy the company of his neighbours.

The acceptance of food is also a powerful symbol of emotional bonds. The Malay villagers who discovered that we were eating more or less the same food as they were seemed delighted. On some occasion when we returned after twenty years, I was offered a particular dish at some ceremonial feast, with the recommendation that it was one I had particularly liked the last time. So with dress. Our wearing of the "kain and baju" of local custom in the evenings was greeted with enthusiasm. To be dressed alike considerably helps along the game of identification. But of course it is only a game, played to aid participation; it is not the same thing. Occasionally, the play goes too far. I remember one evening when I was serving coffee to Raymond and to one of our most trusted and respected informants, a very strong urge came over me to retire into the back parts of the house after the coffee, as a Malay woman would have done, rather than stay talking to the two men. Then I had consciously to remind myself that I was indeed an anthropologist, not just a Malay woman nor a good Muslim wife.

There were other occasions when my behaviour was dictated by intuitive feelings of what was correct. At a meal given on the occasion of celebrating the birthday of the prophet Mohamed, I nearly used a pillow to lean against which, I thought, had been tactfully provided for me in consideration of my being unaccustomed to sit on the floor for long. At the last moment, a flash of doubt restrained me, and I rightly guessed that the pillow was there to take the sacred book of the Koran from which readings were to be made. A more comic occasion was on our return to our old village after some twenty years, when I was invited to bathe on the verandah of the house where we were staying, it being a very hot, damp evening. It was private, but not to the woman of the house nor the children. With shock I realized that since Malays never bathe in the nude, I should somehow have to stand up and take my shower clothed or not bathe at all. I remember my discomfort and confusion as I stood in a nightgown and solemnly poured water from a jar over myself in the correct style, and then attempted to dry and to put on another garment over the wet one. But the sense of shame which nudity had for them had transmitted itself to me. It even prevented me from enjoying a bathe in the open sea when properly covered, since no Malay *plays* with the sea, which is the unpredictable and possibly dangerous source of his livelihood, except as a child. And later, I also felt this to be an impropriety, although when newly arrived, I used to enjoy it.

In the early days of living in a strange community, the stranger is very conscious of the necessity to give up the usual patterns of his previous life, although he is painfully aware that he is ignorant of what should be substituted. As time passes, he begins to notice when he has not behaved correctly, although he may yet be unaware exactly in what way the behaviour was incorrect. Thus he becomes wily at delaying doing many things until he is sure of what is expected of him. As he becomes more assured of the expected patterns, he can even begin to experiment by deliberately breaking the rules or postulating that they be broken in conversation, to see what happens. When two people are in the field together, experimental techniques like this can often be deliberately used to highlight local differences between various individuals' interpretations of group norms. If there is a dispute about correct behaviour, it can be thrown into the open by each observer taking a different side.

The disturbing effect on what is observed caused by the observer's presence can be allowed for by distinguishing situations in which his presence is necessary to throw into relief the social reality of a situation, from those in which from long habituation it is at last genuinely ignored, from the more common ones where people are only partly and intermittently aware of it.

To give a small example of the first condition: We were walking along the beach one evening when we accidentally came upon a group of fishermen handling a new net. The precipitate action taken to prevent us from approaching made it abundantly clear that something of a special, ritual nature was going on, of which we would otherwise not have been made aware. It contrasted strongly in my mind with a performance of a shadow play, complete with musical accompaniment and the offerings of rice and symbolic figures for the spirits common on such occasions, but which had been arranged, at great expense, to take place in the middle of the morning—an entirely novel time —in order that some visiting team of film directors could record it. One of them was attempting to understand the meaning of it all by enquiry; the point is that he could not get at the real significance because he was observing a "fake" performance, whose meaning would be hidden from him just for that reason. The complete stranger observing something he knows little about has no means of assessing its importance. What the anthropologist does by constant participation is to make himself into a sensitive measuring agent for gauging the implications of what he observes. It is not only he who does the experimenting, however, but also the people he is studying will be making their observations and tests, and drawing their own conclusions about him. And only if he can be considered adequately to pass their tests, may we suppose that he is accepted, or at least temporarily "incorporated."

Two examples occur to me. I was offered a gold ornament which belonged to a small child of whom I was fond, in exchange for cash, during the off season in fishing. When the economic stringency improved, the mother asked me to return the ornament, in exchange for cash as before. What this marked really was her acceptance of me as a reliable and able person to hold the property of her child in return for cash which she badly needed to tide her over temporary difficulties. I did not at first see the transaction in that light at all, but in terms of my own culture, in which what I had done was to "buy" something, which for sentimental reasons reminded me of a friend's child. If I had persisted in my construction of the situation and stood on my supposed right to the object which I thought I had "bought," I should have demonstrated empirically that I was still an outsider. The explanations which made it clear to me that I was bound to return the ornament which I wanted, although disappointing to me as a European, were highly illuminating to me as an observer of the workings of the economic and kinship systems.

Another occasion, when it seemed to me that I had markedly failed to behave in the correct fashion, by fainting at the sight and sounds of death when watching the ritual slaughter of a bull, was also used by the Malay villagers to underline our acceptance among them. Far from being treated as an outsider who had shown herself affected by different standards, as I expected, my physical condition was treated with sense and efficiency, while it was explained in terms of locally held values. The old man Pa Che Mat, who was beginning to instruct Raymond into certain magical practices, scolded him for failing to protect me from the assaults of a powerful spirit who inhabited a pool near our house; the spirit would be attracted by the animal's blood and, finding Raymond protected by his smattering of magical knowledge, naturally attacked Raymond's more vulnerable wife. Such explanations were common of relatives being harmed by spirits unable to reach their more powerful male kin; and of course it thus reinforced what the old man was teaching Raymond about the power of spirits. What is also illustrated was that we were beginning to be accepted, since we were found to be subject to the same laws as our neighbours.

The jump from being the Englishwoman who could not stand the sight of blood to the unwitting wife of an apprentice *bomor,* as from the sentimental foreigner to the rich friend who will help with cash in time of need, is not too difficult or painful. But there are occasions when the anthropologist suffers from his two roles, as member of the new society and as scientific observer of it. Such an occasion occurred on our second visit to Malaya.

A neighbour who was clearly suffering from a psychotic illness went into a manic state, precipitated from a depressive one by the shock of accidentally encountering her husband's second wife, of whose existence he had kept her in ignorance. The cries and screams of anguish as this woman was subjected to the mental pressures of the local "witch doctor," the real sense of fear in the presence of mental illness which was shared by my Malay women friends and by me, were a sharp reminder that I had other standards of treatment for the mentally ill and other ideals of behaviour in the emotional crisis of marital relations which were revealed by the affair. That was an occasion on which I sat, a dutiful scientist, watching and recording much of which I did not approve. But on returning to our own house, tired and shaken, to find a crowd of people anxious to discuss some other subject, I leapt out of my scientist's cloak and addressed them as an outraged European: "Go away, all of you, and leave us in a little peace for a bit." Raymond expostulated; he could always remain the scientist longer than I could. But the crowd of visitors moved off, sensing for once a personal need, not explicable by social context. Our housekeeper said afterwards that no one was in the least put out, understanding that everyone sometimes loses his temper.

Raymond and I had long consultations throughout the next night, which was still punctuated by shrill cries from the disturbed woman and her attendants, as to what we might do to bring genuine psychiatric help to her. We made enquiry in the mental hospital which showed that only temporary relief by drugs would be available and that the patient would soon return, without supportive help, to her own community, so we were eventually persuaded that interference with local customs of treatment would be ineffectual and therefore useless.

When the anthropologist is most torn by the incompatibility of his being the friend and the scientific observer of his people, the solution to his conflict is usually a practical one: There is so much less that he can do as a helper than as a scientist that he chooses the more effective role. The poverty of the families whose daily food expenditure I spent many hours in examining often impelled me to try to alleviate it with gifts. To do so continually would have nullified the study of living standards, and so made humanist destroy scientist. But more importantly, it could have had only a temporary effectiveness, and in the end might even have done more harm than good, by raising expectations which it was impracticable long to satisfy. So that, in the end, moral conflicts about helping those he studies usually have an inevitable solution dictated by the situation. The most he can probably hope to do is to avoid exacerbating the situation of his friends, either politically or by carelessness in personal response, by apparent lack of respect and loyalty in his subsequent reports, or by too sudden a defection to his own culture. The extent to which one can go on sending money or other help to informants who are literate enough to be able to request it after one has left the field is a thorny question, harder in proportion as one was genuinely fond of them. It is part, I feel, of the pain which the anthropologist probably has to undergo as he detaches himself again from the culture he has been privileged to experience and has learnt to enjoy, back again to that in which he was reared and in which he must ultimately be most at home.

THE RETURN TO ONE'S OWN CULTURE

I wonder if it is too fanciful to continue the analogy of initiation through the phases of separation, transition, and incorporation into a cyclical pattern in which the field worker on returning home has to go through the reverse operations of transition, separation, and finally reincorporation with his own culture.

We made our first break by leaving the village for three weeks for a run down the east coast, stopping to examine the fishing villages of the adjacent state of Trengganu for general comparative material. It so happened that our reentry to the world of newspapers, wireless, and European company, as we once again took advantage of official and private hospitality, coincided with the disastrous epic of World War II, the defeat of France and the withdrawal of the British army from Dunkirk.

I wrote to my father on June 14, 1940:

We have just heard the news of Italy's entry into the war, verbally, no papers yet. When we got back to our little village last week it all seemed like a lovely but unreal dream, our life here for the past year; a dream which was over but which was just waved before us once again, to tantalise and sadden us by its unreality. A gulf of years seemed to have opened up in the weeks we were in the outside world hearing such grave daily news, which made all seem a mockery here on our return. But although the spell is broken, we have managed to recapture a few stray threads of the old pattern, and to pretend to ourselves that we are as we were. The coming back has been useful; it has given us a chance to finish off a number of things; to pack up in peace, and now that all our routine daily jobs are over, like the daily collection of fish catches, and the daily budgets, we are left much freer for odd jobs, like checking census details and so on. We both feel very strange not to have to rush out every day for fish and budgets; Raymond can hardly restrain himself when he sees a sail on the horizon from rushing down to the beach to record the catch. Instead we are writing up our figures and repairing last minute gaps in our information.

It was a most strange re-entry to our old village, met by Pa Che Mat with the sad news of the death of his own wife, of the famous old "bomor" he had brought to Raymond for most of his instruction in magical practices, and of another respected old rice farmer. It was a shock and seemed to highlight the sense of impending change. On all hands we were greeted with cries of mixed pleasure and sorrow at our return and projected departure, and our old friend Awang Lung, who was leaning over the edge of his boat, positively blushed with pleasure and surprise as he looked up and saw us again, once more walking down the beach together. We went to the house of a woman whose boy had just been circumcised, and because we had missed this while we were away, she made a special meal for the two of us at her house. So we went and ate delectable chicken grilled in spiced coconut cream, curried fish, grilled mackerel, omelette, pumpkin in coconut sauce, and rice, followed by a sweetmeat made of eggs, and curiously scented tea. We sat cross-legged on the floor mats, and I chewed the betel, we both smoked locally rolled cigarettes, and sat gossiping there for some time until a tremendous thunderstorm had spent itself outside.

It was peaceful, delightful, and seemed quite rational to continue living the simple but good peasant life with such charming people, who although ignorant of the outside world, offered us such warm hospitality on the eve of our leaving them. My letter continued:

We both seriously believe we ought to return to war-time England, but I have suddenly been made a temporary coward by being thrown back into the routines of our village after three weeks contact with the outside world. I could almost weep at leaving the familiar beach with its line of painted boats, and all our friends here, to go back to the unpredictable life of war-time England.

Words, so it seems to me, form the avenues through which the anthropologist proceeds from one culture to another; it is through learning their use, and the social and emotional overtones to which they provide the clue in human interaction, that he comes to be a member of a new social group, in somewhat the same way that he became a member of his own in infancy. Words are used differently in different contexts. In those letters to my father, I tried to evoke for him the romantic attraction which Malaya had cast over me.

But just as words can be used to unite, so they can also be used to divide. The scientist uses words for another purpose, to isolate and objectify experience, rather than to give it subjective warmth. When the social scientist returns home and has to reverse his identification and enter his own culture again, perhaps the process of writing up his material helps him, by erecting the barrier of verbalisation between the being and the doing, the screens of theory between sympathy and empathy. In the long analysis of what he has known, he slowly unwinds himself from his involvement with it. For in a nutshell, this is the core meaning of being an anthropologist to me, compounded of a double mixture of involvement and understanding at a personal and empirical level, along with detachment and analysis at a professional and theoretical level.

Whether he be brilliant as a theoretician or just an adequate collector of field data, the initiated professional is, to me, one who has felt as well as seen the alien society he has studied. His involvement with his subjects lies in his capacity not only to identify with them, but also to engage them in identifying with him and his previously incomprehensible curiosities.

I have seen Raymond many times sitting on the steps of some fisherman's house, absorbed with a Malay in unravelling the complexities of some system, such as the distribution of fish or the meaning of kinship obligations. The two men have been equally engrossed by the conversation, using diagrams drawn on the sand with a stick, seeking analogy and illustration in a mutual attempt to present some pattern in a system or some conception which it may never before have occurred to the informant needed explanation. In a way, a good field worker finds another potential worker, as it were, in the community he is studying, whose own curiosity and even identification with "abstract truth" he can mobilise and use himself. In collecting facts and formulating theories, he lives some of the facts at the same time as he collects them; while the local people may be led to perceive a new pattern emerging out of the well-known details of their own lives and so to theorise about how they live.

One result of his methods may be to change the outlook of the field worker in the course of his work, so that he can never look at his own society in quite the same way that he did before he experienced another.

John Berger (1963) ends a brilliant introduction to sociology for the layman by showing how the social scientist comes to perceive men in the model of puppets on their miniature stage "moving up and down as the strings pull them around, following the prescribed course of their various little parts." But, he adds, "unlike the puppets, we have the possibility of stopping in our movements, looking up and perceiving the machinery by which we have been moved." The implication which is made here that pain is involved both in identification and in detachment from a given social system is particularly relevant to the anthropologist. But I think that there is a difference.

Where the sociologist, in his model, may observe the strings overhead which are pulled to move the puppets, the anthropologist may take as his model a set of glove puppets. He studies them by putting his hand inside, as it were, and feeling with part of his own body the stresses and strains of their behaviour as they interact with one another. Returning from the players to record the play, he leaves behind a hollow glove, his second social personality, with which he has been involved from *within*. So he leaves a gap behind him, and may be mourned by the group he has left, as he also may miss the society in which he took a temporary part.

During my last week in Malaya, I had a nightmare dream, in which I *was* a Malay peasant, a woman crouching over the fire to blow up the embers for an evening meal. I awoke in terror, momentarily confused about my own identity, Malay woman or English scientist. Perhaps few anthropologists get to this condition, but many must have been near to it, I feel sure; whether they choose to talk of it is another matter. To me, the experience of becoming an anthropologist includes that of learning to play a part so well that one may occasionally forget whether it is a natural one or not.

The essence of an initiation rite is to make a person feel differently as well as to behave differently in a new role. Field-work experience can have this effect. Insofar as it does, it can have both the traumatic impact and the social force of a rite of initiation.

REFERENCES

BEATTIE, JOHN. 1965. *Understanding an African Kingdom: Bunyoro.* New York: Holt, Rinehart and Winston.
BERGER, JOHN. 1963. *Invitation to Sociology: A Humanistic Perspective.* Garden City, N.Y.: Doubleday.

BOWEN, ELENORE SMITH (LAURA BOHANNAN). 1954. *Return to Laughter.* Garden City, N.Y.: Natural History Press.

FORTES, MEYER. 1962. "Ritual and Office in Tribal Society." In Max Gluckman, ed., *Essays on the Ritual of Social Relations.* New York: Humanities Press.

MALINOWSKI, BRONISLAW. 1962. "Science and Religion." In Valetta Malinowski, ed., *Sex, Culture and Myth.* New York: Humanities Press.

POWDERMAKER, HORTENSE. 1968. "Field Work." In David L. Sills, ed., *International Encyclopedia of the Social Sciences,* vol. 5. New York: Macmillan.

RICHARDS, AUDREY. 1956. *Chisunga: A Girl's Initiation Ceremony among the Bemba of Northern Rhodesia.* New York: Humanities Press.

2 / Did Frank Hamilton Cushing Go Native?

SYLVIA GRONEWOLD

In the lore of anthropology the name of Frank Hamilton Cushing has enjoyed a peculiar status. He is frequently cited as the outstanding example —perhaps the only pure case—of a man who, starting from professional motives, "went native." Cushing, in the familiar account, became a Zuñi Indian while living among these people to study their culture. The drama and distinction of such an achievement are probably magnified for anthropologists by the passing of nearly a hundred years; but the legend remains effective to a fraternity that to some extent still prizes the authentic depiction of an ethnic ritual, acute insight into an alien ethos, or sympathies founded on the intrinsic value of humanity's parochial forms. That even those who do not know his work pass on the story of Cushing is due in part, no doubt, to the way it lends itself to various parables useful in camp, corridor, or classroom.

The point may be that the outsider, especially the anthropologist, can indeed totally educate himself—*will* himself—into an alien culture. Or it may be that the field anthropologist's vaunted "approach," especially his participant observation, is a powerful means of rapport capable of propelling a Cushing in the direction of complete identification with an alien tradition. With Cushing as text, tribal elders have, not infrequently, pointed to the peril of carrying participation so far beyond its proper depth as to drown out detached observation. Here, in fact, another dramatic element enters some versions of the story: Cushing as the tragic hero. The poignant twist is that, having gained admittance to the deeper Zuñi secrets, Cushing learned so well the lesson of sacredness as never to divulge what at last he came to know, not even to fellow scientists. In this reading of his biography, Cushing leaves the world that motivated him, to enter the world he only meant to learn about. In that world, moreover, the original motivation becomes pointless or worse. Thus the classic instance of "going native."

Besides inviting a lengthy gloss on the subtleties of going native, the "Zuñification" of Frank Cushing raises a question familiar in other contexts: If Cushing as portrayed did not exist, would his equal have had to be created?

33

With all its emphasis on simulating the fullest possible stance of the insider, was American anthropology bound to find a Cushing to celebrate? Was some sort of Prometheus inevitable, a culture hero who showed his fellows that one could move in from the edges into the full light of the fire, even if in doing so he himself was to be cut off from the intended use or enjoyment of his achievement? There are other Cushing-like figures in the lore of the field, moreover, and this general question is as interesting as Cushing's particular story. It is, in any case, a fact that many students of anthropology are familiar with the legend of Cushing's going native while knowing nothing else about him. As in a myth, Cushing's person is reduced for them to the dramatic role. But Frank Cushing was a modern man. If he did what he has been widely credited with doing, we need to know, apart from his life among the Zuñi, what sort of man he was. And if he did not do it, why is it so widely credited to him?

Frank Hamilton Cushing was born July 27, 1857, at Northeast, Pennsylvania. Even as an infant he was remarkable. He weighed only one and a half pounds. Today, despite laboratory skills and techniques specially adapted for premature infants, we are able to save only a small percentage of them. In 1857, his survival was almost miraculous and involved long hours of special care. His father, a physician, was fully aware of the difficulties to be faced by a delicate boy. He evidently subscribed to the school of opinion on child rearing which was to influence the parents of Theodore Roosevelt, a delicate lad less than a year younger than Cushing. Frank was never sent to school and was encouraged to spend as much time as possible in the outdoors.

When Cushing's father retired to devote himself to a study of philosophy, he purchased a farm at Barre, Orleans County, New York. Here Frank, a precocious child, showed early traits of the boy genius. He was especially able with his hands, and before he was nine years old had invented and built a boat with wheels which could function both in water and on land. He had also flung himself off the barn (fortunately with no ill effect) in a construction with wings and a wooden frame intended, like that of "Darius Green and his Flying Machine," to enable man to realize the dream of flight. The last half of the nineteenth century was an age of invention. Thomas Alva Edison, another who had received very little formal schooling, was only ten years older than Cushing. Edison took out his first patent at age twenty-one. Cushing's imagination and enthusiasm were diverted to a different interest. When he started on his career as a student of the American Indian, in 1866, he was nine years old.

As he himself tells the story (Cushing, 1895, p. 311), he was first intrigued by the gift of a projectile point which his father's hired man had plowed up on the farm. Immediate and diligent research throughout the area, which was rich in Indian "relics" (Chamberlain, 1900, p. 129), resulted in finds rewarding for the collector. A neighbor who had returned from a journey to California as a "forty-niner" presented him with points made of obsidian. Cushing's swing of interest to the Indian and his "relics" diverted his attention from mechanical invention, which attracted so many youths of that period, to the study of aboriginal artifacts. His first publication, "Antiquities of Orleans County, New York," appeared when he was seventeen years old (Cushing, 1874).

In the interval between the finding of the arrowhead at the age of nine and his first publication at seventeen, the boy wonder had been studying Indian artifacts to some purpose. In 1870 the family moved to Medina, New York, and Cushing located the ruins of an Indian encampment nearby. He was allowed to stay at the site for a week or more at a time to collect artifacts and to see what he could learn about the ruins. Joining to the hobby of "relic hunter" that which we nowadays refer to as "rock hound," Cushing roamed the shores of Lake Erie and Lake Ontario on walking trips, during which he developed a fine eye for rare rocks and fossil formations as well as for Indian curiosities. As he brooded over the Indian artifacts, the imaginative boy used his mechanical skill to try to duplicate their manufacture with such tools as might have been available to the Indian technician. Much thought and insight went into guessing the ways in which various implements might have been used. He invented eight methods by which flint arrowheads might be fashioned (Chamberlain, 1900, p. 130), and in later years discovered that six of these eight experimental techniques were actually in use by one or another tribal group.

In those days everyone who had any interest in aboriginal ways seems to have corresponded with Lewis H. Morgan, and Cushing must have been one of Morgan's younger correspondents. Morgan is said to have encouraged the boy's interest both in Indians and their artifacts and in geology (Holmes, 1900, p. 359).

Cushing's approach to the academic world came originally through his rock-collecting activities, which involved him in an encounter with the scientist L. W. Ledyard (Holmes, 1900, pp. 359–360). The story goes that young Cushing was about to collect a fine trilobite which was embedded in a boulder in Ledyard's driveway. Ledyard, chancing to arrive at the crucial moment, noted the activity with anguish. He explained with great firmness that this particular fossil had already been collected by himself and had been set exactly where he wanted it. When Ledyard discovered that he was talking to no ordinary boy-vandal but to a fellow collector of no mean understanding, his attitude changed. Feeling that Cushing should be encouraged, he sent the boy to Charles Frederic Hartt, a geologist and well-known student of archeology at Cornell.

The slender young man arrived at Cornell only to be assured by Professor Hartt that no Indian relics were to be found in the immediate neighborhood. With the skill which was later to become famous among his colleagues, Cushing promptly went out and gathered a gunnysack full of relics. Hartt is reported to have been so impressed that he shouted to his assistant, "Darby, feed him" (Holmes, 1900, p. 360). He forthwith took Cushing on as a protégé and pupil. Whatever college education Cushing ever had was obtained at this time;

but it cannot have been more than a few months, for he was seventeen when he met Hartt and he was not yet eighteen when at Ledyard's recommendation he moved on to Washington to work under S. F. Baird, the Assistant Secretary of the Smithsonian Institution.

Under Baird's tutelage, Cushing became a charter member of the new Washington Anthropological Society and read the first paper ever delivered to that society, one entitled "Relic Hunting." He was given a position of some importance at the Centennial Exposition at Philadelphia in 1876. He was put in charge of part of the National Museum collection and was able to edify visiting archeologists with his interpretation and demonstration of primitive tool making. Aged nineteen at the time, he was capable of chipping projectile points at the rate of seven in thirty-eight minutes and of manufacturing points from pieces of obsidian or glass in two minutes. Such a record compares very well with timed efforts of crack Apache tool makers. A man with such technical gifts and himself a reinventor of tool-making ways, Cushing naturally believed in the repeated invention of the same techniques, rather than in the diffusion of such techniques from a single area of invention.

While it is customary to speak nothing but praise of a man in an obituary, the technical achievements of the youthful Cushing as listed by Major J. W. Powell, Director of the Bureau of Ethnology and a former employer of Cushing, are impressive even for an obituary address (Powell, 1900, p. 259). Powell considered that Cushing had invented a new method of research into prehistoric archeology, a method which Powell christened "experimental reproduction." He stated that Cushing was an expert at making pottery, stone tools, and baskets, at fashioning utensils and canoes from birchbark, and at making dugout canoes of logs by means of stone tools and fire. The Smithsonian had accepted the Cushing collection of various types of wigwams. Powell credited Cushing for devising a method of weaving which utilized stone weights formerly considered by archeologists to be fishing plummets. Cushing proved the practicality of his own intuitive method when years later, in the West, he discovered similar weights in use by Indian weavers. Cushing had literally thought himself into the mood of a primitive man, making and using such tools.

This quality was challenged later by Paul Radin. In a review of *Les Fonctions Mentales dans les Sociétés Inférieures,* Radin was especially critical of those opinions of Lucien Lévy-Bruhl which, Radin stated, were based only on the claims of Cushing (Radin, 1929, p. 21). Cushing's beliefs about the magical and conservative attitudes of primitive thinkers were derived from his impressions of the magical and conservative feelings of the Zuñi as he knew them. His interpretation has been vigorously disputed by a number of other students of the Zuñi and nearby peoples, such as A. L. Kroeber (1921). In fact, Cushing's reputation stands much higher among the French than among the anthropologists of his own country. Both Lévy-Bruhl and his brilliant pupil Claude Lévi-Strauss seem to have had great respect for Cushing. In fact, Lévi-Strauss

used Cushing's versions of Zuñi mythology with just as much enthusiasm as
he did the less flamboyant studies of such twentieth-century anthropolgists as
Ruth Leah Bunzel, Elsie Clews Parsons, and Ruth Benedict. Lévi-Strauss
credited Cushing with having inspired some of the thinking of Emile Durkheim and Marcel Mauss in their theories about structural space, and he considered Cushing in advance of his time in that his attempt to explain Zuñi society
was less a simple description than an attempt to set up a model which could
explain the structure and process of the society (Lévi-Strauss, 1963, p. 290).
The place of Cushing, according to Lévi-Strauss, was on the right hand of
Morgan. In the hagiography of a thinker as close to Marxian views as Lévi-
Strauss, such a position in anthropological history could hardly be improved
upon.

In contrast, Washington Matthews, an American contemporary of Cushing,
declared that students were much disappointed when "Outlines of Zuñi Creation Myths" (Cushing, 1891–1892)—the work so admired by Lévi-Strauss—
appeared. Matthews indicated that what students of his generation were expecting was a long and detailed descriptive work. He somewhat querulously
commented that in view of the long time scientists had had to wait for Cushing
to write up his material, the result seemed a mere outline, suitable only as an
introduction for laymen. He stated emphatically the hope that more would be
forthcoming (Matthews, 1896, p. 232).

Even in Cushing's lifetime, the impression was strong among his colleagues
that he was withholding a great deal of information to be written up in the
future. Cushing himself contributed to this belief by mentioning in almost
every piece he wrote for scholarly journals that the present effort was a sort
of preliminary jotting down, to be followed later by further detail from his
large store of material. But until after his death, when it was found that little
remained which could be put in shape for publication (see the introduction to
the posthumous *Zuñi Folktales*, 1901), there seems to have been no suggestion
that this information would not eventually be produced.

As for what Cushing did write down about the Zuñi, the opinion of American scholars seems largely to agree with that of Kroeber (1921). Kroeber gave
Cushing credit for keen observation, but declared that he had overinterpreted
his findings, that it was almost impossible to disentangle his observations from
his "imaginings." British scholarly opinion, if one may take Darryl Forde
(1960) as a sample, was more kindly. Forde listed Cushing's *Zuñi Breadstuff*
with Robert Henry Codrington's *The Melanesians* and Henri Alexander Ju-
nod's *Life of a South African Tribe* as early classics. But the most enthusiastic
opinion on Cushing was that of Edmund Wilson, who spoke in his capacity
as one of America's distinguished literary critics. Wilson felt that Cushing's
Zuñi Folktales was a classic on the level with *Uncle Remus* (Wilson, 1956, pp.
17–18). The autobiographical element in Cushing's work appealed strongly to
Wilson, who declared that Cushing's own records of his struggle to adapt to
the Indian way of life (notably in *Zuñi Breadstuff* and "My Adventures in

Zuñi") provided a literary account which was unique. The classic writer to whom Wilson compared Cushing is Charles Montagu Doughty on Arabia.

The description of how Cushing became a Zuñi was written for *Century Magazine*. Cushing's other classic account of day-to-day Zuñi life, *Zuñi Breadstuff,* also appeared as a serial in a magazine for laymen, *The Millstone*. Both accounts employed a familiar, anecdotal style. No one has attempted to claim, however, that the wealth of detail about Zuñi life is anything but factual, even though both accounts were written for popular consumption.

When Cushing first went to Washington to become an assistant to Baird at the Smithsonian, there was apparently no intimation of a trip to the Zuñi. The transition to field worker seems in fact to have been quite abrupt. In 1879, Colonel James Stevenson was about to set out on a collecting expedition to the Southwest. The intention was to obtain artifacts, both ancient and contemporary, by barter and purchase from the Indians of the pueblos. Baird, who seems to have decided it was time for his protégé-prodigy to begin to pick up information about living Indians, sent Cushing along as the party's ethnologist. Cushing stated that only a few days before the party was to leave, Baird gave him these directions:

Make your own choice of field, and use your own methods; only, get the information. You will probably be gone three months. Write me frequently. I'm in a hurry this evening. Look to Major Powell, of the Bureau of Ethnology, if you want further directions. Good-day (Cushing, 1882b, p. 191).

The expedition was launched with the usual pomp and fanfare of collecting expeditions of the time. Upon arrival at the Zuñi, the party camped temporarily upon the property of the Reverend Mr. Ealy, a missionary, and Cushing began his pueblo studies by observing, sketching, and measuring at the nearby village. At the same time he began to try to learn the language. The villagers were markedly reserved in their treatment of the ethnologist. While they admired his colored drawings, they absolutely refused to give him permission to sketch their dances. Cushing attributed some of their lack of enthusiasm to the fact that the party had camped on the missionary's doorstep. The missionary, whom the Indians called "Dust-eye," does not seem to have possessed a personality likely to win friends among the Zuñi, and it is certain that his attitude toward Zuñi religious ceremonial was not conducive to Zuñi confidence that their beliefs would be respected by whites allowed to obtain information about them.

Cushing therefore decided to sling his hammock in the house of the "governor," as the Zuñi householder who occupied the most important political position in the village was called by the whites. The governor agreed to take Cushing in but kept him under continual observation. Relations of the utmost formality were observed. Nevertheless, Cushing felt that he was making some progress in gaining the confidence of the Zuñi villagers.

Frank Hamilton Cushing, by Charles M. Bell, Washington, D.C., July 26, 1879. (Smithsonian Institution National Anthropological Archives)

Having collected as many pieces for the museum as the villagers were willing to sell, the members of the exploring expedition now decided to move on to visit the Hopi. Cushing felt he ought to stay with the Zuñi, especially as more ceremonials were in the offing. He hoped to be allowed more freedom to observe, now that the Zuñi were acquainted with him. Thus it was arranged that the expedition would leave supplies for him with the missionary.

At this point occurred the misunderstanding which was at first to appear a disaster for Cushing. Yet it was to prove most fortunate in enabling him to establish himself with the Zuñi in a confidential position never to be achieved by any subsequent anthropologist. When Cushing applied to the missionary for his supplies, the chilling response was that anything which had been left behind by the expedition had been left for the missionary himself, as partial repayment for his hospitality. Nothing had been said, Cushing was told, of any need to share such provisions with Cushing. Moreover, the missionary did not intend to make himself responsible for Cushing in any manner whatsoever.

Cushing returned to the Zuñi as a sort of outcast from his own society. We are not told what balance of ingenuity and naiveté was involved, but Cushing presented himself to the Zuñi as indigent, helpless until the expedition returned, and cast off by the missionary. Possibly the unpopularity of the missionary influenced the attitude of the Zuñi toward this young man whom the missionary clearly regarded as no friend of his. The governor said solemnly:

Little brother, you may be a Washington man, but it seems you are very poor. Now, if you do as we tell you, and will only make up your mind to be a Zuñi, you shall be rich, for you shall have fathers and mothers, brothers and sisters, and the best food in the world (Cushing, 1882b, p. 204).

Cushing was adopted into the family of the governor, although a stringent testing period had to be endured before his ears were pierced in sign of formal admission to the tribe. His name was declared to be Té-na-tsa-li, Medicine Flower.

When the Stevenson party came back to Zuñi and Cushing might with honor have packed up his information and returned to Washington, he decided instead to stay in the village where he had established such excellent rapport. His preceptors were determined to make a real Zuñi out of him. They warned him against having anything to do with either the missionary (who can have presented no temptation) or "Blackbeard," the trader. In particular, he was to eat no food not Zuñi-prepared nor wear any but Zuñi clothing. Many of the foods he called delicious, but among the items to which he was introduced was rat soup. This delicacy, prepared while Cushing was on a hunting party, entailed squeezing the juice from the entire rat, intestines and all. It is obvious from his account that his Zuñi hunting comrades were gleefully aware that the enthusiasm of his participation was feigned. He explained how at first he found eating very hot food with his fingers excessively painful. Quietly, he kept at his side a horn spoon, itself of Zuñi manufacture, with which to dip up his portion of very hot food. Just as quietly, his "Elder Brother" brought his foot down on the spoon, which was crushed under the impact. Cushing took the

Frank Hamilton Cushing in Zuñi clothing, by John K. Hillers of the Bureau of American Ethnology, date not recorded, 1180–1881. (Smithsonian Institution National Anthropological Archives, Bureau of American Ethnology Collection)

hint and used his fingers henceforth as a proper Zuñi should. The anecdote is only one of many which show that no detail was too insignificant for his mentors' attention. Cushing was trained much as though he were a small boy. His teachers expected conformity even in minute details, such as that of wearing the headband straight.

If "going native" is defined as a deliberate, nearly complete participation, it must be conceded that Cushing went native during this period. Certainly during the rugged ordeal of learning to participate like a native, he was required by his Zuñi instructors to behave more as a genuine member of the society than an anthropologist is ordinarily expected or required to do. His professional rewards, however, were correspondingly great. When he started to sketch the great winter ceremony of Shalako, a group of Zuñi which included both young men and elders indicated their objections by a dramatic threat of force. Ignoring the dissidents, he continued to sketch. Eventually the band which had threatened to knife him decided instead to tear to pieces a dog —labeled a Navaho. How much of the drama was playacting and what weight Cushing's adoption as the son of an important Zuñi family had in the decision to spare him, one cannot exactly assign. Certainly the attitude of the pueblo peoples to those whom they feel are spying on their secrets indicates that the danger was by no means unreal and that Cushing's position as a "Washington" could not in itself have given him immunity from Zuñi anger.

The legend that Cushing went native to such an extent that he refused to reveal Zuñi secrets does not stand up very well, however, in relation to this episode. Even in this first period of his years at Zuñi, he published pictures of the highly secret Shalako ceremony (Cushing, 1882b). He seems to have had the art of dividing Zuñi public opinion, so that, as we shall see later in relation to his publication of Zuñi mythology, he was able to persuade at least some of the elders that his anthropological interests were no threat.

Although the light tone of "My Adventures in Zuñi" does not hide the strain which Cushing occasionally felt in his efforts to immerse himself in Zuñi culture, the one feature about his new people which Cushing seems to have found most difficult to tolerate was their casual cruelty to animals. A burro which wandered into a cornfield not only might be severely beaten but might lose his ears, an eye, or his teeth. Crows were discouraged from maurauding by being captured and tormented, tied with wires, and left to starve with their beaks cut off. Cushing mentioned the futility of intervention:

In pity both for crows and burros, I have sometimes pleaded mitigation of the customary severe measures. My experiences at such times lead me to advise all aspiring ethnologists to mind their own business when corn is in the question. As I have said before, the Zuñis, and probably most other Indians, are touchy on the subject of their breadstuff (Cushing, 1884–1885, p. 211).

No one seems to have interfered with Cushing, however, although he admitted that everyone thought he was behaving like a simpleton, when for two years he fed a crippled burro whose owner had cast him off as useless.

One way of becoming more closely identified with the Zuñi, that of marriage, was twice proposed to Cushing, although the proposal took a symbolic rather than a verbal form. On two occasions, shy Zuñi maidens appeared with presents of ground meal. Cushing's attitude toward the opportunity seems to have been that he felt most fortunate in already understanding the marriage customs well enough to insist on paying for the meal. Acceptance of the corn meal as a gift would have meant that Cushing was formally betrothed.

In 1882, when Cushing, accompanied by a number of Indian elders, returned to Washington, he married Miss Emily Tennison McGill (Chamberlain, 1900, p. 130). By this time his position within the tribe was so secure that the demands made upon him while he was in process of adoption seem to have been much relaxed. On his return to the Zuñi he was accompanied by his white wife, and some of the hardship of village life was ameliorated by the services of a Negro cook (Wilson, 1956, p. 16). The stringent fidelity to Indian custom which was described in "My Adventures in Zuñi" and in "Zuñi Breadstuff" seems to have given way to a style of life much more like that to which anthropologists on field trips are more or less accustomed.

Instead of marrying within the tribe, Cushing sealed his relationship by performing a service for the Zuñi religious orders. He took a group of Zuñi to get water for their sacred ceremonies from the "Ocean of the Sunrise"—the Atlantic. The publicity was worthy of a P. T. Barnum—and indeed the group was actually interviewed by Mr. Barnum. Sylvester Baxter (1882) reports a variety of interviews—eminent scholars, students at Wellesley College, and members of the Paint and Clay Club of Boston, who sketched some interesting portraits which accompany the article. Cushing is shown with his headband worn straight, but he has added a jaunty eagle feather and a quantity of silver jewelry. His blond hair appears to have been shoulder-length, but we are let in on the secret of a little compromise. Since he was to be involved in the ceremonials of Kâ-Kâ on his return, he needed both long hair and the scalp of an enemy, preferably a Navaho. The scalp was easy to obtain through the influence of D. S. Lamb, one of his museum friends (Lamb, 1906, p. 568), but perhaps Cushing feared some of his colleagues might think he had gone native if he appeared with long hair wherever he went. He persuaded the high-ranking Zuñi who accompanied him to allow him to have his hair cut. The shoulder-length swatch which resulted was attached to his headband. Whenever he donned the band, his hair appeared to be of the proper length. Another special dispensation permitted him to appear, when he thought it desirable, in white man's clothing instead of in Zuñi buckskins.

The newspapers took great interest in the pilgrimage. In Chicago, the Zuñi were particularly impressed by Lake Michigan. At Lincoln Park Zoo, they paid homage to the sea lions because they were ocean beasts. In Boston, the mayor rented a steamboat to take the Indian group and a select company of ladies and gentlemen to Deer Island, where the ceremony of dipping the water from the ocean was performed with due solemnity. The gourd container was so old and so holy that the venerable high priest, a man over ninety, had carried it carefully in his hands all the way across the country.

Cushing became a member of the Society of the Bow, one of the influential Zuñi secret societies, and rose to high office in it. His friends among the priesthood seem to have been willing not only to teach him their mysteries but even to cooperate with his desire to explain to American scholars the meaning of Zuñi beliefs. Cushing discussed one of the Zuñi epics thus:

Although oral, this epic is of great length, metrical, rhythmical even in parts, and filled with archaic expressions nowhere to be found in the modern Zuñi. It is to be regretted that the original diction cannot here be preserved. I have been unable, however, to record literally even portions of this piece of aboriginal literature, as it is jealously guarded by the priests, who are its keepers, and is publicly repeated by them only once in four years, and then only in the presence of the priests of the various orders. As a member of one of the latter, I was enabled to listen to one-fourth of it during the last recitation, which occurred in February, 1881. I therefore give mere abstracts, mostly furnished from memory, and greatly condensed, but pronounced correct, so far as they go, by one of the above-mentioned priests (Cushing, 1880–1881, pp. 12–13).

Cushing not only did not mind explaining the sacred myths but also had enough influence with one of the elders who had accompanied him to Washington to persuade him to pronounce on the correctness of his abstract.

Of the visit by Cushing and his Zuñi to the Seneca Reserve, Powell stated:

Here he learned important and obscure facts relative to the social organizations of the Seneca, more especially the "medicine" fraternities. In the latter he found evidence of a society of "medicine priests," functionally identical with a similar organization among the Zuñi . . . (Powell, 1882–1883, p. xxxvii).

The details about the suggested resemblances between Zuñi medicine societies and the Seneca False-faces, we shall probably never know. Like so much of Cushing's information, all was to be revealed at a future date. While colleagues reported him as generous almost to a fault in giving his time and knowledge to help his friends with their own ethnological problems, he never had time enough to write up his own voluminous information. His mannerism, in almost every account he did write, of apologizing for lack of space or time to enlarge upon all he had discovered about the given subject, has possibly led some critics to overlook how much he did actually discuss. But there can be no doubt that much of his knowledge was never written down. It seems to have been lost in lectures and in conversation. The legend that out of some mystic loyalty he kept secret what he did not put down about the Zuñi, the myth of Cushing's supposed conversion to Zuñi notions of the magical strength of secrecy, has romantic appeal; but one cannot easily correlate such ideas with the facts. There was nothing in the archeological discoveries which he made that he was in any way sworn to keep secret.

The Cushing legend has drawn strength from the casual way in which both Cushing and those who discussed Cushing had of referring to his "five years at Zuñi." Five years, with what both Kroeber and Bunzel seemed to believe was only a brief break when Cushing took the Zuñi priests to Washington, suggest a more profound identification with the Zuñi than apparently occurred. Probably no other professional anthropologist has studied a single people continuously for so long a time. Bronislaw Malinowski's long stay with the Trobriands would make him only the runner-up. However, when we examine those five years which are credited to Cushing, we find them full of absences.

Everyone seems to agree that the first stay with the Zuñi was from the autumn of 1879 to the winter of 1881. While much of this time was spent in the ordeal of training to be a true Zuñi, as described in his own tale of his adventures, part of it was spent on archeological exploration which was of professional rather than tribal interest. In January 1881, he made the long visit to the Havasupai which he described in *The Nation of the Willows* (Cushing, 1882a). Although he mentioned that he had become a member of the Zuñi nation, there is no suggestion that the Zuñi who were riding with him had any interest in the trip besides that of assisting Cushing in his professional exploration. He seems to some extent to have been the armed white, riding with Indians not all of whom he could fully trust.

Both Cushing and the Zuñi who accompanied him to Washington were working for the Bureau of Ethnology during Cushing's stay in Washington, and Cushing was still on the bureau's payroll and performing various services beyond those of his own professional interests upon his return. The trip to Oraibi in the winter of 1882–1883, for example, was an effort to persuade the Hopi to cooperate with Victor Mindeleff. In 1922, Parsons printed Cushing's own story of this ill-fated trip (Cushing, 1883b). The Hopi had been convinced by the Mormons that no trust could be placed in the words of any "Washingtons." They were uncooperative in the extreme. One detects echoes of departmental differences at the Bureau of Ethnology. Apparently Cushing originally wrote this account, found among his papers long after his death, because there was a good deal of criticism, and an attempt to lay the blame for this lack of Hopi cooperation on Cushing.

One has similar indications that not all of Cushing's scientific colleagues loved him as the Zuñi did. In a letter from Herman F. C. ten Kate, written from Nagasaki, where he had been making scientific studies when he belatedly learned about the death of Cushing (ten Kate, 1900), ten Kate suggested that it would have been nice if more of the praise and credit so generously bestowed in the "In Memoriam" tribute (Holmes, 1900, pp. 354–380) had been available to encourage the living Cushing. Ten Kate mentioned that his first meeting with Cushing was at Albuquerque in 1883. Cushing and a group of Zuñi were returning from the Exposition at Santa Fe. This busy anthropologist-gone-native was leading his Zuñi to meet scholars and the public a long way from his adopted village. Attending expositions has never been a Zuñi trait, except when the professional interest of an anthropologist has led them there. Moreover, Powell (1882–1883, p. xxxviii) mentioned a number of archeological expeditions which Cushing had taken or was about to take. The famous five years with the Zuñi were full of absences extraneous to Zuñi business and not typical of a man who had deserted his own culture and profession.

One piece of work that was, however, definitely in the interests of the Zuñi was the furore which Cushing raised in the newspapers, especially the Chicago and the Boston newspapers, when whites attempted a land grab of Zuñi property. The whites were influential, but Cushing understood publicity. Presidential intervention finally secured the Zuñi in the possession of the part of their land which the whites had tried to take away from them. It has been suggested (Wilson, 1956, p. 17) that by this activity Cushing incurred the enmity of Logan, the former Civil War hero who finished his career as the powerful Senator from Illinois. Senator John A. Logan's son-in-law, according to Wilson's information, was one of the villains of the land-grab attempt. Wilson also suggested that Logan put pressure on the Bureau of Ethnology to get Cushing removed from the Zuñi. The idea that Cushing left the Zuñi only under pressure, although suggestive of an added smirch in the record of American patronage politics, is at least congenial to the legend of his Zuñi identification.

Cushing himself officially attributed the change to a desire to trace the ancient history of Zuñi through his old love, archeological research (Cushing, 1890). In the years that followed, he gave little appearance of an embittered man cut loose from a chosen life style or a love that had become his whole being. He busied himself thoroughly with sponsors and expeditions. In the summer of 1886, Mary Hemenway, a wealthy Bostonian, agreed to finance an archeological expedition with Cushing as its leader. The Hemenway Southwestern Archaeological Expedition was ambitious in conception and, for its day, lavish in expenditure. Several prominent scientists became associated with it at one time or another. Here we encounter Cushing as an anthropological entrepreneur.

Organization proceeded rapidly and excavations began early in 1887 in the Salt River Valley near Phoenix and continued there and near the Zuñi in New Mexico into 1888. The major site, Los Muertos, a pueblo ruin, was of the epoch which is now known as Classic Hohokam. Unfortunately, Cushing's ill health forced his retirement from participation in the expedition after about two years. Cushing published his theories about the discoveries in an account prepared for the 1888 meeting of the Seventh Congress of Americanists. Illness kept him from attending the meeting, but his notes appeared in its proceedings (Cushing, 1890).

At the time of his death a decade later, Cushing had found time only to write an introduction to a report on the findings of the expedition. J. W. Fewkes published a brief sketch about the pottery some years later (1908). Further publication came after nearly half a century, when new archeological discoveries aroused interest in what could be salvaged about the classical period of the Hohokam from the materials of the Los Muertos site. Emil Haury made an intensive study of the 5,000 archeological specimens that had been deposited in the Peabody Museum in Cambridge, and wrote a report of his findings (1945). He included some excellent photographs which he had located among the scanty records, the unpublished introduction by Cushing, and an eyewitness account of some of the adventures of the expedition by a living survivor, Frank Hodge, Cushing's brother-in-law. The record was now complete.

Although Cushing was very ill for a time after his retirement as head of the archeological expedition, he was hard at work soon after his recovery. He finally published a quantity of his Zuñi material and began work on a volume of folktales, which was not published until after his death. Meanwhile, he became interested in the possibility of a new archeological project. He had long been of the opinion that primitive man would have begun his advance toward civilization by using shell and bone before he took to using stone. He was therefore especially interested in the artifacts of coast dwellers. During his long illness, he was attended by Dr. William Pepper, a man of independent wealth who became interested in Cushing's archeological theories. Together with Phoebe Hearst, Pepper financed what was originally called the Pepper-Hearst Expedition. Making soundings along the coast of Florida, the expedition led by Cushing made a remarkable find. While the discoveries at Key Marco were not of such antiquity as to furnish any backing for Cushing's theories of how man began to use tools, they represented a rich find. Some of the articles were in a remarkable state of preservation because they had remained submerged in water. The material which is in the possession of the University of Pennsylvania includes what some believe to be the most beautiful artifact of the American Indian—the celebrated deer's head. Portraits of this deer, sometimes in a copy of Cushing's original watercolor, have been reproduced extensively.

Cushing's brief account of the Key Marco find is characteristically called "A Preliminary Report" (Cushing, 1897). He never got around to writing any more about his coast dwellers of the Florida keys; but for once he had an impeccable excuse. He died, very suddenly, on April 10, 1900, after choking on a fish bone. All the insight and information which he had never had time to write down died with him. Except for the little book of Zuñi folktales which was published posthumously in 1901, the brief account of Oraibi which Parsons rescued in 1922 (Cushing, 1883b), and the few pages published by Haury in 1945, he is said to have left nothing else that was publishable. One can speculate that, when it came to documenting his material, this fluent talker and pleasant popular writer felt the lack of academic discipline. But he was not yet forty-three. He may have thought that he had plenty of time.

From the details of the life and accomplishments of Frank Hamilton Cushing, one feels justified in judging him a dedicated professional. Although he became, to an impressive degree, a Zuñi, he did not cease to be an anthropologist. Cushing was among the very first ethnographers who sought knowledge directly in the field and who deliberately adopted as far as they could the lifeways of their hosts. In an absolute sense, there is no question of Cushing's going native, just as there is no question of his success in his effort to become a Zuñi. By ethnographic standards, he appears to have had a thorough and uncompromising apprenticeship, a very long one, and a highly successful one. Even native members of a community, whose education is by no means as abnormal as that of an adult outsider who learns in the process of adoption, vary in their adjustment to the life of the community. But what of the apocryphal Cushing, whose "Zuñi-ness" is confirmed not only by the profound cultural mastery but by an unshakable secrecy about some of the teachings imparted to him? Was the professional dedication not at least curtailed by loyalty to Zuñi secrecy? If, despite some evidence to the contrary, there was an ultimate reluctance to disclose certain things Zuñi for fear of betraying a deeply felt personal rapport, this no more proves that Cushing went native than does a similar reticence which might be charged to many anthropologists.

Anthropologists, like others who work intimately with their fellow men, receive personal and cultural confidences they may wish they did not have to keep but about which deep feeling and respect may enforce such discretion. In Cushing's life there can be no question—as the bare legend may suggest—of a man who leaves the world he knows and while becoming ever more familiar with an adopted world becomes ever more mute and uncommunicative about it. Such a cultural crossover would never return to his first world; he would die in the second. Although Cushing wrote regrettably little, he communicated much about the Zuñi world. Even though the circumstances of his departure from the Zuñi are somewhat clouded (he did return briefly), his subsequent life has little hint of exile.

As we have seen, however, Cushing need not lose interest for us because he fails as the archetype of the complete transcultural emigré, the one who burns all his bridges. Like many another man, he is done a disservice by his legend, which claims what is dubious while distracting from a demonstrable achievement, remarkable for its own day, and not without importance for his anthropological heirs.

Much information may have been lost to anthropology by his sudden death, but one is inclined to blame his failure to set down a larger proportion of what he had learned to the lively temperament which kept him constantly learning more. In his time, anthropology was so new that in America there was no anthropological discipline per se. Most of those who practiced the new science arrived with training from other disciplines. Among these men Cushing was unique in that he was a member of no academic discipline. He invented his own methods of work. The same insight and imagination which as a youth he applied to Indian artifacts proved useful to him in his rapport with living Indians. He was always willing to share his information with other scholars. Possibly his intuitive and psychological methods of working could not wholly be shared. He grew into being an anthropologist in a way not unlike the process by which he became a Zuñi—without the kind of formal education that is commonly followed in becoming either.

REFERENCES

BAXTER, SYLVESTER. 1882. "An Aboriginal Pilgrimage." *Century Magazine,* 2:528ff.

CHAMBERLAIN, ALEX. 1900. "In Memoriam." *Journal of American Folklore,* 13:129–134.

CUSHING, FRANK HAMILTON. The first date given is that of writing; the date in parentheses is that of publication.

    1874 (1875). "Antiquities of Orleans County, New York." *Annual Report of the Smithsonian Institution.* Washington, D.C.

    1880–1881 (1883). "Zuñi Fetiches." *Second Annual Report of the Bureau of Ethnology.* Washington, D.C.

    1882a (1965). *The Nation of the Willows.* Flagstaff, Ariz.: Northland Press. Reprinted from "A Visit to Havasupai," *Atlantic Monthly* (1882), 50:362–374, 541–559.

    1882b. "My Adventures in Zuñi." *Century Magazine,* 25:191–207, 500–511.

    1883a. "My Adventures in Zuñi." *Century Magazine,* 26:28–47.

    1883b (1922). "Oraibi in 1883." *American Anthropologist,* n.s. 24:253–268. Foreword by Elsie Clews Parsons.

    1884–1885. "Zuñi Breadstuff." *The Millstone,* January. Reprinted in *Indian Notes and Monographs,* whole vol. 8, 1920.

    1888 (1890). "Preliminary Notes on the Origin, Working Hypothesis and Primary Researches of the Hemenway Southwestern Archaeological Expedition." *Proceedings of the Seventh International Congress of Americanists,* pp. 151–194. Berlin.

    1891–1892 (1896). "Outlines of Zuñi Creation Myths." *Thirteenth Annual Report of the Bureau of Ethnology.* Washington, D.C.

    1895. "The Arrow." *American Anthropologist,* o.s. 8:307–349.

    1897. "A Preliminary Report on the Pepper-Hearst Expedition: Exploration of Ancient Key Dwellers Remains on the Gulf Coast of Florida." *Proceedings of the American Philosophical Society,* 25:329–432. Philadelphia.

    1901. *Zuñi Folktales.* Introduction by J. W. Powell. New York: Putnam's, Knickerbocker Press.

FEWKES, J. WALTER. 1909. "Ancient Zuñi Pottery." *Putnam Anniversary Volume.* New York: Stechert.

FORDE, DARRYL. 1960. "Anthropology." *Encyclopaedia Britannica,* vol. 2, p. 43.

HAURY, EMIL W. 1945. "The Excavation of Los Muertos and Neighboring Ruins in the Salt River Valley, Southern Arizona." *Papers of the Peabody Museum of American Archaeology and Ethnology,* Harvard University, vol. 24, no. 1. Cambridge, Mass.

HOLMES, WILLIAM HENRY. 1900. "In Memoriam." *American Anthropologist,* n.s. 2:356–360, Part 1.

KATE, H. F. C. TEN. 1900. "Frank Hamilton Cushing." *American Anthropologist,* n.s. 2:768, Part 2.

KROEBER, A. L. 1921. "Frank Hamilton Cushing." *Encyclopaedia of the Social Sciences,* vol. 4. New York: Macmillan.

LAMB, D. S. 1906. "The Story of the Anthropological Society of Washington." *American Anthropologist,* 8:564–579.

LÉVI-STRAUSS, CLAUDE. 1963. *Structural Anthropology.* New York: Basic Books.

MATTHEWS, WASHINGTON. 1896. "Review of Outlines of Zuñi Creation Myths." *Journal of American Folklore,* 9:232ff.

1900. "In Memoriam." *American Anthropologist,* n.s. 2:370–376, Part 1.

POWELL, J. W. 1880–1881. *Second Annual Report of the Bureau of Ethnology.* Washington, D.C.

1882–1883. *Fourth Annual Report of the Bureau of Ethnology.* Washington, D.C.

1900. "In Memoriam." *American Anthropologist,* n.s. 2:360–367, Part 1.

RADIN, PAUL. 1929. "History of Ethnological Theories." *American Anthropologist,* n.s. 31:2–33.

WILSON, EDMUND. 1956. *Red, Black, Blond and Olive.* New York: Oxford University Press.

3 / On Being an Anthropologist

A. IRVING HALLOWELL

BECOMING AN ANTHROPOLOGIST

The social scientists of her sample, comments Ann Roe (1953), often show a sense of rebellion against traditional family values. I think this was true of me. Since I had no outstanding talents and evinced no special interest in any of the professions, my conservative parents assumed I would take up a business career. Therefore, after a three-year course in a manual-training high school, I was sent to the Wharton School of Finance and Commerce of the University of Pennsylvania.

In those days, before World War I, the Wharton school had a much more flexible curriculum. It was also then the home of social sciences (economics, sociology, and political science), but anthropology was in the College of Liberal Arts. The school permitted its students to take many electives in the college; so in addition to the required business-oriented courses, I sampled chemistry, history, English literature, and Italian Renaissance painting, though I did not look into anthropology. Above all, I discovered social science and took all the courses in economics and sociology that were offered. I had work with Scott Nearing, and in my senior year I was admitted to a seminar given by Simon N. Patten, a singular economist of that time who is now almost forgotten. In rebellion against classical economics, Patten attempted to deal with problems of change and evolution and tried to open up a perspective emphasizing abundance rather than scarcity (see Patten, 1924).

Soon I gave up all thought of a business career. The social sciences and ideas of social reform absorbed my interest. I wanted to go ahead with graduate studies, but because there were no family funds, and fellowships with stipends were scarce in those days, I entered social work and took some graduate courses in sociology on the side. Since I had been brought up in a protected environment, social work opened my eyes to how "the other half" lived. As a representative of the Family Society, I went into the homes of unfamiliar ethnic groups—Poles, Italians, Negroes. Casework among people with such diverse backgrounds provided me with a wide experience in interviewing.

It was also at this time—the late 1910's and early 1920's—that I was first introduced to psychoanalysis. Psychoanalysis was then a novel, exciting, and controversial topic among American intellectuals, especially in New York. A. A. Brill, the first American psychiatrist to become a member of Freud's group in Vienna, published his translation of Freud's *Interpretation of Dreams* in 1913. It almost immediately stirred up tremendous interest. Many social workers eagerly turned to psychoanalysis for a new illumination of social theory and interpersonal relations. In Philadelphia the Pennsylvania School of Social Work engaged A. A. Goldenweiser, an anthropologist, to give a series of lectures on psychoanalytic theory. Goldenweiser was one of the first social scientists in this country to attempt to apply Freudian psychology to the elucidation of social facts. His lectures had nothing to do, however, with personality and culture studies as they subsequently developed.

During my undergraduate days I had met Frank G. Speck. We were both members of the same fraternity. At the fraternity house I had often listened to his stories about his experiences with Indians. (Speck was a gifted raconteur.) I had also dropped in to hear him lecture. Casting around for courses which were given at a time that would fit my social-work schedule, I signed up for several of his.

I found the general anthropological approach very stimulating as compared with the approach of sociology. I thought the anthropologists' rejection of a unilineal theory of cultural evolution very progressive. The idea of "culture," too, was rather new and it was not in the sociologists' kit. Anthropology opened a vista far beyond the ethnic groups in my own backyard. Abstract and theoretical social problems now had a very broad base.

Another feature that impressed me was the political attitude which characterized the anthropologists of that period. If I may use so old-fashioned a label, it was very "liberal." Perhaps this was due to the dominant influence of Franz Boas. My own attitudes were on the liberal side. I was very doubtful, for instance, about our entry into World War I, and I had socialistic inclinations.

Since I already knew Speck and since his classes were small, we quickly became well acquainted. I became a candidate for a master's degree in anthropology, dropped my courses in sociology, and decided to leave social work for a career in anthropology. At the time I thought this was a radical shift, but now I see a continuity: my move was well within the broad boundaries of the social sciences, theoretical and applied.

Speck helped me to obtain a Harrison Fellowship so that I could devote full time to graduate work. During one semester I made a weekly trip to New York to attend Boas' seminar at Columbia University. All the members of the group, which included Ruth Benedict and Melville Herskovits, were assigned books for seminar reports and discussion. My assignment consisted of Edward Westermarck's *History of Human Marriage* and John Dewey's *Human Nature and*

Conduct, which had only recently been published. A group of us from Boas' seminar also met privately each week with Goldenweiser for anthropological discussions.

With my interests ranging over broad social problems, it may seem paradoxical that the people in whom I became most interested were the American Indians. But these were the primitive, aboriginal people of America—and they were Frank Speck's pets. At this time, he was engaged in "salvage anthropology" among the Indians of the eastern United States.[1] Speck's self-involvement with the study people and their problems was perhaps greater than that of other anthropologists of the period. He was always extolling the sovereign virtues of the Indians and proclaiming the intrinsic values of their culture. Current political events and problems in American life held little interest for him; he was critical in general of the values of American culture. This attitude Speck shared with other anthropologists, for these were the days of Harold Stearns' *Civilization in the United States,* to which both Robert H. Lowie and Elsie Clews Parsons contributed.[2] It was also the time when many American writers and artists were going abroad to do their work.

Speck was about as detached from American culture as one could be. He would not, for instance, buy a car, and he never read newspapers. In a sense, he was also detached from the university and its affairs. I never remember his serving on a committee; his thoughts and energies were entirely devoted to his research among Indians. And I imitated my mentor for a long while. I, too, identified myself with the Indians, and tried to avoid serving on university committees. Anthropology in all its aspects was the overarching thing and Boas was king, for Speck had been not only a student of Boas but also a deeply rooted follower. Boas had said the last word. What one strove for was to follow Boas in his ubiquitous interests—ethnology, archeology, physical anthropology, and linguistics. Anthropology, despite broad areas of specialization, was regarded as an all-embracing study of man which should be conceptualized and pursued as a whole even while the individual engaged in specialized investigations.[3]

FIELD WORK IN THE 1920's

It was in this spirit, following Speck, that I began my field work among an acculturated group of Indians in eastern Canada, the St. Francis Abenaki. These Abenaki, who were related to the Penobscot of Maine whom Speck had studied intensively, lived on a reservation sixty miles east of Montreal on the south side of the St. Lawrence River. They were bilingual but they lived much as the French Canadians did who surrounded them. I set out to recover for the record the remnants of their aboriginal culture. It did not occur to me to study their "community" or any problems of "acculturation." In fact, this latter approach was not articulated in anthropology until the 1930's. These were the days when the major emphasis was on "culture traits" and "trait complexes," such information to be reconstructed from fast-disappearing native cultures (see Beals, 1953).

Thus I collected Abenaki objects of material culture for the Museum of the American Indian (Heye Foundation) in New York. There were more of these to collect than one might suppose—the last birchbark canoe, for example, and a native "slow match." I made a series of physical measurements (unpublished). I also studied the native language, which was still spoken by everyone, made a collection of loan words, and secured some folktales in text.[4] I collected information on their hunting customs and particularly on their hunting territories, a special interest of Speck's, and wrote a paper (unpublished) on the subject. I became interested in the Abenaki kinship system, and I was able to document changes unknown to the Indians themselves. This was made possible through my discovery of an eighteenth-century manuscript dictionary on the reservation. Melville Herskovits (1938) pointed out that my paper (1928) was one of the earliest attempts to demonstrate changes in a kinship system from documentary sources. (Incidentally, the Abenaki system does not belong to the Northern Algonkian pattern, which reflects cross-cousin marriage.)

Although I made quite a few brief trips to the Abenaki, this kind of field work did not satisfy me. A number of years went by while I fretted for an opportunity to work in a really "primitive" culture. Meanwhile, there was the problem of a thesis, and nothing appropriate had emerged from the Abenaki investigations.

Finally, with a lead from J. G. Frazer and with Speck's encouragement, I began research in what I would later call "bear ceremonialism." In the course of studying the variety and detail of local ceremonies, I was soon led to evidence of the occurrence of related ceremonies in the Old World as well as the New. There appeared to be a nucleus of common ceremonial traits suggesting historical connections from Lapland to Labrador. If one took this finding, along with a somewhat similar distribution of other culture traits commonly shared by the peoples of Eurasia and northern North America, an old culture stratum seemed indicated (see Hatt, 1933; Lowie, 1934). With respect to antiquity, I drew attention to the peculiar disposal of bear skulls and long bones at Drachenloch, Switzerland, during paleolithic times and the crudely modeled figure of a bear in the cave of Montespan. Other archeological evidence of an ancient bear cult has since turned up. I realized that there was a local setting for bear ceremonialism everywhere—involving mythology, world view, the hunting of other animals, and so on—but I chose to be selective and to consider the geographical distribution of the associated features of bear ceremonialism in a broad cultural-historical setting.

Incidentally, Bertold Laufer at first discouraged me by questioning my ability to handle the Eurasian data. But things worked out somehow, and later he was extremely complimentary about the final product.[5] The monograph which ultimately emerged (Hallowell, 1926) has created more reverberations in Europe than anything else I have written. At first it was taken up by the Kulturkreise School. Then it helped focus further field work among the Russians. More recently it has been discussed by those interested in prehistoric religion (see Campbell, 1959; Maringer, 1960; Lissner, 1961).

KINSHIP, CULTURE, AND PSYCHOLOGY

Meanwhile, my interest in kinship was further stimulated by the residence in Philadelphia of an Araucanian Indian, J. Martin Collio, with whom both Speck and I had personal contact. I obtained a set of kinship terms from him as early as 1922. At first they were very puzzling to me. Eventually, they turned out to be the Omaha pattern, an ill-defined type at the time. I hesitated to publish my information, partly because the data were obtained from a single informant, but also because I half-hoped that someday I might be able to go to South America and do field work among the Araucanians. Then, stimulated by an article by A. Lesser (1929), I presented my material at a meeting of the American Anthropological Association in 1929. It met with little or no discussion so I put the paper aside. More than a decade later, in 1943, at a lecture he gave before the Philadelphia Anthropological Society, G. P. Murdock remarked that in his survey of social organization and kinship throughout the world, he was struck by the absence of the Omaha pattern in South America, although he suspected its presence among the Araucanians. So I sent my paper, in its original form, to the *American Anthropologist* and it was published (Hallowell, 1943).

Long before this, however, I had made some other excursions into the relations between kinship pattern and social behavior, which led directly to my study of the Northern Ojibwa. In Montreal, in the late 1920's, I discovered some old dictionaries which suggested that cross-cousin marriage had once existed among the North-Central Algonkians. While this finding would excite very little interest today, in the United States in the 1920's the prevailing view, supported by such influential anthropologists as Kroeber and Truman Michelson, was that kinship terms were to be considered as purely linguistic phenomena. Thus, one aspect of the problem was the traditional attitude of American anthropologists toward the study of the functional ramifications of kinship in its total sociocultural setting. At any rate, at the International Congress of Americanists in 1928, I read a paper raising the question of the existence of cross-cousin marriage among the Algonkian (Hallowell, 1930). As I recall now, I received no support for my hypothesis but a rather critical appraisal from Michelson. It was not until shortly after the congress that I learned that W. D. Strong, who had recently spent fifteen months in Labrador, reported the practice of cross-cousin marriage among the Barren Ground band of the Naskapi. So I made plans to go into the field in order to discover whether the kinship pattern together with the practice of cross-cousin marriage actually existed in any contemporary North-Central Algonkian group.

I went into the field both "functionally" and "problem-oriented." My first trip was made in 1930 to the Algonkians of the Lake Winnipeg region. Pursuing my search for cross-cousin marriage among the Ojibwa of the Berens River, I well remember an early conversation with William Berens, my closest collaborator. I hesitatingly asked him whether a man could marry a woman he called *ninǝm*. His reply was, "Who the hell else would he marry?" In a sense, the problem I had come to investigate was solved: the Ojibwa of the Berens River did practice cross-cousin marriage and used the appropriate terminology. The situation among the Northern Algonkians was more complicated, however, because historical circumstances had led to differential changes in terminology and social practice among different groups. Later I concluded that "Northern Algonkian kinship systems are . . . intelligible as variants of a basic pattern that has undergone modifications as the result of acculturative processes and differences in local conditions" (Hallowell, 1937).

My field work among the Cree and Ojibwa of the Lake Winnipeg region had hardly begun when I was drawn into a newly emerging area of research in anthropology: the psychological interrelations of individuals and their culture. From its beginnings anthropology has been influenced by developments within the academic tradition in psychology; but around 1920 it was psychoanalysis with its psychiatric background, its concepts of individual psychodynamics and personality, that challenged anthropologists.[6] This was another facet of the great impact of psychoanalytic theories on the thinking of the modern world, particularly on the sciences of human behavior. As I have said, I first met psychoanalysis burgeoning in social-work circles in Philadelphia. The anthropologists' interest, however, was on a directly professional level, and there was much discussion and many thoughtful reviews of the writings of Freud and other analysts. All of this interested me very much. All through the 1920's I followed the various new developments in psychoanalysis and in psychological anthropology.

Now, in the 1930's I became directly involved in psychological anthropology through Edward Sapir. After Sapir went to Yale in 1931, we became better acquainted and had some stimulating discussions on psychoanalysis and anthropology. Sapir had long been interested in psychoanalysis. As early as 1917 he had reviewed Freud's *Delusion and Dream* and Oskar Pfister's *The Psychoanalytic Method* for *The Dial*. Any and all new ideas in the field he welcomed, so that, for example, he gave C. G. Jung's *Psychological Types* an appreciative and thoughtful review in *The Freeman* (1923). More recently he had been listening to Harry Stack Sullivan expound his ideas on the collaboration of social scientists in the testing of his interpersonal-relations theory. Sapir had also explored various methods of getting at such information in different cultures.[7] It was to be expected, therefore, that when Sapir became chairman of the Division of Anthropology and Psychology of the National Research Council he would set up a committee on "Personality in Relation to Culture." Sapir invited me to be a member. Among the others were Ruth Benedict, Harry Stack Sullivan, Adolf Meyer, and A. A. Brill.

There was strong resistance among professional anthropologists to this psychological approach. There were also many real problems, including the question of how far psychoanalytic concepts were to be used as compared to behavioristic or Gestalt concepts. Another basic question was: From what sources were psychological data, apart from ethnological data, to be derived?

The Rorschach test was relatively new at this time. It had many advantages over other psychological tests of personality: it was a subtle means of probing many of the complexities of personality and it was "culture-free." The scoring system also made comparisons possible on either an individual basis or a group basis. From the scanty literature on the Rorschach, I learned enough to be able to try my hand at administering and scoring the test. On my next trip to the Berens River I stopped in Chicago hoping to see the Rorschach expert, Samuel J. Beck, but I missed him. So on my own I collected a large sample of protocols from both adults and children.

It was after this field trip in 1937 that I met Bruno Klopfer, who became very interested in my Indian Rorschach records. We had several conferences to discuss my material and then decided to collaborate on joint papers to be presented at the 1938 meetings of the American Anthropological Association in New York (Hallowell, 1938; Klopfer, 1938). There was a greal deal of curiosity (a large audience came to hear the papers), and while there was some interest, there was more derision. Who could take playing with ink blots seriously? However, I went ahead with my research in personality and culture among the Ojibwa using the Rorschach test (see Hallowell, 1956).

In recent years there has been a lessening of interest in personality and culture. Anthropologists are busy cultivating other fields, and psychologists have been critically evaluating the Rorschach test (see Lindzey, 1961). However, I should say that my own conception of psychological anthropology has always been a broad one that transcends the study of personality and culture in the narrow sense. There are many psychological areas that should be dealt with. It may surprise some when I say that I never gave a course myself under that rubric; my course was called "Culture and Psychology." Consequently, I fully agree with John Fischer's remarks and the shift he made in the 1965 *Biennial Review of Anthropology* by changing the title of his section from "Culture and Personality" to "Psychology and Anthropology."

Within this broad framework my interests expanded still further. Using my Ojibwa investigations for specific illustrations, I explored such topics as acculturation processes and personality changes (Chaps. 18–19 in Hallowell, 1955), culture and perception (Hallowell, 1951), and the nature and concept of the self (Chaps. 4 and 8 in Hallowell, 1955).

THE OJIBWA

My Ojibwa experience in the early 1930's was a plunge into a new world and involved problems I was little prepared to face. Since Alanson Skinner's preliminary survey in 1911, nothing had been done in the area. It was an

immense region and I had to choose a locale. As a matter of fact, I started with
the Cree and then shifted to the Ojibwa after discovering that, while there was
plenty of evidence everywhere for acculturation, up the Berens River there
were some pagan Indians. These Ojibwa had retained attitudes and a world
view which were "primitive," even though their tools, clothing, and diet were
not. This fact involved the acculturation problem in a modified form, one quite
different from the situation in eastern Canada. I think it was not until about
this time, however, that I realized there were no completely unacculturated
Indians in the United States and Canada. Before anthropologists were professionally trained in field work, Indians everywhere had been transferred to
reservations when the frontier was closed in 1890.

My original attitude toward the Indians nevertheless persisted. I deeply
identified myself with the Berens River Ojibwa. To the small number of white
people in the area I paid practically no attention. I never made friends with
the personnel of the Hudson's Bay Company posts and became only casually
acquainted with the missionaries, among whom I was more friendly with the
Catholics than with the Protestants. Since I was completely oriented toward
Indians and their culture rather than the total community, I did not at first
realize what the basic pattern of relationship was between whites and Indians.
Actually, it exemplified all the basic features of the pattern in the South
between whites and Negroes; for example, the use of first names for Indians
(my friend Chief Berens was "Willie"); a tabu on eating together; the use of
the back door by Indians when visiting whites (missionaries included); dis-
countenance of intermarriage; "passing." I have always regretted not making
a serious study of this relationship pattern. At the time I did not think of it,
for my exclusive concern was the Indians.[8]

Although the Ojibwa I worked with were not "primitives" in the sense of
having a fully functioning aboriginal culture, they were closer to it than I had
thought. There was a graded spectrum on the Berens River, those at the mouth
of the river being the most acculturated and those inland the least. As I found
out later, when I spent the summer of 1946 with a group of students on the
Ojibwa reservation at Lac du Flambeau, Wisconsin, this was only one segment
of a wider acculturation problem. Here I found myself in the position of being
an authority for these highly acculturated Ojibwa on the really old-fashioned
Ojibwa "up north."

It was the gradual realization of this broader acculturation problem that led
me in the end to attempt to interpret and expound the world view of the most
conservative Ojibwa (see Chap. 18 in Hallowell, 1955; Hallowell, 1960). This
became an excursion into ethnoscience—or ethnosemantics, if you will—for
I became aware of how sharply different the Ojibwa world was from our own
and of the necessity for testing the meaningfulness of familiar conceptual
dichotomies, such as natural-supernatural, for example. This process meant
the reintegration of ethnographic material collected under separate and quite

different categories on another level. In short, it involved an attempt to see the Ojibwa world as they saw it—an *emic* as contrasted to an *etic* viewpoint. Ecologically, it led me to the concept of a behavioral environment—a concept borrowed from Gestalt psychology—an environment culturally constituted in such a way that it structures the major psychological field in which individuals act, forming their basic cognitive orientation.

THE LATER YEARS: EXPLORATIONS IN BEHAVIORAL EVOLUTION

All these investigations in psychology and culture inevitably led to a general consideration of the psychological dimension of human evolution (Hallowell, 1950; Hallowell, 1963; Hallowell, 1965). In this endeavor I assumed a more inclusive perspective than the one provided by physical anthropology and archeology alone, one that emphasizes the continuities as opposed to the discontinuities in behavioral evolution between man and the nonhominid primates. I tried to bring together as an integral whole the organic, psychological, social, and cultural dimensions of the evolutionary process as they relate to the underlying conditions necessary for human existence. As Dobzhansky (1962) has pointed out, "Human evolution cannot be understood as a purely biological process, nor can it be adequately described as a history of culture. There exists a feedback between biological and cultural processes" (see also Menaker, 1965). And we may add, there is a feedback between specifically psychological processes and cultural ones: the emergence of ego processes, the development of self-objectification, the socialization of symbolic forms, and the rise of sociocultural systems. In this development there was no "critical point" at which culture emerged, as Kroeber maintained (see Geertz, 1964).

Beyond the world views of man, basic to his life everywhere, there is another evolutionary problem: how man has so fully assimilated subjective and unconscious experiences and integrated them with the acquisition and accumulation of pragmatic knowledge about the external world, in a manner difficult to disentangle. David Beres, a psychoanalyst, departing from the restricted meaning of the term "imaginative" as the obverse of "realistic," extends its psychological connotation to include "a process whose products are images, symbols, fantasies, dreams, ideas, thoughts and concepts." Imagination in this sense is a complex function entering into "all aspects of psychic activity—normal mentation, pathological processes, and artistic creativity." His point is that "imagination is not opposed to reality, but has as one of its most important applications, adaptation to reality." In other words, reality can best be understood, not only as a relatively indeterminate concept, but as one which is *always* infused with imaginative processes. Symbolic representations, derived from such processes, involve mediating ego functions between the external world and the inner drives of man. "To be aware of reality it becomes necessary to have two points of reference—one is the perception of the external world, the other the internal image, the mental representation."[9]

From this perspective, dreams, fantasies, myth, art, and the world views of man, as articulated in cultural traditions, may be interpreted as making positive use of psychological resources in cultural adaptation and personal adjustment. Reliable knowledge of reality in any scientific sense need not be assumed to be a necessary condition for either biological adaptation or cultural adjustment to the actualities of human existence. Man is an animal who has been able to survive by making cultural adaptations in which his own imaginative interpretations of the world have been fed back into his personal adjustment to it.

What I have tried to do in this chapter, in semiautobiographical fashion, is to outline a personal record of my own experience in anthropology, of my changing values and problems in field work. How this personal experience is related to the wider picture of the basic changes and emphases in the anthropological tradition and to changing values in the wider world, I leave to others.

NOTES

1. "It was not an uncommon experience and considered quite a *coup* for a student of Boas to catch the dying gasp of an American Indian language and culture. Sapir in the field of language and Speck in that of natural history exemplify the tradition. Speck, beloved by the Indians and learned beyond most men, sometimes managed to reconstruct a society and its culture from the merest fragments, approaching the feats of psycho-analysts in his study of Delaware ceremonies, which rank among those of the first class in American ethnology" (Fenton, 1953).

2. According to Hoffman (1962), Stearns' book, "which appeared early in 1922, was a historical landmark of the post-World War I years, a curious document of disaffection, pointing to and reiterating the failure of culture, entertainment, family life, religion—of everything but science, and even it scored only a partial success in the survey of American life and institutions" (p. 21). "The twenties were marked by a disrespect for tradition and an eager wish to try out any new suggestions regarding the nature of man—his personal beliefs, convictions, or way to salvation" (p. 33).

3. I am writing, of course, as an American anthropologist. But see Hultkrantz (1968) and the commentaries on that article.

4. The St. Francis Abenaki dialect is still spoken today and presents some interesting problems; see Day (1964; 1967).

5. In his presidential address to the American Oriental Society, Laufer (1931) said: "We owe a model investigation to Dr. A. I. Hallowell . . . into the bear ceremonialism in northern Asia and America where the worship of the bear is widely distributed and practically alike in form and content."

6. For a historical summary of the influence of psychology on anthropology, see Hallowell (1954).

7. For a more extended discussion of the seminal influence of Edward Sapir on personality and culture studies, see Hallowell (1954, pp. 203ff.).

8. As a matter of fact, there is a racial problem in Canada that has been little studied; see the novel by Bodsworth (1960).

9. All quotations in this paragraph are from Beres (1960a, 1960b).

REFERENCES

BEALS, RALPH. 1953. "Acculturation." In A. L. Kroeber, ed., *Anthropology Today: An Encyclopedic Inventory.* Chicago: University of Chicago Press.

BERES, DAVID. 1960a. "Perception, Imagination and Reality." *International Journal of Psycho-Analysis,* vol. 41.

1960b. "The Psychoanalytic Psychology of Imagination." *Journal of the American Psychoanalytic Association,* vol. 8.

BODSWORTH, FRED. 1960. *The Strange One.* New York: Dodd, Mead.

CAMPBELL, JOSEPH. 1959. *Masks of God: Primitive Mythology.* New York: Viking.

DAY, GORDON M. 1964. "A St. Francis Abenaki Vocabulary." *International Journal of American Linguistics,* 30: 371–392.

1967. "Historical Notes on New England Languages." *Contributions to Anthropology: Linguistics I.* Bulletin 214. Ottawa: National Museum of Canada.

DOBZHANSKY, T. 1962. *Mankind Evolving: The Evolution of the Human Species.* New Haven: Yale University Press.

FENTON, W. N. 1953. "Cultural Stability and Change in American Indian Societies." *Journal of the Royal Anthropological Institute,* 83: 169–170.

GEERTZ, C. 1964. "The Transition to Humanity." In Sol Tax, ed., *Horizons of Anthropology.* Chicago: Aldine.

HALLOWELL, A. IRVING. 1926. "Bear Ceremonialism in the Northern Hemisphere." *American Anthropologist.* 28: 1–175.

1928. "Recent Historical Changes in the Kinship Terminology of the St. Francis Abenaki." *Proceedings of the Twenty-second International Congress of Americanists,* pp. 97–145. Rome.

1930. "Was Cross-Cousin Marriage Practiced by the North-Central Algonkian?" *Proceedings of the Twenty-third Congress of Americanists,* pp. 519–544. New York.

1937. "Cross-Cousin Marriage in the Lake Winnipeg Area." *Twenty-fifth Anniversary Studies,* 1:95–110. Publications of the Philadelphia Anthropological Society, ed. D. S. Davidson.

1938. "An Experimental Investigation of a Series of Berens River Indians." Unpublished.

1943. "Araucanian Parallels to the Omaha Kinship Pattern." *American Anthropologist,* 45: 489–491.

1950. "Personality Structure and the Evolution of Man." *American Anthropologist,* 52:159–173. (Presidential address to the American Anthropological Association, 1949; also Chap. 1 of Hallowell 1955.)

1951. "Cultural Factors in the Structuralization of Perception." In J. H. Rohrer and M. Sherif, eds., *Social Psychology at the Cross-Roads.* New York: Books for Libraries.

1954. "Psychology and Anthropology." In John Gillin, ed., *For a Science of Social Man.* New York: Macmillan.

1955. *Culture and Experience.* Philadelphia: University of Pennsylvania Press.
Chap. 4, "The Self and Its Behavioral Environment."
Chap. 8, "The Ojibwa Self and Its Behavioral Environment."
Chap. 18, "Background for a Study of Acculturation and the Personality of the Ojibwa."
Chap. 19, "Acculturation and the Personality of the Ojibwa." (Presidential address to the Society for Projective Techniques, 1950.)

1956. "The Rorschach Test in Personality and Culture Studies." In Bruno Klopfer *et al.,* eds., *Developments in the Rorschach Technique.* New York: Harcourt Brace Jovanovich. Vol. 2.

1960. "Ojibwa Ontology, Behavior and World View." in S. Diamond, ed., *Culture in History.* New York: Columbia University Press.

1963. "Personality, Culture and Society in Behavioral Evolution." In S. Koch, ed., *Psychology: A Study of a Science.* New York: McGraw-Hill. Vol. 6.

1965. "Hominid Evolution, Cultural Adaptation and Mental Dysfunctioning." In A. V. S. de

Reuck and Ruth Porter, eds., *Ciba Foundation Symposium on Transcultural Psychiatry,* London. Boston: Little, Brown.

HATT, G. 1933. "North American and Eurasian Culture Connections." *Proceedings of the Fifth Pacific Congress.* Canada. 4:2755–2768.

HERSKOVITS, MELVILLE. 1938. *Acculturation.* New York: J. J. Augustin.

HOFFMAN, FREDERICK J. 1962. *The Twenties,* rev. ed. New York: Viking.

HULTKRANTZ, A. 1968. "The Aims of Anthropology: A Scandinavian Point of View." *Current Anthropology,* 9: 289–310.

KLOPFER, BRUNO. 1938. "Personality Investigation and Its Variables as Shown by Tests of Berens River Indians." Unpublished.

LAUFER, BERTOLD. 1931. "Columbus and Cathay, and the Meaning of America to the Orientalist." *Journal of the American Oriental Society,* 51:99.

LESSER, A. 1929. "Kinship Origins in the Light of Some Distributions." *American Anthropologist,* 31:710–730.

LINDZEY, GARDNER. 1961. *Projective Techniques and Cross-Cultural Research.* New York: Appleton.

LISSNER, IVAR. 1961. *Man, God and Magic.* New York: Putnam.

LOWIE, R. H. 1934. "Religious Ideas and Practices of the Eurasiatic and North American Areas." In E. E. Evans-Pritchard, Raymond Firth, B. Malinowski, and I. Schapera, eds., *Essays Presented to C. G. Seligman.* London: K. Paul, Trench, and Trubner.

MARINGER, JOHANNES. 1960. *The Gods of Prehistoric Man.* New York: Knopf.

MENAKER, E. AND W. 1965. *Ego in Evolution.* New York: Grove.

PATTEN, SIMON N. 1924. *Essays in Economic Theory,* ed. by R. G. Tugwell. New York: Knopf.

ROE, ANN. 1953. *The Making of a Scientist.* New York: Dodd, Mead.

4 / How *A Chinese Village* Was Written

MARTIN M. C. YANG

If I have made any contribution to the field of social anthropology or sociology, it would be in my book *A Chinese Village* (Columbia University Press, 1945; paperback edition 1965). *A Chinese Village* was not based on speculation nor is it a "secondary source" derived from reading the books and reports of others. It was an outgrowth of a tremendous amount of painstaking first-hand field work. My "field work," however, was not the ordinary kind of observing and interviewing one carries out for the purposes of study. I was born and brought up in the village I wrote about, a bonafide member of it, with all my roots there, and I worked and lived among those people until going away to college. So my field work was my own life and the lives of others in which I had an active part. Any success of *A Chinese Village* as the study of a community is chiefly due to this intimate background, a rich accumulation of personal experience and direct involvement from which I could draw all the necessary materials. In the following autobiographical sketch I want to describe the background and relate it to the writing of the book.

I was born and grew up in a Chinese farm family whose economic status was just above the subsistence level. In ordinary years the family had enough basic food for all the members and a little surplus which enabled the head of the family to think of making some slight improvement in our condition. In my memory, however, there were several times when the family suffered critical scarcity if not outright starvation. But we were never in the position of a poor tenant family.

Before I was graduated from college and had a teaching position in the city, the family consisted of my parents, four sons, and one daughter. Later on, my sisters-in-law and then nephews and nieces were added. Family relationships became complicated and our life was filled with both harmony and disputes. There were enough incidents and examples for a person of any sensitivity to discern the intricacies, the delicate balances of power and emotion, and the ways of maintaining harmony among the members.

As a small boy I experienced affection and discipline from both parents and

63

older brothers but enjoyed extraordinary tender care from an older sister. I witnessed and was deeply saddened by Mother's early death. This loss, however, was later compensated for by the establishment of genuine friendship between Father and me. I was keen and persistent in observing the interrelationships between young husband and young wife and that between the various in-laws within the same compound family. My sisters-in-law liked me most of the time but must have occasionally been annoyed by my being inquisitive regarding their private affairs.

Our home was in the farm village of Taitou, located in the southeastern corner of Shantung Province. The village consisted of about one hundred families. With a few exceptions these families belonged to four clans, or kinship groups. One of the clans was much bigger and stronger than the others. Some of its member families were rich and more cultivated than the families of the lesser clans. But as it turned out, it was the third-ranking clan which sent a

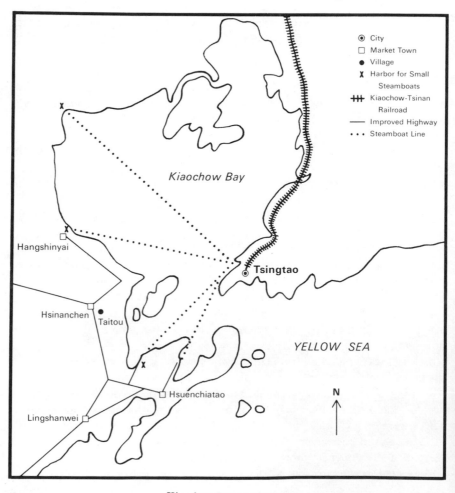

Kiaochow Bay and Vicinity

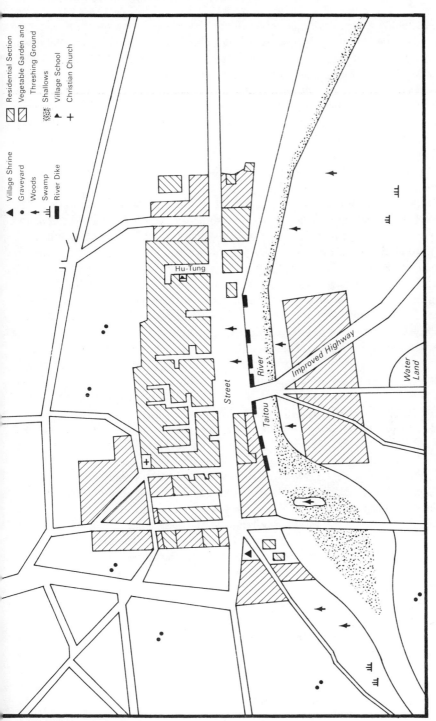

The Village Site of Taitou

Legend:

- ▲ Village Shrine
- ● Graveyard
- ⊢ Woods
- ⊥ Swamp
- ▬ River Dike
- ▨ Residential Section
- ▨ Vegetable Garden and Threshing Ground
- ▨ Shallows
- ▲ Village School
- ✚ Christian Church

Hu-Tung

Street

Taitou River

Improved Highway

Water Land

65

son to college. In our village the families of each clan by and large lived in the same section of the village area. Geographically, therefore, the village was divided into four sections corresponding to the four clans. There were further subdivisions within the territory of each group. Many of the social relations followed kinship lines, but relationships between people or families of different clans were also numerous. Some of the interclan relationships were warmer or more intimate in many ways than the relations between people within the same clan. Many socioeconomic relations were established and maintained on a basis other than kinship.

In the villagers' everyday life it was the neighborhood which counted the most. Kinship relations, religious groups, or other affiliations were important on special occasions, but not in the daily life and work of villagers. The residents of the same neighborhood meant more to each other socially and economically than members of any other group in this farm community.

Outside of my family I was quite popular with the boys in my own neighborhood and those in the nearby ones. We worked and played together, running and playing pranks while taking care of the family cows in the field or collecting firewood on the hills. I always took an active part, sometimes a leading part, in our group activities. I was also welcome among the girls who were somewhat older than I. They treated me as a beloved little brother and let me participate in their group games. For about two years I was under Mother's orders to take care of an infant brother and an infant niece. Because this was usually a girl's job, it obliged me to mingle with the girls in our neighborhood. Because of my close attachment to my older sister, to some of my female cousins, and to a particular girl of a family from another clan, I learned a great deal of the feelings, dreams, and tenderness of the country girls. As far as I can remember, I was the only boy in the village who felt at ease with girls and could enter wholeheartedly into their games as well as boys' games.

At the age of eleven I started to attend a modern primary school in the market town of our district, Hsinanchen. I had to walk about a mile between home and the school two or three times a day. I liked the school very much. It made me quite a different boy from what I was when I had attended the old-fashioned village school. From the second year on I was the most distinguished student of all the boys in the school. We schoolboys came from a number of the villages situated in the market-town area. Going to the market-town school gave a village boy opportunities to make friends among boys from the market town and from the surrounding villages. Through these relations and because my teachers spoke of me with the storekeepers and the local leaders, I soon became acquainted with most of the schoolboy sons of the storekeepers in the town. The boys from the market-town school frequently went in small groups to visit students and teachers in the nearby village schools. The market-town school was considered superior to the village schools and we were always welcome in these visits.

The market town was a service center, and the surrounding villages were

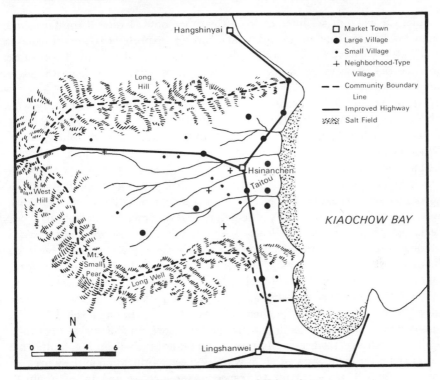

The Market-Town Area of Hsinanchen

linked to it in a town-village interdependence. The town provided a number of services to satisfy the village people's various needs in their daily life and work, and the villagers supplied most of the goods the town people had to have. The town stores owed their existence to the village people's coming to buy and sell and carry on other activities.

Walking between home and school and from one village to another I delighted in the natural scenery. I never tired of the pattern of the fields, unusual features of the terrain, and landmarks of the farm villages. The poverty, disease, natural calamities, and social disturbances suffered by the poor peasants aroused my sympathy and pity, whereas the rural simplicity, the genuine human feelings, and the gaiety of their folklore and local customs were sources of joy as well as material for making inquiries.

Because going to school in the market town kept me away from the village for most of the day, I came to look at the village from an outsider's standpoint, as well as from an insider's. I could see the interrelations of my village with other villages. I could see the direct relations between adjacent villages and the indirect relations with the market town as the link. By this time many of my fellow villagers singled me out, remarking that I was not one of the ordinary country lads. They knew something of my achievements in school, and the teachers told many of the local leaders that I was a boy of great promise.

Actually I was not so different from the other boys. I did all the farm and household chores that any ordinary farm boy was expected to do in those days. I had all the habits, likes, and dislikes of an ordinary village boy. I was more mischievous, however, and insisted more than the others on doing things in my own way.

At the age of fifteen I went to study in a middle school in the county seat, about twenty-five miles from my village. I no longer returned daily to my home in the village, but I spent every summer vacation and New Year holiday there. When I came home, it was not to relax but to work on the farm and the house, helping my father and my brothers. Here again, as at the primary school, I was different from the other students of my group. Upon becoming middle-school students, these boys began to act in accordance with the old traditions, which proscribed a scholar or gentleman from doing menial work or any labor requiring physical exertion. When I was young a person was considered a scholar as soon as he entered a middle school. When my schoolmates returned home for the summer vacation, therefore, they spent their time in the stores and teahouses in town, visited each other, and played chess or other games. Some of the parents actively encouraged the students to act this way because they felt that it was fitting for their boys as scholars. Having a scholar was a family honor. Others, without encouraging this sort of behavior, at least took a tolerant attitude toward it. My father and older brother did not compel me to help with the farm work either; it was my choice. Education in the Christian middle school had taught me to respect manual work and to give help to others. This is not to say that at that early time I had already become a man of high morals. But I did have more sympathy, appreciation, and compassion for the rural people and the rural life, I think, than others of my age and attainments. My behavior, in any case, earned me the disapproval of some villagers and the praise of others.

My attendance at Cheeloo University in Tsinan, the provincial capital of Shantung, took me away from the setting and life of the country except for occasional visits to the village. Moreover, social disturbances and plundering by bandits after each struggle among the warlords deterred me from going to the countryside, although I was deeply concerned for the safety of my kinsfolk. One year when I was home for the New Year vacation the bandits were pillaging the villages and kidnapping villagers for ransom. My father hid me in a haystack, a secret hiding place which had been prepared beforehand for just this purpose. By this time, however, the villagers had organized and equipped themselves with modern weapons of self-defense. It was a very sad experience but at the same time an exciting one.

In my junior year I returned home for another winter vacation. This time I joined my older brother in an attempt to make peace between the two schools of our village. One was the village school of which the teacher was an educated member of the village's leading clan. The other was a Christian school, operated by the dozen Christian families in the village and chiefly attended by the children of these families. Although my brother was a pastor of a Christian church and I was also a Christian, both of us felt that the village could not afford two schools and that they ought to be consolidated to give us a stronger and better village-wide school. Teachers of the two schools and some of the village leaders were invited to a dinner at our home. We tried to persuade the teachers, especially the teacher of the village school, to reconcile their differences and accept an integration plan. We failed. From this impasse and numerous others I learned of the jealousy, rivalry, conflicts of interest, and the different cliques among the villagers, especially among the various groups of village leaders.

As my education progressed, I gained a more sophisticated sense of social justice, ethics, and community welfare. With larger aspirations, naturally, it was easy to be disgusted and disappointed with the rural people. In spite of their selfishness, shortsightedness, and ignorance, however, I felt it would be possible to help them. My zeal for building an advanced and prosperous rural community became stronger and stronger, until I was determined to dedicate myself to the movement of rural reconstruction.

Immediately after graduation from college I became an assistant to two professors of the Cheeloo School of Theology, a branch of Cheeloo University. One professor was in the field of rural sociology, and the other in the field of psychology. With the first I vigorously cultivated my interest in the study of rural sociology. I became anxious to learn how to study scientifically and systematically a Chinese rural community. I was in fact thinking of my own village. I also wanted to learn as soon as possible the best ways of solving the problems of the rural people and improving their living conditions. Thus, in the fall of 1930, I went to study rural sociology at the graduate school of Yenching University. There I was completely absorbed in reading books which dealt with rural life and rural problems. I fully expected to participate in one of the rural reconstruction movements which were popular and strong at the time.

In the summer of 1931, having acquired some knowledge of rural sociology and some experience in a rural service institute, I applied to join a group project in Shantung Province, the Tsou-Ping Institute of Rural Reconstruction Experiment, under the leadership of Liang Su-ming. This man was a great philosopher and one of the prominent leaders during the 1930's in China's rural reconstruction movement. As an entrance test Mr. Liang told me to write a short paper describing the setting, people, and life of my own rural community. I had never done any writing of this kind before. Nevertheless, I tried to recall as vividly as possible my life and work in the village as well as in the larger market-town area. The completed paper contained both descriptions and interpretations, and I also projected into it a certain amount of my own feelings about the villagers and sympathy for their daily life and work.

The writing was successful in two ways. For me personally it was the first time I had been able to put together a systematic description of the people of a village, their ordinary life and their activities and sentiments on special occasions. I also discussed kinship and community organizations and their place in the life of the group. Features I had formerly taken for granted or which had simply been an unconscious part of my background now stood out and I could recognize in them certain relationships with other things. Sometimes things I had never considered noteworthy at all took on special significance. Probably for the first time in this part of the world someone had tried to understand objectively the local people's desires, ambitions, values, anxieties, and problems in relation to the situation as they saw it themselves.

My second success was that I had managed in the paper to convey to others a sense of the village. Mr. Liang said that I had presented a comprehensive and vivid life picture of the community and also revealed several possibilities for improvement programs. The paper was published in a magazine called *Tsun Chih (Village Government)*, which Mr. Liang edited. He wrote a short introductory note saying that it was the first piece of writing in China to use sociological, economic, and anthropological approaches to describe and interpret the many aspects of life in a rural community. He hoped that others would take it as an example and produce writings of the same nature.

This success encouraged me in a decision toward which I had surely been moving for a long time, that of becoming an observer and interpreter of rural life and the rural community in China.

I was engaged for only a short period in Mr. Liang's project. In the fall of 1932 I became principal of a Lutheran-church-supported middle school in Tsimo, the county seat of a rural district in eastern Shantung. Most of the student body of this school came from farm villages or rural towns. One could recognize in these boys and girls many of the attitudes of the rural people—the things they cherished or disapproved—and certain important culture traits still alive in the countryside of north China. During the five years that I held this position, I also served as consultant to the primary schools established by the Lutheran church in the villages and rural towns of a considerable area. On my frequent visits to these outlying schools, I was always interested in talking about rural life and local activities with the village teachers, preachers, and other community leaders. There was no formal plan or purpose to these conversations. I was not deliberately collecting data, just holding casual and spontaneous talks about things that interested me and that I could readily understand. All the same, the results of my visits and conversations greatly increased my insight into rural problems and needs. I was more than ever convinced that I should carry on with my long-term decision to explain and interpret the country people to those who did not know them.

In the fall of 1937, I returned to Cheeloo University to become a lecturer in rural sociology. I had the further responsibility of being Acting Director of a rural service institute then experimenting with a multipurpose program in rural improvement. Specifically, the institute was helping farmers in a rural district to improve their farm technology, establish credit systems, increase production, organize marketing cooperatives, and devise measures for public health and environmental sanitation. The institute also operated adult-education projects and conducted programs of training new local leaders and organizers for community activity.

I always tried to persuade young people to recognize the beauty and good things of the rural life, and so I was very much the rural-life idealist in the classroom. Nevertheless, when I went out to the villages to set up rural service programs, I was not blind to the real conditions. The idealism sustained me as a rural reconstruction worker in the face of practical difficulties that were sometimes formidable. On the other hand, the successes we had reinforced my idealism. This seesaw of enthusiasm and disappointment lasted several years, until the Japanese invasion of China interrupted both my teaching on the university campus and the experimental work in the villages. In the fall of 1939 I was granted the opportunity to do more advanced studies in rural sociology in the United States.

I went to the graduate school of Cornell University, where I majored in sociology and minored in social anthropology. In addition, I also took several courses in social psychology and agricultural economics. I learned the modern and scientific methods of studying a rural community. Anatomy was the first step; the presentation of a whole and living picture the second. In other words, a rural community was first to be broken up into parts, with each part analyzed in detail and then the interrelations between parts closely examined. Attention was paid to the structure and functions of each part and to those of the framework as a whole. Then, based on a knowledge of the parts, the interrelations, and the whole framework, an integrated and live picture of the community was presented. I read a great number of rural-community case studies by graduate students in order to understand just how all this was to be done and to see the results the method produced.

I had most of my training with Dwight Sanderson and W. A. Anderson. They not only taught me scientific methods but further confirmed my enthusiasm. The study of social anthropology taught me how to examine, understand, and appreciate the various institutions and cultural patterns in a rural community. I tried to use Sanderson's methods, philosophy, and enthusiasm in writing my doctoral dissertation, "The Market Town and Rural Life in China."

Early in 1943 Ralph Linton invited me to work on a project entitled "The Study of Modern Chinese Rural Civilization" in the department of anthropology at Columbia University. Professor Linton was chairman of the department and supervisor of the project. The project, which lasted about sixteen months, resulted in my writing *A Chinese Village*. Sociologists consider it a publication in the field of sociology, while anthropologists think it an anthropological study! Whatever its field, I am gratified that it has been effective in giving to readers in many parts of the world an understanding of China's rural life, and I feel honored that it has been used as a model or reference by graduate students in sociology, social anthropology, and Asian studies. It has also been distributed among civic and cultural study groups in many Western countries, and is one of the books used for the promotion of international understanding and cross-cultural studies. For a village boy who learned to observe and think about the country people among whom he grew up, this seems a long way to have come.

The success of *A Chinese Village,* I am convinced, must be attributed first to my personal experience and knowledge and second to my feelings toward the people and life of the community. I shared intimately with my fellow villagers our private and collective activities and acquired as profound a knowledge of our common culture as any of them. I feel genuine sympathy with the people, and I think I have a more than ordinary degree of sensibility toward their ideas and attitudes. I could recognize the emotional context of the situations that arose and could understand much that was left unsaid. By the time I actually wrote the book, however, I had acquired the scientific methods and objectivity which were essential for any balanced community study. I knew my village as only a villager could; yet I could also look at it with scientific detachment.

As for my feelings toward the people and events I was writing about, I can only say that in my imagination I almost completely relived my boyhood and adolescent years. I did not merely recall facts or occurrences, but mentally and emotionally retraced my role in the life of the community. All came back to me—my parents, brothers, sisters; the people of adjacent neighborhoods, of the village, the market town, the market-town school; their personalities, lives, and work; their relations with each other. Experiences recalled moved me perhaps even more than when they had taken place. Alone, I laughed aloud at remembering happy events and wept at the sad occasions. While I was filled with sympathy and compassion for the people of my community, I continually reminded myself that I was writing as a scientist, not a sentimentalist, that I must remain detached and objective, lest prejudice and emotions mar the end product.

As an insider who has written about the small society that produced him, what conclusions can I offer about such studies? An anthropologist-sociologist who wishes to make a real contribution needs an intimate knowledge of the language, a deep understanding of the culture, and a genuine feeling for the people. My conclusion is that it is much easier for a person who was born and brought up in the community to acquire the knowledge, the understanding, and the sympathy than for an outsider. But as this account seems to show, it takes a native-born person more than thirty years and a large amount of effort and good fortune to accumulate the necessary knowledge and experience to write objectively about his group. Being born and brought up among the people do not automatically qualify a person as an interpreter. He must also work to acquire the other qualifications. If the experiences of living in the community are not bestowed with birth, one will have to learn about them from others. The outsider should still be able to secure the materials for his study though it may take him more time and effort.

In conclusion, I should like to summarize the factors that had most to do with my writing a book about Taitou. My love for my sister and girl cousins, my association with village girls at an age when most boys ignore them, I am certain, taught me a different way of seeing the people around me. It was not just feeling close to girls; but from them, I think, I learned to understand their sufferings as well as the happiness of other people generally. I am sure I recognized the longings and unvoiced feelings of the villagers more than did most boys of my age.

Without college, the book would never have been written. But other village boys went to school and college without growing up to be concerned with their villages. School took most of us out of the village. It made us different, made each of us see the people of his boyhood with the eyes of an outsider. In fact, our teachers explicitly encouraged us to do so. This detachment was important for me, but at the same time it did not estrange me from my past. The endless frugality of poor farmers and the backwardness of the country stayed in my mind. I never lost touch with the people and the harsh realities as well as the goodness of their lives. At an age when my mind and heart were developing, that was important. My later determination to join the rural reconstruction movement was actually conceived at that time, I now realize.

Being a Christian surely made a difference. My work with the Lutheran-supported schools allowed me to travel and meet rural leaders, widening my awareness of the hopes and frustrations of country people. In another way, too, being a Christian was important, in that the Christian attitude toward manual work contrasted with the traditional Chinese view. So I did not consider it beneath me to do a farmer's work. Surely it was also worthwhile to write about my farm village.

It is often said that members of a minority are more conscious than others of both their values and those of the majority. Perhaps growing up a Christian affected me this way.

Of one thing I am sure: no single event brought me to the point of writing about my life and my people. If one experience could do that, men from humble backgrounds would more often write about the communities of their youth. All that I have mentioned and some things that I probably do not recognize had a part in *A Chinese Village*.

5 / Contrasts in Field Work on Three Continents

KALERVO OBERG

How easy to say, and how obvious, that in the field the anthropologist must adjust and adapt himself to his new, albeit temporary, milieu. The very words are worn thin through much service, but however poorly they convey it, their truth not only is real but, for the person involved, sometimes requires literally his whole attention. Beyond coping with the practical problems, moreover, the field worker must have still further reserves, for example, to be able to recognize cues to use the unsolicited and unexpected information which comes to him in his day-to-day interaction with the people around him. This information ranges from what may seem trivial conversation and low-keyed bits of behavior to pointed, emotionally charged statements and actions. An inexperienced field worker could easily ignore much of this information, but it often provides insights into the inner meaning of a people's culture and suggests leads for further investigation. The sheer multiplicity of field adjustments and the lack of familiar cues as to how to behave can cause what I have elsewhere described as culture shock (Oberg, 1954). In this chapter, I will indicate some of the varieties of people, experiences, and situations that particularly impressed me in the course of field work in three widely different settings.

My interest in anthropology began while I was still a sophomore at the University of British Columbia. In browsing the library stacks one day I noticed a volume entitled *Men of the Old Stone Age* by Henry Fairfield Osborn, containing color plates of cave art at Font de Gaume and Altamira. I found the whole book fascinating and wanted to know more. The university catalog listed "History 10" as dealing with the prehistory of Europe. I registered for this course in my junior year and it became my formal introduction to anthropology.

Neither the book nor the course, however, was my first contact with other cultures. As a boy, growing up on the remote west coast of Vancouver Island, I learned to fish and hunt with Nootka Indians. I listened with fascination to their folkways and myths, and I learned a smattering of their language. These early associations and interests had brought me into contact with Edward Sapir. Among his many interests, he was eager for someone with training in economics to make a study of the economic behavior of an Indian tribe. Through the years I kept my contact with Sapir and it was thus that, after securing my master's degree in economics at the University of Pittsburgh, I went into anthropology at the University of Chicago. After a year's study there, I was sent to the Tlingit Indians of southeastern Alaska to gather material for my doctoral dissertation.

In 1931 there was practically nothing one could call formal instruction in field-work methodology. Leslie Spier called me into his office shortly before my departure and spent an hour giving me last-minute suggestions about how to work in the field. He cautioned me not to talk too much, but to look, listen, and think. When I asked him about how to organize my field study, he advised me to follow the table of contents of any good ethnographic monograph and added that, since I was to concentrate on economics, I would have to figure out the approach as I went along. He assured me that I would have no great difficulty and that the trip would be a success. This was my launching as a field anthropologist, a career which lasted twenty-five years.

AMONG THE TLINGIT IN ALASKA

Two weeks later I was in Juneau, Alaska, where ten consecutive days of rain literally dampened my enthusiasm. Nor did the attitude of the local whites toward the Tlingit do much for my sagging spirits. To the whites the Indians were beggars, thieves, grumblers, and a nuisance in the community. The Tlingit attitude toward the whites was one of sullen resentment. Later an Indian was to explain to me that the whites had depleted the fur and fish resources to the point where the Indians could hardly make a living. The Indians, he said, would have liked to kill all the whites if they could have gotten away with it. With such ill feeling between white and Indian, easy working relations could hardly be expected. Then I met Father Kashaveroff. This Russian Alaskan, head of the Alaska Museum, gave me some real help. He advised me to spend the winter in Klukwan on the Chilcat River, and in the spring to visit other villages near Sitka and Wrangell. He also gave me the names of the important chiefs and suggested Tlingit men and women who would be good informants.

Preparation for my winter's work at Klukwan was no small task. The Alaska Road Commission had given me permission to live in their large road-camp log cabin some three miles above Klukwan; but since it was used only in summer, I had to ready it for my winter stay. Consequently, I spent some time walling off the front part, lining it with heavy building paper, and chinking the cracks between the logs with strips of burlap. Winter transportation from Klukwan to a nearby town was twenty-five miles by dogsled. The hotel keeper there lent me two young dogs, and an Indian sold me a sleigh and a pair of snowshoes.

The next problems were to acquire a reserve of food for myself and the dogs and to cut a supply of firewood. Late in October, when the temperature was already below freezing, there was a late run of silver salmon in the Chilcat River. An Indian showed me how to catch these fish with a gaff hook attached to a slender, fourteen-foot pole. In a few days I had 150 salmon which, when frozen, I stacked on a platform behind the cabin. My reserve food supply consisted of half a hog, a quarter of a reindeer, and 150 pounds of beef, all of which were put on the platform. Whenever I wanted meat for the next day, I had only to saw off a few pounds with a handsaw. The fish and meat supply kept until the following April.

Field work among the Tlingit of Klukwan was both trying and costly. Informants answered questions I put to them but seldom volunteered additional information. They charged fifty cents an hour, and I was always charged something extra for the right to photograph objects or events in the village. I once paid five dollars to take pictures of the burial ceremonies of one of the old chiefs. Somehow the Indians found out that I had also photographed the body of the chief. The next day a delegation from the village came and demanded my roll of exposed film. The reason they gave was that I would sell the pictures to American magazines for hundreds of dollars. To maintain good relations, I had no choice but to turn over the film, which they destroyed.

American anthropology in that period emphasized the recording of tribal ways, as it was presumed they were doomed to imminent disappearance. From such bits and pieces as might be gleaned, one attempted to reconstitute the past and trace diffusion. This emphasis on historical reconstruction limited field investigation to interviews with older informants. Participant observation was not a suitable technique for such a purpose nor, for that matter, had it been explicitly developed at that time. This point illustrates the direct connection between goals and techniques.

My field work was greatly assisted by the fortuitous arrival of a Tlingit half-breed, Frank Donley, around Christmastime. Having been sent away to an Indian school in Washington State, Donley had now returned after a twenty-year absence. He had spent years in the United States navy as well as in the merchant fleet as an engineer. Keenly interested in the ways of his mother's people, he volunteered to help me in getting information and in arranging for informants who had special knowledge of particular aspects of the old culture of Tlingit. With his help my field work progressed rapidly. In fact, it is hard to say what my efforts without him would have accomplished —surely much less.

I spent May and June in Sitka and Wrangell where field work was much easier because of better Indian-white relationships and, no doubt, because of increasing experience and skill on my part. In Sitka I recorded some Tlingit myths which I later found to be identical to myths John R. Swanton had recorded nearly thirty years earlier. Though laymen and novices at field work sometimes worry that informants are just telling tall tales and supplying false information, I have never found this to be true. While the informant may not understand the questions he is asked or may be poorly informed on the subject, he has not engaged in deliberate deception, in my experience. Checking material with a number of informants will soon bring out discrepancies and result in more accurate information.

My experience with Frank Donley convinces me that a good practice for a field worker is to get a special assistant early in his stay. Such a person can serve not only as informant, interpreter, and guide, but as he comes to know you and understand your purposes, he can also tell you which persons in the community have special knowledge about particular aspects of the native culture. Perhaps this was the most useful thing I learned as a field worker in Alaska. On subsequent field trips my first task was always to find a reliable "man Friday."

My Tlingit informants spoke with a feeling of nostalgia about their great trading expeditions into the interior for furs, about their potlatches, and about their trips to Puget Sound. The old houses lay in ruins, often surrounded by rotting totem poles. I could not help but share in their sorrow, their resentment against the whites, and their feeling of apathy toward the future. For the first time I became aware of the white man's ruthlessness and his unfeeling spoilage of Indian lands and resources. But more important was the discovery that the white man carried on these activities under the self-righteous banner of progress.

In spite of fairly serious practical difficulties, I had no serious problems of psychological adjustment in Alaska. There I was living in an American frontier-type culture not much different socially and environmentally from my home a few hundred miles to the south. As a result, my Alaskan field experience did not prepare me for the totally new demands of dealing with a dynamic African culture or for the culture shock which accompanied it. Like an illness, culture shock has to be experienced to be recognized, and I had not yet experienced it.

AMONG THE BRITISH AND THE BANYANKOLE IN AFRICA

It is curious how chance encounters and past efforts which may have had quite other purposes can shape the course of one's future. In the spring of 1933, one of my fellow students at Chicago invited me to accompany him to Evanston to hear a lecture by Bronislaw Malinowski. That evening we heard the lecture on the campus of Northwestern University and were later invited to the house of Melville Herskovits to meet Malinowski. At the time, Malinowski was recruiting students for African field work to be carried out by the International African Institute. On hearing that I had made a study of Tlingit economics, he inquired if I wanted to attend his seminar in London and explained that he was writing *Coral Gardens,* an account of Trobriand economy. I was glad for this opportunity and in the fall of 1933 I found myself attending the London School of Economics. Malinowski's seminar was devoted to an examination of the functional approach and to field-work methodology. The seminar, along with living in London and associating with advanced students from various parts of the world, made a memorable year for me.

By August 1934, I was among the Banyankole in Uganda, Africa. The context of anthropological field work in British colonial Africa in the early 1930's was so drastically different from that which prevails today, or from what I had encountered in Alaska, that detailing some of the incidents appears necessary. Nothing in my past had prepared me to live within barriers as rigid as those which separated Europeans and natives or to come to terms with the harsh punishment sometimes meted out to natives. Nor could I easily fall in with native restrictions upon my behavior or comfortably accept what seemed to me in some circumstances to be their insensitivity toward each other. The situation allowed for practically no compromise, however: I must both learn and adjust. In retrospect it is easy to see how such conditions enforce conformity and limit the freedom of the anthropologist despite his own moral views or even considerable skills.

It was in Africa that I first encountered culture shock as a personal problem and, I might add, one which also troubled some of the British colonial officials. However, I had the problem of adjusting to two subcultures: that of British colonial officialdom and that of the native people of Ankole. Not only did I have much to learn about being a safari *bwana,* but I found I also needed to adapt to the British colonial society in Ankole. Since the British colonial officials were at the apex of the power-status structure, good relationships with them were necessary for successful field work. During my first two or three months the personnel of the District Office were polite to me but not cooperative. I then realized that to get on more intimate terms with the officials, I had to make an effort to understand their pattern of life and interests. At the time, the government station at Mbarara in the district of Ankole consisted of eight British officials. Life in the station was governed by a strict routine. Office hours were from eight to one, then lunch and a siesta until four in the afternoon. I was soon informed that house visits during siesta hours were strictly tabu. At four most of the men and women went to the nine-hole golf course which formed the center of the station area. Others played tennis and badminton. At six everyone went home for a hot bath, after which they gathered at one of the family houses for the inevitable "sundowner." These visits were made in rotation. Here the men drank Scotch and soda, and the women sherry. At eight everyone went home for dinner, after which it was bedtime. According to custom, one was not supposed to drink before the sun went down nor after dinner except on festive occasions. It was also understood that everyone would serve the same brand of Scotch; Mbarara was strictly a White Horse station.

My relations with the British officials were strained until I adapted myself to their three primary social interests, which were golf, hunting, and the sundowner circuit. I bought a set of clubs, and after six months could play a passable game. Having been brought up in western Canada where most country boys learn to hunt early, I was soon able to swap stories with the others about elephant and water-buffalo hunts. Learning to drink Scotch and soda came a little harder. To most college students of the prohibition era, whiskey was too expensive and difficult to get, so we got along without. It took me quite a while to be able to take the second drink without gritting my teeth. After I gained some mastery over these three enterprises, my social status in the station community measurably improved, which in turn added to my ability to obtain information concerning the administration of the district.

At a sundowner the quiet officiousness of the British was replaced by talkative friendliness. The conversation among the men centered about golf scores, hunting experiences, humorous incidents, and jokes. Being able to hold one's liquor was considered important. But much more difficult than sharing common interests was the effort to react to the verbal cues used to ease the tensions of social intercourse at parties or in situations where no special purposeful action was involved. Small talk consists of words, phrases, and facial expressions to each of which there is a patterned response. It took time to learn this mood-shorthand. Even after I learned to operate within the official community and believed myself to be "in," I was not "of" the community. I think it is important to recognize that, no matter how well you adjust to a foreign society, you are still considered an outsider by its members.

The British had set a pattern of how a white man treated servants and porters on a safari to which I unfortunately had to conform. While I was in Alaska, sleds, snowshoes, and packboard enabled me to carry supplies, to camp in vacant cabins, and to be independent and travel at will. Not so in Africa, where I had to have authority to travel and camp and to depend on food supplies and help from the native people. Custom decreed that the white man have servants, eat off a white tablecloth, and dress smartly. Climate demanded a daily hot bath, boiled and filtered drinking water, and sanitary facilities, however temporary. I arrived with a tropical outfit but it required twenty porters to move it.

Dependence on native help gave the administration control over the movements of white travelers. After making my travel request at the District Commissioner's Office (Boma), I obtained twenty porters selected from the roll of delinquent poll-tax payers. The village or neighborhood chief had looked over his list of poll-tax payers and those who had not paid their 25 shillings' tax were requested to appear before him. Sometimes it took a day or two to get the required number of porters because the tax-delinquent men tried to hide from the chief's tax collectors.

On my first safari I accompanied a British official. At 7:30 on the first morning out, his porters were lined up with their head loads ready. My porters were still asleep in the bushes in spite of the efforts of my head boy to get them out. The Englishman then said, "We shall never get anywhere at this rate. Do you mind if I take your porters in hand this morning?" I could do nothing but agree. After my porters appeared, he lined them up and told the first in line to lie face down. As I stared in shock and amazement, his head boy then administered three lashes with an elephant-grass rod, after which he asked the porters why the first had been whipped. All except one said, "Because we were not ready in time." The exception was told to lie down again, and after one lash he too confessed. I never had any difficulties with porters after that.

My practical relations with my servants and other natives with whom I had day-to-day contacts improved considerably when I came to realize the importance they placed on family ties, status, and the supernatural agents which influence human behavior. When you hire a native servant, he considers himself a part of your family. He expects you not only to take care of him in sickness and in health but to extend social services to his immediate relatives. On several occasions my "boys" asked me to help pay their fathers' poll taxes and to provide money to buy goats for their brothers' bride payments. But along with their belief in rights to your property they also felt obligated to protect your property against strangers. Once when I was away, a thief tried to break into my house and was caught by two of my servants. They took him to the nearest native chief, where he was duly tried and punished by short-term imprisonment. On occasion I would object to their requests for assistance to relatives, but they would justify their requests by saying, "Are you not our father?"

The native servants were very conscious of status, with the important criteria for gauging status being how well their master dressed and how well he dressed his servants as well as the general quality of his equipment. In the early part of my stay, I camped in the bush to be near native kraals, and when I needed to go to the station for supplies, I would get in my car dressed in simple bush clothes. One day my head boy told me that I should dress up to go to town, and when I objected by saying it would take too much time, he brought me a freshly ironed white shirt, slacks, and a tie. After that, we went to the station dressed properly, the boys insisting that they should be dressed in white shirts, white shorts, and white tennis shoes. The British officials had the highest rank and were called *bwana enkoko* which literally meant "rooster *bwana*" because their sun helmets bore the crested crane, the state emblem of Uganda. White men who traveled with a truck, a car, many servants, and much equipment were called *bwana mkubwa* ("big *bwana*"). A gold or tin prospector who traveled in a box-body car with two servants was just a *bwana*. Native servants bask in the reflected status of a good master long after he has left their country. My first cook spoke endlessly about a *"bwana* Wickham." I never found out who Wickham was, but to my cook he was a *bwana* against whom all other *bwanas* were judged.

In the native view, human actions are not accounted for by individual will but by forces outside the individual. For instance, when I became angry with a servant or refused a request by a native, I was surprised to find that he held no ill will against me. I once refused to drive a couple with a sick child to the station clinic, saying that I would do so the following day. The child died during the night and, instead of being angry, the parents said that my refusal to take them to the clinic was a sign that the child would die. On another occasion I finally had to have one of my servants imprisoned because of his fighting with the others. After he got out of prison he wanted his job back, saying that the evil *ihanu* ("force") was not bothering him any more. My anger, too, was attributed to my having been under an evil influence.

My insights into the attitudes of the natives toward the animal and human world were acquired largely through practical experiences. Sometimes the natives would contrast my attitude with theirs. It is usual with white men, when out hunting, to put a wounded animal out of its misery as quickly as possible. Once when I had shot an antelope without killing it outright, I asked the natives to kill it with a spear because ammunition was expensive. Instead of carrying out the request, the native hunters made a fire and began lighting their pipes. After my repeated requests, one of the hunters laughingly asked, "Do you kill a man when he is badly wounded?" On another occasion a wounded water buffalo tossed and gored a native hunter. The natives told me that they would come back next day to pick up the body because it was too dangerous to go into the bush while the wounded buffalo was still there. I kept insisting that the man might still be alive and that we must get him out. After much argument I persuaded the local headman and some of his men to follow me into the bush. Soon we heard moaning and eventually we managed to get the man out, but he was so badly injured that he died an hour later. Who is right in such situations is a moot point. To the native life is precious but his ability to prolong it is limited.

Sometimes the natives made statements that struck at the core of the differences in men's views of the world. After much dickering, I managed to acquire a magic horn from a magician and brought it back to my camp. These cattle horns are filled with the most potent magical objects and are greatly feared by the natives. To their surprise I began pulling out the bits of bone, plants, and hair from the horn, at which they fled in panic. After they returned, I tried to assuage their fears by saying that there was nothing in the horn to be frightened of and that I was not afraid. One of the boys then replied, "Oh, yes, *bwana,* you are not afraid of magic because you do not believe it."

To the Africans I was a friendly white man who was interested in their ways, bandaged their sores, gave them aspirin, and supplied them with meat when I had been hunting. Once I learned their ways of greeting and listened patiently to their troubles, I was welcome in their cattle kraals and homesteads. I attended their religious ceremonies and magic rites, observed spirit possession, and noted that some individuals were under strong emotional tension. Although I could understand what was going on, I could not share in the inner

Kalervo Oberg with Banyankole tribesmen in Uganda, 1935.

meanings of these performances. There were times when I was deeply impressed, but I was not certain whether I had caught what they felt or had just projected my own emotional response. The gap between my own value system and theirs was too great for complete participation.

Perhaps the most significant statement about the white man was made by my interpreter, a very intelligent, mission-trained man. After a long discussion, he said, "We fear the white man's eye; we don't want to look in his eye." Thinking that he was referring to the evil eye, I pressed him further by saying that white men were not mean and that in general they treated the native people quite well. He then said that he did not mean that and added, "We do not like to look into a white man's eye because we do not understand it; it makes us feel troubled." I have since given this matter of the eye considerable thought. I believe this young African had touched on something quite fundamental. Eyes reflect individual moods, but at times they also reflect the meaning of one's culture and become symbolic expressions of it. While we view the world through the mechanism of vision, our perceptions of it are filtered through the prism of culture.

AMONG STUDENTS AND OFFICIALS IN BRAZIL

Early in 1946 I went to Brazil as a member of the Institute of Social Anthropology of the Smithsonian Institution to carry on university teaching and the training of Brazilian students in field-work methods in cooperation with the Escola de Sociología e Política of São Paulo. Six of my eighteen years in Latin America were spent in teaching and research among Indians in Brazil. The remainder of the time I was the "anthropologist" in the foreign-aid program attached to the American embassy.

Only after I had begun to teach Brazilian students, did I realize that the classroom in a foreign culture calls for an adjustment in style and organization of ideas somewhat comparable to the adjustment required in field situations. Furthermore, during the six years of teaching I also learned a great deal about the finer nuances of the Brazilian national character. For example, after I had explained a point of view, the students would want to know whether I believed it, generally not being satisfied by the reply that it was not a question of belief but rather of understanding. Or they would dispute a point I had made by making me read a contradictory statement by an old French or German author. Brazilian students rate brilliance and lightness in lecture presentations more important than content. They tell the story of a French professor who after many years in Brazil still continued to lecture in French. When asked why he did so, he replied that he could never be brilliant in Portuguese. Brazilian students think it odd that American professors insist on lecturing in Portuguese after a year's stay in Brazil. I had tried the light-touch form of lecturing on American college students but had felt that they considered me frivolous.

In June of that year, accompanied by two students and armed with letters from the Escola, the Smithsonian Institution, and the American consul in São Paulo, I went on a short survey trip to southern Mato Grosso. After visiting several Indian service posts, we decided to spend a week among the Guato tribe, who lived on the shores of Lake Guaiba on the upper Paraguay River. On this first trip to Mato Grosso, I was arrested by the Brazilian military. This is how it happened.

Late one afternoon, after a twenty-four-hour trip up the river in a motor launch, we arrived at a village. On inquiring about a place to stay, we were informed that we had better see the sergeant. The sergeant, who happened to be just behind us, took us to his post, which consisted of a radio station and a number of adobe houses. After assigning us to a two-room house, he told us to report to his headquarters. He looked over our documents and said that we were to stay at the post until he could check our papers by radio the next morning. We did not take the matter seriously until we noticed an armed guard standing before our quarters. It all turned out very well, however, for after a few days the sergeant's wife was cooking for us. I later learned that Brazil has a zone fifty kilometers wide along its borders in which the military exercises surveillance over foreigners. For instance, noncitizens are not permitted to own land in this zone. As Bolivia was just across Lake Guaiba, we had definitely been in this zone.

The Brazilian government was suspicious about foreigners wandering around in the unsettled interior, particularly Americans, who were thought to be looking for petroleum and other natural resources. Once, while I was staying in a hotel in Cuiabá, the capital of Mato Grosso state, several local men asked me what I was doing there. They asked me whether I was a missionary, a businessman, or a miner, to which I replied in the negative, adding that I was an anthropologist. This reply, as usual, stumped them, and as I moved away I overheard one of them say, "He can't fool us; we know he is seeking gold for Truman."

Arranging field trips to the interior involved considerable understanding of the Brazilian attitude toward foreigners and of the administrative structure. While in Uganda I had needed only the permission of the administration and the help of the local people. In Brazil I needed these in addition to a link with a national institution in the field, such as a Brazilian Indian service post, a field expedition, or some national agency with a field office in the area in which I wanted to work. Behind the Brazilian attitude toward foreigners is the fear of exploitation and a sensitive national pride. They are reticent about admitting that the best anthropological work in their country has been done by foreigners. An American photographer whom I met in the field said that he had been told I was a Brazilian anthropologist of German descent from Rio Grande do Sul. I soon learned that I was better received by the local officials if I identified myself as a professor of the Escola de Sociología e Política rather than as a member of the Smithsonian Institution.

Another factor which complicates field work in Brazil is the tendency of Brazilian anthropologists to lay exclusive claim to Indian tribes. One Brazilian anthropologist went so far as to ask me to turn my field notes over to him, as he "owned" that particular tribe. In addition, there is competition between Brazilian universities and research institutions, particularly between São Paulo and Rio de Janeiro. In 1948 I had great difficulty in getting to the upper Xingu River, for the National Museum in Rio claimed that research in that area was under its control. In the end I managed the trip, but only after much begging and pleading.

SUMMARY

Each field situation comprises new sets of living conditions, different modes of travel, one or more foreign languages, and various patterns of behavior that call for adjustment and understanding on the part of the anthropologist. The first example from my field experience among the Tlingit demonstrates how the attitudes of two local groups of the larger society can influence the working relations between an anthropologist and the people he studies. Probably because the American frontier-type culture did not differ either socially or environmentally from that where I grew up, I had no serious psychological problems in adjusting. During my stay in Alaska I learned the value of having a special assistant who can act as informant, interpreter, and guide. Such an assistant can also aid in obtaining informants.

In East Africa, where I first encountered culture shock as a personal problem, there were two subcultures to which I had to adjust. In order to gain the cooperation of the British colonial officials at the apex of the power structure, I adapted myself to their social interests—golf, hunting, and the sundowner circuit. The Banyankole who were my servants as I traveled to the isolated villages in the area expected me to maintain a certain life style befitting my status as a white man. I came to realize the importance they placed on family ties and on supernatural forces thought to influence human behavior. They considered themselves part of my family, and the kinship obligations I was expected to fulfill were numerous. Although I observed many of the Banyankole rituals at kraals and homesteads and could understand what was occurring, I could not share in the inner meanings these performances held for their participants. As with the British, I was in the community, but not of it.

The importance of understanding government policy and structure became clear as I carried out my research among the Indians of interior Brazil. Here my adjustments were even more numerous. I dealt with the expectations of Brazilian anthropologists as a subculture, the expectations of university students about their professors, and the expectations of Brazilians in general about foreigners resident in their land. And in Brazil, travel was even more uncertain than in previous field settings.

Over the years a long-term field worker in foreign lands undergoes a process of cumulative learning. To understand a people, one has to learn not only the oral language of formal communication but also the subtle idiom of facial expressions and bodily gestures through which moods and feelings are expressed. Once an individual grasps the significance of this latter language, he is well on his way toward understanding the inner core of a people's culture. Not knowing this is one of the principal causes of culture shock.

Although I have stressed processes of adjustment, there is a limit to how far one can go in this process. Adults enter other cultures with a set of norms learned in childhood. Complete adjustment would mean not only understanding a different culture but identifying oneself with it. The effort can cause severe psychological stresses and tensions, because of the conflict of basic values. There are cases where this attempt has led to alcoholism, nervous breakdown, insanity, and even suicide.

I have known individuals who claimed that they had never experienced culture shock. Close observation revealed that many of them never really lived in a culture different from their own but withdrew into a self-centered cocoon and associated only with their fellow countrymen. Missionaries also survive well over long periods in alien societies. Here the lesson is quite clear. A missionary's objective is to persuade people to give up their religious beliefs and to adopt his belief and value system. The best-adjusted foreigners whom

I have met in strange lands have been individuals with a strong "missionary" motive, in religion, science, or welfare programs. If one lacks this motivation, the best he can do is to understand another culture and to become aware of the nature of his psychological adjustment to it. I doubt that one can escape culture shock in a new situation except by knowing what causes it and what needs to be done to overcome it. This recognition seems to ease the tension and shorten the period of adjustment in each case.

Whether such knowledge can be fully transmitted out of context to a prospective field worker is a moot question. Many of the American technicians who came to Brazil had gone through an orientation course in Washington in which my paper on culture shock was required reading. They told me that although the paper was interesting, it had no special meaning to them. It was only after six months to a year in Brazil that they began to appreciate the problem. At that point the knowledge of what others had experienced and how they coped with the problem became significant.

Anthropological field work can become a way of life, and it seems appropriate to ask what type of person might be drawn to this area of human endeavor. Certainly a young anthropologist must have an abiding interest in and curiosity about the lifeways of other peoples. He has to develop adaptability, sensitivity, and tolerance. In my own experience this adjustment to new conditions and different customs had to be made in each new contact with the societies in question. But after the first adjustment in Alaska, each new adaptation became easier because I knew what I had to do. In each case the anxiety lessened and the pleasure increased. My ultimate goal was to view the world as fully as possible through the prism of another culture. Although the lifeways differed widely in accordance with variable cultural forms, the human motives and aspirations were the same. I found that greed, envy, and aggressiveness were balanced by a search for security and happiness—a finding which, in the end, has given me a greater degree of tolerance and philosophical calm.

Reference

Oberg, Kalervo. 1954. *Culture Shock.* Indianapolis: Bobbs-Merrill. Reprint Series in the Social Sciences, No. A-329.

6 / Past Perfect

JAN van BAAL

I was having lunch one day with a friendly East European delegate to the UNESCO general conference at Paris. Feeling that I was beginning to find common ground, I casually commented that, as a former colonial governor, I felt a black sheep in this noble company of benevolent and progressive well-wishers of developing nations. Although not a single unkind word passed her lips, her startled look told me that, momentarily at least, she was thinking of the wolf in sheep's clothing. The spectre of the proud and selfish ruler of poor and oppressed coloured nations suddenly slipped up to our table and sat down between us. I had seen the same look before, in the eyes of young people preparing for careers as technical-aid specialists in developing nations. They plainly wondered what an old colonial bore could teach them, serious young men who were going to the former colonies with infinitely better intentions than any colonial servant of yore had possessed.

Yet I never really felt I owed these young people an apology. For one thing, the young man who takes up technical aid as a profession today does so with a salary far more attractive than that of a junior civil servant in 1934 when I entered the colonial administrative service of the Netherlands East Indies. I think money must have had very little to do with the appeal of a colonial service career. The young men of my generation were as convinced of their mission as agents of progress and advancement as any anticolonial junior expert sent out by a technical-aid agency today. We were resigned to low salaries and never guessed the secret of the colonial government in resisting improvements in the pay scale of the junior and intermediate ranks of the administrative service. Years later a cynical top administrator of the Colonial Office explained it to me. "Why pay a high salary for an attractive job?" he asked. And an attractive job indeed it was. The civil servant, especially as a junior administrator, had a well-defined and fully integrated function in a society which urgently called for action. He could feel he was needed. When I entered the service, I originally did so with a firm resolve to quit at the first opportunity for a more scholarly pursuit. But when my chance actually came,

I did not take it. Once I had the job, the job had me.

At the time nobody guessed that decolonization was so near at hand. The omens were there, but it is easier now to recognize them than it was before the war with Japan. The idea of the colonial government as an agent of oppression never entered our minds, though we were critical enough of many of the government's actions. We acted not as members of a dual society, as representatives of the dominant section, but as functionaries of one well-knit whole in which the progress and well-being of the district under our administration, with all its races and subgroups, were our personal responsibility. This responsibility, combined with a diversity of contacts and a close interaction with other people, made the work of the junior administrator, the controleur, a fascinating job. I think this held true even of one of the most controversial activities of the controleur, his role in the administration of justice.

In most of the districts outside Java the administration of justice was to no small extent in the hands of the controleur, as the head of a subdivision. The legal training of a controleur was inadequate by professional standards; and as an administrator, moreover, he could be supposed to be less impartial, at least in criminal cases, than a professional judge would be. After all, the controleur was responsible not only for justice within his subdivision but for the maintenance of law and order. The system certainly conflicted with the doctrine of the *trias politica,* and some of the shortcomings were easy to recognize. Nevertheless, a presiding judge, with a long career both at the Bar and on the Bench, once assured me that, in spite of its defects, this imperfect organization was preferable to one more in harmony with the doctrine of the separation of powers. In most primitive societies the local conditions underlying conflicts are very specific and differ from district to district. The professional jurist with several districts under his jurisdiction must necessarily sometimes be unaware of these specific conditions. His more legalistic approach would result in unrealistic decisions at variance with the people's sense of justice, while the alleged partiality of the controleur, even with his imperfect knowledge of the law, could usually be counted on at least to reflect local conditions and local sentiment. The sentences given by the controleurs, moreover, were subject to strict supervision. They could not be executed before they had been scrutinized in the office of the resident, a procedure known in legal parlance as revision. In practice this meant that all relevant documents were examined twice, first by the assistant resident, the controleur's immediate superior, and then at the resident's office. From experience I know that both authorities were accustomed to take this task seriously.

In Java, unlike the other areas of the Netherlands East Indies, the judges in almost all cases were trained jurists. The exception was civil-law cases involving sums not exceeding 20 guilders (then the equivalent of 8 dollars) and those involving more than 20 but less than 50 guilders (20 dollars). Such cases were tried, respectively, by the district court and the regency court. The district chief presided over the district court; the regent or his deputy, the

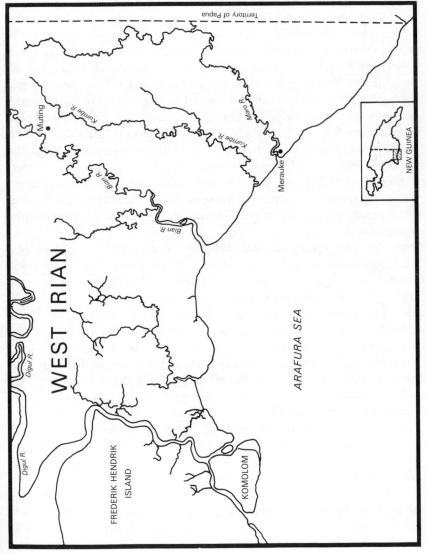

Merauke and Hinterland

patih, over the regency court. The supervision of both courts was entrusted to the resident, but at the time I served in Java this supervision had fallen into disuse, owing to the policy of emancipation which had shifted many of the executive functions to the native administrative service, the regents and the district chiefs under them.

Early in 1939, however, the resident of Banjumas, under whom I served as principal secretary, decided to review the records and sentences of the courts under his supervision, and the examination, not surprisingly, fell to me. On the whole, the records proved to be well kept. There were many errors of form, to be sure, which led to our drafting a long list of objections, but the administration of justice had generally been effective and reasonable. The principal discrepancy was that district courts appeared to have been extremely partial to borrowers against moneylenders. Some of the claims of the latter had been dismissed on the flimsiest grounds. The district chiefs evidently shared with Europeans their dislike of the harsh practices of moneylenders. What the district chiefs had not understood, however, was that, by denying fair treatment, they had increased the moneylender's risk. These one-sided sentences inevitably contributed to a further increase in the rate of interest. The records provided a ready explanation of our failure to reduce the interest charged by moneylenders.

Despite such interesting discoveries about the real workings of the legal system, examining records of court sentences was not very exciting. Compared to sitting in court it was sheer drudgery, and I had had ample acquaintance with the courtroom, especially at Merauke, where I was controleur from 1936 to 1938. I will never forget one case in which I was involved.

Some documents reached me one day in 1937 from the district chief of Muting, a small government station in the interior, near the upper course of the Bian River. The documents were puzzling if one accepted the facts as presented. Actually, I had no real reason for doubt, as the district chief, Mr. Pirsouw, an Indonesian from Seran, was a man of experience with a fair knowledge of the ways of life of the Papuans in his district. The papers described the case of a man who had been apprehended because with a stick he had so thoroughly belaboured a fellow Papuan as to break the victim's arm. Worse yet the victim had died a few days afterwards, and the district chief had the culprit arrested on the grounds of assault resulting in death. Though on the face of it the case was a simple one, there was more to it than met the eye. Pleading guilty, Sesam, the defendant, advanced the plea that he had ample reason to thrash his victim because a few weeks earlier, aided by another man, the deceased had given *him* a beating. Summoned to Pirsouw's office, the surviving assailant readily admitted the charge. Of course, he and the deceased had given Sesam a thrashing! Had not Sesam thrown stones at their uncle's house, threatening the old man with assault? To this charge Sesam once more confessed. Naturally, he had threatened the old man—fully justified, he felt, by facts, which he then set out at length. It was a touching story the way Sesam told it—or at least the way Pirsouw understood it.

Sesam was a native of the upper Bian valley. There he had been married, but his wife died soon afterwards. As a widower, he went to the upper Kumbe River, where he was adopted by Kakik, the old uncle of the case, and his wife Mo-iwag. He was in fact adopted as their future son-in-law. The old couple

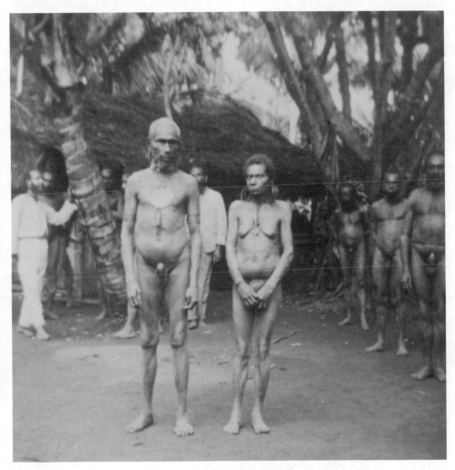

Kakik and his wife Mo-iwag, upper Kumbe River, 1937.

had a young daughter whom they pledged to Sesam, he said, as his bride-to-be. Because of her age, however, he had to wait; meanwhile for seven long years he worked for Kakik and Mo-iwag. Then without warning the girl was given away in marriage to somebody else. Sesam, enraged, threw stones at his foster father's house.

The analogy here with the Biblical story of Jacob and Laban was by no means lost on Pirsouw. He was deeply impressed and felt that Sesam had a right which should be vindicated. Through Pirsouw's diligence, I consequently received three sets of papers dealing, respectively, with the cases of

1. The government versus Sesam on a charge of assault resulting in death.
2. The government versus the man charged with having caused light bodily injuries to Sesam (the thrashing given Sesam by his late victim and the latter's kinsman, who admitted the act—an offence summarily triable according to the penal code).
3. Sesam versus Kakik and Mo-iwag in a civil breach-of-promise case (the matter of their daughter who had allegedly been promised to Sesam).

It all seemed quite simple, except for one thing: in the civil case of Sesam versus Kakik and Mo-iwag, Sesam himself did not make a specific claim. It was evident that Pirsouw had put the case together on Sesam's behalf, but, unable to formulate a claim, had left that part to me. At the time our knowledge of Marind-anim marriage customs was poor. The one thing we did know for certain was that there was no bride-price, which meant that a simple settlement by reimbursement was out of the question. Sesam was in the right; but what could be done about it? Despite current notions about colonial servants, I was no Turkish pasha and hence could not simply take the girl away from her present husband and give her to Sesam.

At that point a Roman Catholic missionary came along who knew the area well, and I brought up the case to ask his advice. "Oh," he said. "Pirsouw does not understand these people at all, and of course he has misinterpreted the case." He proceeded to tell me a long story (and a perfectly good one), but I immediately forgot the gist of it because the way Pirsouw's opinion was waved aside annoyed me so much that I listened with only half an ear. Moreover, because of a long-standing conflict between Pirsouw, a staunch Protestant, and the Roman Catholic mission, the mission was never known to let slip an opportunity to lay something at Pirsouw's door. The conflict between them dated back to the time, some ten years before, when Pirsouw was a district chief in the Tanimbar Islands. During that time two teachers, a Protestant and a Roman Catholic, came to blows. I do not know whether they taught in the same village or in neighbouring hamlets, but the story has it that the Protestant teacher leveled a shotgun at his Roman Catholic colleague, though taking care to miss his target. The event did not pass unnoticed. The Protestant teacher was brought to trial and convicted, whereupon the Protestant mission decided to remove their man to another island. Well and good, but the Protestant flock deeply resented the conviction and the loss of their shepherd, and a prayer meeting was organized on his behalf. On that occasion the spirit moved Pirsouw, himself at one time a Protestant teacher, and he led the prayer meeting, galvanizing the group's sentiments through his uncommon eloquence. His partisanship in this affair nearly ruined his administrative career. Well aware of what had happened, the local priest reported everything to the authorities.

Pirsouw was reprimanded by his superiors and removed to another post, more or less simultaneously with the teacher. That would doubtless have been the end of the affair had not he and the priest met again in South New Guinea, the latter as supervisor of the Roman Catholic mission which also had a station in Muting, where Pirsouw had just been posted as district chief. I knew the background, and the renewed accusation against Pirsouw therefore made me mad enough to overlook the factual information which the missionary (and later friend) supplied.

I decided that I would hear Sesam's case *in loco,* that is, on the Kumbe River, three days by motorboat from Merauke. After rereading the papers, I regretted my disregard of the story given me by the missionary. What to do with Sesam's civil suit? I could not ignore it, because it was the first cause of all the other developments. Upon arrival, I met Pirsouw, who had come a few hours earlier. He had made the entire two-day trip from Muting on foot, bringing Sesam with him. I told him bluntly that I had been informed that there was something wrong with the civil lawsuit, though I did not remember exactly how his report was said to be in error. I sincerely hoped that it *was* in error, moreover, because I was at a loss how to handle the case if by chance Sesam should be in the right. For that reason I wished to deal with the civil suit first and *ab ovo.* Pirsouw, who was an exceedingly reasonable man, cheerfully agreed. And so I held my court under a palm tree, feeling hardly happier than Adam Bede.

Sesam was summoned and I went through the usual procedure.

"What is your name?"

"Sesam, Sir."

"Good. Where were you born?"

"In the bush, Sir."

"In the bush?"

"Yes, Sir. With a stick, Sir."

There was a complete misunderstanding between us. Sesam was wholly preoccupied with telling me how he had struck his unfortunate opponent. He had no idea of the civil lawsuit in which he was supposed to be the claimant. The one thing he assumed he would have to do was to describe the fight which had ended in the other man's death and resulted in his own arrest. As a consequence, it took an hour and a half before the court could find out where Sesam had been born, that he had been married, and that, as a widower, he had come to the upper Kumbe to marry Maria, the daughter of Kakik and Mo-iwag.

At last I had a hunch. "What is your clan, Sesam?" I asked.

"Mahu-zé," he answered.

"And Maria's?"

"Also Mahu-zé."

"Also Mahu-zé? How on earth could you wish to marry her?"

"Well, Sir, that could never be," the claimant acknowledged.

From a technical point of view I could at this juncture have dismissed the whole case. However, I wanted to know the source of the confusion, and with some difficulty I refrained from asking the logical question: why in the first place he had stated a claim. (Of course, it was Pirsouw who had filed it, not Sesam.) It took me another two hours to ferret out the background. Marriage on the upper Kumbe is by sister-exchange (as it is on the upper Bian). The story told to Pirsouw had been false. Sesam had been adopted not as Maria's future husband but as her brother in an exchange procedure. I then asked whether the man Maria had married had a sister. Yes, he had one. Pressing the matter further, I enquired whether the young woman was present. Indeed she was. The whole village (and part of the neighbouring one) had gathered to watch the proceedings, and the young woman, without a moment's hesitation, declared that she and Sesam wished to be married, a statement reaffirmed by Sesam.

At this point I again felt tempted to ask Sesam why he wanted to bring his claim, but a question of this kind would only have added to the confusion. I simply dismissed the claim in order to return to the basic problem of the criminal case. What was the cause of the conflict which had arisen between Kakik and Sesam, leading to Sesam's being thrashed by the two young men? To this question Sesam gave no answer. He had not been talkative before, but now he became positively mute. The same was true of old Kakik—indeed of everybody concerned in the affair. Whatever I asked or suggested, nobody offered a word of comment. The situation was not unfamiliar. Once a people like these feel that a conflict is no longer the government's business—because the parties concerned have found a way to settle their dispute—they obstruct the progress of the court session by observing a collective silence. This was happening now, and here I was, with Pirsouw and young Gerrit Uneputty, my assistant, surrounded by some two hundred local people quietly squatting under the palm trees, each one perfectly able to supply the answers to all my questions but instead curious to know whether I would be able to extricate myself unaided.

I looked round the circle. Nobody spoke. The moment I showed signs of anger I would have admitted defeat; so I quietly resumed my questioning, inviting the main parties to stand nearer the table. Dusk was falling and I ordered a lamp to be brought. The lamp arrived but there was no break in the situation. It was no longer a matter of holding court but a contest of will with a couple of hundred secretly amused onlookers. I told them to think it over quietly. "I have a world of time," I added and ordered my evening meal. The table was laid and leisurely we began to eat. Everybody was now aware that I had no intention of giving up. Then, suddenly, Mo-iwag came forward, an almost completely naked and unbelievably ugly old hag, knock-kneed and with one blind eye. She seemed quite angry. "Well, Sir," she shouted, beating her flaccid breasts, "if nobody cares to tell you, I will. He"—pointing to Sesam— "has copulated with me." A roar of laughter arose from the spectators to the profound humiliation of the young man who had had intercourse with so old and ugly a woman. For one moment she stood there and then disappeared into the crowd. Sesam winced. Embarrassed, he raised one finger. "Once only, Sir," he pleaded. Pirsouw, who had so far said nothing during the session—certainly no triumph for him either—chose that moment to intervene. Sesam had hardly finished his feeble exoneration when Pirsouw matter-of-factly said, "You lie. Twice." Sesam winced again, and after another roar of laughter from the crowd, he gave in, raising a second finger, and said: "Indeed, Sir. Twice."

I adjourned the session till the next morning. We quietly walked back to the launch, and while going aboard I asked Pirsouw what had made him guess that Sesam had twice committed adultery with his foster mother. Pirsouw chuckled. "Well, Sir, it is two days' walking from Muting to this place and during those two days I talked a bit with our friend Sesam. He confided to me that he had twice copulated with Maria; but when I heard the old woman it suddenly dawned upon me that it was really the mother instead of the daughter."

The next morning the trial presented no problems. No causal relation could be proved between the victim's broken arm and his subsequent death. But that in fact did not affect the practical outcome, as even for murder I could not have sent Sesam to jail for more than eleven months. Once again the reason was not to be found in law books or formal administrative procedures but arose from the local experience of a controleur in fitting the system to the situation.

Any sentence of a year or more meant that a culprit had to serve his term at Ambon. Confinement so far away from New Guinea and home meant a very great likelihood of death for men whose most serious crimes could often be described as no more than a tenacious attachment to custom. Once I knew the lethal effect of overseas imprisonment on Papuans from the interior, I never sentenced such offenders to more than eleven months. For one man only, who had committed a really brutal murder, I made an exception; he got five years. (Such a sentence still avoided the formalities and extensive reports required for the death sentence.) To my dismay I found that my forebodings at convicting him were even more justified than I had supposed. Seven days after the sentence had been pronounced, the man was dead. The autopsy pointed to a set of symptoms we had repeatedly seen in the sudden death of prisoners. Of this peculiar sickness let me now relate my experience.

I saw my first cases almost as soon as I took up duties at Merauke. Three out of a group of fifteen prisoners who had been brought in from the middle Fly region were dead within a fortnight. In each case I ordered an inquest, and to my amazement all three deaths appeared to be the same. All three men had worked outside the prison on the day before they died. Returning to the prison, each had complained of a hard belly and the next morning all three were found dead on their sleeping mats. With each of them the main arteries of the heart were seriously enlarged as with sufferers of what is commonly known as beri-beri of the heart, an acute form of vitamin-B deficiency. We now know that these are also symptoms of shock, but in Merauke in 1937 we knew nothing about shock. Be that as it may, the sickness alarmed me. I had read

Rivers (1922) on the depopulation of Melanesia and I guessed that, whatever the mechanism responsible, these cases had something to do with a deep mental depression. Nor was this an unlikely reaction among these poor frightened men from far inland. Their disorientation to the town and to imprisonment is in nothing more strongly suggested than in the cause of their arrest, headhunting. Thus I felt I had good reason for my misgivings as to any simple organic cause of their deaths. The regular prison fare surely made a vitamin-B deficiency most improbable. This I pointed out, together with the other relevant circumstances I could collect, in my letter officially requesting a reduction of terms for the remaining prisoners—varying from two and a half to five years —to about six months.

The effect of the letter was surprising and it brought me into sympathetic contact with one of my models of the intelligent colonial administrator. At that time New Guinea was not a separate administrative division but formed part of the very extensive residency of the Moluccas. The then resident was the late Bouke Jan Haga, a very scholarly but also a very vigorous man. Haga had upset everybody in the Moluccas with his energetic measures for modernizing the administration of this remote corner of the archipelago. Here for many years time had seemed to stand still as successive administrations dozed their way through a routine as placid as the tiny townships far up the deep-blue inlets of island after island. Some of these lovely places recalled the visions of a dream. Banda, which I visited in 1936, was indescribably beautiful in its glory of withered old palatial countryhouses once bustling with life during the heyday of the East India Company when the Moluccas had the world monopoly of nutmeg and cloves and Banda itself was a mighty emporium. The decaying buildings slumbered now amid an exuberantly rich vegetation bordering the deep-blue waters of the magnificent bay. Silence prevailed, a silence so perfect that we thought to walk on tiptoe.

Whatever his feelings about the charm of the division, Haga did not walk on tiptoe. Since he had become resident, the administration suddenly jumped to the double, much to the discomfort of all the old hands who loved the tranquillity. Haga traveled more than any resident who had ever been there. He managed this quite handily because he could weather any storm; and when everybody else on board the government steamer was sick or suffering headaches from the rough sea, Haga, unperturbed, would be sitting at his desk writing letters, making notes, or summoning sick controleurs or assistant residents to confer with him. On his visits the "old man" even startled the village teachers. In a time-honoured custom the resident on an official visit was welcomed by the village school children singing in Indonesian two stanzas of the Dutch national anthem. The melody of the old "Wilhelmus" lends itself exceedingly well to a broad largo which the Moluccan teachers delighted in stretching into a solemn lento. This ceremonial interval was longer than Haga could bear. At the last line of the first stanza he stood poised. With the final note and before they could commence the second stanza, he literally shot forward, grasped the teacher's hand, thanked him cordially, and, waving to the children, darted off, a retinue following in his wake, straining to keep up with his pace.

I greatly admired the "old man" (he was not that old, actually) and knowing him, I had some hope that my request for a remission of sentences for my Merauke prisoners would be passed on to the governor general for a decision. This time Haga acted with a swiftness beyond what I had thought possible, even for him. Within a month I received a cable that the sentences had been reduced as suggested and that the prisoners were to be remanded to the small backwoods prison of Muting where security arrangements were quite informal. But I was perplexed: the sentences in question had been confirmed earlier by the resident, and it was a long-standing rule that, once entered into the record, a sentence could be changed only by the governor general's exercising his prerogative of pardon. Though not a simple procedure because the governor general had to consult the High Court, it was nevertheless for this purpose the best available legal means. Of course I was delighted with Haga's decision and quickly carried out his instructions; but all the time I was worried that his action was *ultra vires*. My uneasiness was confirmed in a few weeks when I received a copy of the short dispatch which had been sent to the resident by my immediate superior, the assistant resident of Tual in the Kei Islands. This worthy gentleman dryly noted therein that the resident had not followed the advice given—that is, *my* advice—for he had not referred the matter to the governor general!

A month later Haga paid a visit to Merauke. He inspected the jail at his usual slow run. I told the "old man" how happy I was with his decision, adding that I nevertheless wondered about its legitimacy. He stopped short and spun round. "Phew! Illegitimate? No, Sir, no," he gruffly expostulated. "No, no! The worst you can say of it is that it is questionable. Questionable, all right. But what would have happened to the poor devils if I had acted upon this great piece of advice of yours and involved the governor general? Those doting old gentlemen of the High Court would still be studying the papers by the time you buried the last of your fifteen prisoners." He turned brusquely and we resumed our trot till, a hundred yards farther down the road, he suddenly stopped and said quietly, "Look here, young man, remember that the resident of the Moluccas is responsible for good government. If possible, within the law; if not, without it." We hurried on to the next stage of his inspection.

Haga was also a man of ideas. He was one of the first to point out (*Indonesische en Indische Democratie,* 1924) that in many cases the tyranny of native princes was a product of modern conditions and that the rulers of these states were originally kept in check in many ways by the nobility as well as by their dependence on the opinion of the people at large. He also suggested a noteworthy solution to the problem of modernizing the customary law. Adat law (the current term for customary law in Indonesia) played a very important part in the administration of justice in the Netherlands East Indies. In civil lawsuits all natives were subject to the rules of adat law, except in cases involving nonnatives, in which cases the European civil code took precedence. There were other exceptions. For example, all natives had the right to submit voluntarily to European law, either in general or for a specific case. A more important exception was that in many ordinances a clause had been inserted making their provisions applicable also in areas where customary law prevailed. In criminal cases adat law was of lesser importance. In large parts of the Netherlands Indies the penal code was applied to natives and nonnatives indiscriminately, and in those parts where customary law also included criminal cases, many sections of the penal code (together with the penal provisions of many ordinances) remained applicable as well. Moreover, even in cases which had to be adjudicated on the basis of adat law, the penal code served as a kind of reference book. Although seemingly unwieldy, the system on the whole had important advantages. It made it possible to meet the people's sense of justice by punishing actions which were not punishable according to the penal code or to exempt people from punishment for actions deemed criminal by the penal code but not by customary law. At the same time, the custom that in every case the corresponding article of the penal code had to be cited, or the absence of such a reference explained, promoted a gradual penetration of the penal code as the conscious norm of the system and thus contributed to a welcome generalization of the rules of conduct.

The customary law had originally been recommended as the basis for administering justice because it was expected that the informal nature of adat law would provide for a gradual adaptation to changing conditions. This did not work out as predicted, in part because of the overscrupulous supervision of the sentences of native courts. Proponents of the customary law had hoped to develop a body of rules by insisting that in every sentence the relevant rule of adat law be cited. In some areas, to be sure, rules of this kind actually existed —south Sumatra and Bali, for example. In other areas, however, the rules were in fact formulated by controleurs, contributing to an increasing rigidity of customary law. The growth of inflexible rules and the tendency to standardize the terms of jurisprudence in local reference files made adaptation to change difficult.

Again it was Haga who attempted a solution. In areas where adat law prevailed, he explained, there were other influences at work besides custom and tradition alone. The very presence of the Netherlands Indies government (in many parts of the archipelago established as recently as 1905 or 1906) was so new as to have a dramatic impact on the people's concepts of justice and much else. These altered notions should be accepted in court as their new adat, their new customary law. Haga's solution seemed sound enough in light of a case which was tried in Nias (one of the islands west of Sumatra) about 1937. Here an unwed mother had killed her baby but was acquitted because the case did not come under the articles of the penal code applicable in these parts and because her action was also legitimate according to adat law. Early in 1937 the assembled chiefs of Nias therefore decided that in future the killing of a baby would be punishable by adat law. As in similar circumstances the legitimacy of this change was once again contested, not by the people but by the jurists, on the ground that decisions of this kind could only be made at the time of a rather complicated traditional feast. One exponent of adat law published an article in which he applauded the original sentence and discounted the legitimacy of the subsequent ruling of the chiefs; but he failed to see that such a position necessarily led to the complete immutability of customary law. I must add, to the author's credit, that he was not blind to one more immediate consequence, suggesting a change in the law which would make the relevant articles of the penal code applicable to Nias (see Luyks, 1939).

Haga's idea of a new adat was never generally accepted, on the ground that its introduction would lead to legal ambiguity. Native courts could introduce any new principle they wished simply by presenting it as a new adat. Any controleur might similarly influence the court he presided over. I must admit that there was substance in this objection, certainly as far as the Merauke area was concerned, for there the native court was unmistakably personified by the controleur, there being no Papuan spokesmen of a sufficient standard of education or with enough traditional prestige to fill the Bench of a full-fledged court. As the reviewing judge, Haga instructed me more than once to use the fiction of the new adat in ambiguous cases, such as that of the participants in *otiv bombari*, the *jus primae noctis* exercised by the men (often to the number of ten or more), in respect of a bride. The custom had been forbidden for a time because venereal granuloma prevailed. Punishment was then possible on the basis of the so-called Epidemics Ordinance. At a later date this ordinance was suspended because a program of public health had considerably reduced the extent of the disease. This situation confronted us with the problem of how to deal with a custom which could easily lead to a flare-up of the epidemic so long as the illness had not been eradicated. Besides, *otiv bombari* met with serious objections among the members of the younger generation who had become Christians, and this constituted the one acceptable ground for intervention. Under the circumstances the notion of a new adat offered a solution, though not an attractive one, because it could hardly be maintained that the new *mos* had been accepted by the community at large. It must be granted that so long as new rules are applied wisely and with discretion, no harm can ordinarily be done. The norm in a society passing from stone-age morals to some form of Christianity—even a diluted one in our eyes—is a problem to which there is no easy solution. Admittedly there are situations in which no amount of wisdom will suffice, and on this point I must return once more to the prison deaths in Merauke.

Not everyone shared my theory of mental depression; the doctor, for one, did not agree. I happened to have a prisoner by the name of Kariu, a man who had seriously injured one of his fellow villagers on suspicion of sorcery. One night Kariu fled—easy enough where the prison consisted of simple wooden buildings on a site surrounded by barbed wire. (One thing which continually amazed me was that prisoners always made their escapes at night. It would have been simpler during the day while working outside the prison under very loose surveillance. They must have felt sorry for their guards!) Kariu had presumably fled to his village, and six policemen went to look for him there, some twenty miles westward along the coast. It took them two weeks to get him to give himself up. He spent a few days in one of the two cells and then returned to routine internment. After two months he broke out of jail again but this time he did not flee alone, for five others disappeared with him. I was much annoyed by this serious new breach because the informal prison system we had depended heavily on the voluntary cooperation of the prisoners. At whatever cost, I therefore decided, this man should be recaptured. I was even more annoyed when, after two weeks' time, my policemen returned empty-handed. A few hours later, however, Kariu was brought in by the chief of his own village, who informed me that he had not wanted the police to catch Kariu because they would handcuff him. Handcuffing was something which ought not to be done to a human being, he explained.

Grudgingly I gave the chief the reward I had promised and after dismissing him sent Kariu to the doctor. The prisoner looked haggard but he had to be punished all the same. I had to set an example to the remaining inmates if the prison system was not to fall apart. The relevant ordinance permitted twenty strokes with a rattan, provided the doctor declared the prisoner fit to undergo the punishment. The doctor found nothing wrong with Kariu, but I had misgivings. The doctor stuck to his opinion that twenty strokes would not do the prisoner any harm, but I finally decided to reduce the punishment to ten. "And even so he will probably die," I mused.

"Oh, no." replied the doctor. "He is as strong as a horse."

"Yes, but it is not the beating I mean. He will probably die afterwards, of heart beri-beri." The doctor scoffed at this prediction, and we made a wager.

For some time it seemed as if the doctor were going to win the wager, for all went well. A week before Kariu had finished his sentence I met him during my inspection of the prison. I gave him some tobacco and congratulated him on returning home next week. When I turned around, I saw the doctor standing outside, grinning. "Good for you; you win," I conceded.

But he did not. Four days later at eight o'clock in the morning he stepped into my office, a bit gray in the face. "*You* win; he is dead," he said.

I stared at him, incredulous. "How?"

"Beri-beri of the heart," he said with a shrug.

Now, at least, thought I, I am fully aware of the problem; but I was wrong. In the jail I had seven men from Muting. They had killed an old woman whom they suspected of sorcery. I had sentenced the leader of the group to eleven months, the six others to seven. Petrus, the leader, had worked in Merauke for a couple of years and therefore should have known better than his fellows the government's view of homicide. Two months later a serious epidemic of influenza broke out in the area, and the doctor and I each went to different places to see what we could do. It was not much. On one of these trips I visited Muting, where 26 per cent of the population had died. When I came back, one of the first things I did was to enquire after my Muting prisoners. The news was alarming. Five of the seven had influenza, three of them quite serious cases. "I have given up two of them," the doctor told me. I went to the prison where the men were lying under a couple of blankets. I told them how many people had died at Muting, mentioning some of the names I recalled. I looked at the two men who were worst off. "Listen, you there. You have to realize that you simply can't die. They are waiting for you, expecting you. You can't do this to the people of Muting. They just can't have you die after so many others!" And I told them to follow the doctor's instructions to the letter. A week later they all were well again. It may be that the doctor's pessimism was unfounded, but I flatter myself that my pep-talk made an important contribution to the recovery of these men. I still felt that way when I left Merauke a few months later. In paying a final visit to the prison, I went through an odd little ceremony. Petrus made a valedictory speech on behalf of his fellow prisoners to thank me for the good care I had taken of them. Never was there a more ironic valediction. Three months later I received a letter from Merauke. The other prisoners had returned to their village at Muting, leaving behind Petrus whose sentence was longer. Six weeks after their departure Petrus was found dead: beri-beri of the heart. It was as if I had personally committed a murder, I who prided myself on understanding this very possibility.

Past perfect. For the present generation of young whites there is no longer a role to fulfill in colonial areas such as the one which we were privileged to undertake. It was a privilege for the very reason that it was not an easy life. We had tasks to which we could devote all of our energy because they set us in the very midst of events and developments. We made serious mistakes. My story here has concluded with one. Yet where we were and where we acted we felt part of a whole, members of a society in which we had a function. No longer can any of us have such a function today, but thirty years ago we could. Whenever the popular caricature of the callous, self-serving colonial servant is invoked, there comes to my mind the memory of men I have known, men like Bouke Jan Haga, a brilliant illustration of dedication and insight into the lives of the people for whom he was responsible. I am happy to cite him as representing the sort of men I have in mind, moreover, as he cannot speak in his own behalf. After his term as resident in the Moluccas, he went on to become governor of Borneo, where the Japanese invasion caught him and he and his wife were beheaded.

REFERENCES

LUYKS, W. A. L. 1939. *Tijdschrift voor Indische Taal-, Land- en Volkenkunde*, ed. by Het Bataviaasch Genootschap. 69: 262.

RIVERS, W. H., ED. 1922. *Essays on the De-Population of Melanesia*. New York: AMS Press.

7 / Return to the Longhouse

WILLIAM N. FENTON

"THE ONE WHO SLEPT IN A TENT"

At the moon of midwinter, 1968, I revisited my Seneca friends of Coldspring Longhouse, on the Allegany Reservation near Salamanca, New York, where I had commenced ethnological field work in the summer of 1933. Now, some thirty-five years later, I was hoping to see once again the ceremonies that mark the Indian New Year. From time to time I had returned, and in particular I had followed the affairs of the Seneca nation during their tragic struggle against the building of the Kinzua Dam on the Allegheny River, and I had chaired an advisory committee to the nation. I had described the rebuilding of their homes, but I had not attended the doings at the new longhouse where recently they removed their fire. This modern structure near Steamburg was built with funds received from the United States Congress in partial compensation for 9,000 acres taken for the reservoir. The old settlement at Coldspring which I had known was obliterated. Not since Sullivan's army destroyed their towns and crops during the American Revolution had the Seneca people suffered such cultural loss. I wondered how the shock of being uprooted would affect the performance of their ceremonies.

I reached "New Coldspring" on the morning that "Our Uncles, the Big-heads" traditionally go out at dawn, progressing from house to house, hailing the men as nephews, and urging them to renew all obligations revealed through dreams. I immediately learned that the Uncles did not go out that dawn, and I inferred that they no longer made the circuit of houses and that I could probably expect other radical changes. Ed Coury, the speaker of the long-house, confirmed my first inference. "There was no one at home to receive them," he said; "their nephews were either at the longhouse or at work."

It was good, nevertheless, to see familiar faces among the small crowd assembled in the longhouse. For a moment seeing these old friends diverted me from the startlingly modern surroundings. Among the people were some I had known from the first summer I had spent in the community, thirty-five

Iroquois Reservations of New York and Ontario

years earlier when I slept in a tent at Jonas Snow's. Somehow I felt reassured: with these experienced persons on hand things would go about as usual.

Except that the doors opened westward toward the road, the interior arrangements of the new building and the placement of the windows recalled the old longhouse. There was still a stove for each sex at opposite ends, and there was even a ladder at the men's end giving access through a hatch to the attic for storing and retrieving ritual gear. I recognized the old benches, and a higher bank that circled the room providing elevated seats behind the benches had been reproduced.

But the building contained some strange innovations for a longhouse. To be sure, it was a frame structure, clapboarded and painted white, but the cement-block foundation afforded a complete basement. The doors were doubled and there was a hardwood floor, perfect for dancing. The architect thought the old

Tent at Jonas Snow's, where William Fenton slept, 1933.

The Old Coldspring Longhouse near Salamanca, 1933.

The New Coldspring Longhouse near Steamburg, 1968.

ladies would appreciate a basement kitchen, but they had insisted on a separate cookhouse—equipped with gas. At an outdoor fire where the kettles hung on wooden poles, I heard Alta Cloud complain that she missed the crane in Jake Logan's brick fireplace at the old cookhouse. Inside fluorescent lighting from a false ceiling contrasted favorably with the bare bulbs or kerosene lamps I had known. The room was paneled with birch plywood in which electrical outlets were spaced at regular intervals. I thought these would be ideal for tape recorders now owned by several singers; but Dorothy Jimerson told me that the outlets were for the old ladies to plug in hotplates for warming corn soup at socials. The final touch was a fresh set of corn pestles which the Uncles carry, made as replacements for the old pestles, which were given to a museum. Besides having unfamiliar, new equipment, the Uncles did not know their lines and mumbled the chants.

Presently Ed Coury stood, removed his hat, spat in the nearest can, and commenced the thanksgiving address which greets and thanks the Creator for all of the things that he has left on earth for man's use and enjoyment. Then he announced the opening of the Midwinter Festival and the dressing of the Uncles. Although Ed has more white genes than red, he had mastered the speaking style of Seneca preachers just as earlier he had learned the ritual songs. As I closed my eyes to concentrate on the old words, for a moment there was the illusion of the old longhouse and Henry Redeye speaking.

The midwinter ceremony deals with both halves of the subsistence cycle:

hunting and meat, which ends at midwinter; and the maize cycle, to which the people look forward after a period of hunger. The other concern is with "good luck" and health—both physical and mental—and this is why the ceremony persists today. The next four days are devoted to ceremonies of friendship and to renewal of the medicine-society's dream obligations. The obligation to fulfill these rites and the ties of joint participation bind the generations, age-mates, and persons of opposite sex in Seneca society as long as either partner lives, helping to keep the ceremonies themselves alive.

On the fifth morning the speaker announced that the door now stood open to admit all kinds of ceremonies revealed through dreams—Bear, Buffalo, False Face, which he mentioned, and others. The bear dance has always been the most popular of the dream dances. During the opening songs, as the words of the invocation rise on the smoke of burning tobacco begging the bear spirits to listen, the conductor passes a small pipe to the members and then throws a spoon of berry juice out of doors. The saying is: "The bears will come and get it at night."

At dusk several performances of the False Faces disclosed substantial changes in the rite. In their new ranch-style houses people objected to the maskers' scraping their rattles on the varnished doors, marring the woodwork, and tracking in mud. The two head women thereupon quit because this objection meant that the circuit of houses at midwinter would no longer be observed, and they had to abandon spring and fall "housecleaning" throughout the settlement. The rites of the maskers now centered at the longhouse.

As the False Faces crawled and stooped toward the women's fire, I noted that their behavior lacked enthusiasm. Only Herb Dowdy, who was properly raucous, and Ham Jimerson, who danced while scooping hot ashes, moved the patient's head on its axis, and pumped her arms, came up to expectations. At the men's end one could scarcely hear the invocation by Art Johnny John. One lady sponsor was wearing curlers, which embarrassed her, since under the old rules she would have left the ashes in her hair for three days. I thought audience participation was quite limited: I saw no frightened children and no cases of hysterical possession; nor did anyone crawl to the fire. When the doorkeepers cleared the benches, requiring everyone to join the dances, only the older people knew the steps. But it was too early in the festival to form a judgment.

The sixth day is the climax. Events had started that morning before I arrived. The Bowl Game, now also confined to the longhouse, had gone rapidly and was over, save for the announcements, and the rest of the morning was free. People came and went. Four restless boys of thirteen chattered in English and wriggled on the bank behind me. Ed Coury announced that the Great Feather Dance in honor of the Creator would take place the following day. I have to concentrate to follow such discourse, and the distraction was such that, partly as an experiment, I turned to the noisy lads and remarked in Seneca, as the old people sometimes do when conversation is loud, "Swadáonkdiyos!" ("All of you, listen!") This quieted them for a moment, but presently I felt a finger in my shoulder and then in English the taunt: "You can't understand him anyway. Tell us what he is saying." I then related the gist of the announcements. This was too much. Unable to contain themselves, they went outside and caucused. Soon they were back in again. By then the men around me were aware of what was happening, and I sensed their amused approval. Quiet lasted only a moment, when again I was nudged. "We got you figured out. You must be the one the old people tell about. Long ago you came here and slept in a tent."

That the grandchildren who impersonated "Our Grandfathers," the maskers, would have something further in store for me had not occurred to me as I reached the longhouse that evening for Husk Face night. The benches were beginning to fill with visitors from Steamburg and Jimersontown; then contingents of Seneca arrived from Cattaraugus and Tonawanda, among whom I recognized old faces, and a carload came from Six Nations Reserve in Canada. Soon every seat was occupied. A dozen white people attended. I felt part of the homecoming to Coldspring since every community in Iroquois where I had lived and made friends was represented. It was interesting to meet the new generation because I had always been curious about the learning process in this society that afforded so few formal teaching situations. I recalled how anxious Johnson Jimerson was to learn everything of importance concerning the Coldspring ceremonies, how he constantly practiced his songs, and I was anxious to see how being a speaker at Newtown had affected him. I was also fascinated to witness the learning that had been transmitted to his son, who proved the winner by acclaim in the False Face beggar contest. Johnson had indeed, to use his words, "raised him right." The power of symbols and of certain stereotypes, much of it nonverbal, must be operative in this process. The masks are impressive enough when seen in museum collections, but they really come to life when worn by impersonators of the spirits that they represent.

The False Faces, as everyone expected, led the program. Small boys meanwhile went out to the cookhouse in twos and threes to return as masked beggars. Among them were my new friends who had challenged me that morning. The first beggar was dressed in white coveralls and wore a Negro mask. Crossing the room to where I was seated, he thrust his stick at me and demanded that I sing for him to dance. Such a confrontation is a recognized contest between the generations, between singer and dancer, and I had obviously made myself liable by exercising moral authority that morning. Now it was their turn to test me. Years ago someone had taught me a simple False Face song, and I recalled one other from my recordings. The beat was easy, and Clifford Crouse of my generation urged me to keep it going to tire the dancer. Accomplished singers try odd beats to throw the dancer off. Dancers prefer a fast tempo and short songs, so the game is to stretch the beat, keeping the dancer at it until he tires and begs for his stick, at which the singer may speed up the beat again. This byplay appeals to the Iroquois sense of humor, in which an element of kindly torture persists, and these contests are looked forward to and are remembered long afterward. Surely having contributed another incident to local legend, the lad and I were both glad when I ran out of songs.

SNOW STREET 1933

The friendship between the Fenton and Snow families in western New York goes back several generations. There is a hemlock ridge at the back of the Fenton farm in Conewango Valley, which is halfway between Cattaraugus and Allegany. Here for generations Seneca hunters stopped to camp in the fall on the way to the big woods of Pennsylvania, and they frequently paused with their families on the return trip. One winter day in the 1860's my grandfather, then in his twenties, who was running the farm with his widowed mother, saw smoke rising from the ridge in the swamp. It was bitter cold and the snow was deep. His mother suggested that he go down and see how the Indians were faring. He took an ax and went afoot, thinking that he might split up some firewood that he had felled. He found an Indian family encamped in a hemlock leanto: a man, an old woman, and a young girl with a newborn baby. When he came back to the farm for dinner, he reported what he had seen to his mother, who insisted that he hitch the team to the pung, fill the bed with straw, and go fetch that family to the warm farmhouse. By suppertime the Indian family was installed in the hired girl's room off the kitchen. They stayed for a week until the weather improved. When they left, the old lady thanked my great-grandmother for shelter, sustenance, and hospitality, saying that it was the first time they had been invited to sleep and eat in a white home. It was the Indian custom, she said, to return thanks. It was also the Indian custom to bind friendship with a present, whereupon she produced an old burden strap, an obvious heirloom, decorated with dyed deer hair and porcupine-quill embroidery worked in a geometric pattern, and handed it to my great-grand-mother.

The Indian hunter was stout, jovial Amos Snow, who became a lifelong friend of my grandfather: companions on squirrel- and pigeon-shooting expeditions, trotting-horse fanciers, and good for some shared labor on the farm. Amos used to show up with his young family. At one point he entrusted to my grandfather two wooden False Faces, both very old, which he produced from under the wagon seat in a wooden cheese box. Later it was a string of wampum that recalled an alliance of war with some tribes in the old Northwest. These items, however they came to us, were the nucleus of a growing family ethnological collection that was kept "up attic" in a special museum room which I was privileged to visit on rainy summer days. Often there were visiting collectors present—sometimes Indians. It was then that Jonas, a son of Amos's, and my father discovered a common interest in the arts—the one a painter and the other a gifted carver of masks. Going to the reservation to visit the Snows and their neighbors were summer outings that we particularly cherished during my childhood. It was only natural that I should remember Snow Street years later when I was about to do my first field work in ethnology.

For a year I had prepared by going through F. W. Waugh's notebooks on Iroquois medicines, which Diamond Jenness sent me from the National Museum of Canada. Ethnobotany seemed a good opening subject, being close enough to everyday life not to arouse anxiety. It involved linguistic terminology, and it might be expected to survive. At a more difficult level I might do something to extend Arthur C. Parker's sketches of the medicine societies. Before I left New Haven, Professor Sapir, who had procured $500 for my field fund, advised finding a field of concentration early so that I should have a subject for a dissertation and not just field notes. He recommended religion and ceremonialism, with asides in material culture. He advised avoiding negative leading questions, which invariably evoke monosyllabic answers. I was urged to make a census to get acquainted and for the data it would afford on social organization, which I might then use in observing ceremonial usages. Sapir also loaned me a book on the phonetic transcription of American Indian languages. George Herzog, for whom I had agreed to make some recordings of music, produced an old Edison mechanical recorder, instructed me in its use, and told me where to write for wax cylinders. These hints to the novice field worker proved a boon. I was soon to learn, however, that the Seneca would control my learning and that my success would be governed by their interests.

Snow Street was a dirt road connecting Highway 17 toward Steamburg with a north-south road running past the longhouse, parallel to the Allegheny River, toward Quaker Bridge. That summer when I camped in the dooryard of Jonas Snow's household yielded entries for a journal which is a miscellany of family life, medicines, rattlesnakes, turtles, drunks, feuds, friends, ball games, singing societies, mutual aid, adoption into the Hawk clan, and socials at the longhouse—far too long a list to detail here. One or two incidents will serve to show how my progress was affected, not by any of the good advice I was given by my professors nor any strategy that I had devised for my field work, but by being annexed to a family and participating as well as I could. It was all quite confusing at first because everything kept coming at me in bits and pieces, and I lacked a scheme for sorting it out and putting it together. The Snow family were helpful enough, but they were engaged in activities of their own that they scarcely had time to explain.

Although I soon commenced formal work on medicines with an informant, and I took genealogies as opportunity afforded, it was not these systematic efforts at ethnology that were most rewarding, nor did they introduce me to Seneca society. It was the informal, after-hours activities that I engaged in with members of my "family" that brought me in touch with the culture as a going concern. Mornings, from the vantage point of my umbrella tent, I watched the comings and goings of the community along Snow Street as I wrote up my journal. Evenings, with the Snow boys, I traversed the network of paths that cut through the brush to the ballground where we fielded grounders or practiced lacrosse. Beyond was the river crossing where we poled over to Crick's Run in a john boat or went "torching" at night, to the gravel pit to swim, or to some house where people met to play games, sing, or just gossip. Inevitably we stopped somewhere.

On the first Sunday of my visit I was told that the group of men and women who had passed on the road that morning were members of a "society" on the way to hoe an old lady's garden. That evening Windsor Snow and I stopped to see Amos Redeye (Windsor's "friend") about borrowing his boat for fishing. Going on through the brush to Ed Coury's, Windsor volunteered that rattlesnakes were hunted for their oil, that the tried-out fat made an excellent liniment, but that it was no good if the snake was mad when killed.

Returning, we stopped at Sarah Armstrong's, because we heard singing from inside. At the back of the house, six men sat facing each other on two rows of chairs. One, who held the small water-keg drum, closed his eyes and lined out a verse while the others kept time by bumping their heels and beating cow-horn rattles in the palms of their left hands. Then they repeated the song together, drum and rattles vibrato, simultaneously maintaining the slower, measured tempo with their heels. Youngsters sat on a nearby bench, hands clasped between their knees, gently moving their heels and humming; they were learning the song. Someone told me, "This is 'The Women Shuffle Their Feet'; these songs belong to the Women's Dance. The men like to sing them. They are a society who meet to help one another, and when they have finished working, they sing for pleasure."

Presently the speaker stood. He thanked the men and women who had helped Sarah Armstrong, our hostess. In return, she had set down a kettle of corn soup for the society. While the women served first the singers and then the women and children with bowls of steaming corn soup which Mrs. Armstrong ladled from the kettle, the speaker continued: next time they would meet across the river. He asked the men to assemble the following week to cut brush in the tribal cemetery. After that, they would go in a body to put roofing paper on Alice White's house. The hostess passed me a brimming bowl of soup, a spoon, and a salt shaker, saying: "His face is white, but maybe he likes soup. Perhaps later he may learn to sing." Soon after, the leader gathered the cow-horn rattles and the drum, put them in a hand basket, and paused at the door to say to me, "We are glad that you came. You are welcome to sit with us. We will let you know where we meet next Tuesday."

At midnight Jonas Snow, his son Linnus, and I walked back along Snow Street. The night sky was brilliant. I had found the Seneca, as described, a charitable people. What was more, the singing society was common to all of Iroquois, and through that summer of learning to sing at Coldspring I would find a passport that would give me entry at Tonawanda, and later at Six Nations, for the drum is to the Iroquois what the violin is to the gypsy.

So it turned out that these evenings of listening to the Coldspring singers had consequences for my field work that were only gradually apparent. I was told to listen and hum the songs, not to worry about the words—"They don't mean anything"—though I discovered that these nonsense vocables ran in distinct patterns. The singers liked the idea of my recording them because they were constantly composing new songs which they wanted preserved. The women attended and wanted to dance. On Sunday nights we joined the rest of the community at the longhouse, where the social dances started "when they turn the lamps up" if the people were in the mood.

These social occasions were also the setting for much conversation. For example, I was asked which clan I was going to join. It was assumed that the Hawks, the family of Jonas Snow, his sister Emma Turkey, and her daughter Clara Redeye, was the logical choice, although the question came from two members of Snipe clan who were married to Hawks. I would only gradually come to understand that the clan functionally includes a fringe of spouses.

These same people wanted to visit their relatives at Cattaraugus. Of a Sunday Jonas Snow, his daughter and son, and Jonas's current drinking companion (the village villain), and I set out for the lacrosse match at Pine Woods. After stops at the back of taverns to visit bootleggers in Randolph and Lawtons, our progress included calls on Jonas's maternal relatives. In the pauses my vehicle served as a taxi between drinks and the ballground for various friends and relatives, introducing me to the elite of Seneca informants.

On a visit one stops with one's clansmen. We paused at a log house, the home of Hanover Bennett and his wife, who was Jonas's mother's sister. The old lady, bedridden, had had several strokes, but she was especially glad to see me when Jonas explained who I was. Her face brightened. She was the one, she told me, who was born in the shanty on the hemlock ridge in the big swamp and who had been brought to my great-grandmother's house. Before we sat down to dinner she insisted that I read from the Bible. At the time I thought she was a Christian, but later I realized that her request had been a courtesy to me, for she was later buried from the longhouse. The old log house (which was spotless), the grounds with their fine garden, and the reunion of Hawk and Bear clan lineages presented subjects for my camera. Whatever the reunion might mean to the real members of Jonas's mother's family, to me it was a symbolic reinforcement of my own family's link to the Seneca. I was beginning to encounter difficulty in sorting out my role of anthropologist from my role in my adoptive family.

After this bright moment I was to see a darker side of Seneca character. The afternoon nearly ended in disaster when the lacrosse game turned into a brawl in which my host and his now drunken companions joined. The bloodshed was fortunately cut short by a violent thunderstorm which cooled tempers rapidly, after which we made tracks for Coldspring.

That Sunday visit to Newtown provided both prelude and climax to a summer's field work. In the next two months I became more involved in the affairs and concerns of the Hawk clan. They did not get around to giving me a name at the Green Corn Festival, which postponed my formal adoption until I returned at midwinter. The bereaved relatives turned to me, nevertheless, when the old lady I had met died in September. This was my first opportunity as an anthropologist to attend and observe a longhouse funeral and surely under rather unique circumstances. When we drove the forty miles to Newtown that evening, I suddenly realized that the people riding with me regarded me as next of kin. And that is how I was treated when we arrived. I sat with the mourners half the night, and after the midnight meal we went aloft to sleep. I was assigned a bed near the wall, and I still have the vision of "my family" bedding down on the floor around me. Once we were awakened by drunks, who were dismissed by the women. And toward dawn I awoke to see not three feet away the beautiful face of the young woman who, throughout the long illness, had cared for her grandmother and was now snatching a few moments of sleep before the funeral, secure in the taboos of exogamy, in the common bed of the Hawk clan.

A MESSENGER OF THE TONAWANDA CHIEFS

I was introduced at Tonawanda, which is the central hearth of the Handsome Lake religion, under the best of auspices by the Coldspring "Keepers of the Good Message," as they call the prophet's words, whom I drove from Quaker Bridge to Akron for an annual convention of their peers. They introduced me to the local leaders and to the great ritualists and chiefs from Six Nations Reserve where I was afterward to work. I did not then anticipate spending two and a half years at Tonawanda as Community Worker for the United States Indian Service, which gave me daily contact with the Seneca and constant practice in the language. I seldom missed any of the events at the longhouse, so that it seemed natural for me to be appointed to go with Chief Eddie Black to carry the message sticks to Canada announcing the next convention of Handsome Lake preaching at Tonawanda. This embassy gave me entree to the chiefs of Onondaga Longhouse, where Hewitt and Goldenweiser had preceded me and where I was to feel at home after 1939 when I took up Hewitt's work at the Bureau of American Ethnology until 1951. Hewitt's texts, which I learned to read and translate, contained the words of the old men, and I was welcomed by the next younger generation who wanted to learn with me. With the advent of electronic recording machines, we put down the sacred words for posterity. These were of a quality that lent themselves to published albums by the Library of Congress.

Considering the publicity in the media to the fortunes that popular singers reap from hit recordings, one can understand why questions arise about earnings from my Iroquois recordings. The Iroquois all have television sets, and they visit and participate in various tourist attractions. They occasionally hear my recordings of their grandfathers being played under circumstances that are

Chief Edward Black carries invitation wampums to Canada.

hardly educational, although the Library of Congress intended that they be limited to educational use by museums, libraries, schools, and television. Who is to prevent the proprietor of a roadside alligator park in Florida, who hires a Seminole Indian to wrestle a 'gator, from playing them as background music? I have heard that one Canadian station uses the Medicine Song as the theme song for a cartoon series. If these allegations are true, both the Iroquois and the collector are being damaged. Such incidents contribute to the decline of rapport between one ethnologist and the grandchildren of informants with whom he once enjoyed excellent relations.

THE HEADS OF OUR GRANDFATHERS ARE BENEATH THE GROUND

One would scarcely expect the reentry to field work among a people with whom an ethnologist had previously worked to be more difficult than his first field trip. Nearly eighteen years elapsed between my last field trip to the Six Nations Reserve in 1951 and my return in 1969. My first brief trip, in January, coincided with the midwinter ceremonies at the Onondaga Longhouse, and I asked whether I would be welcome to attend, as I had in the past. To my dismay I learned that Onondaga Longhouse was closed to white people, including anthropologists! I found myself in the odd situation where research is possible but field work no longer feasible.

To be sure, admission to Iroquois "doings" had always been a privilege granted by the local longhouse officers, never a right. And over the years at Six Nations Reserve there were irritations, particularly with certain journalists, some of whom, from the Indian standpoint, wrote without sympathy or understanding and even with ridicule. For the latter reason, the Lower Cayuga Longhouse has been closed since the late 1930's. Nevertheless, the chiefs admitted me in 1945 to observe a Condolence Council, of which I published an account (Fenton, 1946). I honored their invitation to a repeat performance at Onondaga Longhouse in 1951 and was received under most cordial circumstances, although I was unable to attend on later occasions. So it did not seem to me inevitable that I should be excluded at Onondaga, even if the longhouse were closed to the general public.

Possibly Six Nations Reserve has had a surfeit of anthropologists. The list is as long as it is illustrious, beginning a century ago with Lewis Henry Morgan, Horatio Hale, and J. N. B. Hewitt and running on through Alexander A. Goldenweiser, Frederick W. Waugh, and Frank Speck. Upper Cayuga, where Speck observed, is still open; but Onondaga, where I succeeded Hewitt and Goldenweiser, is now closed. This anomaly may not be unrelated to the fact that at least seven anthropologists later spent from a summer or two up to three years on the reserve, collecting material for doctoral dissertations at major universities here and abroad. In the course of their researches many aspects and details of Iroquois life were subjected to examination and published—mythology, foods, law, factionalism, the longhouse ceremonies, conservatism, public health, the emerging elite, language, and so on. Like the Navaho, therefore, the Iroquois may have come to feel that they scarcely had a breather from being "studied," and perhaps they tired of answering questions or trying to guess the ulterior purposes of seemingly well-heeled, middle-class white observers. They protested that continued study made them self-conscious and that their privacy was being invaded. They suspected that investigators would go home and write books about them and make a lot of money. It did not escape the Iroquois that several anthropologists who first came as poor graduate students had gone on to remunerative jobs in universities and museums. Others seemingly forgot all about the Iroquois and never wrote. There was once a comfortable collaboration, based on mutual respect for a valued heritage, between older Iroquois who still knew and appreciated their traditions and the often eminent scholars who came to record and discuss them. For the new generation the importance—even the recognition—of this intellectual collaboration has become quite negligible.

Although my former sponsors were in favor of my gate-crashing the longhouse assembly and facing down any opposition, I decided not to attend any ceremonies unless and until I was invited. I did, however, offer to show for a longhouse audience, during my next visit, slides of objects that I had found in European museums, which had aroused considerable interest among the educated public.

During my courtesy call on the superintendent of the Six Nations Reserve, he suggested that the council would like to hear from me. I therefore arranged to appear at their monthly meeting in April to seek permission to reside and carry on my work during the next twelve months. Addressing the chief, the councillors, the superintendent, and the public present, when my turn came, I stated that my appearance before them was more in the nature of a report than a request. It was then more than thirty years since I had first visited the reserve. I reiterated the times and the conditions of my residence among them and observed that I had always been made to feel welcome. I explained my present position as a university professor, which enabled me to resume my former work among them. I recalled that in 1955 I had appeared before them in the interest of borrowing the Queen Anne communion service for an exhibition in Albany at the state museum, of which I was then assistant commissioner, and that three councillors (whom I named) had come with me to watch the service. A lady councillor at the center table interrupted, "That was my late husband, who died two years ago. He always spoke well of you and of that visit to Albany where he said the councillors were royally treated." (This was a most fortunate break, as I later learned, because this woman had recently objected to studies proposed by other anthropologists.) I went on to reassure them that recovering old texts in no way concerned present conditions on the reserve. I was not making a survey and I would not pry into their business. I would be concerned with their affairs to the extent that they wished me to know about them, and I would be of what limited service I could as a guest among them. (This was a good plea.) Later, if they approved, I hoped to return with students who I thought might be trained among them as I had learned to be an anthropologist while working among their old men. Indeed, I acknowledged, as was so often alleged—"Fenton has made his living off us Indians"—that I owed my whole career to them. I mentioned a portrait of a Seneca which hangs in my office at the university—how I tell inquiring visitors that he was my mentor under whom I wrote my doctoral dissertation. (This brought a laugh.) I said that what I was really asking for was "a hunting license for the year 1969." And this was substantially what I was granted.

Within ten days I fulfilled my promise to show the pictures of collections in European museums. We met in the dining room at the Onondaga Longhouse after supper. As might be expected, the audience kept straggling in during the showing, which progressed until, toward the end, a slide jammed, one of several old pictures of local personages I had inserted. I could hear a sudden inspiration of breath among some of the audience as each image had appeared, and it occurred to me that someone might construe it as an omen that the projector jammed just then. The incident brought my talk to an abrupt halt in any case and prevented reshowing the first tray that latecomers had missed. I offered to hold a second showing another night. Then the meeting was opened to questions.

None of the questions related to the pictures or to my remarks. The questions came from younger people who had come in last and they all related to my role as an anthropologist. "What is your work?" "Are you not the one who made recordings of Indian songs here twenty years ago?" Then my young inquisitor leveled the charge that I had not paid the singers, yet had made a lot of money from the recordings. I explained that I had always paid the prevailing wage rates. "I suppose it was then about sixty cents an hour," the young man retorted. "Anyway you should know how much you paid." No one admitted knowing that payments had been made by the Library of Congress for releases, and my explanation of a nonprofit cultural institution was greeted with disbelief.

Then a young matron seated on the floor to my right accused me of selling her grandfather's sacred songs to some television program. She said that she had heard his voice as background music to some cartoon that her son was watching, although she could not identify the song or the program. "I shall never forgive what you have done to my grandfather." She stormed out of the room, saying, "I don't want to hear any more from you or see those pictures. You are just like all the others." But her mother, the daughter of the old chief, who was seated before me where I could see her face, questioned me quietly and at length about the releases. At first she did not believe that he had received any such payment, but at the end she shook my hand and thanked me, saying, "My father always spoke well of you."

It is not difficult to understand the frustration that adherents to the old system of "life chiefs" must feel, when something they know and respect is not acceptable to a large segment of their own people and is completely misunderstood by Canadian society at large. The longhouse warriors (the young men of the Handsome Lake faith) abhor the elected council, the official government of the reserve, and they have twice locked it out of the council house in Ohsweken. My first questioner had read the report in the *Brantford Expositor* that I had appeared before the elected council and requested permission to reside and work on the reserve. "Why if you know so much about us," he asked, "did you go to that council? You should know that it does not represent most of the people. Why didn't you go to the proper council of the Confederacy?" Touché! There was no use explaining that I was locked up in official protocol, being an American in Canada. And my offer to appear before the life chiefs was never taken up.

So what I had hoped might be a pleasurable evening turned into a confrontation. Only afterward did people come up to me, one by one, and express interest in my remarks and in the pictures. Perhaps some regarded the photographs as another proof of the white man using the Indian. In any event, the occasion was exploited for venting aggression and hostility toward a representative of the white race.

The Iroquois enjoy cutting someone down to size. Characteristically, when criticism arises, no one stands to defend. Only men of prestige among the chiefs, men who spoke with confidence, and dared to do so, used to assume the role of public defender. I thought of this as I was being attacked, and when one of my accusers interrupted me, I reminded him that in all of my experience in councils of their grandfathers no man ever spoke while another was still talking. And this remark ended the attack.

One cannot be objective about such an experience. In writing about it, my tendency is to make it look better than it probably was. Howard Sky, an informant from my early work, consoled me next day. "I was really disappointed in the people last night. Those young people are trying desperately to be Indians, and they don't know quite how. They don't succeed in making their viewpoint clear because they don't know how to speak. Young men like the secretary of the council who questioned you last night get so mad when they go anywhere to speak that no reasonable body will listen to them for long." When I commented that I recognized in the disturbed young people what we face in the young militants in the universities, he replied, "Yes, I think you are right. These people don't know really what they want. But they are against all whites."

Hearing of my experience, one of the elected councillors who had formerly been with the old chiefs, showed little surprise. To him the impatience and intolerance of the young crowd were an old story, which he said went back to a previous "do" (as he called the counterrevolt of some years ago); then he pleaded for moderation, saying that there was a proper way to raise objections. "They are the same hotheads," he went on. "Then they would not listen. That is when they started putting white people out of the longhouse. And there has been trouble ever since." The councillor went on to outline his policy of religious tolerance. "I believe in letting the white people in because we go to their affairs off the reserve. Sometimes we don't understand what is going on, but we go anyway. Serious people should be admitted [to Seneca Longhouse, where he is speaker], and if they want to write about it, they could request permission. I believe in what you are doing because that is the only way that we are going to preserve the old words. Those young people won't listen to anyone—not even to the old people—so they will not listen to you."

Twenty years and a new generation had brought changes in attitude with dimensions and intensity that I had not foreseen; unwittingly, I had walked into a hornet's nest. Field work is difficult now, yet research is still possible. The ethnologist's work matters to people who care about preserving the old lore. As my friend and colleague Howard Sky put it, "There are people down below who are waiting for you to finish this work in which we are engaged. They need it. And they cannot get it anywhere else. No one can recite Dekanawidah clear through."

REFERENCES

FENTON, W. N. 1936. "An Outline of Seneca Ceremonies at Coldspring Longhouse." Yale University Publications in Anthropology, No. 9. 23 pp.

——— 1936a. "Some Social Customs of the Modern Senecas." *Social Welfare Bulletin,* 7:4–7. Albany: New York State Department of Social Welfare.

——— 1941. "Masked Medicine Societies of the Iroquois." *Smithsonian Institution Annual Report, 1940.* Pp. 397–429, 25 pl. Washington, D.C.

——— 1941a. "Tonawanda Longhouse Ceremonies: Ninety Years after Lewis Henry Morgan." Bureau of American Ethnology, Anthropological Paper 15, Bulletin 128, pp. 139–145, pls. 9–18. Washington, D.C.

——— 1942. "Songs from the Iroquois Longhouse: Program Notes for an Album of American Indian Music from the Eastern Woodlands." Smithsonian Institution Publication No. 3691, Library of Congress, *Folk Music of the United States,* vol. 6.

——— 1946. "An Iroquois Condolence Council for Installing Cayuga Chiefs." *Journal of the Washington Academy of Sciences,* 36:110–127.

——— 1950. "The Roll Call of the Iroquois Chiefs: A Study of a Mnemonic Cave from the Six Nations Reserve." Smithsonian Miscellaneous Collections 111, No. 15. 75 pp., 12 pls. Washington, D.C.

——— 1953. "The Iroquois Eagle Dance: An Offshoot of the Calumet Dance . . ." Bureau of American Ethnology Bulletin 156.

——— 1967. "From Longhouse fo Ranch-Type House, the Second Housing Revolution of the Seneca Nation." In Elisabeth Tooker, ed., *Iroquois Culture, History and Prehistory.* Albany: University of the State of New York, State Education Department, New York State Museum and Science Service.

FENTON, W. N., ED. 1944. "The Requickening Address of the Iroquois Condolence Council" by J. N. B. Hewitt. *Journal of the Washington Academy of Sciences,* 34:65–85.

——— 1968. *Parker on the Iroquois.* Syracuse, N.Y.: Syracuse University Press.

Part II / INTRICACIES OF FIELD WORK

8 / Field Work in High Cultures

MARGARET MEAD

Whenever anthropologists are asked to work within high cultures, their own or those of other nations, either as members of multidisciplinary teams or for special pieces of cultural diagnosis, they encounter the peculiar problems of transferring a field method designed to cross a wide cultural gap to a very different situation. I believe that if anthropologists themselves and those who work with them were more conscious of what this transfer process involved, their tasks would be easier.

The model to which all of us refer, whether explicitly or covertly, is that of a highly trained, intellectually disciplined ethnologist working with a primitive people without a written language and without full participation within a great society, although they may have made a long-time adjustment to such a larger society, as have the Bedouin tribes of the Negev. But dependence on an oral tradition and ethnic isolation, which almost universally also implies visible racial differences, has been intrinsic to the model. The great social, technological, and intellectual distance that must be traversed has been an essential part of the situation.

Members of societies whose experience of members of high cultures—usually European, but this applies also to ethnologists of Japanese, Chinese, or Indian origins—has been in most cases negative, and in many cases very negative, are able to extend a peculiar type of welcome to the visitor from another intellectual world who states his interest in them, their language, their culture, their world view. Instead of attempting to convert, recruit, educate, or cure them or to alter their traditional way of life, which has already come under some criticism by the time he reaches them, the ethnologist gives that tradition support and dignity by his interest and respect. This respectful attitude, plus the intellectual equipment provided by training in transcribing language and music, analyzing kinship, and working out the patterns of the culture, is in fact the anthropologist's chief stock-in-trade. Furthermore, he is a stranger who will stay for only a short time; he does not propose to marry into the group or establish permanent status there, and any intimacy that is established can be confined within this carefully defined relationship. For while it allows for respect and warmth, such a relationship does not involve the same kinds of friendship and love as those formed by educated men and women with their social and intellectual equals. This condition is truer of women anthropologists than men, as educated men have more tolerance of close relationships which do not involve intellectual or spiritual interchange of any kind. Nevertheless, I think we can say that the model is a relationship which depends on distance in which marriage and comparable relationships are ruled out. This very ruling out then permits—as it does also between priest and laymen where celibacy is taken seriously or between psychoanalyst or psychiatrist and patient—a degree of intimacy and emotional freedom which, in some respects, is greater than between marriage partners or close friends and colleagues who lack such protective barriers.

Furthermore, an essential ingredient of the informant relationship is its collegiality: the field work depends on the sophisticated comment of the informant at every step of the way. In the ideal field worker–informant partnership, the informant grows in his knowledge of his own culture and in his understanding of cultural analysis as the field worker learns. It is upon the intellectual delight that such work brings that in the end the field worker has to depend for a kind of intensity of effort which money could never buy.

When one works in a high culture, as an American working in France or Spain, all of these conditions are lacking. The dependence on an oral tradition vanishes, and it is hard to explain to a sophisticated and educated member of a Western culture, one's own or another, why one should ask questions instead of reading books or consulting appropriate experts. Informants have their own culturally limited view of their own culture, but it is a highly sophisticated one and one that they are not in the least interested in exchanging for a different level of cultural consciousness. Every relationship formed contains elements of possible involvement, status rivalry, erotic complications, lifelong obligation or friendship. Although these conditions are somewhat moderated when contacts are made across great cultural distances—as between European and Americans on the one hand, and Chinese, Japanese, or Indians on the other—the anthropological insistence on equal respect for all cultures contains implicitly the possibility of pursuing any such relationship as deeply as possible, which means marriage and intellectual equality.

So where, superficially, field work in a high society may look like field work in a primitive society, it never is. This is so whether work is done among members of one's own class or of other classes. If the anthropologist works with ethnic minorities, or with a class lower than that to which he belongs, or with his own rural or provincial relatives, he cannot rid himself of the implications of potential or actual membership in the society he is studying. This is one reason why work in ghettos, slums, and remote peasant or mining villages is such a different undertaking from work in a primitive village. Such a relationship is tenable only if the anthropologist can assume, legitimately, some helping role which justifies the choice of a temporary participation in a group who consider themselves discriminated against, less educated, less privileged than he. Pure anthropological field work in its primitive form is virtually impossible.

Margaret Mead in Manus.

I came to realize some of the implications of the contrasts between working in a high culture and primitive field work in the 1930's, when we first began to introduce actual anthropological field methods into various branches of the adolescent study being conducted by the Commission on Secondary Education of the Progressive Education Association. My colleagues from other disciplines were delighted at the idea that someone might study adolescent groups by anthropological methods, which, I rapidly discovered, they interpreted as spying. At last the adults would know what the adolescents really thought! Attempts to get them to see what we meant by participant observation—a phrase that was just coming into popularity at that time—and how different it was from spying were very unsuccessful. But presenting them with the ethical dilemma of a twenty-two-year-old girl who looked sixteen mingling with teen-agers as one of them and dating a sixteen-year-old boy did something to bring them up with a start and to show them how a failure to declare one's intentions could result in a human betrayal. But ordinary, clear anthropological statements about any of the institutions we were interested in—the status system in a school, the attitudes of teachers, the methods of selecting students —also seemed like some kind of a betrayal. The studies of schools that were done with the help of highly placed members of the groups sponsoring the research were never published. Where patronage by the chief assured one an entry in a primitive ranked society, it acted, in these American studies, in the opposite way because of the sophisticated resistances of foundation officials and committee chairmen. Initial, unreal cooperation was followed by rejection and the use of power to suppress publication.

Comparable conditions occurred in England in the late 1930's. Those in power arranged for studies to be made, in cultural terms, but then repudiated the results, and in ways that would have made publication a breach of hospitality and friendship.

There also were, and are, realistic questions of class and social sophistication. "How," demanded one of my colleagues in psychiatric social work, who is experienced in the relationships between middle-class sophisticated professional workers and upper-class members of boards of social agencies, "can an anthropologist study members of a class higher than his own?" How indeed? And how could the best-intentioned patron secure an entree into European society for those who handled their knives and forks incorrectly or whose appreciation of social nuances was nil. Of course some of these distinctions held in colonial situations. Alfred Haddon used to comment on those of his students who were "gentlemen, and the natives know it," but it seems more likely the natives were responding to subtle differences in the behavior of the other Europeans toward the anthropologist. Differences in wealth as well as in breeding or genealogical credentials can also be difficult. In our Columbia University Research in Contemporary Cultures, we used young, relatively impecunious graduate students of Eastern European origin as field workers among very wealthy, very unintellectual Syrian Jews, and my dreams were filled with attempts to provide them with mink coats, after listening to outraged discussions of Jews—Jews!—who didn't encourage their sons to go to college. Here difference in wealth, and ethnic differences within the wider cultural range, both constituted barriers, which had to be lived out within social settings where social equality was a necessary assumption.

During World War II, I had my first taste of the problems of working within another high culture where my introductions were personal—that of England. I was sent over to explain Americans to the English. Although I had an English husband, an English nurse for my child, two English wartime foster children, and many close English friends in many parts of the world, I had never lived or worked in England or been part, even for a few days, of an English household. The problems that usually plague the field worker were all absent. I could speak the language—with only a few terrible errors—if I was careful to avoid slang. I was warmly received by an array of friends, colleagues, and relatives-in-law and was given the kind of deep acceptance characteristic of English people. Everyone was willing to talk with me; there was no problem in drawing them out on any subject as I tried to explore those cultural differences most relevant to my current task. Their comments and explanations were embarrassingly explicit as they decried the Americans, and I learned to include in my lectures the important fact, for example, that Americans did not think standing bolt upright at all times and in all places was a test of character. Field work went very fast, and wherever I was I could collect local, authentic statements about the relevant American-English differences I needed for the next set of lectures.

But there was one great gap. Although the English were such ready talkers, they could not be transformed into informants without a violation of the terms on which they accepted me. I could not discuss their culture with them; this would have been to take intolerable liberties. (I remember years later sitting in the theatre with Edith and Osbert Sitwell, who were protesting that *Death of a Salesman* took unbearable liberties with the audience.) Yet all my fieldwork training had consisted of discussing what I learned with the people from whom I learned it, as well as, at a still different level, with other anthropologists in the field and in correspondence. Letters from England were all likely to be read, reproduced, and circulated; so instead of their being an outlet for my growing knowledge, they had to be constructed very carefully for their probable audience—censorship and security. I felt strangely bottled up, cut off from normal human relations, and perhaps a little like the spy that my colleagues had wanted to send among the adolescents, just because I couldn't tell my friends what I was learning from them about their culture. In a way this affected, a little, for me, the quality of my friendships which I felt could have been deeper had I not had a professional wartime task of cross-cultural analysis on my hands.

The solution I found to my own personal sense of field-work isolation proved generalizable later. I had made two friends, both analytical intellectuals, a social psychologist and an economist, both, as it happened, Viennese, and both acutely, professionally interested in understanding English culture. English culture—discussed, dissected, reconstituted, enjoyed, and puzzled over—became the substance of my friendships with them, kept me feeling human, and provided some of the necessary interplay that is part of testing out just how far one has come in understanding. I ceased to feel a temptation to discuss their own culture with my English friends.

At the end of the war, Ruth Benedict was made a member of a panel on human resources of the Office of Naval Research; each panel member was encouraged to develop a relevant piece of research. During the war, she and I had both worked intensively on studies of other cultures as seen through the eyes of individual informants in this country. A group of us had developed a number of techniques: interviewing a social scientist on his own life history and asking him to comment on it theoretically and professionally at the same time; setting up hypnotic sessions with members of other cultures and asking both hypnotist and subject to comment later; group interviewing of persons who occupied different statuses in comparable bureaucracies; and the like. Ruth Benedict had worked with Romanians, Thais, and Japanese in addition to doing a number of smaller studies among other nationals. On the basis of our experience and that of a number of other anthropologists—including Geoffrey Gorer, Gregory Bateson, Rhoda Metraux, and Clyde Kluckhohn—we had built up an image of how distant cultures could be studied by working with single informants, with groups, and through literature, films, and so on. Columbia University Research in Contemporary Cultures was designed with these wartime experiences, as well as regular field work, in mind.

In setting up the project, which was designed to deal with several different cultures of different degrees of accessibility through informants in the United States, we also wished to have a structure that would represent anthropological methods of work, nonhierarchical and holistic in style. The groups were structured around the project—groups arranged by cultures in the center and those arranged by disciplines around the periphery, with all members occupying at least two different statuses. All participants—some sixty at any one time—met as a group every two weeks and shared common materials. Informants were chosen, not because they represented particular disciplines, but because of their interest in the research topic and their special relationships to the cultures involved.

We had found, and have continued to find, that if a group is made up of members of two high cultures, especially high cultures between whom there has been a great deal of contact, it tends to get stuck in bicultural interchange and to develop stereotyped responses to the dyadic relationship. So in addition to including members of the culture being studied—French, Russian, Polish, as the case might be—we also included a member or members of a third culture to break this kind of deadlock. We did not strive for any symmetrical arrangement of participant disciplines, but only for a group of people with divergent skills and interests whose discussion and analysis of shared materials would supplement and complement each other.

And it was this "whole" approach to the studied cultures that held our center, culture-based groups together. The small peripheral, homogeneous groups of various disciplines achieved no such unity.

During this period of the late 1940's and the 1950's, multidisciplinary projects multiplied, and a tremendous number of difficulties developed. Groups were ordinarily organized around the initiative and interests of a principal investigator, with individuals recruited on the basis of their disciplinary competency. Graduate students were added as a way of providing them with stipends. The projects themselves were problem-oriented, and the contribution each traditional discipline could make was heavily emphasized. In the mid-1950's, an evaluative plan was developed. Before each of the annual meetings of the societies most involved—anthropology, sociology, psychology, and psychiatry—workshops were held, and the course of the projects analyzed. Although the final project publications were bland in the extreme, the workshop sessions revealed for the participants how tremendously filled with tension and strain the projects had been. Members of each participating discipline reported how difficult it was to get acceptance of their particular contribution. One such project team, to which I became a consultant, had spent an entire year arguing about the frame of reference without collecting a single piece of data. Another, which included an invaluable set of interviews, was so fragmented that no other member of the group had ever read them. Projects dragged on and members left for other projects or better jobs. By the end of the 1950's, there was tremendous dissatisfaction with group multidisciplinary projects and with the quality of their results.

I believe that some of the allowances we made for our anthropological experience, and for the predominance of anthropologists within Research in Contemporary Cultures and its associated projects between 1947 and 1955, were to some degree responsible for the different style that prevailed. We assumed that research workers went into projects because of a deep and consuming interest in what they were doing. (This must be so for field anthropologists if they are to be carried successfully through the rigors, the exacting hours and physical circumstances, and the loneliness of work in the field.) We assumed that people should be self-selected, not recruited to fill in formal gaps. We assumed they would also be attracted and held by the human factors involved—the enjoyment of working with the other participants and with their special groups. Husband-and-wife teams were welcomed, and a place was found for spouses who later wanted to join. There were many volunteers, and the senior people were paid little or nothing for their participation. (In one of these projects volunteers paid their own way from other cities to participate.) Many people had worked together before, especially during World War II, and old and new friendships, strong teacher-pupil ties, present and former love affairs (and lovers' quarrels), and, sometimes, love-hate rivalries occurred. But they were vicissitudes that characterize any group whose participants are acting as whole persons, not as overprofessionalized partial contributors, as is often the case when unknown and uninvolved people are enlisted on a professional basis alone. The fact that some individuals were more experienced, some much more gifted, some much more brilliant served to diversify the group, with the same sort of consequences that one finds in families where the children have diverse gifts, instead of sidetracking or disrupting it with arguments about the superiority of the methods of one discipline over another.

Each group was open-ended; 114 people worked in Research in Contemporary Cultures over the whole period, but many of them came and went according to the circumstances of their professional lives. No group became so closed that a departure or an addition was disrupting. Ruth Benedict's death, the year after the first project began, was experienced as a tragedy in the way the death of a leading figure in a village is experienced, and by each participant in terms of his or her respective culture. Political differences were often extreme; we had one participant who had been hanged by the Nazis, cut down before he was dead, and released under the legalism of double jeopardy. The Chinese and Russian groups were sensitive both to the pressures of the McCarthy era and to changes in national and party lines. It later proved that the extreme precautions we had taken to protect our informants—they were coded and their names known only to the field worker who interviewed them—had been very necessary.

The anthropological principles involved were: a lack of hierarchy within the working groups and between field worker and informant; protection and respect for the informants; shared materials so that each member of a group was working with all of the materials collected by other members; and a special combination of the anthropologically enjoined types of participation. Where the individual worker in a remote primitive village lived his or her whole life in disciplined but intense day-by-day relationships with a whole village and with selected informants within it, and where I had found in England that it was complicated to try to create field-work conditions when I worked in a high culture with people to whom I had deep personal ties, in this research the personal ties were among the members of the research group, while the informants represented isolated and controlled contacts. Each field worker worked with a separate set of informants, and the informants practically never met each other as informants. The field worker brought a written record of an interview—and his own lively version of it—to the research group, where informants were referred to by the field worker's link: "John's Mr. X." As each research group, with the exception of the French, had permanent members from the culture being studied, the commentary and elucidation which the anthropologist received from his informants in the field, and which I had to search for and find in my Viennese colleagues in England, were provided within the group. In a primitive field situation, relationships to informants have to be governed by strict rules, the simplest of which is, I think, that no informant should ever be fitted into a fictive primary relationship—child, parent, sibling, spouse, or lover. Here, however, the only rules that had to be applied were protection of privacy and preservation of formality. Informants were not paid, but each field worker had to establish sufficient rapport to obtain the necessary information, continued participation, and, in some cases, consent to projective tests.

We did find, however, that within the research group we had to bar controlled relationships, such as those between therapist and patient, analyst and analysand, and social worker and client. Reliance on full human warmth, friendship, and love and on involvement of the total personality was incompatible with these more restricted, specifically charged, and self-conscious relationships. It was members of the therapeutic professions who had the hardest time establishing the kinds of nonhierarchical, symmetrical interviewing situations on which this kind of field work depended. When the customary props of the practitioner's role and patient's or client's declared need were removed, the highly trained specialist was often at a loss. The implicit insistence on leaving the informant free and abjuring all manipulation, however benevolent and protective, is one that those trained to make every moment of a verbal interchange promote a therapeutic end find very difficult to learn.

Another anthropological style we followed in the big projects, and which I have subsequently incorporated into small field-training projects for graduate students, was the need to so structure the research that the loss of any member of the research team, the interruption of the project at any point, or the failure of one planned aspect would not prevent some results. Most multidisciplinary projects are planned with a series of interlocking enterprises for which members of different disciplines are given exclusive responsibility—medical examinations, social surveys, series of projective tests, home visits, growth measurements, and so on. The failure of one facet of the whole sometimes wrecks the design completely, or the need to substitute a new research worker in the middle of the project may be disastrous. The anthropological model here is familiar to every anthropologist, especially to those who work far away where travel costs and the initial cost of equipment are very high. All of us know the haunting fear of personal illness, of a natural or man-made catastrophe—earthquake, epidemic, war, revolution—that will cut short our field work. This hazard has increased rather than decreased through the last fifty years, as it has been possible to travel farther, costs of equipment have been multiplied a hundredfold, and political complications have grown. But under the old circumstances of month-long journeys or under the new conditions of expensive air trips, the risks are there and the prudent field worker keeps his research in such a state that if it is interrupted, he will still have something to show for it. This ensurance of results involves writing up in the field, refusing to postpone essential matters like mapping or listing and photographing informants, and periodic assessment and analysis of the progress of one's work.

In our research on contemporary cultures, we accomplished this task in several ways. Interviews were typed up and distributed to the members of the groups involved, and there were periodic thematic presentations on such subjects as "the house," "money," "friendship," on which each group worked separately, and then cross-cultural presentations were made to the projectwide seminar. A series of subgoals of this sort assured us that what was known at a given period in the research would be organized and integrated. At the same time the basic materials—interviews, analysis of literature, films, and so on—and the stenographic or taped records of the group discussions were and are available for reexamination. We found what every field worker knows—that it was necessary to go back to the original material, not to coded, derived versions of it, if new questions were to be answered. We had, in fact, to abandon one plan, which was to have summaries of material prepared, because the summaries were never useful for a later theoretical stage.

Different cultures provided different problems. We were never able to find a French man or woman who was willing to be a permanent member of the French group. So the French participants had to work, outside the group, more intensively with individual informants to whom they had more personal ties. This was a drawback, but one typical of the French characteristics of great clarity combined with an unwillingness to treat French culture as one among many rather than as a prototype of high culture itself.

The Syrian group which worked with a variety of Middle Easterners (Christian, Jewish, and Moslem), who in the United States form a conglomerate of self-styled "Syrians," had its own problems. It was easy to establish relationships within small groups, but each small group was possessive of its own field workers. Those who worked with the Chinese found that extremely smooth and rewarding relationships also contained a *quid pro quo,* so that two years later the field worker was suddenly called upon to arrange a wedding or intervene in a court case. The Eastern European Jewish group suffered from the very voluminousness of the records. The Russian group had the largest number of political nuances to adjust to. Here again, the opportunity to compare such contrasting field problems provided immediately what the lonely field worker acquires only through several field trips or, at best, through postfield discussion with colleagues—a sense of cultural relativity about the processes of the research itself.

Another problem which has assumed new and disturbing proportions in recent years, and which was necessarily part of our work, was the relationship to security. Most of us who worked in Research in Contemporary Cultures had worked within rigorous security regulations during World War II. We had also participated in postwar discussions regarding the damaging effects of participation in "black activities" (activities in which the source of information is falsified so as to exploit trust) and psychological warfare. While it was true that we needed the same kinds of information on contemporary cultures for war as for peace, for building national morale and for subversion, the way in which research materials were gathered, stored, and exploited was exceedingly significant. This experience was used in setting up the new research projects, which were specifically designed to give us more information about the cultures of our allies, those from which many informants had been drawn during the war, and those, like the Soviet Union and parts of China, that were inaccessible for direct field work. We knew we would be working with foreign nationals, with refugees, with political defectors, and with those whose future political allegiances were in doubt. Not only our informants, but our research workers needed protection in a period when one's loyalty might be attacked if one were seen buying a book at the Four Continents Bookstore in New York City. The arrangements we made were, I think, appropriate for the period. Research on the Soviet culture, and to a certain extent on the Chinese, later on the Polish, could only be conducted with safety from witch hunts within the framework of the defense establishment. At the same time, secrecy and involvement in security problems would be, we felt, fatal to the type of research we wanted to do. The research was openly sponsored by the Office of Naval Research, Rand, and, through a subcontract with the United States State Department, Columbia University and the American Museum of Natural History. Informants were told this. No participant within the project was cleared, and many people could not have been. (Some of us, of course, held clearances in relation to other government appointments.) There were no locked safes and no secret files of any sort. Our informants were protected by anthropological ethical standards. There was only one oversight: we did not foresee that verbatim interviews might conceivably prove damaging to the interviewer, making suspect the simple grunts of encouragement characteristic of ordinary rapport. In another such enterprise, I would code the interviewer also.

Today the very conditions that made it necessary to locate open research within the defense establishment make it necessary to advocate the removal of all research, no matter how open and how ethically conducted, from such sponsorship. Trust and credibility have seriously deteriorated; episodes like Camelot have been widely discussed. The basic problem, however—the vulnerability of socially relevant research to political attack—still remains. The 1969 attacks on foundations that engage in socially relevant activities reaffirm the danger of trying to conduct such research in any context open to Congressional political debate—whether it be government research, done inside but not secret; research within the defense establishment; open research financed by government funds; or research financed by tax-exempt institutions. The more skillfully the results of such work are presented, the more they take into account the whole of the culture within which recommendations have to be carried out, the less the danger of political interference. But the danger remains.

It has been observed that small social-science groups formed around innovations—sociometry, projective tests, group dynamics, psychoanalysis—tend to founder on their own insights. The field of culture and personality is not exempt from this danger. But I believe, looking at it from a perspective of more than a decade, during which I have again been concerned with primitive traditional types of field work and with attempting to simulate field conditions for graduate students, that the extent to which this particular set of projects avoided the pitfalls of too great an emphasis on the culture-and-personality approach, with its temptation to incest, was due to the way we drew on general anthropological style and on the ethics and requirements of field work, rather than on the inevitable overemphasis of any particular approach. Crises, both within and without the group, were, in fact, associated with culture-and-personality emphases, as in the violent reaction to Geoffrey Gorer's swaddling hypothesis which mobilized resistances within sponsoring agencies, other scholars in the Russian field, Russian Jews, and anti-Freudians of all sorts. As we worked, we became more skillful in presenting results in a form that was acceptable to the members of the culture being studied and to the members of other cultures. Today we know this to be an absolute requirement if anthropological materials are to be used constructively in the contemporary world.

Many of us who worked very hard to establish full membership in the human race of primitive people with whom it was a long and arduous task to establish such a relationship are inclined to feel somewhat bitter when young nationalists and young radicals accuse anthropologists of having collaborated with colonialism—because they necessarily worked within colonial framewords—or of having insulted primitive people by treating them as "guinea pigs" or merely objects of study, or of having laid too much emphasis on the primitive past instead of the progressive present. Such criticisms are vividly illustrated by the anachronistic reactions to Bronislaw Malinowski's diary. The use of the outmoded descriptive term for black people interested readers more than did the heartbreaking accounts of the illness and loneliness that accompanied Malinowski's pioneer work—work which dignified modern discussions of primitive law and mentality. But it may well be that this contemporary uproar, promoted in most cases by those who are ignorant of the conditions of real field work, may be simply one more expression of the basic premise of anthropology—that we do not have subjects, we do not treat people as objects, we do not experiment with human beings, and we treat those with whom we work as full collaborators. However, definitions of treating others as full collaborators change through the years. The demands that college students are making today differ drastically from the demands of just a few years ago, although not from the demands that I have made all my life, first as a student who participated in curriculum planning in the early 1920's and later in relation to my own students and research assistants. It is perhaps inevitable that some of the very justified furor about the rights of youth, black people, American Indians, and young nations should spill over into a reexamination of anthropological methods, and the legitimacy of the premises on which we have built our research, both among primitive peoples and in contemporary societies. This examination becomes the more urgent when such activities as the Peace Corps and the poverty program are under reconsideration; when psychiatry is being taken to the community; when T groups are being formed in prisons where young conscientious objectors, youths arrested for possession of marijuana, hardened offenders, and old and new prison staff sit down in equal converse. In such a period we need every ounce of sophistication that we can get as we try to combine research with action.

REFERENCES

LUSZKI, MARGARET B. 1958. *Interdisciplinary Team Research: Methods and Problems.* National Training Laboratories Research Training Series 3. New York: New York University Press.

MEAD, MARGARET. 1947. "The Application of Anthropological Techniques to Cross-National Communication." *Transactions of the New York Academy of Sciences,* 2:133–152.

———. 1948. "A Case History in Cross-National Communication." In Lyman Bryson, ed., *The Communication of Ideas.* New York: Institute for Religious and Social Studies.

———. 1954. "The Swaddling Hypothesis: Its Reception." *American Anthropologist,* 56:395–409.

———. 1962. "Social Responsibility of the Anthropologist." *Journal of Higher Education,* 33:1–12.

———. 1965. "The Anthropology of Human Conflict." In Elton B. McNeil, ed., *The Nature of Human Conflict.* Englewood Cliffs, N.J.: Prentice-Hall.

———. 1969a. Research with Human Beings: A Model Derived from Anthropological Field Practice." *Daedalus,* 98:361–386.

———. 1969b. (Participant.) "Secrecy and Dissemination in Science and Technology: A Report of the Committee on Science in the Promotion of Human Welfare." *Science,* 163:787–790.

———. 1970. "Field Work in the Pacific Islands, 1925–1967." In Peggy Golde, ed., *Women in the Field.* Chicago: Aldine.

———. In press. "The Art and Technology of Field Work." In Raoul Naroll and Ronald Cohen, eds., *A Handbook of Method in Cultural Anthropology.* New York: Natural History Press.

———. In press. (Participant.) "Hearings on Psychological Aspects of Foreign Policy." Report of the Proceedings of the Hearings Held before the Senate Committee on Foreign Relations, June 20, 1969.

MEAD, MARGARET, AND PAUL BYERS. 1968. *The Small Conference: An Innovation in Communication.* Paris and The Hague: Mouton.

MEAD, MARGARET, AND RHODA METRAUX. 1953. *Study of Culture at a Distance.* Chicago: University of Chicago Press.

MEAD, MARGARET, WITH MARTHA WOLFENSTEIN. 1955. *Childhood in Contemporary Cultures.* Chicago: University of Chicago Press.

9 / Entering the World of the Aymara

WILLIAM E. CARTER

Learning to live among a people as isolated and as little researched as were the Aymara fifteen years ago, the ethnographer finds that he can neither plot the course of events nor control their outcome. The best he can hope for is flexibility to adjust to them and sensitivity to learn from them. Eventually he may discover, as I did, that the events have as deeply affected him as they have the people he has studied.

My initial experience with the Aymara was in the summer of 1952. I was living in Uruguay at the time, and decided to vacation in highland Bolivia and Peru. On first reaching Ancoraimes, a little town alongside Lake Titicaca, I was overwhelmed by the sparse beauty and deep tranquillity of the place. It gave me the uncanny sensation of having returned home. Home for me had been a staid, conservative Midwestern city, though my father had been reared on a farm, and, as a boy, I had spent many summers there. The immenseness of the cultural difference that separated me from my vacation surroundings escaped me entirely.

So fascinated was I by the Altiplano that I arranged for a position in the Ancoraimes Methodist mission school to begin the following year. It served almost exclusively Aymara students from the surrounding countryside. During that first year on the Altiplano, my life was limited almost entirely to the school. From time to time I ventured into the countryside to visit a pupil's family, but the true life of the community remained unperceived. Rather than attempting to discover the basic values of the Aymara, I zealously worked to implant my own, beginning with what to me were the most obvious ones—cleanliness, sobriety, and honesty. My actual participation in Aymara culture did not exceed occasionally watching festive music and dance groups perform when they came into town. Much as I admired these groups, I had no real idea of what was actually going on. The drunkenness on such occasions I found to be perplexing and even revolting; its meaning escaped me entirely.

Sometimes my pupils would refer to secret rituals carried out in their homes, and the director of the mission clinic often commented on the ill effects of

133

witch doctors. Indigenous religion fascinated me, and I tried to learn as much as I could about it. My pupils were poor informants, however. Not only were they reluctant to talk about the subject; they themselves were unaware of many of its subtleties. Nor did my identification with a mission group make for easy communication about their religion.

Being the teacher of these youths, however, was a deeply satisfying experience. That I was an educated white man elicited an immense esteem. My pupils had scant notions of where I had come from or what life was like in my homeland, but they could not doubt that I enjoyed both power and wealth far beyond their own expectations.

The adulation of my pupils deluded me into feeling that I had succeeded in making a remarkable adjustment to Aymara culture. I felt completely confident with them, because I always met them on my ground, not theirs.[1] I often traveled with their kin in the back of a truck as it roared over the countryside, but only rarely did I eat in their houses, and I spent not a single night in their company. At the end of the day I always made certain that I was in safe quarters either in distant La Paz or in my own comfortable apartment within the school compound.

The spring morning I left Ancoraimes was shiny bright, as only Altiplano mornings can be. Classes had ended and a few of the schoolboys came to see me off on the truck. "Why do you have to go?" they asked. "We are afraid that if you go away, you will forget about us completely. You will never come back." Such an accusation was unsettling. I resolved that, some way or other, I would return. The year I had spent at the school had been one of the most satisfying of my life.

Upon my return to the United States, I completed a degree in theology that had been left unfinished four years before. My obsession, however, had become South American Indians. Indeed, I talked about them so incessantly that some of my colleagues suggested that I return to spend the rest of my life with them. After several years' graduate study in anthropology at Columbia University, I received a research grant from the National Institute of Mental Health and I returned to Bolivia.

When I discussed the goals of my project with Julia Elena Fortún, the Bolivian national director of folklore and ethnology, she immediately suggested that I consider doing a study in Tiahuanacu, where her husband had been engaged in archeological research for a number of years. An added advantage was the fact that the archeological team had been granted the use of an abandoned, but refurbished tourist hotel on the edge of town, where a full-time cook provided meals, so that no time would be wasted on the housekeeping chores. The situation sounded ideal, if for no other reason than that it provided an immediate solution to the problem of setting up a field station.

My first week in Tiahuanacu was spent in getting a feel for the town and the surrounding countryside. Before long, however, I began to sense a real strain between the personnel of the center and the townspeople. Rumors were myriad, one of the most vicious being that the personnel of the center had plans to dynamite all the houses belonging to members of Falange, a national minority party. The fact that the director of archeological research was simultaneously the executive secretary of the majority M.N.R. party's *comité político* did not help matters, for this committee was charged with controlling all political forces opposed to the regime.

Greater frustration came when, after reviewing the agrarian-reform dossiers for all the major former haciendas around Tiahuanacu, I tried to get into the countryside itself for research. Though I had an acute awareness of the importance of the language, my Aymara was still practically nonexistent. The antagonism between Mestizo and Indian in Ancoraimes had convinced me that one of the major reasons for the dismal picture of Aymara personality reported by ethnographers was the fact that they had used Mestizos as interpreters.[2] To overcome this deficiency, I made a thorough search for a rural Indian field assistant who, in addition to his Aymara, had a fluent command of Spanish. For weeks the search proved fruitless.

The attitude of center personnel discouraged me even further. One afternoon, when I spoke of spending the evening in a former hacienda so that I could establish better personal relationships there, the assistant director informed me that such would be impossible. The guard who was posted at the gate to the center's compound had orders to shoot anyone who entered or left after 8:00 P.M. Immediately my mind went to the fascinating work Tschopik had done on Aymara religion, and I realized that, as long as I lived under such regulations, I could never hope to do anything comparable, for practically all Aymara ritual is conducted at night.

The experience that led me to consider permanently abandoning Tiahuanacu occurred when I tried to get some idea about the flow of goods in the regional market. I had finally been able to persuade a local Indian, who was moving into the intermediate Cholo status, to help me with the language problem. We went together on the appropriate day to the market site located in the middle of an open pampa several miles southeast of Tiahuanacu. Trading regularly took place there from 9:00 in the morning to 3:00 or 4:00 in the afternoon. We arrived before 8:30 so that we could see the first marketwomen bring in their produce. By 9:15, there were more than one hundred stalls, and it was then that I began to walk among them, admire the products that were being displayed, and solicit information. Aware of possible distrust, I tried to make my questions as innocuous as possible. "How interesting your things look. You must have worked hard to bring them here. Did you grow them yourself? How far did you have to come?"

The reluctance with which the marketwomen answered my questions did not surprise me. What did cause consternation was that sellers on the edges of the market farthest from me began to pack up and leave. There was no open protest; rather the vendors merely slipped away. Within thirty minutes, no one was left save myself, my interpreter, and a few stragglers who were busily getting their things together. I could only conclude that somehow my presence had been responsible.

The experience was shattering. Between the time spent in Ancoraimes and Tiahuanacu, I had been on the Altiplano for some fifteen months. Through reading, I had steeped myself in anthropological research methods, and had tried to be as diplomatically cautious as possible in establishing relationships in the field. All these efforts, it was now clear, had come to naught. I was as far as ever from knowing how to relate to the culture I had come to study. Not a single person in Tiahuanacu grasped my purpose. Even the archeologists in the center failed to understand my role as ethnographer.

A series of serendipitous events finally solved my problem. A few days after the market fiasco, I learned that a central meeting was being planned for some new 4H clubs which were getting started around Tiahuanacu. When I expressed interest in attending, the man who told me of the meeting invited me to accompany him. The group that came together was small, not more than ten young men, and made up entirely of Indians from surrounding communities. In an attempt to establish rapport, I shared experiences I had had as a boy on Midwestern farms. The men were astounded that a white foreigner had ever tilled the soil. My ploy worked. When they began to make plans for attending a regional rally the following week, they invited me to go along. It was to be held in Irpa Chico, a free Aymara community located only thirty miles from La Paz.

Since Irpa Chico was so near the city, I took advantage of that fact to drive into La Paz and invite my family to spend a couple of days in the country. Together, we approached the community's boundaries at mid-afternoon. The year had been unusual in that September had brought drenching rains to the region; the roadbed into Irpa Chico was a quagmire that periodically had to be tested before one could proceed. At one spot, surrounded by lagoons, it gave way entirely, and the jeep lurched on its side into one of them. As water began to flow into the vehicle, we had to climb perpendicularly out the doors to escape.

After two hours of attempting to free the mired jeep, we were convinced that nothing could be done until the next day. It was then that a Toyota appeared and, since it was lighter than my American vehicle, slid successfully through the mire. It was driven by a priest, accompanied by two teaching nuns, all of whom were returning from the 4H-club rally. They tried to pull my vehicle out of the mud but failed, and the priest then insisted that my family and I accompany him to his rectory, where we could dry out and be fed.

The following morning, after seeing that my family had safely returned to La Paz, I walked the ten miles from Viacha, where the rectory was located, to Irpa Chico. As I entered the community, I was amazed to discover that the jeep had disappeared during the night. In my rudimentary Aymara, I tried to learn where it had gone, and was directed immediately to the schoolhouse, some two miles up the road. I had no inkling of what had happened. There were no other tracks on the road, and I had taken the ignition key with me when I had gone to Viacha. Yet there the jeep stood in front of the school-house, defiant in its muddied resplendency.

A group of curious young men surrounded me when I entered the school-yard. Some spoke good Spanish and quickly gave me a clear picture of what had happened. As part of their 4H service to the community, they had assembled at the abandoned vehicle at dawn with plowshafts and oxen. After righting it, they had lifted it bodily onto the road. Lack of the ignition key was no obstacle to one of them who got the engine going and drove with a full load of rescuers back to the school where he parked the vehicle, to await the appearance of the owner.

By the time I arrived at the schoolyard, the 4H rally was drawing to a close. I attended the last sessions and, when they had finished, thanked the men who had rescued my jeep and said that I would take it to La Paz for necessary repairs. The leader of the rescue team, M.M., asked immediately if he could go along since he had business in the city.

As we drove away from the community, M.M. inquired why I had come to Irpa Chico in the first place. Thoroughly discouraged over my past difficulties in communication, I said simply that I was interested in learning about the customs of rural folk, about land tenure, and about the effects of the Bolivian agrarian reform. "Oh," said M.M., "then you must be a rural sociologist." Such perception on the part of a peasant Indian amazed me. "I am something very similar to a rural sociologist," I replied; "I am a cultural anthropologist."

"Oh, yes," said M.M. "I studied cultural anthropology in normal school. It was one of my favorite subjects."

Here, after so many frustrating months was some positive response. M.M., the son of a former Irpa Chico headman, had grown up in a monolingual home, through diligence and talent had learned Spanish, and had completed a normal course roughly equivalent to our high school. Although reared in the traditional Aymara manner, he was at the same time sufficiently conversant with Bolivian national culture to act as broker and interpreter. Where I had previously been met with distrust and hostility, there now appeared interest and understanding. Here was mutual opportunity, for his curiosity was as limitless as mine. We made plans to meet in his town house to exchange information on Aymara and North American culture.

My new friend and I worked together daily while my jeep was being repaired. In my first three hours with him, I learned more about traditional Aymara culture than I had learned in nearly a year and a half on the Altiplano. I was concerned that the information be reliable, however, and knew that I would still have to take up residence in a dispersed, rural community. Tiahuanacu seemed like such a hopeless site that I began to think of moving to Irpa Chico. Previously, the basic problems in making such a move had been the fact that those Aymara communities which were never converted to estates are closed and corporate. Sale or rental to individuals outside the community is forbidden, and the only way an ethnographer can establish residence there is to be invited as special guest of a birthright family. Given the intrinsic hostility and distrust of the inhabitants, securing such an invitation is extremely difficult. Any light-complexioned stranger is automatically taken as a potential *terrateniente,* or estate owner.

When I first suggested taking up residence in Irpa Chico, M.M. was cautious. Before the week was out, however, he invited me to spend a few days in his home. During those first few days, I engaged in participant observation of several cultural events which M.M. had verbally described to me, and this experience convinced me that he was an incredibly detailed and accurate observer. I have never since found such a reliable informant.

The initial test to which M.M.'s family put me came during a family wake for the patriarch of the lineage. Until that moment I had been abstemious. I had learned enough about Aymara culture, however, to realize that the drinking of distilled cane alcohol is important for social relationships. What I did not learn until later was that communal drinking is the principal means for breaking down social reticence and distrust and that such drinking symbolically separates the sacred from the profane.

To initiate the death ritual, a bottle of alcohol was brought together with a single shot glass and set on the ground in front of the corpse. The ritual leader began his ceremonies by proffering the drink to each person present, insisting that he down three shots in a row. When my turn came, I hesitated. Those present, noticing this hesitation, quickly made clear to me that I must drink and that I must do it properly, first spilling a few drops on the ground as a libation to the spirits and then downing what remained with one gulp. I followed their orders and winced at the vile-tasting liquid; it came from the sugar refineries of the Bolivian Oriente and contained some 89 per cent ethyl alcohol. M.M.'s family was kind. Though some of them drank to total oblivion, they approached me with the shot glass and bottle only three times that night; a mere gesture of accepting their ways seemed sufficient. By the time the night was over, the elders of the group were profusely thanking me for my presence and telling me what an honor it was for them to have a white man share their poor hospitality.

Food often presents a real problem to the field worker. The Aymara are justifiably noted for their lack of hygiene, and plates of food I was given on occasions such as this often contained so much dirt that I could feel grit between my teeth as I chewed. I had begun to accept meals offered to me during my sojourns into the countryside while I was still in Tiahuanacu, and now the consequences caught up with me in the form of typhoid fever. This came as no great surprise, for during the year that I had taught school on the Altiplano I had come down with a very serious case of hepatitis. In both cases, it meant losing at least a month of work and, with the case of typhoid, this loss came at a particularly frustrating time, for, after months of abortive attempts, I was finally beginning to gain successful entry into an Aymara community.

Just before taking ill, however, I had offered M.M a twelve-month position as field assistant, and he had generously countered by moving his wife and children into a wing of his parents' house and giving me the use of his own quarters indefinitely, on a rent-free basis. The typhoid meant that I had to return to La Paz where I could receive proper medical attention. M.M. followed me and, as I began to recover, we worked as many hours a day as my strength allowed. He assured me that his family would be gald to have me back, once my health returned, and that his house was still at my disposal. What he did not tell me was that, in my absence, he and his family had dug a well so I could have pure drinking water, had put down a cement floor so I would have protection from the dampness and inconvenience of tamped earth, and had provided the house with a latrine—a convenience shared by no one else in the entire vicinity. I was beginning to learn how protective and concerned an Aymara family can be, once they accept a stranger.

Mutual acceptance and respect between M.M. and myself formed the initial cornerstone of my research edifice, and without it I could never have penetrated the life of Irpa Chico. This acceptance and respect quickly broadened to include M.M.'s nuclear and extended families, and finally his quite extensive kindred. Thus, what was originally a shamefully slim informant base soon became one which included more than sixty individuals.

The first five months in Irpa Chico were spent gathering basic data on landholding, crop-rotation patterns, division of labor, life-crisis ritual, and child-rearing practices. By the time these initial investigations were over, I felt that I had succeeded in establishing remarkably good rapport with my informants and neighbors. Strong evidence of it came when M.M.'s younger sister was formally betrothed in a ceremony known as the *Irpaka*. Symbolically, it played out the initial antagonism of the families of bride and groom and the gradual resolution of this antagonism through stylized hazing and ritualized drinking. In preparing me for participation in the event, M.M.'s father explained that the groom's family must come and encounter the bride's family sleeping, around 11:00 at night. After waking the bride's kin with the proper courtesies, they must proceed to prove their merit by presenting the bride's kin with abundant gifts of food and alcohol. For their part, the bride's parents must examine both bride and groom and make recommendations as to how they should conduct their impending union. As a member of the bride's family, I should wait until aroused by members of the groom's party. Only then could I join the others in the bride's father's compound.

The knock came at my door at about 11:15 P.M. Two members of the groom's party entered; each gave me three shot glasses of alcohol and then begged that I join them for the *Irpaka* which was to follow. In compliance, I went with them to the neighboring house compound, and there joined the bride's parents and other members of the immediate kindred. In a large room opening onto the compound two 16-liter cans of alcohol, immense pots of hot food, and a pile of quartered mutton were conspicuously displayed, all intended as gifts to impress the bride's family. Drinking began immediately, as members of the bride's family were systematically called one by one to a platform at the end of the room to receive three shot glasses of alcohol at a time. As the night wore on, the effect of the liquor increased until, around 2:00 A.M., large plates of hot spicy stew were served to "sober us up." Following the meal, the young couple were accosted by the bride's parents with a series of riddles, accusations, and recommendations. Then the drinking rounds began again. At about 4:00 A.M. a brass band, which had been brought by the groom's family to provide background music for dancing and singing, went, for the first time, into the houseyard to play, thus announcing to all the neighborhood that a bride was about to be carried away. Drunkenness by this time had reached an exaggerated peak, and quarrels broke out between men of the bride's family and those of the groom's. The bride's father, in traditional fashion, wanted to accompany her, but his kin were doing everything to prevent it. Should the father of the bride succeed in leaving with her, it would mean that the groom's family would dominate the union forevermore. Thus a struggle so often interpreted as simulated bride capture appeared in this case to be one over impending loss, not of the bride at all, but rather of her father.

My peripheral connection with the bride's family permitted me to accompany the groom's party with impunity. We crossed the fields during the deepest dark of the predawn hours in a state of near total inebriation. Individual members of the group repeatedly stumbled and fell, some into the numerous water-filled depressions that covered the plain. Weaving in and out of the group, an ancient, wrinkled woman whined the tune of the betrothal song, *Irpastay,* gasping and wheezing as she did so. Members of the group hung onto my shoulders, and I to theirs. My clothes reeked with coca-stained saliva and alcohol, the residual result of frequent drink-stimulated embraces throughout the night. Two of the younger members of the group began to speak their minds. "The Mestizos and Blancos of the cities," they said, "are not true Bolivians, for they are lazy and debauched. The true Bolivians are the Indians." They drew me closer. "You are not like those vile Spaniards; you are a true Bolivian," they said. "Those haughty Spaniards would never share our life the way you are doing. We have much love for you, for you live in our houses, you eat our food, and you accept our coca and drink." Through the fog of my inebriation I felt a slight elation.

On arriving at the groom's house, we waited while the band played and the bride was instructed by her future mother-in-law to prepare breakfast for the party. The ancient female singer continued her squeaky *Irpastay,* the alcohol continued to flow, three shots at a time, and a few teetering people tried to dance. A little boy sidled up to me and said, "Señor, you look sick." I hastened to assure him that I was. At the beginning of the evening, I had begun to count the shot glasses of alcohol I downed, and had lost count after eighty-four. The boy brought me a green apple, saying that this, if anything, would help to settle my stomach and clear my head. A little later, *chuño,* potatoes, and hot pepper were served for breakfast, and these helped even more. Then the drinking was resumed. M.M., at my side, dropped like a fly, and others soon followed his example. I left at about 9:00 A.M., with men and women lying in disordered heaps around the houseyard, and staggered across the field to the house M.M. had loaned me. The Andes, in the distance, took on unbelievable shapes. I barely made it to my cot and, as I flopped onto it, asked myself why men value such experiences. For the moment, neither the concept of cultural relativity nor of functionalism seemed adequate as an explanation.

Periodically I awoke to gulp enormous quantities of water, but it was 2:00 in the afternoon before I finally dragged myself from bed. What, I wondered, would be the aftermath of the previous night's binge? I walked to the house compound of the bride's parents and found the mother hard at work in the houseyard as if nothing at all had happened. When I inquired as to the whereabouts of the father, I was astounded to learn that after three hours of sleep he had gone to the stone quarry, where he too was hard at work. Subsequent experience with all-night rituals convinced me that such rapid recovery from similar excesses was usual. The physical stamina of the Aymara, given their protein- and vitamin-deficient diet, is little short of the miraculous.

The symbolic importance of alcohol was brought home to me on numerous occasions during the ensuing months. On one occasion I had heard that, on the other side of Lake Titicaca, there was to be a special fiesta which would bring together some unusual musical and dance groups. Since I was making a collection of folk music, I decided to go, and took M.M. as an interpreter. We arrived a little early, and only one musical group was in the plaza. After exchanging some pleasantries with them, we explained that we had an interesting machine which could preserve whatever they would play and that we would like to use it. With that, we demonstrated how our tape recorder worked. Their response was that it was all very interesting, but that they would never allow me to record, for I was a foreigner, and therefore a Protestant. M.M. argued (contrary to the facts) that I was not, and this sent them off into a huddled conference. They returned; their leader put a few meager drops of alcohol in the bottom of a shot glass and offered the drink to me. When I took it with no protest and downed it with one gulp, the members of the group sighed, "It is true; he is not a Protestant." Their attitude changed immediately. They asked me what I wanted to record, and played for over an hour. Alcohol, again, had broken down hostility, distrust, and social reticence.[3]

Experiences such as these were giving me remarkable insight into Aymara culture, but they were not solving the problem of quantification. If I were ever to understand demography, the relative importance of various land-tenure patterns, leadership structure, and marriage preferences, I would have to obtain a comprehensive census of Irpa Chico as well as detailed land-use maps. When I suggested such needs, however, I encountered truly violent opposition.

During my months in the community, I had become acutely aware of the formal power structure and had developed more than a glimmer of understanding regarding the informal structure. My first step in implementing the quantitative aspect of my research was, therefore, to present the idea to the council of headmen—eight individuals representing that many zones within the community.[4] I had taken care to establish a personal relationship with each of these men long before suggesting the census and land survey so that, when I presented the idea formally before the council, there seemed to be no difficulty. The headmen indicated, however, that before making a final commitment, they preferred to consult their constituency, and that we should all plan to reconvene within a fortnight.

Up to that time, I had worked essentially in only three of the eight zones that made up the community. Irpa Chico covered some 15,000 acres, and its settlement pattern was a highly dispersed one. I found it physically impossible to contact most people personally, for even when I visited their house compounds they were either traveling or working in some distant field. News soon came to me, however, that when the headmen had gone to their constituency, negative reaction to the quantification idea had been so intense that the next council meeting would have to be open, with everyone in the community invited to participate.

Of the nearly 3,000 residents of Irpa Chico, some 500 attended that meeting. It was held in a large room of the central schoolhouse. The wall opposite the entry door held a wide platform, where I was asked to sit together with the council of headmen. To my right, along one wall, sat the former headmen of the community, and facing us was a mass of irate household heads, together with a sprinkling of wives and widows. It looked as if my situation were about to become very serious indeed.

The first few speakers in the meeting revealed what I had already begun to suspect: There had developed a split between the young leaders, who had achieved status through formal education, and the older ones, who had achieved it over many years through traditional fiesta sponsorship. The young men, most of whom were schoolteachers, were determined to defend me, and their elders were just as determined to oust me permanently from the community.[5]

The debate began with a series of accusations and suspicions. If I wanted to take a census, it was because I intended to impose new taxes. If I wanted to measure their land, it was because I intended to confiscate the land and set myself up as a new landlord. I was about to dispossess them of half their clothing, half their tools, and half their children. I was a capitalist! I was a communist! I was a Falangist!

Fortunately, I did not have to answer all these accusations directly. M.M.'s kindred and the core of local schoolteachers handled many of them for me. When a question was directly put to me, however, I did my best to argue that my activities were in the best interests of Irpa Chico. I pointed out that an intensive study had never been made of an Altiplano community and that such a study was imperative if the government was ever to develop an awareness of peasant problems and to attempt to solve them. Gradually, opposition subsided and, after four embattled hours, I was given permission by the council to proceed with my plans.

What I did not realize at the time was that I had aroused the antagonism of one of the most powerful elders of the community—a man who had gained leadership on purely traditional terms and who deeply resented the favoritism increasingly shown to the bilingual young men who were products of the local schools. During the next two weeks he gradually built his case and gathered support. As a result, when the time came to initiate the actual census, I found myself confronted with yet another council of headmen, attended by a far larger group of householders than had come to the previous meeting. The same accusations were repeated, only this time they were made much more viciously. It was soon obvious that unless some help appeared, my cause would be lost. At the end of two hours of acrimonious debate, assistance came from one of the zonal schoolteachers. He described to the group the serious doubts he himself had had with regard both to me and to my study. He had questioned whether I was telling the truth, for it seemed indeed strange that I should want to know how many people, animals, houses, and lands were in the community if I was planning neither to tax nor to confiscate. He had reasoned, however, that if what I had said was true, it should be written down somewhere. So he had gone home to consult his library, which consisted of some fifteen volumes (more than half of which were comic books), and had systematically perused each of these until he had come to the minutes of an indigenous congress which had been held some years previously in the city of La Paz. There (and he held up the book) he had discovered an entire page devoted to a discussion of the need for censuses of indigenous communities. Until such censuses were made, said the book, it would be impossible for the governments of Latin America to be aware of the needs of rural Indians, much less to respond to them. "Is it not wonderful," he then asked, "that the Bolivian government has finally begun to awaken to our needs, and that they have sent this man here to help us discover them? We should help him in every way we can, for he is fulfilling the task which was outlined as of utmost urgency by the Inter-American Indigenous Congress when it met in our country."

Following this remarkable speech, the entire mood of the gathering abruptly changed. My opponent immediately lost all his support, and the very men who had been attacking me began to attack him, asserting that he was an obstacle to the progress of the community. One headman after another then offered to accompany the census takers as they visited from house to house to ensure that respondents answered truthfully. They simultaneously expressed their concern that the topographer make an accurate map and indicated that, once the census was completed, each of them would serve as unpaid assistant in measuring house plots, pastures, and fields of cultivation for his portion of the community. Such offers of help were sincere and strictly within the community tradition. The role of headman is built around service to the general welfare to such an extent that during their year in office most turn over their agricultural chores to members of their immediate families. During the next two weeks, Irpa Chico's headmen worked ten hours a day until the entire community of nearly 600 dispersed families was entirely censused. Then, one by one, they volunteered services over the next five months until the surveyers had completed a detailed map of land holdings for each zone.

Other community members reflected similar changes in attitude. With few exceptions, I was now received openly wherever I wished to go, and informants went out of their way to be sure that I correctly understood whatever they were trying to tell or show me. A few holdouts remained, however. One of these, P.C., was disturbed that valuable secrets of the community were being turned over to an outsider, and so took every opportunity to speak against my research. When, during the first week in Lent, P.C. invited me to his father's house for a fertility ceremony, or sheep marriage, I was greatly relieved, for I believed that this invitation indicated an end to his hostility. As soon as we arrived at his father's, he plied me with alcohol and invited me to join the group of musicians who were circling the house yard. As I took up the drum and fell into line, I congratulated myself on finally succeeding in smoothing the ruffled feathers of a vociferous opponent. This self-congratulatory spirit increased when, as the sun was setting, P.C. asked me to drive him and his wife to their home and to spend the rest of the evening there, drinking, eating, and playing music. He climbed into the back seat of my jeep, and his wife took the front, immediately to my right. On reaching the house, P.C.'s wife attempted unsuccessfully to open her door; she had apparently never ridden inside a vehicle and could not distinguish the door handle from the window crank. I reached over, from the driver's seat, and flipped the handle so that she could get out.

I had often been told by informants that the Aymara are very sensitive about body contact, but this had not prepared me for the events that followed. The atmosphere in P.C.'s house was one of camaraderie and gaiety until his moderate inebriation gave way to heavy drunkenness. Then, of a sudden, he began to scream at me with all his power. He first accused me of trying to convert his beloved community into a slave-type hacienda, and then he attacked my morals. Just like all other white men, he stormed, I had no respect for Aymara women and their families. I wanted to destroy his marriage; I had sexually accosted his wife.

"When did I do such a thing?" I asked in all innocence. I could not imagine what he had in mind.

"You did it when we were getting out of the jeep," he replied. "I saw you put your arm across my wife's bosom."

Immediately it came to me that I had probably violated one of the basic precepts of the society, albeit totally unawares. I remembered how M.M. had told me of cases where white lovers who ventured into the countryside had sometimes been stoned simply because they were walking hand in hand. But such recall came too late. Already P.C. was coming at me, whip in hand, and screaming that he was going to kill me.

So many things happened in such a short period of time that it is impossible to remember the exact sequence of events. I do recall, however, that M.M.'s mother suddenly appeared and stood between me and P.C., shouting to him to desist, and to me to remove myself as quickly as possible. When she saw that I was standing my ground, she added that my very life was in danger; P.C. was quite capable of murder. Her urgent insistency convinced me that I had better take her advice. As I jumped into the jeep and started to speed away, P.C. broke away from two men who had begun to constrain him and, lunging after me, succeeded in smashing one of the windows of my vehicle with his whip.

Once I was back in the safety of M.M.'s family, I sought out his mother to ask her what had happened and how she had known that I was in trouble. She replied that she had been very concerned about me when she had seen that I was going to P.C.'s house in spite of her previous warnings about his family and her detailed descriptions of the various murders committed by his immediate progenitors. She had thought that I would have problems there, and when she heard the shouting and screaming, she knew she had been right. She hoped that I had learned my lesson and that I would never again get involved with such worthless people.

A few pointed questions made it clear that M.M.'s and P.C.'s families had been at one another's throats for years; I had stumbled directly into the most intense of interfamilial rivalries. The saving grace was that M.M.'s family carried the day. Within a week, the headmen of the community demanded that P.C. appear before their court of inquiry. There they found his actions to be indefensible, informed him that he would be stripped of his current office of *camana,* or overseer of the crops, and that he would simultaneously have to forgo his lifelong dream of becoming headman. In the presence of assembled heads of households, they made him kneel, removed his whip and his black poncho (both badges of office), and hung them on a peg in the zonal school-house. They then made it clear to him that he was on a long period of probation and that until he proved himself worthy of the community's trust, he would never again be considered for a post of responsibility.

The defrocking of an important community official on my account gave me a rude shock at the same time that it gave me a certain sense of security and acceptance. More than ever before, I began to feel like an Irpa Chiqueño. From that moment until the end of my field research, relations were incredibly positive and pleasant. There was no doubt that the community had made a major commitment to cooperate in every way possible.

A few weeks after the incident with P.C., I learned that the wife of Víctor Paz Estenssoro, President of the Republic, was planning to visit me in Irpa

Chico, at the invitation of the national director of folklore and ethnology. The council of headmen met and discussed the proper way to receive such an illustrious visitor. Some pointed out that though a fiesta should be prepared for the occasion, to do so would be disastrous, for it would fall in the middle of Lent. The playing of music or dancing during Lent would offend the spirits of the hills, and in retaliation they might destroy the crops.

The desire to present their community in a good light won the day, however, and a full-scale fiesta was planned for the visit. When Mrs. Paz Estenssoro arrived, each zone within the community brought gifts of food and drink and presented musical and dance groups. In return, she presented playground equipment for the central school. The spirit that prevailed was one of utter euphoria.

The mood did not last long, however; that night, true to predictions, the crops were devastated by a killing freeze. Yet the reaction of most of the community was surprisingly mature; they had discussed the danger of holding such a fiesta during Lent and had decided to take the risk. This was the first time that a person of such distinction had ever visited their community, and they were obliged to receive her properly, regardless of the consequences. The crops were seriously damaged, but through no one's fault but their own.

That freeze was the last critical point in my long struggle to win sufficient confidence to allow me to penetrate the inner workings of an Aymara community. From then until the end of my field work, some six months later, I found nothing but cooperation wherever I turned. When neighboring communities, jealous over the attention Irpa Chico had begun to receive, threatened to boycott and even to attack the community, Irpa Chiqueños, rather than turn against me, prided themselves that they had been progressive enough to merit an anthropological study. As my research drew to a close, I was feted by various families in the community; was given an ancient textile, the heirloom of one of the former community headmen; had a soccer team named after me; and was accompanied into town and even to the airport by various community members. Our parting was filled with emotion.

From 1965 to 1967, I trained several Peace Corps groups for service in Bolivia. One of the most frequent questions these young people put to me was, "Will I be accepted?" It is a question which every ethnographer asks, at least implicitly, when he goes into the field. However, as the Irpa Chico experience shows, inasmuch as the question is dichotomous, it is invalid. In a social situation there is no such thing as total acceptance or total rejection. The basic question should not be whether one is accepted, but rather *how* one is accepted.

The whole of the field situation makes for a complex study in status and role. The ethnographer may have goals in his own mind which seem both clear and logical. Generally these will entail certain behavioral patterns—indeed will reflect certain statuses and roles—that did not formerly exist in the society he wishes to study. His lengthy period of adjustment to the situation consists mainly in his discovering the esteemed roles in the host society and in learning

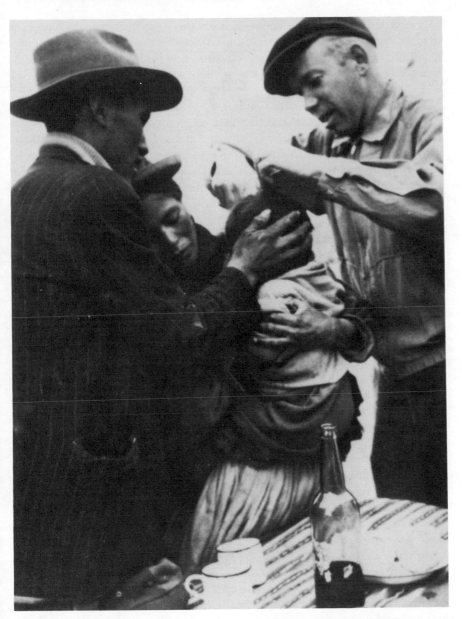

William E. Carter, as godfather to an Aymara youth, officiates at first haircutting ceremony.

to perform them to the extent that he can without prejudicing his basic research objectives. The types of information to which he is given access will correlate directly with the types of roles he learns to perform satisfactorily.[6]

In situations like that at Irpa Chico, ethnographers are easily placed into preconceived molds based on the actions of other educated white men who appeared on the scene before them. Many of these predecessors may have been in some manner exploitative, so it is understandable that the ethnographer may face initial hostility. Only by breaking the unwritten rules which separate social classes and ethnic groups can he hope to get beyond surface pretense and shallowness.

Another lesson that the Irpa Chico experience teaches is that the ethnographer is not a free agent in selecting his community. Indeed, the residents of Irpa Chico chose to work with me fully as much as I chose to work with them. This provided a near-ideal field situation. Young people in the community who had been educated in Western-oriented Bolivian schools opened the doors for the beginning of my research. But their influence in the community was not so great that it impeded the study of traditional Aymara culture. They represented a new cultural wave which, since my original field experience, has increasingly been felt in local affairs. My unusual good fortune was that I entered at a time that outside influences had softened the traditional prejudice against the outsider, but before these same influences had demolished the major outlines of traditional culture.[7]

Even under favorable circumstances the presence and activities of an ethnographer constitute a threat not only to the community as a whole, but to its residents as individuals. In my case, the person most deeply affected was my field assistant, M.M. At the time that we began to work, he was well settled in a position of young leadership in his community and was collecting a modest but locally competitive salary as a teacher in the central school. By working with me, he began to gain a more objective appraisal of his surroundings and to set his sights on rising above them. At the termination of our field work, he made it quite clear to me that he could never again be satisfied to work as a rural schoolteacher and that he certainly did not intend to spend the rest of his life scratching a bare existence from the recalcitrant soil his ancestors had worked for centuries. He had learned, furthermore, that he would rather work with North Americans than with Bolivians.

Before leaving the country, I succeeded in getting M.M. employed by a branch of the United States Agency for International Development (AID), and since that time he has floated from one short-term American-sponsored project to another. Unfortunately, he has been seized upon by a succession of North American social scientists as their field assistant or research-team member. For M.M.'s sake, I am pleased that these openings were possible. From the standpoint of social science, however, I have grave misgivings, for no matter how fine a given field assistant may be, the fact that he is employed in a whole series of what should be independent research projects means that too many basic field data are filtered through the eyes of a single individual. Through no fault of his own, M.M.'s conscious and unconscious screening of basic data has become magnified to an intolerable degree.

In a sense, while I was attempting to cross a cultural boundary in one direction, M.M. was attempting to do so in the opposite. He may have been more successful than I. A year and a half after returning to the United States, I was surprised by a long-distance call from M.M. in Miami, Florida. He was on his way to Israel, where he planned to enroll in a six-month course on cooperatives. Following this experience, he returned to Bolivia as one of its specialists on the cooperative movement, and has traveled to all corners of the country by jeep, train, and air. His wife, though still monolingual, has not lagged far behind. She too has permanently left Irpa Chico and now occupies a solid house in the midst of one of the "Indian" neighborhoods of La Paz. On her own, she has launched a trucking business, and on my last visit to Bolivia proudly showed me the new Toyota that she had just purchased. Her new wealth and social status are conspicuously displayed through the use of showy velvets, brocades, and silks which would be the envy of any woman back in Irpa Chico. Her children are being educated in the American Institute, a costly private school which has traditionally served the Bolivian elite. M.M. and his wife clearly have no thought of returning to Irpa Chico to live. Even if they wanted to, their reception would be questionable, for the Irpa Chique-ños resent the fact that M.M. has crossed over into urban society. They interpret his actions as a betrayal. As for M.M. himself, he no longer feels comfortable in the role of a mere peasant.

The psychological cost of such boundary crossing can be great. Once a person is an adult, he cannot realistically expect to completely absorb a total cultural configuration different from that in which he was reared. On the other hand, once he dips deeply into that configuration, he can no longer wholeheart-edly accept his own. If he was not marginal in his own society before crossing into the other culture, he is likely to become so afterward. Not even being an anthropologist makes him immune.

NOTES

1. Beginning with his dissertation, John Hickman (1964) has produced a series of writings on Aymara biculturalism. He sees it as a defense against any real communication across the societal and cultural boundary between the Aymara and the Spanish-speaking castes of Bolivia and Peru.

2. The most thorough previous attempt to delineate Aymara personality had been made by Harry Tschopik. His interpreter was a young Mestizo, born and reared in the village of Chuquito. On the basis of information obtained through this medium, Tschopik concluded that the Aymara were anxious, hostile, submissive, disorderly, and utilitarian (Tschopik, 1951, pp. 143–187).

3. A recent article on Aymara death ritual discusses the role of alcohol in depth. The giving of drink is one of the principal means by which the Aymara cultivate trust (Carter, 1968).

4. For a more detailed description of community structure, see Carter (1965a).

5. In spite of the apparent openness of the younger, formally educated men, there is consider-able evidence that schoolchildren hold fast to traditional Aymara values (Carter, 1966). My support by the younger men may have come because, as an academician, I represented a model which they had been taught to respect in the school system.

6. The concepts of status and role have occupied a prominent place in anthropological thought since their introduction in Ralph Linton's *The Study of Man*, published more than thirty years

ago. They have been refined in a number of approaches, one of the most interesting of which is found in Schwartz's analysis of the Paliau movement in Melanesia. There he argues that the basic problem of communication revolves around the "idioverse"—"that component of the individual's personality derived from experience" which determines "that individual's version or portion of his culture." Shared experiences produce common understandings and interpretations, and these constitute and "intersect" (Schwartz, 1962, pp. 360–61). In a field situation, it is only when the ethnographer's experiences form "intersects" with those of the people he is studying that meaningful communication becomes possible.

7. Most of the young men who had received considerable formal education were sons of traditional community leaders, an especially fortuitous combination. This relationship is discussed in some detail in a previous article (Carter, 1965b).

REFERENCES

CARTER, WILLIAM E. 1965a. *Aymara Communities and the Bolivian Agrarian Reform.* Social Science Monograph No. 24. Gainesville: University of Florida Press.

——— 1965b. "Innovations and Marginality: Two South American Case Studies." *América Indígena,* 25:383–392.

——— 1966. "Factores socio-económicos en el desarrollo de la personalidad Aymara." *Proceedings of the Thirty-sixth International Congress of Americanists,* 3:367–381.

——— 1968. "Secular Reinforcement in Aymara Death Ritual." *American Anthropologist,* 70:238–263.

HICKMAN, JOHN MARSHALL. 1964. *The Aymara of Chinchera, Peru: Persistence and Change in a Bicultural Context.* Ph.D. dissertation, Cornell University, Ithaca, New York.

LINTON, RALPH E. 1936. *The Study of Man.* New York: Appleton.

SCHWARTZ, THEODORE. 1962. *The Paliau Movement in the Admiralty Islands, 1946–1954.* Anthropological Papers, vol. 49, part 2. New York: American Museum of Natural History.

TSCHOPIK, HARRY, JR. 1951. *The Aymara of Chuquito, Peru.* Anthropological Papers, vol. 44, part 2. New York: American Museum of Natural History.

10 / **Two Dollars**

NANCY OESTREICH LURIE

If you're going to work with Indian people, there is something you should understand. You see these two dollars? If I give these two dollars to an Indian, he'll be glad and take them and spend them, and he'll have two dollars' worth of enjoyment. And when they're spent, they're spent. He got along before he had those two dollars and he'll get along after they're gone. Even when he's broke some time, he won't think back and regret he spent those two dollars. Now, if I give these two dollars to a white man, he'll take one dollar and put it away and maybe he'll spend the other one. But he won't enjoy spending it because he's only having half the enjoyment he knows he could have. And he'll make himself sick worrying he's going to lose the other one, or that someone will steal it before he gets to use it.

Maybe you don't understand what I'm saying now, but when you really understand, then you will understand how to get along with Indian people.

The old man was totally blind but in no way the aged and infirm informant eager to talk to the anthropologist because he feels lonely and neglected. John C. was a busy man who took an active and interested part in the life around him. There was little that escaped him, and he had no compunction about exercising his privilege as an old and wise person to speak his mind and call the wayward to task. Everyone agreed, however, that he was a good talker in both Winnebago and English and, because of his formidable bilingual talents, even those who had cause to resent him on other occasions would seek him out as a spokesman in difficult dealings with whites. John C. was more than an interpreter. He approached cultural differences with the same dispassionate, intellectual interest he brought to finding just the right English phrase to convey its Winnebago equivalent.

He had received little formal education, and it was now some thirty years since he could see well enough to read. He had never before acted as an anthropological informant. Questioning me closely about what I was trying to do, he must have reached two conclusions early in our relationship. First, while he knew about people who collected old stories and wrote books about Indians, he was gratified to discover that anthropologists did more than retrieve and describe, that they actually tried to grapple with the problems of differences and similarities among peoples that had long engaged his own interest. Second, he realized that I was not yet an anthropologist but only learning to be one; and he decided to be my teacher, not just to tell me facts about the Winnebago but to instruct me in the proper practices of ethnography, at least among his people.

It was not until long after my first field trip that I fully appreciated John C.'s unusual intellectual grasp of the problems of Indian-white relationships. I do not know whether some culture-bound remark of mine prompted the parable of the two dollars or whether John C. simply knew his white people well enough tc decide I needed the lesson. Throughout our discussions, he tested, assessed, kidded, and corrected me. But he never belittled me, though it must have been hard to resist the temptation at times, I'm sure, when I recall the self-satisfied sophistry and academic pretentiousness of my youth. He accorded me genuine respect for what I was trying to become rather than for the scholar I thought I was.

It was 1944 when I met John C., so designated by the community to distinguish him from the many Winnebago men named John Decora. I was still an undergraduate. My major professor at the University of Wisconsin, J. Sydney Slotkin, considered it unfortunate that most students got their first taste of field experience at the same time they were beginning serious, theory-oriented research on their dissertations. Courses and texts on field methods were not yet a regular part of the anthropological curriculum—certainly not for undergraduates. Slotkin simply gave me all the good advice he could think of and sent me on my way. Our review of Murdock (1941) had determined the choice of Winnebago among the Wisconsin Indian groups because they had been scarcely noticed by scholars since Paul Radin's classic studies many years before. Slotkin imbued my practice run with seriousness of purpose beyond mere learning of field techniques and impressed upon me my responsibilities to my chosen career. If I could learn to observe and record accurately in regard to one Winnebago community for a few weeks in 1944 and *publish* what I had learned, I would be making a small but real contribution to knowledge in a neglected area. Field funds for this noble enterprise were my own lookout.

Will C. McKern, then Director of the Milwaukee Public Museum, and an old friend, suggested I go to Door County because I could earn my summer's keep while doing my research. Door County is the peninsula jutting into Lake Michigan, famous for its orchards, particularly cherry trees. The growers there relied heavily on Indians, especially the Winnebago, as a dependable itinerant labor force. However, World War II was in progress and many Indians were in the armed services or working in defense industries in the cities. With the prospect of a bumper crop—the season that year lasted an almost unprecedented six weeks—a call had gone out for students to work in the orchards.

I had no trouble finding a welcome at the orchard where the largest group of Winnebago customarily congregated, some 42 families in 1944, as well as one family each of Menomini, Potawatomi, and Ojibwa. The understanding was that I would sleep in the "girls' dormitory," an old barn loft, and buy my meals like the other student workers at the orchard dining room. I could work in the Indians' section of the orchard if I didn't distract people from their work with my "research," and I could visit with the Indians in the evenings and on weekends at their camp. Both Slotkin and McKern agreed that these arrangements were a reasonable enough approach to the ideal of "living in the community as much like the local people as possible." My family offered no objections to the project. Knowing my aversion to anything resembling hard work, they were confident that I would be home in three days.

My first day in the orchard I was assigned a regular partner, a young widow with several small children. Mrs. Cloud welcomed adult company because the method of work consisted of each family group stripping a tree and moving on to another. With two of us, we could keep up with the other families and she could keep track of her children when they tired of picking cherries and wanted to play with other children. Actually, we did drop behind that first day because what I thought would be easy work required more skill and stamina than I had expected. Furthermore, when Mrs. Cloud let me pick out our second tree, I chose a huge one that took a long time to strip. She chided me pointedly, "I guess you white people always think 'The bigger the better.' " But, good-naturedly, she taught me how to count to ten in Winnebago and how to say the Winnebago words for the things around us—cherries, pails, trees, tree frogs.

By the end of the afternoon, a few people in nearby trees began to join in the game of teaching me Winnebago words. My efforts were always greeted with laughter although I thought my pronunciation was not at all bad. But I kept in mind Slotkin's dictum: "Remember, your novelty value as a stranger can be an asset; don't be overly sensitive." At least people were talking to me! I thought all this happy rapport resulted from their appreciation of my novelty value and from my willingness to afford entertainment in what I found to be hard, dull work. I also concluded sagely that Indians must harbor natural resentment against whites and thus I should expect a certain amount of hazing. Eventually, in some polite, indirect way, John C. set me straight. The novelty and humor for the Winnebago lay in their being on the teaching end of the relationship, and their laughter was not at me nor a mask of hostility but delight and even a certain self-consciousness on their part. He could have pointed out that I was obviously so young and naive as to be no threat to anyone, for if people did not like having a white person in their part of the orchard, they could easily complain to the owner. Their labor was more important to him than my research! John C. chose to instruct me about the positive aspects of the relationship, sparing my youthful sensibilities.

As the day ended, I was hot, tired, stiff, and sticky. The very air was sickly sweet from cherry culls fermenting in the July sun. I had decided I would simply write up my impressions and collapse into bed. Mrs. Cloud and I had not spoken for quite a while because I was too exhausted to talk and silence did not seem to bother her. As we were putting down our ladders and stacking our pails, she said tentatively, "I've been thinking. There's a little shack at our camp. Only big enough for one person and no one is living in it. You could move in there and do your own cooking. Save you money and you wouldn't have that long walk every night. You could borrow a little stove and a lamp and some dishes from the orchard boss. I'll show it to you when you come by tonight." By the second evening I had made my arrangements with the white overseer and his wife and had moved into the shack.

People in the camp teased me about being afraid to be alone among the Indians, but they also said approving things and understood far better than I why I should be there. "Now we can really get to know each other." "It's good you're living here; you'll get to understand us." All I could think was that now I was *really* an anthropologist living in my own "field quarters."

There was one hitch. I did not need my wartime ration books to eat at the orchard dining room. My mother was so sure I would not go on working in the orchard in order to stay with the Indians that she would not risk sending my books for fear I was already on the way home. Discovering at the meagerly stocked local store that canned baby and junior foods did not require ration stamps, I managed to survive. I suppose I should be thankful that mashed peach with liver and puree of peas and carrots prepared me for the absolute *worst* in the way of field foods thereafter. Unfortunately, they also conditioned me for life to approach any food with almost total indifference, the idea being to get it down to stay alive.

Upon settling in the camp, I took note immediately that Mrs. Cloud and other new neighbors seemed to keep mentioning a John C. Decora as very well informed. I was, of course, eager to talk to him, having thus cleverly discovered a key informant in the community so quickly. Nevertheless, I approached his shack my third evening with a certain trepidation, not wanting to impose myself and risk losing his cooperation. Rapport, I knew, was a delicate thing. So is Indian indirection. He was waiting for me at his front door. His wife silently brought out a stool for me to sit on and withdrew. People wandered by, silently watched us, listened a bit, and ambled on. It was my first formal interview with my first real informant. He interviewed me.

He was a vigorous old man whose blindness was more nuisance than handicap. Even his facial expressions were those of a sighted person, spontaneous and genuinely appropriate to the situation, not the vague, almost vapid smile so often worn as a perpetual expression of the blind. As it grew dark I finally took my leave, gratefully accepting his invitation to return for more conversation. John C. usually chose the topics of our discussions, stopping often to ask if I had any questions. If a question was too far off the present subject, he would sometimes say he wanted to think about it to refresh his memory or talk with other people about it, and we would discuss it later. We always did. Sometimes he suggested I take a question to some other person in the community who was better informed on the subject.

Before the end of the week I wrote a long and triumphant letter to Slotkin detailing *everything* that had occurred since I had stepped off the bus with my sleeping bag and suitcase. Unconcerned about my sensibilities, he shot back a scathing reply. Apparently staggered by the detail and worried about the tremendous amount of data I had forwarded to him on the peyote religion, he said he hoped I wasn't going around notebook in hand and offending people with my nosiness. Moreover, I should realize peyote was a "controversial subject" not to be plunged into as the first topic of inquiry, and certainly not by a novice!

As a matter of fact, I had used my notebook only to jot down Winnebago words to help me remember them or when I sat down to a formal session with John C. or others in regard to defined topics. Slotkin simply did not realize that I came from a family of irrepressible raconteurs and brought to the field a developed talent for recall and a compulsion to retell vividly. The field diary in which he told me to keep a record of each day's impressions and remembered conversations was remarkably complete. Furthermore, while I attributed my "success" to my impeccably professional approach, the truth was that I could not have picked a better family than my own to grow up in as preparation for work with people like the Winnebago. I had been the cherished but disciplined only child in a household which included parents, grandparents, and, until my thirteenth year, a great-grandfather. I accepted oligarchy as the natural order of family life. I could not have done otherwise than to relate easily to John C. and other people older than I, and it was they who determined whether I would be a welcomed guest.

It was my age peers among the orchard group who gave me serious field anxieties with their scornful teasing. I often found them incomprehensible in their seemingly aimless, hedonistic outlook and total lack of middle-class career expectations. Interestingly, the publication which resulted from this first field experience (Oestreich, 1944) is concerned largely with the contemporary scene and the problems of change and adjustment, with emphasis on the young and the future. These were the controversial subjects into which I plunged with the novice's foolhardy zeal!

Slotkin, of course, had no way of knowing from my letter that my "chief informant" was really a self-appointed instructor in field technique who had the advantage over Slotkin of being on the scene. But, crushed and chastened by Slotkin's letter, that evening I went over to John C.'s house without my notebook. Suddenly he asked, "Why aren't you writing this down?" Astonished, I blurted out, "How do you know I'm not writing?" "Can't hear your pencil scratching!"

Naturally, I thought he knew I had been taking notes because people would have told him. Instead of belatedly asking if he minded, I was so upset by

Slotkin's criticisms that I had decided I was doing everything wrong. Evidently I was supposed to depend entirely upon memory and write all my notes in the privacy of my shack. When John C. asked again why I wasn't writing, I confided the contents of Slotkin's letter. He was vastly amused. After he had recovered from laughing, he said sternly, "Well, when I tell you something, it's important and I expect you to write it down so you get it right! You're not an Indian and don't know how to listen carefully. You've learned from paper all your life. It's your way." I went back for my notebook.

But John C. was not one to discredit my other teachers, especially not Slotkin, who had sent me to the Winnebago. He expressed approval of Slotkin's concern that I not offend people. John C. further consoled me that I should remember that he, himself, had opened the subject of peyote. He said he had done so because he considered it a good thing to have "honest writing" about it, his interpretation of my prim concept of "objectivity." John C. also took this opportunity and many other occasions to observe that he hoped I would write books telling white people what Indians were really like, particularly in regard to peyote, to help stop the "persecution" of the Native American Church. John C. set the terms of a contract which I did not recognize as such at the time; but I have been bound by it ever since: cooperation exchanged for the promise of reliable reporting.

John C. also did more than instruct me in ethnographic method. By his influence and example, he educated our small community in the ideal role of the anthropologist. He was the closest the settlement had to a leader in expressing community sentiments and liaison with whites. If John C. accepted the notebook, at least other peyotists would have no objection. I was to learn that the traditionalists were far less eager to have their religion studied and publicized, although they shared John C.'s appreciation of the need for accurate information about Indian people in regard to other matters. That I wrote down what people said because what they said was important invested the notebook with dignity rather than snoopiness. By the end of the season a few people would actually approach me with the comment, "I just remembered something you ought to write down."

Significantly, I never attended a peyote meeting that summer, although several small ones were held for a sick man in the camp. John C. took an active part in them and gave me full reports. I did not feel excluded and it never occurred to me to ask to be invited. John C. implied I was just not ready to understand fully.

As willing as he was to instruct me and as high as his hopes were for my future, he knew what I would resentfully have denied had he mentioned it: this might be no more than an interesting summer in the life of a very young person. I would have to prove the depth of my commitment to be fully trusted and instructed. But John C. set out bait by not inviting me to an actual peyote ceremony that summer. "Some time, when you come back, . . ." As it happened, I only saw John C. once again, when I visited him briefly a few years

later at his home at Wittenberg, Wisconsin. He was satisfied that I was pursuing my career as planned at other Winnebago communities.

By the end of the cherry harvest, my family had undergone nearly six weeks
of misgivings about whether they had gone too far in pushing me from the nest
in their determination that I not be an overprotected only child. They had been
saving gas coupons so that my mother and grandmother could drive the several
hundred miles to see where I had spent the summer. Too polite to comment
until we were driving home, they were nevertheless appalled by the squalor of
the camp, with its flimsy shacks, the flies, the single handpump supplying all
our water, and the sagging community outhouses. Casual references in my
letters to occasional drunken uproars in camp were recalled with horror by my
grandmother when she discovered I could not lock my shack from the inside.
However, she reported something I had not known. John C. had made a point
of engaging my grandmother in a long conversation while my mother and a
cousin who had come along for the ride took a stroll through the camp with
me. John C. had told my grandmother, "I know you must be worried about
Nancy, but you needn't be. We could see right away she came from a good
family. She is polite to everyone and knows how to respect people. We watched
out for her so no one would bother her."

Those poor people! My nuisance quotient must have often come close to
outrunning my novelty value or any potential value John C. and others could
find in me. How many evenings had old Mrs. Brown appeared, silent and
glowering, at my door, broom in hand, when a group of boisterous young
people or an occasional drunk had stopped by to visit. If she spoke any English,
I never heard it. A few words in Winnebago or just that reproving scowl was
enough to drive out my guests. She would then depart in silence. While I had
fretted that I was responsible for annoying her and disturbing her sleep and
had worried about my precious rapport in the community, she had been
concerned about me!

It came home to me that even my exasperating peers and the often drunk
and belligerent veterans in camp treated me as a community responsibility.
When a slightly tipsy fellow visiting from another orchard appeared to be
taking too much interest in me and I began edging away, a huge, darkly
ferocious, and quite drunken fellow from our camp moved into action. (He is
the only person I have ever seen actually open beer bottles with his teeth.)
Getting a firm grip on the visitor's collar with one hand, he lifted him off the
ground and shook him, wagging a reproving finger in his face with the other
hand. "Lishen you, she's no *girl.* She's an anthropologisht!"

In 1944, however, I would have said the Winnebago were often impolite and
definitely not very respectful of people, John C.'s comments on the importance
of such attributes notwithstanding. Honest mistakes were noted with derisive
laughter and repeated teasing long after they occurred. And minor injuries, at
least, met with no sympathy. "You cut your finger slicing bread! Shows you
never work!" They even poked fun at physical disabilities I had been brought

up to feel pity for or to pretend not to notice. I was shocked to hear a youngster call out one day, "Here comes Mrs. John C. Decora and Mr. John No-See Decora!" John C. just laughed. What I regarded as remarkable personal compensation for his handicap, even overcompensation because it embarrassed me, was culturally predictable behavior. One evening John C. realized I was hesitant to mention that it was too dark to take notes. His wife had gone out, neglecting to light the lamp. Smiling at his own joke as he told me to light the lamp, he said, "No point in neither of us being able to see!"

What really distressed me was what I considered a cruel game played by his four-year-old great-grandson, who had the job of leading him to the outhouse. The little boy delighted in taking the most difficult and circuitous routes he could find. Once he even led the old man into a line of wet wash. I now understand that John C. respected a child's natural wish to have some fun in the course of bothersome duties and he went along with the game, scolding loudly that he was in a hurry but losing no dignity as the whole community looked on at his apparent discomfort and smiled indulgently at the little boy.

Ordinarily John C. got around perfectly well, tapping efficiently with his cane. He even climbed ladders to pick cherries. But the "Men's and Women's," as the two community privies were called, were in a state of progressive disrepair, offering even the sighted increasing hazards with each use. It was the orchard owner's responsibility to keep them in repair, and the people in camp put up with them while registering frequent complaints at headquarters. I was vaguely puzzled that the skilled carpenter in our camp did not just go ahead and fix them. He had remodeled my shack shortly after I moved in because I had casually observed that I was cramped for writing space and a place to store papers. Obsessed with concepts of rapport and empathy, I did not realize that I "belonged" to the community, not to the white power structure.

John C. was my first Winnebago teacher but not the only one to instruct me in field methods during that summer. One man sought me out, motivated by the same kinds of interests that underlay John C.'s cooperation. His assessment of me must also have been much like John C.'s. Mitchell Redcloud, Sr., worked at a different orchard but had heard about me and one Sunday came over to visit. He was more knowledgeable than John C. about the formal aspects of anthropology and was familiar with Radin's work. At first, I thought his criticisms of Radin were substantive in regard to ethnographic accuracy, but it turned out that Redcloud was acquainted with some of Radin's old informants in Nebraska, and he felt that Radin had taken advantage of people. In later years, when I got to know Radin, I was appalled at his candid admission that he had systematically gotten into his debt the various nephews of old men who would not speak to him on sacred matters. He could then send the nephews to obtain the information he wanted and report back to him. Radin felt justified and, in fairness, I cannot criticize him.

Although the census figures were already beginning to show a slight upward trend in Indian population when Radin did his field research, the popular view was that the Indians were bound to vanish. The greatest part of Radin's field work was done in Nebraska, where he witnessed the dramatic impact of the newly introduced peyote religion. The excesses of some converts at that time even led them to burn their medicine bundles and other traditional paraphernalia. Radin believed the old religion was in imminent danger of disappearing. He was not the only anthropologist to assume that the almost total replacement of Indian material culture with items of white manufacture clearly meant rapid acculturation leading to total assimilation. He felt that the few old people who possessed special knowledge should be exploited by any means, no matter how they might feel about it, before their precious knowledge died with them. Even Redcloud admitted that some information might have been lost had Radin not recorded it.

It was Radin's theory that the compact Nebraska reservation community would preserve more of their original culture intact than the Wisconsin people who lived on scattered homesteads. On the contrary, the Wisconsin people depended on their ritual cycle and special ceremonies to maintain group cohesiveness. Unknown to Radin, moreover, the Wisconsin people also represented an interesting social selection of the resisters and holdouts against white domination, which is why they are still living in their old Wisconsin homeland. Although peyote was introduced from Nebraska and clearly made inroads, a stable core of traditionalists remains, continuing to initiate members into the Medicine Lodge and perform the old ceremonies.

Redcloud felt that Radin might have collected his data without sowing resentment toward anthropologists generally if he had gone about his work differently. It was now almost impossible to get certain information which Redcloud thought should be available for general study because of its philosophical depth and beauty. However, since Radin's time, the followers of the old ways were more determined than ever to keep their secrets. This solved in part the mystery of the gap in the Murdock *Bibliography*. Actually, two anthropologists had worked briefly with the Wisconsin Winnebago since Radin's time, and Redcloud had acted as informant to both of them. He was disappointed that one died before she had really done much work and what notes she had taken were presumably lost and that the other had changed his career, never returning or even publishing what information he had collected.

Redcloud recognized that the Winnebago had changed and were changing rapidly in material aspects of culture, and he deplored many features of modern Winnebago life—drinking, brawling, and most particularly peyote. But even among the peyotists there were matters of the spirit which were ineffably and durably Winnebago. There was much for white society to learn from Indians which ought to be reported accurately to bring about greater respect and fairness in Indian-white relationships. He saw literacy as a means of perpetuating Winnebago culture, not just for reading the record of the dead past, but for stimulating new pride and interest among the young. It was simply impractical for economic reasons in these days, however, for people to spend the great lengths of time necessary to learn entirely by ear, particularly when they often had to be away from their communities for long periods to earn a decent living. Redcloud was intrigued with the useful possibilities of mechanical recording although they were then still costly and unwieldy. Records were even better than phonetic writing, with which he was familiar, because they could capture the dramatic oratorical style of good Winnebago speakers and even music. Today, tape recorders are almost standard equipment in even very humble Indian homes.

Redcloud's basic philosophy and opinions were communicated gradually over a period of two years. On that sunny August Sunday, he contented himself with observing that in his opinion Radin was a poor anthropologist because he did not understand that "You can build birdhouses for birds, but they don't stop being birds." Although I faithfully recorded it, this cryptic remark, like John C.'s lesson of the two dollars, took one a long time to understand.

Redcloud, the instructor in ethnographic method, also expressed his concern during our first conversation that I would get an unbalanced picture of the Winnebago by living in a temporary camp with so many peyotists from the settlement near Wittenberg. I had, indeed, been under the impression that everyone in camp and virtually all the Winnebago who weren't mission Christians were peyotists. I assumed the few families from Redcloud's home area, Black River Falls, were also peyotists only not as skilled in English as John C. and some of the others. They were pleasant enough but not very communicative and I did not exert pressure. Slotkin had counseled me well about patience. Redcloud described himself as "conservative," believing in the old ways although he admitted there was much he did not know about them. There were people at Black River Falls I might, with patience, get to know who would talk to me about some of these things. I was to learn, ruefully, that even when I had achieved the necessary age and trust, I would never have Radin's linguistic talent to deal with the esoteric language of Winnebago ritual. My consolation is that, while it may be changing and much has probably dropped away since Radin's time, this aspect of culture is not "dying," and the Winnebago themselves are taping the old knowledge for their own purposes.

Redcloud walked with crutches, explaining that an old hip injury had not healed properly, but if it bothered him too much in getting around and working he would go to the hospital again. That fall, my senior year, he became a patient at the Wisconsin General Hospital in Madison. Notebook in hand, I spent many hours at his bedside. Redcloud had a strong mystic streak which I found embarrassing. John C. had been much more businesslike, describing even his peyote visions as matter-of-fact "miracles" because he could see them although he was blind. Redcloud's abhorrence of peyote made him refuse any "dope" at the hospital whenever he had the choice, and his pain probably explains his vivid dream which bordered on a true vision in the Indian sense. I figured in the dream. His pain stopped when I appeared because a voice told him to call for me, and we then stood beside each other and watched the sun set, our arms in friendship across each other's shoulders. He even drew a picture of the scene for me. I secretly wished he had not told me or drawn the picture. It seemed somehow unprofessional for me as an anthropologist to have been viewed in this fashion.

Redcloud, like John C., must have also wondered whether I would ever really become an anthropologist, truly capable of understanding his people. He knew he would not live long enough to find out. As John C. had done, he also set out lures, speaking of the old ceremonies performed by some of the people at Black River Falls and preparing me in his discussions for the right to observe them.

His "tuberculosis of the bone" was really cancer, and in the spring, when surgery proved of no avail, he was sent home as being beyond hope. I visited him during a three weeks' reconnaissance trip to Black River Falls in 1945 in preparation for research on my master's thesis the following summer. It distressed me to see how wasted he was, but I was deeply impressed by his determination to stay out of bed and remain active as long as he could. We wrote to each other during my first year in graduate school at the University of Chicago, and Redcloud provided accounts of matters of ethnographic interest; but his main concern was to help me establish contact with people who could continue the work he had begun with me.

Ironically, one of the first traditional ceremonies I attended, long before I attended a peyote meeting, was the four-night wake for Redcloud. I was invited because Redcloud had told people—what I took at first as only a symbolic gesture of friendship—that he considered me his adopted daughter and he had given me a name from his clan. Redcloud's legacy was uncles and aunts and other kinsmen I could approach directly and respectfully for information without having to buy off nephews as Radin had done.

A first field experience is something like a teacher's first class. Every face, every name, every object, and every personal anxiety and small triumph are recalled in detail when recollections of later field studies and the endless succession of classrooms have begun to blur. A person can never again be so conscientious, so observant, so informed, and so insightful in such a short period of time—nor so incredibly obtuse.

The distinctive individuals of one's early research begin to take on the function of type specimens in the biological sciences. We note differences and similarities in relation to the familiar types, and we begin to find recurrent patterns which at first seemed highly individualistic traits. When we have seen things often enough and in enough variations and examples to understand the deeper meanings, we begin to have theories, insights, moments of exciting revelation about the nature of human behavior in this or that culture or in the world at large. Sometimes, if we are honest, we recognize that we have claimed as our own profundity what was in fact the abstract knowledge of our informants and which we did not even grasp at first!

It is hardly surprising that *they* should have a better working knowledge of the reality of culture than most of *us*. In our times, usually they *must* know themselves systematically in relation to our alien system simply in order to survive. We usually do not have to know them except for some special reason, such as in connection with anthropology. Even this requires only that we learn to formulate facts of culture but, except in the field, without the necessity of doing so directly for the purpose of living. The compulsion to understand and be understood is much greater on their side than ours. They are often chary because they have long recognized that they cannot ordinarily expect the compulsion to be reciprocated. We should not deceive ourselves that we succeed primarily because of our methods for reaching out to them. They are reaching out to us, and our methods are only the means to effect the contact so they can teach us. The best informants are simply good teachers, people who are not only well informed but who have the capacity to convey the obvious most clearly and the ability to help clarify the difficult, the obscure, and the abstract.

We may not always be as likable personally as we think and may often, like a perennial house guest, be an inconvenience at times to have around. But we can do creditable work if we are acceptable instruments to amplify the sound of their message: let us understand and accept one another as we are. This is not to deny that there may be esoteric data, jealously guarded from even the most trusted outsider. But knowing this, and knowing that to pry ruthlessly is to destroy, is a valuable insight into the nature of culture, though obviously no substitute for the concealed but significant minutiae of a human tradition.

In the isolated, unthreatened community the anthropologist is apt to find his outstanding informant in the role of a fellow intellectual exchanging knowledge, rather than a self-conscious mentor. The intelligent stranger brings a new stimulus to conceptualization and communication. Even in a situation of cultural upheaval, Radin enjoyed such a relationship with Jasper Blowsnake, elder brother of the man whose autobiography Radin published in 1926 under the title *Crashing Thunder* (see Lurie, 1961, pp. 96–98). Radin never spoke of Blowsnake except with sincere affection and deep admiration for his remarkable mind. Blowsnake must have responded similarly to Radin, the scholar and philosopher. Perhaps he could therefore overlook Radin's sometimes ruthless tactics as a creature of the science of his era, determined to wring out data by any means because he thought it would otherwise be lost forever.

For the most part Radin benefited, and admittedly so, because there were people eager to teach him the truth about the peyote movement, an extremely controversial subject at that time. They recognized that he could serve their ends by honest and sympathetic reporting. If Radin ever thought he might also approach the long-beleaguered conservatives as a patient student and ultimate spokesman for their cause, he considered their cause doomed anyway. Time seemed to be running out and all too rapidly. He saw his first obligation to the cause of ethnology and he got the data. Radin had a certain advantage. His generation was not plagued with all the soul-searching about conflicting ethics we must now go through in our field work and writing for publication. Most of Radin's informants were, furthermore, illiterate; and if they trusted him, they could not do otherwise than trust that he would write to their satisfaction. Such is seldom the case today, certainly not in North American Indian studies.

Because I was very young and had many more years of schooling ahead of me when I did my first field work, I responded as a student to my informants, albeit unwittingly and despite my own scholarly pretensions. Now I see that in becoming a real anthropologist, one simply becomes a more mature, experienced, and self-aware student.

In 1967 June Helm and I returned to the Dogrib Indians in northern Canada, where we had worked in 1962. She had written our chief informant of our plans, and he looked forward to working with us. When we arrived, a white resident in the area greeted us with what he considered a terribly amusing story about our informant, whom he viewed patronizingly and with a certain scorn. The old man had said he was going to be *"teaching"* during the summer! We may have been fully educated white people and our informant an ignorant old man in the eyes of the white shopkeeper, but our Dogrib friend correctly understood the situation.

References

LURIE, NANCY OESTREICH, ED. 1961. *Mountain Wolf Woman: Sister of Crashing Thunder.* Ann Arbor: University of Michigan Press.

MURDOCK, GEORGE PETER. 1941. *Ethnographic Bibliography of North America.* Yale Anthropological Studies, 1:1–169.

OESTREICH, NANCY. 1944. "Cultural Change Among the Winnebago." *Wisconsin Archeologist,* 25:119–125.

11 / On Objectivity and Field Work

THERON A. NUNEZ

Our professors in graduate school and our peers recently returned from field work had told us what it should be like—to do ethnology in the field. Ever since Malinowski had gone it alone on the Trobriand Islands during the second decade of this century, the art and science of ethnology had left the armchair and had become part of the experience of those who would pass on the mystique of the "participant observer" in the alien culture to their students and their friends. There were several rules: one must learn and work in the language of the people to be studied, one must spend a long and more or less continuous residence among them, one must participate as much as possible in their daily round of life, one must establish rapport and become as much as possible accepted as a part of the social landscape—and most important— one must remain objective. This ultimate injunction served to validate the scientific nature of our work.

I submit that to follow all of these rules except the last may be *relatively* easy. However, if one finds them easy to follow, the last admonition becomes even more difficult. We are taught and urged to do a variety of things which logically inject us into the lifeblood of a community; yet we are expected, ideally, to remain objective after we have become part of the plasma. I suspect that many of my colleagues have, during the course of field work, experienced a loss of objectivity in some fashion or in some degree. The three experiences recounted here portray my deepening involvement in the life of the community I had set out to study.

OBJECTIVITY BY IMITATION

On the very first day of my initial field work in a rural Mexican peasant community, I had scarcely settled in when I met Don Ramón, a Mexican novelist who spent his weekends writing in a one-room adobe retreat he had recently had built there. Shortly after we had begun talking, three rockets broke the quiet of the afternoon, exploding into the sky at about one-minute intervals. Don Ramón sighed resignedly and said, *"otro angelito"* (another little angel). My thoughts moved quickly to the literature I had consumed for months in preparation for the field and I remembered that the term *angelito* referred conventionally to a child who died before confirmation in the church. I asked some questions and Don Ramón answered them hospitably and intelligently, for he was the author of several "folk" novels. He understood my curiosity, although he knew little of my mission, and he agreed to help me seek out the *angelito* in a nearby precinct of the village.

The three rockets had served to notify friends and relatives of the death and readiness for viewing of the child, as well as to open the heavens to the child's soul. We arrived to find the body, covered with flowers, lying on a small table in a courtyard. Friends and relatives of the bereaved family were milling about, greeting and chatting with each other in a rather casual social fashion, and the mother, father, and siblings of the dead child evidenced no grief whatsoever, for it was not customary to do so.

I made careful observations of all that was said and done, of all that I could see and understand. I took note of the bowl of sliced onions beneath the table where the child lay (to absorb the bad air of death, I would later find out), of the crown of flowers adorning the *angelito's* head, and much more. Later that evening as I typed up my notes and filed them under the appropriate categories designated by Murdock *et al.* (1954), I congratulated myself on my first day's work and on my objectivity. I had felt no more emotion about the dead child than his parents had shown.

OBJECTIVITY THREATENED

Some months later, death was to become a more personal matter. Before he died, José Maria had been a vigorous, self-confident man in his middle twenties, married and the father of four. When we first met, I thought that central casting might pick him as the stereotype of the Mexican *pistolero*. He wore his Texas-style straw sombrero low over his eyes, almost concealing his hard, steady gaze. He had the ubiquitous black mustache of the highland Mestizo, but his wardrobe of jeans and khaki shirts, purchased in the United States where he had worked as a *bracero,* set him apart from the other men of the village; and he habitually wore boots instead of sandals. He carried at his hip at all times a nine-millimeter German-made automatic pistol, with a magazine of 15 rounds, and two spare clips of ammunition on his belt.

The sight of men bearing side arms is not uncommon in west-central Mexico. In fact, most of the men in José Maria's village and vicinity owned pistols. What distinguished him in this regard was the potency and fire power of his pistol and the fact that he practiced marksmanship. I found out early on that he had been accused of cattle rustling. Nevertheless, he was a good informant, although really responsive only in matters having to do with livestock and the

Theron A. Nunez and his friend Señor Suarez.

out-of-doors. As we became better acquainted, he would invite me to accompany him on horseback journeys into the hills to look for lost cattle or horses or to other villages on small matters of business. We would often stop at cantinas along the way or upon our return. After a while, I noticed that he drank only soft drinks, while I habitually refreshed myself with beer or tequila, when available. One day, I casually asked why, adding that of all the Mexican men I had come to know, he alone apparently did not drink. He pulled up his shirt, pushed down on his belt, and exposed a chest and belly dotted with bullet scars. He said, "I owe too many lives."

I later verified the fact that José Maria had violated a principle of local conflict resolution, which states that if "A" kills "B" in a spontaneous pistol duel (usually involving a matter of honor), then "A" must leave the community and not return. Should he fail to leave or should he return, he is the legitimate enemy and target of any male kinsman of the slain man. José Maria had chosen not to exile himself and had experienced the consequences; but he had achieved the status of the marked man, somewhat like the Hollywood stereotype of the Western gunslinger, who of necessity must always be on the alert, ready to defend himself. This was his existential dilemma and his reason for abstaining from alcohol. By remaining in the village with his family, José Maria had precipitated what was called *"una cadena de muertos"* (a chain of deaths) and he was attempting to postpone adding his link to the chain.

One evening when the village was celebrating a fiesta in the central plaza, with much gaiety, fireworks, music, and drinking, José Maria and a friend slipped a skiff into the lake which bordered the village and quietly rowed across the water some four kilometers to a smaller village on the opposite shore. There, they drank through the night until the light and sound of the fiesta had died away. Then, thinking they might return, unmissed and safely, before daylight, they set themselves to rowing.

I was awakened in the morning by a knocking at my door and, upon opening it, was greeted by four men whom I knew. They announced themselves as the *compadres* of José Maria and, as a delegation, told me that he was dead. Somehow, just before beaching the skiff, José Maria and his companion had overturned the shallow craft. José Maria, perhaps drunk and undoubtedly hampered by boots, pistol, and spare ammunition, drowned in two meters of water. His companion recovered the body. His *compadres* had come to me at the request of his mother, who had no photograph of her son. Would I, since I had been a friend—and owned a camera—come and take a photograph of the corpse. I took several photographs, to make certain that at least one would be successful. The prints showed a boyish face, in repose, and a body unadorned by boots or pistol. I felt that I had lost a friend, not an informant.

OBJECTIVITY COMPROMISED

It is axiomatic in anthropology that culture and cultures change, just as people do though time. A few months after the foregoing events, José Maria would not have been able to wear his pistol openly in the streets of his village. Law and order had come to the community. The state governor had initiated a campaign of *despistolización* and dispatched three-man teams of *rurales* (rural constabulary), armed with carbines and .45 calibre pistols, throughout the state. Such a team took up residence in my community, immediately confiscating a few pistols. Many others were hidden. It was not long before the *rurales* had nothing to do. They decided or were ordered to make the village their headquarters, meanwhile checking out other, more remote communities.

My first encounter with the sergeant of the *rurales,* which more or less set the tone of our later relations, involved his attempt to commandeer my horse for one of his missions. His two subordinates had already acquired mounts and he wanted to be better mounted than they. It was known that my horse was one of the better animals of the village. When he made his request, I responded with a well-known saying: *"Caballo, pistola, y mujer—a nadie se deben prestar."* (Horse, pistol, and woman—to no one should they be lent.) The adage reflects an ideal; in reality one may lend a horse to a friend or *compadre.* I had made it clear that he was neither. My behavior was consistent with local attitudes, for the *rurales* were from the very first considered outsiders, and outsiders are habitually regarded with suspicion or resentment, or both. I had unconsciously acquired insider sentiments, although at that time I hadn't realized how completely I had incorporated them.

I had been pleased with my idiomatic response and had mentioned it to several of the men of the village so that the incident soon became general knowledge. Shortly thereafter, the sergeant entered a combination grocery-cantina where I was making a purchase. Although it was midmorning, he offered to buy me a tequila. I knew that I had been challenged to a ritual drinking bout, and for reasons which are clearer to me now, I accepted the challenge. Appropriately, in terms of the culture pattern, we alternated buying shots of tequila, and by midafternoon we had attracted an audience. The conversation (what I remember of it) was superficially amiable but careful although it eventually became somewhat incoherent. Realizing the degree of my intoxication, I excused myself, vowing to return immediately. My house was nearby, I said, and there was something that I had to do there. My intention was to eat as much greasy and substantial food as quickly as possible, before I returned to drink with the sergeant. By late afternoon, we were both quite drunk. At some point, for some now obscure reason, the sergeant handed me his pistol and asked me if I would like to try it out. He then put his head on the table and went to sleep. I put the pistol beside him and walked unsteadily home to sleep.

Thereafter, the sergeant and I avoided each other for several weeks—until the incident of *la gallona.* To refer to a man as a *gallo* (rooster) is to say that he is capricious and quick-tempered, easy to take offense. Such a description would rarely apply to a rural Mexican woman, for women are supposed to be socially subordinate to men, quiet, modest, and self-abnegating. However, there exists the occasional exception, the marginal woman, one who may act like the *gallo.* But since there is no such thing as a female rooster *(galla),* the term *gallona* is used for such a person; such a woman was Doña Augustina, proprietress of the village's sole café. She had been known to throw a pan of searing grease at a customer who insulted her, and she had once run a man out of the café at rifle point. Although she was married, her husband worked in highway construction and was seldom in residence. She operated the café with the help of her eldest daughter and a hired girl. For the last few months of my field work, I took most of my meals there.

One day, after almost fourteen months in the field, I rode my horse into the plaza and dismounted in front of the café. Doña Augustina's daughter met me at the door; tearfully, she related the following: The sergeant of the *rurales* had come by the café shortly after Doña Augustina had swept some debris into the plaza street. He had told her to clean it up, that the *rurales* were trying to clean up the town. (They had begun to impound pigs and burros which traditionally foraged in the streets.) He had been rude, I was told, and Doña Augustina had responded by cursing the man soundly and with expertise, using the word *buey* (ox) with special vehemence. To be called an ox is an explicit reference to castration and infers that one is certainly something less than a man. Infuriated, the sergeant arrested Doña Augustina, placing her in the filthy one-celled jail in the courtyard of the town hall. She had been lodged there several hours by the time of my arrival at the café. The formal elements of what follows are comic in the main, but the humor became evident only afterward —the scenes were played in a manner of high seriousness.

Upon hearing the full story of Doña Augustina's dilemma, I remounted my horse, galloped across the cobblestone plaza, reined up sharply in front of the town hall, dismounted, and entered, my spurs jangling as I walked. I confronted the ancient village clerk, whose function it was to record births, marriages, deaths, and other community matters of legal interest. Announcing that I had come to get the prisoner out, I demanded to see the mayor, who was sent for and who arrived shortly. I reminded the mayor that "we" did not customarily jail women "here," that if there were a charge there had to be bail or a fine, and that I was prepared to pay it. He said that he didn't have the key to the woman's cell, that the sergeant had it. I asked him to fetch the sergeant.

I was angry and arrogant. I had learned to be angry and arrogant in Spanish, most of which I had learned in the village. I had lived there for more than a year. I had gone to mass almost every Sunday, had helped now and then with various chores when my friends needed or asked for help. I could visit and gossip in quite a few households with ease and confidence and could go about my appointed rounds, soliciting data from informants, hardly being noticed as I passed in the streets. Doña Augustina had fed me well and was a friend, and "they," the outsiders, had no business putting her in jail. Her husband was out of town as usual and she had no male kinsmen. Anthropologist or not, I felt I simply had to free Doña Augustina.

The sergeant arrived, grinning, having been undoubtedly informed of the situation and my chagrin. We discussed the matter. It had to do with disrespect for an officer, he said. Did I know what she had called him and the significance of that consummate insult? I tried to be moderate at first, then clever. I said that such a word, indeed, was a serious insult, but that everyone knew the lady to be a *gallona*. Therefore, this should be taken into account and, since she had already spent most of the day in that stinking cell, she should be released. He said, "Not yet." I turned quickly to the mayor and asked him what he thought an appropriate bond would be (which would be automatically forfeited). He replied, "Ten pesos." I took a ten-peso note from my pocket, held it out to the mayor which, by force of habit, he took. Turning to the sergeant, I said triumphantly, "The bond has been paid. You must release the prisoner." Then came his quick trump: "I'm sorry, but I don't have the key. One of my men has it and he is off somewhere." I asked him to find his subordinate and return with the key. I must have waited almost an hour before I sent a young boy to find out what was going on. He returned with the report that all three of the *rurales* were playing cards in the sergeant's quarters. Incensed, I turned to the mayor and stated that if he did not obtain the key from the *rurales* immediately, I would go to the capital and speak with the governor—whom I had never met.

The key was promptly returned and I opened the cell myself, escorted Doña Augustina across the plaza to her café, where she stood me a beer and prepared an excellent meal. When I finished eating, we exchanged thanks and I mounted my horse to ride out of the plaza to my house, two blocks away. By the next day, the story had spread and people were greeting me on the street as *Señor Abogado* (Mister Attorney).

EPILOGUE

Within two days of this incident, I had sold my horse, given away most of my household goods, packed my personal belongings into my battered station wagon, and left for the United States border.

During the two-day interval, as my emotional lenses began to clear, I examined my behavior carefully and became somewhat frightened and confused. I couldn't be sure that I had done the correct thing. I concluded, however, that I had behaved rather like a *gallo,* a precarious role even for a Mexican, but one which is understood and accepted, if carried off successfully. But I had not behaved very much like the social scientist; I had temporarily lost my objectivity. I knew then that I would have to leave that place and those people, who had started out as my subjects for study and who had come to be my friends and enemies. Hopefully, I could return another time, to combine objectivity and subjectivity, to learn more than I had in trying to be completely objective, abjuring the subjective, and being unsuccessful at both.

The episodes recounted in this chapter occurred while I was collecting data for my doctoral dissertation. The dissertation was as objective as I could make it, and these incidents were not part of it. They are part of me, however—part of my anthropological experience. Like the loss of innocence, the loss of compulsive objectivity may be ultimately salutary.

REFERENCE

MURDOCK, GEORGE P., ET AL. 1954. *Guia para la clasificacion de los datos culturales (Guide for the Classification of Cultural Data)*. Washington, D.C.: Pan American Union.

12 / Talking to Strangers

JAMES B. WATSON

In many parts of the Eastern Highlands of New Guinea, the initiation of boys is a ritual cycle of two main phases, each lasting from one day to several days. These events were reported to me secretly a number of times during 1954 and 1955 by various Agarabi and Tairora men. Once they knew me, it was no problem to find men willing to talk about initiation. Most of them, in fact, volunteered information. As a rule they spoke of this particular topic with animation, which was certainly not true of every topic. I concluded that they liked to recall initiation as a stern test they were proud of passing; or else, as the rites were infrequent and much of the ritual secret, surreptitiously admitting me to this knowledge appealed to their sense of masculine comradeship. Male initiation, to be sure, is the ritual high point of the culture.

Yet even a dozen different accounts did not yield a clear or comprehensive picture. In any single description numerous details were omitted, even major details; and it was hard to reconcile different versions or to place activities in a consistent sequence, let alone to discover their approximate duration. Some of the principal roles could only be guessed. Not only loose and perfunctory, most of the descriptions were distinctly one-sided as well. Despite all that a man might leave out, he usually mentioned the pain experienced or the reactions of the frightened boys. Initiates who fainted or fled would not infrequently be noted while central parts of the ritual itself were ignored.

The emphasis on fright and pain doubtless reflects a reality of male initiation in Agarabi and Tairora life. I acknowledge the significance of its repetition, but an ethnographer with a limited time in the field cannot be indifferent to redundancy. In the interest of exploring other aspects of Agarabi and Tairora life, I could hardly justify collecting exhaustive data on "The Spontaneous Recollection by Male Subjects of the Male Initiation in Agarabi/Tairora Society." Intensive and systematic sampling—polling the relevant group on every relevant matter—would doubtless be ideal but it is simply beyond the resources of the average ethnographer or ethnographic team.

Just trying to reconstruct the initiation ceremony was time-consuming

172

enough. The men almost always found tedious any effort I made to go beyond the familiar high points. Their animation would fade, their eyes grow dull. With waning interest, their answers became mechanical and untrustworthy. A number of them may have regretted bringing up the topic. I suspect some felt about as follows: "Here I tell you something secret and exciting, something which would greatly interest any man. You, however, must be either ungrateful or stupid, for you abuse my friendship to plague me with tiresome and obvious details!" Indeed, sometimes I felt a clod to press them further.

There finally came a point where my best efforts at questioning were no longer productive. I lost enthusiasm for any further clandestine accounts. I would still listen, to be sure. When so little information of any kind was freely offered, it seemed reckless—quite apart from discourteous—to appear indifferent. But eventually I stopped making notes. Once I stopped asking all but polite and obvious questions, I suppose, our conversations came closer to what was expected. For my part I hoped that being the interested listener was at least a contribution to rapport. Otherwise, the exercise was by that time quite without point.

Gradually synthesizing a "proper" description of the cycle by comparing the different accounts I had collected earlier, I could finally recognize the major and constant ritual elements and most of the minor or variable ones. I could generally distinguish the roles of different participants. I constructed the ritual sequence—albeit idealized; and I came as close as it seemed I was apt to come to the approximate schedule and duration of the episodes that comprised the total cycle. In effect, I could now provide a better composite depiction, I felt, than a Tairora or Agarabi—much better, certainly, than any ever provided me.

With most of Agarabi/Tairora beliefs and practices there was at least no problem of redundancy! In fact, wherever I lacked an acknowledged practice or an observed event to provide a point of reference, my general, open-ended, or searching questions tended to produce more frustration than enlightenment. No few matters, indeed, were brought to light only through stubborn persistence, even sometimes in the face of impatient denials. As I have since complained to fellow ethnographers, should one be fortunate enough to *know* the answer beforehand, he could at best hope to get it verified! Otherwise, the villagers appeared to be endowed with a far greater tolerance for ambiguity—both theirs and mine—than for answering questions. Redundancy or ambiguity—at times they seemed an interviewer's nightmare.

The experience of ethnographers appears to vary widely in different fields, so my characterization of Eastern Highlanders has sometimes been challenged. More than once suspected of hyperbole, I now hold in reserve for the doubting Thomas a particular telling case. I was asking some Agarabi men one day about the causes and cures of sickness. Was ill health ever the result, I inquired, of some foreign object—stick, stone, leaf, dirt, bone, or the like—being present in the body where it did not belong? No, they told me. Such a thing was quite unheard of. I elaborated, expanding the range of possible illustrations. The answer remained the same. Was cure ever effected by removing from the body a foreign object—stick, stone, and so forth—after which the sick person got better? Again negative. Their impatience showed. I pursued this issue to the point where I felt, so far as interviewing alone could be relied upon, that sickness from intrusive objects must be no part of Agarabi belief or practice. This was in fact conceivable, for important other sources of sickness were known—perhaps sufficient to account for all the diseases Agarabi recognize.

Six months later in a Tairora village, I encountered illness from intrusive objects and cure by removing them. The local version was almost identical to the hypothetical one I had earlier sketched in querying Agarabi. After some months I returned for a final visit to the Agarabi village, having in the meantime assembled a list of apparent contrasts between the cultures. Once again I described the illness and cure the Agarabi had previously denied. They remembered and confidently reconfirmed the denial. I then pointed out that the Tairora had such a belief and sometimes effected cures accordingly. Mildly interested (perhaps because they had always insisted there was little to distinguish between their two cultures), my hearers asked me to describe the Tairora belief and practice. I could hardly do so in fresh terms, so close was the resemblance to the hypothetical model of illness-from-intrusive-objects I had originally used. They shook their heads once more, however, apparently surprised that, contrary to claim, there was such a difference between Tairora and themselves. One man asked me what the Tairora called this kind of illness or the cure for it. Turning to my notebook, I gave him the name. "Oh!" said he, "that is what we call such-and-such," citing therewith an obvious cognate of the Tairora word. It was indeed interesting, I observed, that their own name for a sickness so resembled that of Tairora, and I asked if they could describe for me the Agarabi syndrome and the treatment to which their own name applied. I was dumbfounded! I was given—quite blandly—a description that hardly departed from mine of six months earlier or from the one I had just now repeated! If there *was* a difference, it was practically imperceptible!

The only possible conclusion seemed to be that if I had been able the first time to call by name the Agarabi sickness, I could readily have confirmed its part in the local ethno-medicine. Providing an accurate general description evidently was not enough. Even a cue containing—let us say cautiously—more than half of all the "correct" information and, so far as I could see, containing no "incorrect" information, would not guarantee recognition—not if one happened to omit what, for the local listener, was the *crucial* information. In this case a specific name was apparently crucial. But if one had to know the crucial local terms *to begin with,* the prospects for pioneer ethnographic exploration were sobering, to say the least!

My point has never been that this behavior was either scatterbrained or cranky, much less evidence of a "primitive mind." Much better reasons can be suggested. For practical purposes, the abstract reasons did not matter: most of the villagers were simply not "good informants." To be able to put together a satisfactory description of some segment of their belief or behavior, therefore, gave me a sense of purely personal achievement. It was, after all, a triumph over obstacles. Persistence, intuition, general knowledge of things human and cultural, and just plain luck seemed to be the factors that counted, surely not the meager and unreliable assistance of the villagers. I have no reason to suspect that their resistance was deliberate; still, any success was generally achieved against their indifference, lack of insight, or intellectual inertia.

On my second long field trip to New Guinea, I returned for a few days to visit the Agarabi village where, among others, I had first collected accounts of male rites. For me it was mainly a chance to renew friendships and to find out what changes had occurred since my work there ten years earlier. Soon after my arrival two old men I had known before appeared. Referring to their previous help, they told me they wished to place themselves at my disposal, to devote all the time it might require to review me on everything I knew of Agarabi kinship, folklore, sib alignments, local history, rituals, crop and plant nomenclature, and so forth. In effect this was the total range of matters, as they perceived them, which comprised my interest in the village. Jokingly they said they would be my "teachers"! As delightful as it was unexpected, this offer was not exactly what I had come for. With but a few days to visit I needed to talk, for instance, to some of the village coffee growers and to the man who now had a small retail business, using a part of his house for a trade store. But how refreshing a contrast, at least, from the pursuit of elusive information with uncomprehending "informants" to the present open-handedness. I could not resist the chance to talk with the two old men, whatever the yield, if only to find out what their offer could possibly mean.

The tutorial character of our several meetings was touching. It pleased my teachers that I had learned my lessons well, but they conscientiously corrected me on any point where they sensed omission or obvious misinterpretation. The two always appeared together, so that they could prompt or correct each other, they said, if either of *them* made a mistake. The village at large seemed to approve the arrangement, as it were, with a nod of responsible concern. Once started, I regretted that it was not possible to stay on the job. Besides lacking sufficient time, however, I did not even have my notebooks with me from the previous field trip.

Two features surprised me about these meetings. The first was the offer itself and the tutorial dedication that apparently lay behind it. From my earlier experience I could not in my wildest optimism have expected any such involvement from the village. It is still hard for me to realize that it happened. The second surprise, of which I was soon aware, was the bland assumption of my tutors that our present sessions were but the continuation of an earlier relationship. My vivid recollection of that previous visit was, to say the least, nothing of the sort. Interviewing had never produced a situation remotely resembling "teaching." Hardly anyone had concerned himself—if he even noticed—when I missed the form or point of some custom, belief, or practice. A loose approximation was sufficient, and even then I myself usually had to force the question. Stressing that completeness and accuracy were important in the work I was doing had made little impression. Without dependable "feedback" from the people, gathering data through interviews thus required unusual concentration and large amounts of nervous energy, an exhausting business which left me to fall wearily into bed at night and reluctantly to drag myself out again in the morning. As with the accounts of male initiation, moreover, I could almost always expect a glum face if it became necessary to probe or cross-question villagers very far for fuller detail. They were unable to elucidate the obvious because of their inability to realize that what was to them "the obvious" might need elucidating.

How retrospect had altered the view of my tutors! Every so often we would come to some matter where I clearly recalled a hard-won discovery, something I had either dragged out of people or composed almost entirely from unaided observation and inference. Now, however, it was: "As we explained when you were here before . . .", or "When we told you about that the last time . . ." How incredibly casual! Some topics had not even been acknowledged by most people during my first visit, let alone freely discussed. The reasons included village anxieties about alleged government or mission sanctions. Even these topics, one was now to suppose, had been methodically explored expressly for my enlightenment. While it was fascinating to have my earlier hunches and formulations confirmed, it was also frustrating to have had to work so hard to elicit what, ostensibly, was now readily within reach. How much difference ten years had made, even in men already middle-aged and who could still speak to no white man except in their own tongue.

I do not want to suggest that the two old men had become classical "informants." To some extent our conversations could move along briskly, I am sure, because this time I already knew a good part of the answers to a good part of the questions; I now had the key terms. Things had not changed that much. Nor had the problem of securing an orderly account of complex activities— male initiation, for example. I was quite content, in fact, to resist their several invitations to explore that particular topic. Tutorial motives could take my elderly friends well beyond what anyone had been able to do ten years before, but their information was nevertheless still given in bits and scraps, and their ability to point out relationships remained embryonic. They were no "village philosophers."

Late in the afternoon of my second day in the village a young man approached to shake my hand and to inquire if he could be of any help. About seventeen years of age, he would have been about seven at the time of my first visit. Now a handsome, clean-cut youth, his clothing, his bearing, and his excellent pidgin, deliberately interspersed with English, betrayed that he had been to school and had also worked for a time in a town or on the coast. It was a pleasure to meet him for he had an attractive manner. As an index of change in the village, moreover, he was surely as important as the 10,000 new coffee trees, and much more interesting. What gave me pause, after we exchanged brief pleasantries, was what he wanted to talk about. He asked me, of all things, if I would like to have him tell me about the male initiation rites!

It was late in a day most of which had already been spent in working with my two tutors and visiting and interviewing other villagers. I was tired. It would soon be dark. I could quite happily have called it quits for the evening cup of luke-warm Scotch. Of all the topics he might have suggested, moreover, initiation was one of the lengthiest and most involved if one really tackled it seriously. As I have already admitted, it was for me long since also a redundant, tiresome, and frustrating topic—to be blunt, a kind of *bête noir* that I hoped I had done with. So I hesitated. An excuse could easily have been found. Conceivably I could have suggested that he accompany me to some part of the vicinity I had yet to revisit. But something made me curious. Perhaps it was the eagerness I sensed or his being so pointed about the proffered information. His sophisticated and direct manner was hard to resist. So once more I gave in to curiosity.

We went to the meeting hall to get out of the dew. This four-sided, thatched building of native materials seemed large enough to hold the entire village, about 400 people. It had been erected since my first visit, there being no need or precedent for such meetings then. Except for children, dogs, or chickens, it was even now empty most of the time, and so it was at the moment. There were only three or four small windows, but early evening light still came in the doorway and through numerous cracks in the roughly boarded walls. We sat on the edge of what appeared a stage, our feet on the dirt floor. I opened my notebook to the last few unused pages left in it, scarcely doubting that they would be enough for whatever was to come.

"The First Day," the young man announced like a title, flashing me a self-conscious smile. He began to detail the preliminaries of the ritual. That was a novelty. Most accounts propelled one directly into the midst of the action, taking for granted all such business as the making of ritual costume and paraphernalia, the collecting of food and firewood, the involvement of different people, or even the assembling of the boys. I hardly had time to wonder if he would remember to indicate when we came to "The Second Day." The description continued without hesitation, and I was soon fully occupied just trying to keep up. Detail followed detail in logical order, requiring neither prompting nor query and with only such pauses as he himself made when he guessed that my writing was lagging behind. Lag it did, and I had to ask for other pauses now and then. I scarcely interrupted him at all for further information as his account, as given, was clear and, from what I already knew, could hardly have been more complete.

The children peering in the windows, the hens scratching the dirt floor for their chicks, the meeting hall, and the stage on which we sat all receded. My attention narrowed to hearing and recording the young man's unstoppable flow of words. His voice and the slip of the ball-point on the paper, punctuated as I turned the pages and inserted carbon paper, blotted out other sounds. How long, I wondered, could it go on? As I neared the end of the notebook, I began to wonder also if it would be like breaking a spell to stop for more paper. Would an interruption somehow cause us to revert to the pattern of painstaking question and perfunctory answer, almost the only kind of information-giving to which I had previously been exposed? What was happening was simply unbelievable. To me the impressive detail of ritual act and folk rationale almost became secondary, so amazing was his feat of detailing it coherently.

My hand began to ache from the uninterrupted writing, even with switching from fingers to wrist-and-arm in propelling the pen. I had to drop my arm and shake it for muscular relief from time to time. At this action the young man appeared to smile, as if he saw in it an acknowledgment of his virtuosity. Perhaps it even spurred him on to greater explicitness and descriptive detail.

I finished the last unused leaf of the notebook and now, fascinated and reluctant to stop, continued the notes on the inside back cover, then on the outside. The speaker soon saw what I was doing. He had probably written in copybooks at school and was thus himself aware of the linearity of the written medium. As I neared the bottom of the outside back cover, he stopped to ask if I did not have another book. By chance I did, though I had not expected to need it on my visit to the village, having foreseen neither the elderly tutors nor any such phenomenon as this boy. I called out to the house where we were staying for someone to bring me the book. A quarto-sized, English copybook, the same as I had just finished, it had pages numbered in pairs up to 100. It was designed for slipping a sheet of carbon between the successive pairs of pages as one proceeded, thus yielding a copy of each page with the same number on the original and the copy.

The interruption had no effect whatever on the young man, and, with the new notebook, there could hardly now be a problem of sufficient paper. We picked up where we had stopped. I now became aware that the light was getting dim. Continuing to write, I called out for the pressure lamp to be lighted and brought over, leaving preparations for supper in semidarkness. The cooks could better proceed by firelight than I could write in the dark. We were not quite through "The Second Day" at this point, and I knew that it would be a while before the job was completed. Supper would be very late, and I was hungry. Still reluctant to disrupt this remarkable encounter, however, I dismissed the idea of recessing until morning. The young man, exhilarated by his prowess and by my obvious recognition of it, evinced neither hunger nor weariness and for his part would surely not propose a halt. We went on, so far as I could tell, at an undiminished pace.

My eyes were straining now from seldom looking up. Page by page we noted all the events of "The Second Day," finally reaching the third. The children and onlookers had long since departed for their houses and their evening meal. With their usual squawking and fussing, I was dimly aware, the chickens had found roost for the night in the thatch overhead. The village had fallen silent.

My young informant and I were alone on the stage in the circle of light from
the hissing lamp. It had already become an endurance test for me, but now
I was also the spectator betting as to how much longer the performer could
sustain his stunning act. Through growing fatigue I could still appreciate the
quality of this account. For my collaborator, I felt, it must be the pleasure of
a man who knew that his competence was fully visible.

At last the session ended. It was almost eight o'clock. We had been at it for
well over two hours. My few questions had elicited relatively minor addenda,
nothing to suggest an important omission. My collaborator told me cheerfully
that he would be available tomorrow for any further questions. I felt it un-
necessary to say how impressed I was with his exposition of the ritual, but I
said I had never before had such a complete account. It was true, he replied;
when the older men try to tell anything, they usually "halve it." He didn't
know why. I thanked him again and he left. I pumped the lamp, which had
been getting yellow, and gathered up my gear. Light-headed and slightly numb
with hunger and fatigue, but bemused and elated to have been witness to the
feat just concluded, I stumbled back to join my family for supper. In the wet
grass my enormous shadow from the swinging lamp I held seemed to fit my
mood.

Not the account but the performance itself, I concluded, was the more
significant. What an amazing thing! Sure that I knew the village well ten years
ago, I had found no one like this, no one who could help me learn village ways
and beliefs, except to some degree in spite of himself. Could the equal of this
young man have existed then? Had I overlooked valuable assistance, perhaps
by having sought help within too narrow a circle? Some younger person?
Surely not. I knew some of the youth of that time, too. Lively and interesting
in talking about their own schemes and problems, they were no better than
their elders at putting together an orderly account of any length or complexity.
Like the women, in fact, they nearly always deferred to older men as the only
authoritative source for important matters. And no elder I had ever talked to
could do what had just been done.

No, I concluded, "young versus old" informants was not the explanation.
It was the "age" of the community that made the difference, not the age of
a particular person. A young man of today has had experiences different from
those of any youth of the same age a decade ago. He has grown up in a village
in which word of the white man's ways is commonplace. He has grown up
hearing and speaking pidgin, even without ever leaving the village, quite likely
speaking it with the gang of boys among whom he rambled—using the outsider's language, perhaps, to ape an older brother, to demonstrate sophistication to his mates, or to keep secrets from the girls. He may have had enough
schooling to learn to read and write and even to learn some English. He may
have worked outside the village in a job calling for such skills or have lived
where he could assert them. He is seventeen or eighteen years old but histori-
cally he is older than his predecessors. He knows outsiders and deals with them

calmly if not with ease. He no longer sweats, probably, if they shout at him.

This must be the new wave. For the first time I had experienced an *informant,* the sort of individual for whom the label was presumably devised. Here was a collaborator such as the older students of American Indian groups perhaps took for granted, able to discourse for hours at a sitting, exploring his own language or life memories for the instruction of a practiced listener. My young Agarabi informant or his village contemporaries might have some way yet to go in becoming "professional" in the North American mold, like "those informants who were influenced by anthropologists to become anthropologists" (Holmberg, 1958, p. 12). The Agarabi potential is nonetheless clear.

But what of the elderly tutors who took charge of reviewing me on Agarabi culture? In what sense were they a part of a new wave? Neither of them, to be sure, would in their lifetime equal their young fellow villager. Still, their acceptance of my need for information and even more their wish to give it—their assumption of the responsibility—were unprecedented, too, in my experience of the village. For them, of course, no command of pidgin, no school, no work experience outside the village could account for the new orientation. It could only be the passage of time, bringing increasing familiarity with the postcontact world; surely that had helped. Within the very community in which they were born, they have now watched a whole generation arise who have never discharged an arrow in the direction of an enemy, never even seen it done—young men who speak the white man's tongue, perhaps read and write his alphabet, grow coffee for sale to his buyers from the town, buy and sell his trade goods—a generation, in short, who cannot be thought of simply as "villagers" or "sib-mates" in the old sense because they do not have the old assumptions. Living through this period of change could make it easier for my two elderly friends to conceive of tutoring me. Could they doubt that now the younger people, their own fellow villagers, themselves require "teachers" to understand things they would once have witnessed or learned directly from practice? Parts of Agarabi life are fast becoming "memory culture." To survive at all, they must do so in an explicit, vocabular form, without local precedent. What is no longer seen or enacted, in other words, is either verbalized or surely lost to oblivion. The recent past of the village is increasingly another culture, then, though one not yet extinct. In that sense everyone is today to some degree marginal. The old men are marginal to the present. They have had to live with younger people who, on the other hand, are marginal to the past.

How much can now be said in that familiar shorthand which, if one takes it only literally, furnishes the barest clue of the communication? Where once no hearer needed more, he may now sometimes fail to understand. Eventually the time may come when Agarabi folktales will cease to be so skeletal, with setting, motive, and characterization almost wholly assumed. Perhaps the people will also gradually drop their curious readiness, in recounting the interplay of persons, to attribute words to a man solely on the strength of what they feel certain were his thoughts. The attribution will be harder, at any rate, when they cannot feel so confident that they know each other's thoughts.

My brief revisit to Agarabi thus produced multiple ironies. No stranger, I had returned to find I could talk readily with the people, elicit once difficult information with unprecedented ease. They for their part knew much more about white men, surely magnifying the acknowledged advantage of the ethnographer's revisit. While the distance had shrunk between the villagers and me, that between some villagers and others had widened. Much had happened to set young and old apart, in a village which, to the best of their effort and insight, had qualified for—and proclaimed—its entry into modernity. Talking to fellow villagers was now in some respects not unlike talking to outsiders. As a constant condition of life, you recognized that you did not know all that your younger neighbors knew. And, of course, they did not know all that you knew, for they were born too late. You had to realize that your views and values could not in all cases be theirs. Simply in order to communicate with them some insight was needed. So the surprising experience with my tutors by no means arose solely from the fact of my previous visit, not even if one discounts their greater present familiarity with the outside world. The change that so impressed me came in part from within the village itself. Learning from having to understand their own children, older Agarabi have apparently acquired some facility in understanding strangers. Meeting villagers today, an inquisitive outsider would quite likely feel relatively little frustration. They would probably find his questions comprehensible, even interesting. They would grasp at once his lack of background and need of explicitness. If they wanted to, some of them could explain to him the premises he must recognize in order to understand their answers. They could *talk* to him, and he might therefore never realize what it was like before, for them to talk with strangers.

REFERENCE

HOLMBERG, ALLAN R. 1958. "The Research and Development Approach to the Study of Change." *Human Organization*, 17:12–16.

13 / Learning a New Culture

SOLON T. KIMBALL

Soon after the beginning of my graduate-student days, I began to collect a set of guiding principles about the behavior which I would follow if I ever became a field worker. It is now no longer possible nor would it be of very great significance if I were able to pinpoint the source and situation in which these principles were accumulated. There can be no question, however, that their apprehension was by bits and pieces and not by any orderly transmission and acquisition.

Surely the most inclusive of these prescriptions was the insistence that the successful field worker must adjust to the way of life of the people he studies. Modification of behavior toward native style should be as near total as possible. This process would include, for example, changes in dress, food habits, eating patterns, speech, greetings, gesture pattern, and walking. These were counted as the more obvious culture traits which, if acquired, would reduce the differences setting the ethnographer-stranger apart from his group and hence would facilitate the collection of the data he sought.

Immersion in the cultural life of the natives beyond that necessary for collecting information required adjustments of a more fundamental sort. The rationale for such an objective is clearer today than it was then, but the purpose to be served remains the same. It was believed that only as the field worker became able to view objects and happenings from the same perspective as that of the natives would it be possible for him to understand the cultural context which gave them meaning. This dictum bears the unmistakable stamp of Malinowski.

Exactly how far one should go in adopting the native way of life was never made clear. The danger of "going native" was an unlikely possibility. What was more probable was that some unwitting violation of a religious or social taboo would place one in jeopardy. If the field worker observed the suggested limitations on his behavior, such dangers would not arise. These cautions were not urged as much to protect him from the threats to his physical or mental health as they were to ensure his effectiveness in gathering data and the success of the project. Some behavioral guides contradicted each other, particularly those which set limitations on the degree of involvement. Opinions contrary to local views or that might identify one with a local controversy, for example, were not to be expressed. Partisan alignments with religious, political, or familial factions were to be avoided although the existing divisions were to be investigated. Sexual or romantic involvement with native women was to be strictly avoided. As Lloyd Warner once explained it to me, a sexual linkage with a female of one moiety of the Murngin immediately involved you in a whole set of obligations with her kinsmen as well as in their quarrels with the opposing moiety. An angry tribesman of the opposite moiety who was seeking to avenge some insult to him by a newly acquired distant kin of yours might throw spears at you. Such a powerful joining of anxiety, fear, and pragmatism should restrain all but the most lubricious male.

That these directives should be heeded I quickly learned in my baptism to field work in Ireland. At a late-evening gathering of supporters of the political party which favored close ties with Great Britain—a fact I had not yet discerned—I called for a free Ireland, bringing my innocence to a sudden and unhappy end when I found that I was in the wrong crowd for such a sentiment. I attempted to recover the lost neutrality by reciting Lincoln's Gettysburg address. Near-mute wariness was the watchword from then on although I made other mistakes from which I also learned.

Through strict neutrality it was presumably possible to avoid the status identification that would limit access to all segments of a population. Although it didn't occur to me until much later, such status anonymity must create confusion among members of a society who have been trained to identify and respond to others primarily upon the cues of status. I also learned quickly enough in the field that the preservation of neutrality created an ambiguous and ambivalent position for me, with resultant social and psychic tensions from which there was no release. Even the intimacy of friendship did not engender full freedom of expression. The unwitting report of your private view might do great harm.

It had been drilled into me that neutrality and success were inextricably linked. Success would be evident in fat piles of field notes. But I recall nothing being said about the effect on the novice enthnographer of long-term isolation from his own kind combined with a restricted involvement in the affairs of a host culture. For me, the acquisition of a native perspective was slow, erratic, and often traumatic, but I was driven by the near-complusive conviction that the costs of transformation were the inescapable price paid for success in one's research. Whatever comfort contemporary students may derive from knowing that such suffering is normal and can be labeled "culture shock" was not then available. Certainly I was unprepared for the recurrent attempts to incorporate me in the lifeways of a West Ireland county where I conducted my first major field research in 1933–1934. The process of induction was both subtle and direct and I must also admit, effective. Although at the time I believed that control of my cultural destiny resided in my hands, hindsight suggests that the reality was something quite different. The guiding principle which prescribed no overt entanglements became increasingly pro forma as I became more deeply enmeshed in Irish culture. In fact, the transformation at the psychic level seemed to have moved quite beyond any conscious control. At least, no other explanation seems as valid for interpreting the event which I shall describe here.

My introduction to Ireland came on a cold, gray morning in April 1933 at the small, West Irish port of Galway. A handful of steerage Irish and I disembarked from a North German Lloyd steamship to a small lighter which deposited us at a nearby quay where a dozen or so hackney drivers solicited customers for their hotels. My destination was the Queen's Hotel, Ennis,

Abbey Street with Queen's Hotel in background, 1968.

County Clare, about forty miles away, where I was to be met by my co-worker, Conrad Arensberg. After some minor misadventures caused primarily by my ignorance of local custom and my inability to comprehend the thick Irish brogue of western Ireland, I employed the driver of an ancient Ford to carry me to my destination. By late afternoon we managed to get within sight of the Queen's Hotel when the last of several blowouts occurred and the driver, his helper, and I trudged the final two blocks laden with my luggage. Arensberg, who had failed to receive word of my coming, had gone off to visit friends in England and did not appear until several days later. But the hotel personnel and guests were friendly, and the bar sold drinks on tick. Thus began my stay in Ireland which was to end some thirteen months later.

The process of my transformation and incorporation into Irish life was affected by experiences both in the town of Ennis, where the Queen's Hotel was the base of operation, and in the countryside. I lived with two farm families on four different occasions, each for periods of several weeks. Arensberg returned to Harvard about two months after my arrival, so that the companionship which had been so valuable during the early, stressful period of adjustment to a strange way of life ended. Although the townspeople were friendly and helpful and I entered into many of the summer activities, I knew that I could never understand the Irish people until I became directly involved with the seemingly remote and different life-style of the small farmers. A direct approach seemed utterly impossible. This feeling may have been the result of the townsmen's appraisal of rural folk. To them the country fellow was "deep," "cute," "untrustworthy," enmeshed in kinship obligations which excluded outsiders, and suspicious if not hostile to strangers. Furthermore, their ways were considered to be uncouth and at times even barbarous. However typical these attitudes may have been as an urban stereotype of the countryman, they were just that and nothing more. Later I was to discover that the country people reciprocated with equally uncomplimentary ideas when they warned me about the evil ways of the townsmen.

During the early fall, arrangements were made for me to take up residence with a family of the small-farmer class in the townland of Rynamona near the village of Corofin in North Clare. This move was accomplished in a manner which the Irish understand so well and which they phrase as "Everything goes by friends and friendship." The local district health officer, Donough McNamara, a man much interested in the history of the county and a friend, secured the help of the local schoolmaster, who found a suitable location for me. Thus it was that with a bicycle for transportation and wearing a black suit that was appropriately respectable for Sunday Mass, a country-style wool hat, and farmer-type brogans, my other belongings stowed in a pack on my back, I left Ennis one midmorning on a new venture. Two hours later in time, but what for me was a century in cultural difference, I wheeled down the narrow borheen toward the modest thatched cottage where John and Mary Quin lived with Mary's older widowed sister, whom I came to know only by the respectful title of "the old lady."

The Quins were middle-aged and childless, as was "the old lady." After her husband's death she had brought her younger sister to live with her, and in due course, John Quin married into the house and farm as husband of the younger sister. A dowry always accompanies the in-marrying individual, but it is usually somewhat larger with a male since the name on the land has been changed in the process.

In layout the house displayed a pattern distinctive of West Ireland, with a central kitchen and small bedrooms on both east and west ends. At the western end of the rectangular kitchen was an open hearth where food for both humans and animals was prepared and around which evening visitors gathered for warmth and conversation. There the family concluded the day with its recitation of the rosary. Furnishings were few and simple, including a dresser with its display of seldom-used delftware, a benchlike settle bed along the north wall, and a deal table and sugon (caned straw seat) chairs by the one small window on the south. On the wall was a small shrine displaying a brightly colored lithograph of the Sacred Heart of Jesus.

John Quin was a stalwart man. Big-boned, he stood better than six feet. He moved with the easy, deliberate pace common to the countryman. He paid serious attention to his farm duties and had learned to perform the tasks required of the small farmer with skill and despatch. But he was also full of lightheartedness and wit and took part in the country dances or turkey-gambles with zest. Quin responded well to the happenings of the moment, but he was a poor informant on past customs. When I attempted to get him to tell me about country matchmaking, his response was to condemn the practice as a bad old custom. My probings into other ways of life of the past met with similarly brief replies.

At first I thought that my inability to collect information from John Quin might be due to a defensive reluctance to talk about matters which he felt were no proper concern of the stranger. Later on, after the bonds of friendship had developed between us and he still showed no inclination to talk at length about the past, I concluded that for him the natural flow of life was the present. From the vantage of time and distance, however, I now appreciate that John Quin led me to a deeper understanding of Irish life than I could ever have obtained through direct and full replies to my queries. I was not at the time aware of his effect on my behavior and thinking. Nor do I believe that Quin's course of action was consciously planned, although I later learned he had a genuine concern about my welfare. Quin became my tutor of the proper ways of behavior, though I never thought of myself as pupil. He became my guide to the small farmer's world.

His own position was somewhat marginal since he had not been born in the townland but had come to it through marriage. He did not have a solid place among the elders, nor could he be counted as one of the young men because of his position as head of a household. But he was fully welcome in both groups, and I came to know their members as we made the almost nightly visits to the locale of their gatherings. Round the hearth of old man O'Donoghue's house gathered the responsible small farmers whose deliberations rendered the decisions and set the policy for Rynamona. Occasionally the young men and women gathered at Moroney's house for a songfest and dance, a country form of entertainment condemned by the stricter clergy who believed these gatherings might threaten the moral virtues of the young. It was there that I learned the Irish country dances and heard for the first time the poignant laments of the Irish soloist. To Oscar's, a genial country laborer of great physical prowess, came another category of men, those whose marginality excluded them from easy association with other small farmers. In these diversities there was a rich spread of the variety of Irish country life.

I took part in many of the activities connected with Quin's daily work, tending animals, crops, and field. But there were less-frequent events to which I was also introduced. For example, Quin and I gathered with the other men when the sheaves of wheat were brought to the steam-powered threshing machine. We took our stand at the winter sheep fair in Corofin and, after our animals were sold, joined in a communal drink with other men in the local pub. From the peat bog several miles away we hauled a creel of dried turf for the household hearth. And on Sundays we walked the mile or so to the parish church and waited outside with the other men until the pealing bell announced the beginning of Mass, when with the others we entered and took our seats.

Meanings were conveyed much more fully by the doing than by explanation. I learned to return the country greeting with an appropriate reply, to praise no human, animal, or object without appending the proper "God bless" to remove any suspicion of envy or evil intent, and to call out "God bless all here" as I crossed the threshold of a house.

My gradual acquisition of the small farmer's behavior pattern moved along smoothly enough. Once I had recognized some piece of behavior, I could then practice it. But in the early phases of learning, it was sometimes difficult to remember the appropriate behavior for each situation. Sometimes focus on one item obscured its connection with others. Style of walking can serve as an example. I was aware that the townsman walked differently from the countryman and that my American style was still another variation. My goal was to pick up the gait of the countryman and drop whatever I had learned about town walking. I thought that all I need do was observe the style of walking and then consciously imitate what I saw. What I didn't perceive at first, however, was that walking and talking were sequential rather than simultaneous. If you have something important to say, you come to a halt until the subject has been covered. When talking started and walking stopped, I would at first stand with the others only because I wanted to remain with the group, but not because I recognized the obligatory nature of this practice. After the insight came to me, I practiced the behavior. Returning one night from the men's gathering, I brought my two companions to a halt to initiate a topic for discussion. A few moments later we resumed our homeward course. The incident had not been momentous, but I felt a glow of triumph.

I should mention some of the difficulties, real or imagined, that accompanied the gradual acquisition of Irish thought and manners. A degree of anxiety always seemed to be present. There was the ever-present danger that an unforgivable offense might bring acceptance to an abrupt end. Warnings of this possibility had been given in graduate-school days, and there was sufficient distrust and insecurity among the Irish themselves that the belief had support in reality.

There was widespread acceptance of supernatural causes as explanations for even ordinary events, and this belief could work either to one's advantage or to one's disadvantage. I was always fortunate in this regard. For example, the first night after my arrival at Quin's house, one of his cows was ready to calve, and I was fully aware that a stillbirth might mean the end of my welcome. Luckily, the new calf was a healthy little animal, and I was told that I had brought good luck.

Identification of psychological states such as paranoia, depression, or hysteria is more difficult to make. We know that individuals do suffer stress in cross-cultural situations, but the separation of cultural factors from the idiosyncratic is not easy. I experienced the most severe stress at my second visit to the Quin household during the Christmas–New Year holiday season. There were clearly marked periods of inertia, and it became increasingly difficult for me to seek out others or to plan a departure. At the end of five weeks the unexpected arrival of an American colleague rescued me from the situation. I have sometimes wondered if this period was basically one of accelerated absorption into Irish culture.

Departure was always difficult. Somehow I had failed to learn the behavior which permitted one to disengage himself with a minimum of stress to his hosts and himself. But ignorance of the ritual of leavetaking was only part of the problem. Weeks of close association had forged emotional links of some strength, and these were not easy to break. Departures tended to be abrupt, unsatisfying, even touched with anger. There were elements of sadness, but the joy that came with escape and freedom was more powerful. Escape and freedom were only momentary realities, however, because the Queen's Hotel at Ennis was at the other end of the line.

Reentry into the life of the town was never easy. There was the need to reestablish relationships and to exchange the outlook and manner of the countryman for those of the townsman. The immediate transition was helped immensely by a hot bath, a change of costume, and a few stiff drinks.

During the late winter I made two additional excursions of several weeks each to another small farmer's household in a different part of the county. My objective was to gather comparative material and to extend my knowledge of the countryman's way of life. The contrast in life-style with Rynamona was not great, but I was made much more aware of the deep connections between life's happenings and supernatural powers. These periods of living in the country must also have affected my attitude toward the town, for the Queen's Hotel became home and refuge.

By early spring my entire effort was concentrated on research in the town. In addition to the usual pursuit of information, there were a number of affairs in which I was invited to participate. One of the more dramatic of these events was the week-long mission, or religious revival, which a local physician invited me to attend with him. I viewed the invitation as a friendly act on his part, but it might also have been interpreted as an interest in my conversion and later I learned that the good sisters of a nearby convent had offered prayers toward that end. These gestures toward me I took to be evidence of an increasing acceptance and understanding of my purposes, and my broadened activities also contributed to my progressive acquisition of an Irish perspective. These experiences might also be viewed as prologue to another event that spring which took place without warning and with unexpected consequences.

One midweek night I had talked late with one of the town's doctors about his family history, and it was past 1:00 A.M. when I returned to my hotel. The Queen's Hotel was situated on a corner where a narrow side street joined Abbey Street, which was barely wide enough for two cars to squeeze by each other. It was, however, a main artery lined on both sides with two- and three-story buildings and ended at the height of the street where the monument to Daniel O'Connell stood. The main door of the hotel faced up the street. On the side-street side there was a utility pole which also held a street light. It was a dark night with an overcast sky, and all the street lights had been off for more than an hour. If a guest of the hotel arrived after the main door had been locked, he rang the outside bell and in a few minutes the porter appeared and let him in.

This night was no different from the others and I had rung the bell and was waiting for the sound of footsteps in the hall to announce the coming of the porter. Suddenly a figure appeared from the side street and stopped about three feet away. My first thought was that this was a member of the Civic Guard who patrol the streets at night and take the names of those who are out after midnight. I greeted the presumed guard with a "Hello," but there was no reply and I thought the figure began to move toward me. My sense of danger and my reaction were almost simultaneous. I kicked with all my force at the midsection of the approaching threat. But there was no connection with anything solid. Instead my foot went through the air and I was nearly thrown off balance. The figure moved backward a foot or two, and I had the sense that I had repelled what was intended to be a friendly advance. The figure then disappeared. In the meantime I had reconnected with the bell and was pushing with all my might. In a few moments the porter arrived and opened the door. As I stepped quickly inside, somewhat shaken, I said in what I tried to make an off-hand manner, "I have just seen a ghost outside the hotel door."

The news of my adventure preceded me to the breakfast table, via the porter and his fellow hotel employees, I presume. I repeated the story several times to interested residents of the hotel, but the reaction was something for which I was not prepared. Several of the more permanent guests of the hotel began to relate supernatural experiences they had had. I learned that the hotel possessed quite a collection of ethereal inhabitants. One ghostly monk was such a persistent visitor to the room of a schoolteacher that she finally sought the assistance of the Franciscan fathers, whose spiritual powers relieved her of his nightly presence. One of the land commissioners kept a light burning throughout the night since the occasion when he had awakened to find a figure standing at the foot of his bed. More otherworldly but apparently harmless presences were recounted. It was presumed that the husband of the widow who ran the hotel, a man who had hanged himself some years earlier, was another of the nightly wanderers, but he was never specifically identified.

Word of my experience also passed into the town. I have no idea how extensive was the network of communication that carried the story. But a few days later a man, then unknown to me, sought me out in the hotel and confirmed for some, at least, the identity of the ghostly creature I had met. He said that some years previously a Tim Malloy had been kicked to death by a drunk along that side street. He himself had seen Malloy's apparition on a number of occasions in the vicinity of that street, so that undoubtedly it was Tim Malloy's spirit I had encountered.

Some of the aftereffects of the ghostly encounter should be mentioned. I found myself the center of favorable attention, for now I had had a legitimate Irish experience. Moreover, I needed to have no hesitancy in reporting all the details since the experience was wholly mine. Nor did I need to fear adverse repercussions about the legitimacy of the story, for I have never met any Irishman who scoffed at the possibility of supernatural occurrences. On subsequent occasions I asked questions about supernatural experiences with none of the constraints about invasion of privacy or broaching sensitive subjects that I had felt earlier. Now that I had been through this serious, even dangerous experience, I seemed to acquire a new status which entitled me to considerations not previously granted. Perhaps as a consequence or even because of other reasons less explicit, extensive changes in my relationships appeared along a broad spectrum of activity. Barriers no longer seemed formidable.

The ghostly incident raises two interesting questions, and I have puzzled over both. Many people asked, and so did I initially, a question which assumed an answer based on a certain premise of reality. Was there in fact a disembodied figure at the door of the Queen's Hotel on this particular night, or was I subject to an hallucination? If you are a transcendentalist, you can argue that possibly there was a spirit there, perhaps the lonely soul of Tim Malloy. If you are a materialist, your conclusion might well be that I was hallucinating, or that it would be possible to explain in quite another manner why it was that I thought I had seen a ghost. Neither transcendentalists nor materialists can ever provide that solid proof that would clinch the argument for their side. They can engage in the game of speculation, but after a while that too loses its novelty. Since no answer about the reality of the existence of the ghost can be given, the question is unanswerable. But there is a question that can be framed within the context of behavior and meaning that is worthy of our consideration.

I did not clearly formulate this second question until long after I had returned from Ireland. In fact, its explicit statement was delayed until I began to share, along with other colleagues, an interest in the cultural transformation which an anthropologist in the field undergoes. The phrasing of the problem has now been expanded to include his impact on and sequential modification of his relationships with members of the host culture as he comes increasingly to resemble them. The specific problem is how far my ghostly encounter may be considered as some index or measure of the extent to which I had absorbed the Irish perspective and been incorporated in Irish culture.

As we know, the capacity for supernatural experience as well as its form and content is culturally learned. The visions which the Sioux youth receives, including prayers, songs, and sacred designs, all fall within culturally known limits. The same statement can be made about ghostly and spiritual doings for other cultures. From this perspective it is quite irrelevant whether I actually did see a ghost or whether it was pure hallucination. The point is that I thought I saw one, and the Irish also believed so. Some months later, upon my return to the United States, I told my colleague, Arensberg, of this experience. His immediate reply was that the Irish had made me one of them. For a variety of reasons I disliked this idea, although I now realize I was responding to my biases. In fact, I might have been more willing to accept some mystic genetic linkage with Celtic ancestors as valid explanation. But anthropologists have long known that culture is learned and transmitted, not inherited.

But there is no known device that measures the degree of penetration into an alien culture. It is relatively easy to observe and conform to many items of behavior, but outward appearances may be largely superficial. Change would not be significant until it began to appear at the psychic level in the patterns of cognitive and emotional response and in the unconscious manifestations through dreams and visions.

We must also take account of the incorporative processes associated with interaction and group identification. Among the country people it was much easier to place an individual if you knew his kin connections, and on one occasion a whole set of these was invented for me. But when a half-serious effort was made to find me a suitable country girl as wife in the pre-Lenten matchmaking period, it was time to remember the principle about avoiding entangling sexual alliances and to take evasive action. The invitation to take part in the mission services might also be viewed as an incorporative act. The proselytizing was never insistent or offensive, so that polite joking about the matter could prevent any hard feelings. In these and other areas I maintained a polite aloofness which announced my intended separateness.

The direct participation in the supernatural world was, however, a quite different matter. I became the central character of an event in which my involvement was outside my conscious control. But if one were to choose an identification with powerful and positive overtones of acceptance, it would be difficult to find an area that was more deeply embedded in the Irish past and present than belief in the supernatural. Is it possible that unwittingly in this precipitous and dramatic fashion I had declared a fully Irish cultural perspective?

The question was asked more to evoke interest in a line of inquiry than to solicit a reply. Is it not likely that there is a regular course, a natural history, which each anthropologist experiences during his initial and perhaps even subsequent episodes of field work? Orderliness is further confirmed by some striking parallels between the *schema* of *rites de passage* and the introduction, involvement, and eventual withdrawal of a researcher in a culturally different environment. The time may have arrived when we are ready to undertake systematic observations of the processes of induction and involvement in another culture. We are far more sophisticated today about research in the field than we were in the early 1930's; and with the continuing increase of our self-conscious concern with what we do and its effects on ourselves and others, it should not be too long before such a venture is attempted.

REFERENCE

ARENSBERG, CONRAD M., AND SOLON T. KIMBALL. 1968. *Family and Community in Ireland.* 2nd ed.; Cambridge: Harvard University Press. Ch. 10.

14 / A Day at the Office

ANTHONY F. C. WALLACE

There is a contrapuntal relationship between the anthropologist's experience of his own culture and his analysis of an alien culture. The prime principles of the relationship are two. First—and this has been so long and so widely known as to be now a truism—to understand the structure of one's own civilization, one must know at first hand the structure of one exotic to it. Second—perhaps as long and widely known as the first principle, but less publicly acknowledged by anthropologists—to understand the functioning, or nonfunctioning, of another culture, one must have some intimate awareness of how one's own, or an aspect of it, functions or fails to function. Although these rules do not guarantee "objectivity," only by following both of them can one go beyond a superficial, predictively adequate, in only limited domains, behavioristic description of culture.

In my own work as an anthropologist, the relationship between these two perspectives has been relevant both to studies of the Iroquois and other northeastern Indians and to an interest in the theoretical problem of the organization of diversity. The aspect of American life which has been most significant is the business of bureaucratic administration. Like many academic people (despite our protestations of disdain for administrative work), I have devoted considerable time to being a minor bureaucrat. My bureaucratic career began when I became the administrative secretary of an interdisciplinary enterprise known as the Behavioral Research Council, at the University of Pennsylvania. Next I served as the Director of Clinical Research, at the Eastern Pennsylvania Psychiatric Institute. Currently I am chairman of the anthropology department at the University of Pennsylvania. And throughout this bureaucratic career, I have been a member of miscellaneous advisory and administrative committees in private and government agencies. Far from being a sacrifice, these experiences have been extremely valuable in giving me a view of how some administrative systems really do operate in our world. This awareness, sharpened I would like to think by anthropological training and some field work and historical study with American Indians, has in turn contributed to my scholarly work.

For instance, consider the Iroquois. I have been writing a life-and-times of Handsome Lake, the League chief who in 1799 became the "pagan prophet" of the Seneca tribe, and whose brother was Cornplanter, the political leader of the Allegheny band. Much of the subject matter is politics and administration, in the problems of which the Iroquois were and are intensely interested. There is an old saying among the Iroquois: "A chief must have a skin seven thumbs thick." The intent of the aphorism is obvious: A political leader cannot avoid raising issues and participating in decisions which arouse dissent; indeed, his very status makes him the target of jealous criticism, gossip, and intrigue. He cannot rely on status and authority to protect him; in the colonial period extreme pretensions to power were not seldom met by personal retaliation, including community-sanctioned assassination at the hands of kinsmen (an arrangement which aborted the blood feud). He *must* be able to put up with all the troubles of office without extreme discomfort; if he cannot, he suffers disabling pain, or he drinks, or he goes into rages, or his decisions will not be made "objectively" but with an eye to placating whomever he fears most or from whom he has the most to gain at the moment.

What can one say about this old Iroquois saying? On the one hand, it is patently not a parochial observation; administrators in other cultures, including our own, have the same technical problem of compromising their amour propre and prospect of gain for the sake of making ultimately wise decisions or recommendations on behalf of dependent individuals or a group. This much any administrator knows: handling one's own feelings is a problem. But perhaps for the Iroquois the task was especially agonizing and at the same time familiar. The Iroquois national character, as it appears in the historical record, required that men who had been raised to enjoy great parental indulgence and personal freedom would, in adult life, be extraordinarily stoic, self-sacrificing, and public-spirited. There was a pervasive cultural dialectic between dependency and self-indulgence on the one hand, and independence and responsibility on the other. One of its syntheses was the masking ritual; another was jealousy and witch-fear. For the chief, the need to suppress personal, egotistical motives and to put up with jealous criticism, in the interest of consensus and the welfare of the community, raised the dialectic to crisis. And so the culturally thematic prescription: A chief must have, not just a thick skin, but a skin seven thumbs thick—a mask all over his body.

How does all this apply to my subjects Handsome Lake and Cornplanter? The answer to this question is that looking at these men as generic administrators has been just as profitable to me as looking at them as carriers of a unique Iroquois culture. The cultural innovations proposed by both men were reasonable and understandable if one sees them as ad hoc policies suggested by thoughtful administrators trying to figure out how to cope with very practical problems. Their occasional and modest exploitation of opportunities for personal or family gain represents the classic compromise between conflicting interests. Even their depressions, witch-fears, and hallucinatory inspirations seem generally believable as the responses of officials harassed by insistent and contradictory demands from their constituencies. In other words, the cross-cultural perspective requires both a disciplined analysis of another culture in its own terms and an empathic understanding of constancies in human nature; and the latter depends radically on an awareness of one's own rich intracultural experience.

Personally, I found it difficult to write about Handsome Lake and Cornplanter before I had some administrative experience myself. Furthermore, I discovered that practical politicians and business executives who lived near the reservation and knew the historical records had a much surer instinct for relevant data, and a much closer empathy for the problems, than I had when I approached Iroquois politics as a relativistic ethnologist. All of which leads to the point that in the field neither interviewing nor participant observation is quite enough. One needs not merely to question, observe, and imitate; one needs to be able to feel that one has done a similar thing "for real" back home. In other words, in order to translate, one must speak both languages. It is probably one of the difficulties of the cross-cultural sciences in dealing with administrative behavior (if not with other domains) that so much of the descriptive work is done now by young graduate students who, like myself when I began Iroquois work, have not had much administrative experience and are ideologically or esthetically opposed to it anyway, and who therefore suffer from a trained incapacity to empathize with administrative roles.

THE GENERIC ADMINISTRATOR

As I am using the term here, "administrator" refers to a person who is responsible for coordinating the activities of a group (other than a household) committed to one or more goals. He does not necessarily set the goals or determine the procedures; goals and procedures are not necessarily shared by all members of the group involved; he does not necessarily have coercive authority; and he may come to the role by any one of a number of "political" processes.

The bureaucrat is one kind of administrator. Bureaucracies began in earnest with the urban revolution and have proliferated in urban cultures ever since. They are characterized by a complex hierarchical authority structure and by the fact that the bureaucrat is a professional who depends on his administrative job for all, or a substantial part, of his income.

But nonbureaucratic administrators are important in pre-urban cultures and probably can be identified in every human society, even the most primitive. In simple cultures, the role is occasional, part-time, and limited in scope by the requirements of the task. Perhaps the oldest administrative roles are those of manager of religious ceremonies and director of communal hunting groups and war parties. No doubt of similar antiquity are a variety of positions associated with community councils: chairmen, official speakers, keepers of records, and the like, who coordinate the group process of communication and decision.

Among the Iroquois, a neolithic people, communities ranged in population from a few dozen to about a thousand; the Allegheny Seneca, with whom Handsome Lake and Cornplanter were affiliated, amounted to four hundred people in the period 1798–1815. The number of administrative roles in this population was very large in relation to the population size. There was a community council, consisting of from one to four males, chiefs from each of the eight matrilineal sibs (a sib could have multiple chiefs), the total roster averaging in number from about sixteen to about twenty. One of the men regularly acted as chairman. He called meetings, prepared the agenda for meetings, officially welcomed visitors, managed the course of discussion, and between meetings handled communications with whites and neighboring Indian communities. Two young men were deputized by the council to serve as police to ensure compliance with council resolutions against the use of alcohol. From two to four senior women were recognized as "female chiefs" and acted as liaison between the council on the one hand, and the warriors and women on the other. Handsome Lake, a member of the Allegheny council, also served as one of the forty-nine chiefs of the League, whose council fire was at Buffalo Creek, another reservation; and after his visions in 1799, he was the leader of a religious movement. He in turn used his nephew Blacksnake and two or three other young male kinsmen as deputies and advisers. On the religious side, there were four religious chiefs, a man and woman from each moiety, who were responsible for the timing of the ceremonies on the annual calendar. And there were sixteen "faithkeepers," a man and a woman from each sib, who managed the practical affairs of the ceremonies: cooking food, cleaning the longhouse, notifying participants, and so on. There were at least half a dozen medicine societies each of which had an official responsible for the care of ceremonial paraphernalia and for convening members. There were perhaps a dozen war captains, who had been in the past, and potentially would be in the future (as in the War of 1812), responsible for leading both war parties and diplomatic missions concerned with issues of war and peace. And finally, in each sib, there was at least one matron who headed a distinguished lineage and on occasion was responsible for calling together the female heads of families and nominating chiefs. All in all, there were on the order of seventy part-time administrative positions to be filled in a community whose eligible adult population was about two hundred. Even allowing for some overlap in personnel, it is evident that between a quarter and one-third of the adult population was *at any one time* filling an administrative role. Evidently during an individual's lifetime, his chances of being an administrator were better than even.

Viewed from this vantage point, one peculiarity of modern urban industrial society may be that an extraordinarily *small* proportion of the population is

involved in administrative roles, despite the number and size of the bureaucracies. Alienation and antiestablishmentarianism may, paradoxically, be the
product of a situation common to advanced civilizations in which a few
full-time administrative specialists take over roles hitherto played part-time by
the mass of the population. If this is so, then the administrative experience is
becoming rarer and rarer, and whatever human insights and satisfactions go
with it are decreasingly available to the average citizen.

What is "the administrative experience"? I believe that it has certain generic
features which pervade the diverse forms it takes from culture to culture. In
our own time, unhappily perhaps, both the academic and the literary community have been preoccupied with other interests and there is relatively little
serious interest in the role of the administrator. Academic people tend to
deplore administrative work as an unworthy distraction from higher callings;
to popular intellectuals, "bureaucracy" is an obscene word. Few serious works
of fiction, apart from C. P. Snow's, and some war stories, like *The Caine
Mutiny,* even attempt to deal centrally with the administrator's problems of
administration; in most novels about administrative types, the administrator's
work life is scantily analyzed while his other, "personal" life is explored at
length. (This may actually be in part because administrative work really *is*
regarded by modern authors as more sacred, and more taboo—hence more
dirty—than other activities.)

One approach to characterizing the kind of thing an administrator does is
to list activities, such as consulting with other people, planning actions, making
decisions, analyzing why things don't work the way they should, organizing
communication networks, recruiting and discharging personnel, calculating
"budgets" of money, time, resources, and so on. But such lists are fuzzy at the
edges and convey little information. One can also point out that, far from being
a mechanical sort of activity in which the administrator automatically responds to standard signals with a signature, a rubber stamp, a yes or no, a
thumbs-up or thumbs-down kind of response to initiatives from the helpless,
administrative work is mostly taken up with figuring out what to do in ambiguous situations. Decisions must be made on a diversity of questions, and the
considerations that go into many of these decisions are complex. Moreover,
the emotional issues raised by these questions, both for the administrator and
those affected, are deep. In a bureaucratic system, the social structure constantly has to be redesigned and decentralized; and the administrator must
continuously find for himself anew the narrow path that (hopefully) will run
between overinvolvement with those affected by his work and depersonaliza-
tion and withdrawal.

But these generalities still convey little. My images of administrative work
are personal, and it is really these that are first evoked when I try to understand
someone like Cornplanter or Handsome Lake. The abstractions come later. So
let me try to describe the kind of administrative day which is my touchstone
for recognizing other people's.

A TYPICAL DAY

One way of describing administrative activity is to make a diary. In diary form a day may look something like this:

10:05–10:10	Phone call from National Institute of Mental Health concerning site visit to Los Angeles.
10:10–10:20	Coffee.
10:20–11:00	Talk with first graduate student about his academic and personal problem.
11:00–11:20	Sorting out the mail, which consists of (1) letters letting me know of job openings, (2) book advertisements, and (3) my pay check. Write two letters: one to a publisher declining to edit a general text in anthropology, and the second to the secretary of the American Anthropological Association concerning his forthcoming visit to discuss locating the editorial offices of the association at the University of Pennsylvania.
11:20–11:30	Talk with second graduate student concerning permission to audit my course.
11:30–11:35	Phone call from Rochester asking whether our department has candidate for job in anthropological linguistics; make two suggestions.
11:35–12:00	Coffee break.
12:00–1:30	Faculty meeting with sandwiches and coffee. Complaints from conservative wing about recent firing of departmental secretary; present reasons. Discussion of problems presented by increasing pressure of undergraduate enrollment, both in undergraduate and mixed graduate-undergraduate courses. Am urged to get money from dean for additional appointments.
1:45–2:00	Talk with third graduate student about academic and personal problems.
2:00–2:15	Call home.
2:15–2:45	Read galley proofs of paper.
2:45–3:00	Headache; take aspirin; coffee.
3:00–3:30	Sort through notes to compile bibliography for course.
3:30–4:30	Discussion with group interested in research on calcium metabolism in relation to psychopathology.
4:30–4:40	Write letter recommending appointment of husband and wife to faculty next year.
4:40–5:00	Talk with fourth graduate student concerning her plans for dissertation.

This one-day diary is obviously both terse and a small sample. It would have to be continued over the course of a year in order to yield data for analysis of the full administrative process involved in my particular job. But its terseness leads to the point of relevance here. Each of the entries refers to an event, or events, in which the overt communicative behaviors (talking and writing) are merely selective responses to rather convoluted and sometimes emotionally charged cognitive operations. The events float past one's eyes rather like a procession of icebergs; the objectively perceptible part of each rests on a hidden mass many times as large.

Take, for example, the talk with the first student. He is in his first year of graduate study and has made an appointment with my secretary for 10:30. He comes in a bit early and I see him early because if I start to go through the mail first I may have to stop in the middle of dealing with something brought up by the mail. He is a third-year dropout from a graduate physics program, which, I recall from an earlier talk, he entered because his physicist father forced him to. He has been having major problems of identification and has been in psychotherapy. But he is bright, has a good deal of scientific training, and if he works through his problems may become a productive anthropologist; it's worth a chance. He comes in and sits down and talks about the problems. It boils down to a request for a leave of absence from graduate school next year because of a complex of difficulties: money (he has no scholarship or fellowship); trouble in some of his courses; and the emotional pressures involved in psychotherapy. He also wants to engage me in philosophical discussion of the meaning of religious experience and the role of religion in human evolution. I decide to avoid this because the undertone is a request that I play some ill-defined sort of father-therapist role and I have a personal policy of not mixing this kind of thing with administrative relationships. So I slide out of this discussion but agree to recommend a leave so that he can sort himself out. He asks whether I would talk to him some time about his religious theories and I agree without much enthusiasm. He gets up to leave and I walk to the door and tell my secretary to type up the form letter to the graduate school recommending the leave of absence. All sorts of associations are being evoked while the overt discussion is going on: a kind of grim annoyance at the fact that the students who fail to get Ph.D.'s generally do so not because of lack of intellectual ability but because of complicated emotional reasons which are partly the result of problems they bring with them and partly the result of some inadequacy in our own training program; recollections of my own time as a graduate student; comparisons of this student with other refugees from the hard sciences and from practical professions like medicine, law, and engineering; curiosity about how his father feels about all this; speculation about the relative amounts of damage done by real social and economic deprivation on the one hand, and an indifferent indulgence on the other; uncertainty as to whether it would have been wiser to refuse the leave and demand that he shape up or get out. And I wonder what *he* thinks: how much nervousness does he feel in talking to me about an issue absolutely crucial to his career and his identity; whether he is hurt because I don't want to discuss religion with him; whether he realizes why. . . .

All this is going on very fast during the interview, and at odd moments later in the day, and occasionally in later days and weeks, the discussion returns to mind. It contributes to my own growing conviction that the conventional system of graduate education is incredibly inefficient and wasteful and that redesign is needed, not so much in the direction of staff becoming parental surrogates, as in presenting a clear program for training along lines specialized for each student and with a manifest intention on the part of the department to get every student through to the Ph.D., once admitted, rather than regarding the process as a means of weeding out unworthy candidates. But this is not the way in which all of my colleagues define the problem, so that there is in the background always the somewhat murky chronic political-intellectual struggle over what sort of reform of curriculum, examinations, and administration would be most desirable.

The point of presenting all these reflections—which could, after all, be greatly expanded anyway—is not so much to reveal their particular content as to illustrate a characteristic process. The administrative day consists of a series of such transactions, rarely of a final or climactic kind, and of varying emotional intensity. After—or rather during—an exchange of information, verbal or written, there is a complex internal process of feeling and thinking about the implications of both the communication and the possible responses the administrator can make. His official, overt response alternatives are apt to be limited, but the complexity of the considerations involved in choosing the response is large. They involve matters of personal motive, the articulation of policies, and social relationships which *must* be brought into awareness each time if responses are not to be in error. The concept of error is essential even if it is ambiguous. Any old administrative response will not do: there may be several "wrong" responses, and there may be a considerable number of more or less "right" responses. The rightness of a response can be estimated in advance less by its conformity with standard operating procedure, although this is something of a guide, than by its anticipated effects. And the effect, in general, should be to coordinate the actions of several different people in the direction of a goal or goals within the group's repertoire. In effect, a "right" decision organizes diversity toward the accomplishment of objectives meaningful to all participants. But the complexity of the task often far exceeds any reasonable advance specification of which goals or procedures or personnel to involve.

A "PRIMITIVE" ADMINISTRATOR

Let us now look at the experience of a "primitive" administrator. The person is Cornplanter, a Seneca Indian resident at a town on the upper Allegheny River, in the year 1794. Cornplanter had been a war captain during the American Revolution, fighting on the side of the British, and was now the speaker and chairman of the village council. On July 30 and 31, the village was visited by John Adlum, then engaged in surveying ceded lands for a land speculator who wanted to obtain clearance and protection for his surveying parties from the local Indians. Cornplanter's first day of the visit, insofar as Adlum recorded it in his journal, went as follows:

July 30, morning   Cornplanter (previously informed of Adlum's pending arrival) collects armed warriors and chiefs on bank of river for ceremonial welcome to visitor; stations warriors, dressed and painted "as if for war" in a receiving line; gives instructions for firing salutes when visitor's boat arrives.

July 30, about noon Cornplanter shouts order to fire salute.

Cornplanter and other chiefs shake hands with visitor, greet him, escort him to council house at once; Cornplanter sits on his right.

Cornplanter lights pipe at council fire, puffs, hands it on to visitor, who hands it on to his left, and so on around circle of chiefs.

Cornplanter asks visitor what news he has; accepts credentials (Secretary of War's letter and commission from governor of Pennsylvania) from visitor, breaks seal on letter, returns it to be read aloud and translated by interpreter.

Cornplanter stands up and reproves hostile young Indians who fart loudly, interrupting the reading of the letter.

July 30, afternoon   After Adlum completes reading, Cornplanter asks if he has anything more to communicate.

After Adlum explains his surveying mission, Cornplanter informs him the council will talk about it with him the next morning.

Adlum is housed in Cornplanter's house.

Council deliberates, with Cornplanter as chairman, the answer.

In this ceremonial welcome to a distinguished visitor, Cornplanter as council chairman and speaker is the master of ceremonies. The ritual as performed under his direction follows Iroquois standard operating procedure in a general way. But Cornplanter does have to make some independent decisions, and these are dictated by the peculiar and ambiguous political situation in which Adlum and the Indians are working. The decision to assemble the warriors in line for a ceremonial salute is not *de rigueur;* and the insulting reception at the council house (using, however, a standard gesture of disrespect) violates Cornplanter's and the council's policy, and he and others publicly reprimand the young men. The general circumstances which Cornplanter has to take into account (and which are expressed clearly in the exchange of speeches between him and Adlum on the following two days) are that the United States and the Indians of Ohio are at war. The policy of the Allegheny band, led by Cornplanter, has been to cooperate with the Americans by trying to persuade the western Indians to make peace and at the same time to persuade the Americans to make various concessions to Indian demands. But this policy is not unanimously supported by the young men at Allegheny or the other reservations;

many of them want to fight the Americans. Cornplanter therefore has to coordinate in some way the interests of the Americans, the policy of his own group, and the anti-American sentiments of many of the young people: the show of force for the salute (eighty shots were fired from guns loaded with ball, some of them passing a few feet away from Adlum) to demonstrate Seneca readiness to fight; the assembling of the whole group an effort both to impress the visitor and to induce consensus in policy; and the reproof of the disrespectful young men necessary in order to continue good personal relations with Adlum. The record is certainly not full enough, even with Cornplanter's speeches of the next day, to validate much more than that these considerations had to be behind his actions. But even this much reveals Cornplanter as the usual harassed administrator trying to find a way of serving everybody's interests, if possible, within the constraints of existing custom, if possible.

But he was willing to recommend changes in custom if custom blocked policy. For instance, the effectiveness of Cornplanter's demands that the Americans adjust certain treaty terms in the Indians' favor depended in part on Indian willingness to support the Americans if necessary with a force of warriors. At a certain meeting the Indian women undermined the credibility of this implied promise by refusing their consent, which was customarily needed before war parties would go out, since a venture undertaken without their consent would be ill-fated. Cornplanter, Adlum noted,

eventually got tired of the obstinacy of the Woemen and to do away [with] the superstition of the men respecting it, rose and made a speech against superstition, he called it folly and nonsense, and was surprised that men of understanding, had so long submitted to this ancient custom handed down to them by their ancestors, and now was the time, for men to decide for themselves and take this power from the woemen, —He was grieved to see their nation divided on a point where they should be unanimous. . . .

CONCLUSION

The methodological procedure which I have been trying to make explicit is perhaps intuitively obvious, but it is so easily taken for granted that its practice often escapes critical review. In order to recognize and understand the behavior of a person acting in an alien culture, one must at first—and will perforce even after long acquaintance—use experience in one's own culture for comparison. And to translate depends on the assumption that there is a generic kind of behavior common to the two (if not to mankind). To assume that a culture is understandable only in its own terms would, if carried to its logical conclusion, require that ethnography be written only in the native language. Even the effort of "cognitive anthropology" to understand the thought processes employed in other cultures does assume the possibility of translation. I have used the notion of administrative work as an example from my own experience: I can talk sensibly in English about the behavior of a Seneca Indian because English speakers recognize in his behavior the lineaments of a pan-cultural role.

But I chose administrative work for my example, rather than some other, because I have an interest in the subject for its own sake, and am planning a book on administrative structures, which have been largely neglected in anthropological writing. One of the main features of the contemporary world is the widespread dissatisfaction, most loudly expressed by students, with established administrative structures, particularly with bureaucracies. This discontent comes at a time when, because of the proliferation of technology, the rise in population, and the concentration of people in cities, bureaucracy is an increasingly necessary form of social organization. It is inconceivable, for example, that a city could exist without extremely reliable and rapid transportation and communication systems to service the distribution of water, food, medical care, fire-fighting equipment, manufacturing supplies and products, education, entertainment, and so on and so forth. These systems cannot function without the organized efforts of many people, and the form which that organization takes is called bureaucracy. But today horizontal ideology—the ideology of left and right—is becoming trivial, and the intellectual conflict increasingly focuses on the problems of vertical ideology—the ideology of administration—with positions ranging from a sort of administrative nihilism to a concern with the perfection of management. In other words, the interface between bureaucracy and its clientele, rather than the interface between classes per se, is increasingly perceived as the major problem which does not disappear under *any* horizontal ideological system, but in fact increases steadily with technology, urbanism, and population, in both capitalist and socialist systems. In this world setting, anthropologists may be able to make some contribution in the way of description, analysis, and design of administrative structures.

At least this weary chairman hopes so.

15 / Ambiguation and Disambiguation in Field Work

MARTIN G. SILVERMAN

Having rediscovered the ancient truth that a sense of transcendent virtue can be engendered by the public confession of sin, anthropologists have been moved to bare, in print, their lesser doubts and blunders. I join the chorus to promulgate and demonstrate two simple and well-known points: First, that the data don't speak to you unless you know where to kick them. And second, that within and behind those tedious, ethnographic one-liners—the X's are patrilocal, the Y's plant taro, the Z's appease their ancestors—there is often more than meets the eye.

It is rare these days for anyone to go to the field with an anthropological *tabula rasa*. Chances are that some research has been done in the area, either in the society directly under scrutiny or in related societies. To some degree one knows what to expect and perhaps more surely what *not* to expect. The hors d'oeuvre tray of ethnographic wisdom and paradigmatic examples (such as the Nuer and the Kachin), from which graduate students have been compelled to sample liberally, serves a vital function: it acquaints one with the general range of variation in the institutions and beliefs of human society and culture and with ways of studying them (see Kuhn, 1962). Even in setting out for "the heart of darkness" without a hypothesis worthy of the name, one has internalized much of the range of variation and the categories which have made human behavior intelligible to his forbears—kinship, marriage, religion, environment, and slightly less commonsensically, perhaps, descent system, alliance, liminal period, carrying capacity.

This intellectual equipment can expand rather than narrow the field worker's world. A single observed behavioral act can have a variety of anthropological interpretations. A single formulated regularity can fit into a variety of patterns. Like any puzzle-solving activity, field work is a process of disambiguation—or better, perhaps, of both ambiguation *and* disambiguation. The process should be both continuous and explicit, because each hypothesis or line of interpretation (and the good field worker always tries out several alternative ones) calls for new observations and questions to confirm or invalidate. (Thus the three-months rule: If I only had three months more . . .) The interpretation in fact often goes on for the rest of one's professional life in one fashion or another—not only because one tries to get as much mileage as he can out of a period of field work, but also because new thoughts or new approaches start one moving in a different direction, assuming that one has a reasonably open mind.

Ethnography is very much a practice of creating a picture which disambiguates behavior. Things have a "place" within the interpretation—not that the things are not, on the surface, conflicting. There is always apparently conflicting data, such as "contradictory" statements by individuals or variant practices. These are the stuff that ethnography is made of, and coping with them explains in part the satisfaction that a field worker feels. For what one tries to do is harmonize the apparent conflicts and contradictions, if only to make of conflict or contradiction the key to the puzzle.

But certain things often do not seem to fit—anomalous behaviors or regularities which are ethnographic irritants. At the level of a single observation (a person screaming in a time of religious repose) or even a regularity (chieflike functionaries in an otherwise egalitarian system), one may "solve" the problem by ascribing it to something which is really outside one's operational frame of reference. For example, one may invoke deviance (thus using personality, in a study not really dealing with personality), or change (in a study not really dealing with change). In rare cases the anomaly may lead one to scrap the frame of reference for another one. In others, it may be suppressed, repressed, or honestly consigned to a footnote. More generally one is led not to scrap the framework but to reformulate it, or at least tinker with it, so that the recalcitrant datum is not left completely uninterpreted.

My major irritant has been postmarital residence, a subject in which I have no interest per se, but that only makes matters worse. It has found something of a place in a line of interpretation, but only after I learned, the hard way, the verities I have enunciated. I will now try to reconstruct the process.

THE SETTING AND THE PROBLEM

About two thousand people live on Rambi Island, which is in the Northern Division of Fiji. Rambi was settled in 1945 by the indigenous community of Ocean Island, a part of the Gilbert and Ellice Islands colony. The native name of Ocean Island is Banaba, and thus its people are known as Banabans. The Banabans, when they moved to Rambi, were accompanied by a number of Gilbertese and a few Ellice Islanders, who were married to them or were friends. The Banabans speak Gilbertese but regard themselves as a distinct people.

Postmarital residence is not one of their major worries. Their primary public concern is getting what they think is rightfully theirs. Ocean Island is very rich in deposits of phosphate of lime, and outside interests have mined the island since 1900. The Banabans have been receiving some return for the use of their lands from the outset, but from their point of view, the return has been pitifully and fraudulently small. They maintained land rights on Ocean Island when they moved to Rambi, and the interconnected issues of having their rights to the phosphate recognized and of achieving the autonomy and well-being of Rambi Island are their dominant public concerns. (I will give no more of the history here; the interested reader may consult Silverman, 1971.)

My interest in the island was excited by H. E. Maude, of the Department of Pacific History at the Australian National University. Maude had been close to the Banaban situation in his days as a member of the British colonial service in the Gilberts, and with his wife had written an excellent reconstruction of traditional Banaban social organization (Maude and Maude, 1932). I knew Maude at the university, where I was a Fulbright student in 1960–1961, diffusely interested in culture change. I had become fascinated with the study of relocated communities as a problem in change, and the Fulbright people agreed to let me go to Rambi. That visit lasted from June to November of 1961. I was to return to the island for two longer periods later. After some traveling and graduate study at the University of Chicago, I was back from June 1964 to February 1965, and after a critical reprise in Chicago, again on Rambi from June to December of 1965.

The initial five months on Rambi in 1961 one might kindly call a reconnaissance. My material on descent, kinship, and residence was mixed up with everything from the way taro is planted to the ages of schoolchildren. I was an ethnographic vacuum cleaner. Fortes' charming term "eclectic functionalist" (Fortes, 1969, p. 48) might characterize my orientation. But I did have as an important aid Oliver's (1958) distinction between three aspects of behavior: the normative (what should be), the suppositional (what people think actually is), and the historical (what the observer finds actually is). I did not write an account using these categories, but they were, and still are, important in my thinking.

My only anthropological training up to that point was an undergraduate major, a summer's stay in the Andes, and some study in Canberra. I was acquainted with some of the items on the hors d'oeuvre tray, but not enough. My intellectual passion as an undergraduate had been concepts of space and time and, secondarily, culture change. It turned out that, to make some initial sense out of the Banaban situation, what I needed to know most about was kinship, and that is what I knew least about. My brief initial stay was not a total disaster because the Banabans engage in a good deal of self-ethnography.

It was not until I returned and discussed my material with the anthropologists at the Australian National University and then went on to Chicago that I realized that the Banabans' phosphate mine had within it an ethnographic gold mine, as it were. At that point in anthropological history the subject of bilateral descent was very à la mode; it began, and still is, an ethnographic irritant, for reasons which Schneider (1965) has made clear.

When I arrived on Rambi, the Banabans were in a state of concern over their descent system, and that is how I got drawn into looking at it. Quite early on it seemed that among the Banabans, both in traditional times and in the present, there were bilateral descent groups (groups of people descended from a common ancestor through both male and female lines), or bilateral descent "somethings" (because often when you went looking for the "groups" that people talked about, you could not find them). People spoke of something that sounded like an uxorilocal rule or emphasis in residence (a man, after marriage, going to live in his wife's household). The descent system seemed to demand study because the Banabans seemed so concerned about it, and the Maudes, in their 1932 paper, had referred to a *patrilineal* descent system. I was little concerned with the postmarital-residence question, but the statements which people made seemed also to contradict the Maudes' account, which spoke of patrilocal residence (specifically, a couple lived in the husband's hamlet). I did some limited census work for the current situation on Rambi, which showed that most married couples were not living with their parents. But in the relatively small number of cases where a child-in-law seemed to be living in a parent-in-law's household, it was the son-in-law in about three times as many cases as it was the daughter-in-law. But where it was the son-in-law, I heard no remarks that the behavior was incorrect.

One of my problems was to harmonize my information with the Maudes'. The possibilities which suggested themselves were that (1) I was misconstruing the information I was getting; (2) I was getting deviant information; (3) things had changed; or (4) the Maudes had misconstrued the situation. I cannot go into the details of how some parts of this problem were ultimately solved. Suffice it to say that I invoked factors of succession and authority within the descent unit, and the special position of the Maudes' major informants, to explain why those informants would have made patrilocal statements. Why specifically uxorilocal statements should be made now (or in the past) was still an open question. Why not statements that the couple lived with either or neither set of parents?

It seemed to me, perhaps naively, that a residence rule which stipulated residence with one side or the other side was somehow out of gear with a bilateral system. It seemed to contradict the logic. Having had an undergraduate flirtation with ecology, I tried to think out ecological explanations of a uxorilocal emphasis for Ocean Island and for Rambi, but they did not work. There were water-caves and wells on Ocean Island which some said women inherited, but for a variety of reasons that was not enough to make me comfortable about reducing the puzzle. If I had known better, I would have sought a common explanation to account both for the idea of uxorilocal residence *and* for the association of women with wells and water-caves, but I did not know better.

At Chicago I worked most closely with David Schneider, and my interests in social structure shifted so that they were, in retrospect, more consonant with my earlier interests in space and time. I became interested in social structure as a system of symbols and meanings. *Meaning* became the key term, rather than the concrete arrangements of people on the ground. I learned about the problems involved in the analysis of bilateral systems, and the symbolic framework was especially attractive because it helped make better sense out of my Banaban data. I had begun to sort out the kinship material in Australia, but I was there only a short time after the first period of field work. The things tied up with descent and kinship among the Banabans seemed more important as symbols, as loci of meaning, than as continuing, functioning, on-the-ground social groups.

I noted above some preliminary census work. With the symbolic focus, the question of deriving a statistic of instances of uxorilocal residence versus instances of other kinds of residence, for example, receded in importance before the question of what residing with particular people meant to the members of the society. I did not abandon the more on-the-ground concerns, however, and in early 1965, with the cooperation of the Banaban Trust Fund Board and the Rambi Island Council, I supervised a sociological census covering practically everyone on the island. By now I know the complexity of using such data, and it is impossible for me to make statements from the data until the computer and I have worked out some of our residual problems.

Thus far, one of the mistakes in the census forms has provided one of the most useful insights. In spite of what I thought were reasonably complete instructions to our local census takers, a number of people, sometimes whole nuclear families, were listed as belonging to more than one household. In some cases a couple would be listed by the parents of both man and wife. I had expected to find "households" as exclusive, unambiguous units, but the Banabans would not support my fantasy. People seemed to be moving about a good deal.

PHASE 1: OBLIGATION

I have oversimplified somewhat. At the time I returned to the field in 1964, I had yet to complete unscrambling the question of residence as a problem in the concrete location of concrete people from residence as a problem in meaning. Thus in presenting some extracts from my field notes, to show the relationship between data and interpretation, I can group together those from the 1961 trip and the first return in 1964. The "extracts" are either paraphrases or direct quotations. I will have to beg the reader's forebearance concerning the people who gave the information, since describing them and their circumstances would require a very long paper in itself.

I should note here that, during the 1961 trip, I first worked with a Banaban interpreter-assistant, and toward the end of the stay my knowledge of the language advanced comparatively rapidly. I found on my return in 1964 that although I had forgotten some vocabulary, my command of the grammar was much better than when I had left in 1961. I still worked with an assistant, but in Gilbertese.

I first set foot on Rambi on June 21, 1961. Intimations of my problem were not long in coming.

1. June, 23, 1961. *Eriu:* "In the old days, a couple lived with the mother's side. Now they live where they want. This is a change."

2. July 4, 1961. *Tito:* "How much time the couple stays in the wife's house [where they go after the marriage is consummated in the groom's house], or again in the husband's house depends on them, the families, and circumstances. If someone is sick at the wife's house, for example, they may stay there to care for him."

3. July 11, 1961. *Iotua* [my assistant]: "On the first night of the wedding, at midnight, the couple goes to the boy's family's house. After a few days, they go to the girl's. Unless you build your own house, you have to live with your wife's family. You are glad to have daughters—then the sons [that is, the sons-in-law] come in. Your father-in-law speaks to your wife about your work. He can't ask you for too much—then you might pick up and depart."

4. August 4, 1961. *Te buraen riri* (The man follows the woman). In the Gilberts, the woman is the traveler. [This note of mine relates, I think, to something of a challenge I had had from the Banaban Adviser, the local British official, who was familiar with the Gilberts. He told me that there was a phrase about residence that the Banabans had, which was different from that in the Gilberts, and he invited me to find it out. Operating on the principle that the easiest way to get information is to ask people, I asked someone, and he came forth with the phrase, *te buraen riri,* which contrasts with the expression used in the Gilberts. The latter indicates residence with the husband's family. I do not know whether I knew it then, but the phrase literally means "the strands of the skirt."]

5. August 25, 1961. *Iotua:* "Even here [on Rambi], a man goes to live with his wife. He may visit his own family. He especially goes to live with her if she is the only child in the family: the house will be hers. Going to the woman seems to be the only old custom that sticks. Now, some parents want to see their children on their own. A man might live at his wife's house and not do any work! The man and his wife may quietly decide between themselves to go out on their own. If both families agree, they will help them in building their house. If a man has three daughters, people say he is lucky— he will have three sons, too. But if he has only sons, they say he is unlucky. They will all go away. When a man lives with his wife's family, he works for that side."

6. [Unforgivably, no specific date and no speaker, but probably September 1961.] "When the young couple go back to the girl's side [after a wedding is over], the boy's family try to get food and lots of fish. It has to be taken to the girl's side with beef and sacks of rice, flour, and sugar. [Perhaps on my query:] The girl's side bring nothing to the boy's side. He feeds her. She is only a girl, and cannot cut copra and so forth."

Most of these observations were made while more general subjects were under discussion. In the second period of field work, having at least become somewhat interested in the matter, I was asking more direct questions.

7. [I recall one pertinent conversation which I think is from the second field-work period (1964–1965), and which I know is in my notes, but my fast survey of them did not turn it up. Kawate was chatting with me, and I mentioned "American custom" as one in which the married couple do not trouble themselves with economic obligations to their parents. "In that way the man cheats," Kawate observed comically. "He sleeps with the girl, and he eats too (that is, concerns himself with his and his wife's food, but not that of her family)."]

8. June 21, 1964. [I was at a meal at a church meetinghouse, and some of us were talking about the order in which people ate.] Ioteba noted that the old men ate first. Ioteba and Tokamaen, in conversation with me, said that this was the custom: the old men first, the preparers of the meal last. In the old days in the traditional meetinghouse, only the men spoke. The women ruled the household. And later, I was talking with Ioteba in his house, and he said that in marriage the man is the traveler. He mentioned *te buraen riri.*

9. July 9, 1964. [I was talking with Barereka about marriage procedures.] He turned to a woman whom I thought to be his Gilbertese wife and asked her assent to the point that in the Gilberts the man leads the woman, whereas here the woman's place is, as she put it, their true place. I asked him why this was so. He replied that he had stayed awhile in the Gilberts, and according to what he saw and heard, it was because among the Gilbertese the woman was the worker, whereas among the Banabans, it was the man. The wife might agree to some of his money going to his father, but it might all stay with her family.

10. August 15, 1964. [I was going over some kin terms with a young married friend, Tane, who with his wife and child lived most of the time with his parents.] He said that he calls Natua [his wife's stepfather] and Nei Kaiamakin [his wife's mother] "my father" and "my mother." When he goes to their house, he said, it is just like home because they are good to him. He has to work all the time according to the custom, but they let him rest.

11. October 2, 1964. [A conversation with Y, on pregnant women, went on to the following.] "The woman runs the house," he said, "and you have to give the money to her." "Why?" I asked. "It is the custom," he answered. Some men keep the money and drink. He is lucky with his wife, because she is kind to his mother [who lives with them]. He would like to travel, but this is difficult because he is caring for his mother. His younger brother married a Rambi girl, and relying on him to take care of their mother is difficult because his younger brother has his own wife's family to worry about. "If your wife only wants to give your money to her parents, it's up to her. If she agrees to give some to your parents, that's all right."

I note in passing (although I did not realize it at the time) that all the statements I have on this specific subject up to this point came from men.

When I returned to Chicago, I wrote a 32-page, single-spaced paper on the relations of solidarities and symbols in Banaban organization. I considered the family, the church, the village, and the community as a "national" solidarity.

Of the family I said the following—based on information additional to the extracts presented above.

In the family, authority is generally expressed by senior over junior generations. Grandparents are expected to lavish kindness on their grandchildren, but must be respected, rather than respect. Parents are spoken of as "working for" their children when young, and when the children get older, they are supposed to work for their parents, "to repay the debt." There is some element of delayed return, but continuing cooperation and love are expected. A person should work for and respect his spouse's parents, but because they *are* his spouse's parents, not because they are "my father" and "my mother": which for some people is a sufficient explanation of the way they should treat their parents; "After all, he's my father!" After marriage, the man is under a particular obligation to work for his wife's father. People say that "in the old days," after marriage, a man went to live in his wife's household. A male child is the worker, a female child merely a helper around the house. The male has less of a debt to repay, as he has already worked for his father. The debt of the female child is repaid by her husband.

But both son- and daughter-in-law should recognize the authority of their parents-in-law. At the same time, the husband has authority over the wife, except, in one conception, with regard to money. He should give his wife his wages, and if she wants to give them to her parents, it's up to her. A man considers himself lucky if his wife favors his parents, whom he is expected to favor. His heart, as it were, is in his family, not his wife's family.

I presented the question of postmarital residence in the context of obligation: of a woman to her father, of a man to his wife and to his father-in-law. I wrote the paper as a way of getting my thoughts rather than my notes in order. Note in particular how I overstated the case. The various hedges and qualifications which the Banabans had in fact made were screened out of my mind. I was operating under the critical delusion that the nature of norms was such that they could be stated as unqualified one-liners. I had either forgotten or had not read Goodenough's "Residence Rules" (1956). I suspect that my naive view of norms was developed through taking undergraduate examinations when, at times, one had to match a left-hand column of tribes with a right-hand column of types (for example, patrilocal residence, matrilineal descent).

Schneider and a few others of the advanced social-anthropology seminar had read my paper before the seminar convened. Although unaware of how I had overstated the case, they found other causes for dissatisfaction. The emphasis on the female side seemed unaccounted for. Furthermore, a really important question had not been addressed: If an obligation to the family of either spouse was involved, why should it be fulfilled by means of *residence?* Why the emphasis (of some sort) on the man's *living* in his wife's household? Ocean Island is only three square miles; Rambi is bigger—twenty-seven square miles, but the distances between areas of settlement are not generally great. It was not as if a man from New York were marrying a woman from California and had no postal service through which to send his father-in-law a regular check. Why residence?

Now note very carefully one thing that I overlooked. "Postmarital residence" was my category, not the Banabans' category. True, they did have a maxim which referred to it *(te buraen riri),* but it was not a category which emerged spontaneously as, say, "the family," "family gatherings," or "custom" did. I do not recall whether the next step in reducing the puzzle was inspired by looking at the data again or whether looking at the data again was inspired by an idea on how to reduce the puzzle. I was probably fingering my notebooks like some kind of intellectual ouija board when it occurred to me that postmarital residence was, first, part of a ritual sequence, part of *te katei,* "the custom"; and it was in that sense that I would have to conceptualize it. I think I had been operating up till then with two anthropological categories, "postmarital residence" and "ritual," picking things out as applying to one rather than the other.

PHASE 2: RITUAL

Let us repair to the data.

12. June 23, 1961. [This was only two days after my arrival. See note 1 above. Before making the statement that in the old days the couple lived with the mother's side— which we may now interpret as a statement being made from the point of view of the children of the marriage—Eriu was talking about the *baronga,* a general term for "group" which also applies to bilateral descent units and groups. We were speaking in English, and he called it a "tribe" on Ocean Island.] "People know these *baronga,*" he said. "The *baronga* shows in marriage now. People of the *barongas* related to the married couple come to the village where the marriage is taking place; they are notified beforehand. They bring presents, which these days are presents of money. They are greeted at the door of the house, and their feet are washed. They recite the generations, the 'heads' through which they are related in the genealogy. Groups within the *baronga* send representatives. If they cannot make the proper genealogical recitation, they are thrown out and are ashamed." [He then went on to make the statement about residence.]

13. July 4, 1961. [See note 2 above. Before making the statement on staying in the wife's house, Tito, Eriu's elder brother, had been describing the custom of marriage. This was the first description I had heard in any detail, and here is how he described it.] "The sister, brother, parent, or grandfather of a boy may say, 'How about this boy getting married to that girl, a nice girl?' They have a meeting with some relatives, and write a formal letter to her family. Her family calls a meeting of a lot of relatives; they wait if the relatives live far away. Someone opens the letter. [Probably on my query:] It does not matter much who opens it. The girl may be out in the kitchen and someone whispers to her, 'Do you want to marry him?' She says, 'Whatever you decide.' They may think he is a naughty boy, and write a letter back saying that they do not think the girl is ready for marriage yet. The parents may say to the boy, 'You are naughty. Maybe you didn't grow up right; change your ways.' They call a meeting of a few

people, and decide to go to the girl's people. The mother and father go with a few relatives. They plead and plead. The girl is asked, 'Are you in love with him? Do you want to marry?' The girl says, 'Whatever you decide.'

"They may agree there, and the couple is then engaged. A small meeting is called to announce it. The boy's family decides on a day for the arrangements to be made. Just three people may go. If there are more, the girl's people will have the expense of making preparations for all of them. When they arrive, the mother goes out and gets some near relatives who are around. The girl's family has food for the visiting party and cigarettes and matches for each. The visiting party brings some things as gifts, which they give in return. They eat and drink.

"Before the wedding, there are two rejoicings going on: at the boy's house, there are the relatives of his father and mother; at the girl's house, the relatives of her father and mother. They eat, drink, and sing. The celebrations start at each place about a week before the wedding.

"The marriage night is spent at the bridegroom's house, and they are there for three or four days with all the relatives. People are still partying at the bride's house. Then people say, 'It is time to go.' After the three or four days, the bridegroom and the bride go to the bride's family's house. After one night, the relatives say, 'It is time to go.' When the couple wake up in the morning, the relatives are almost all gone. Both the husband's and wife's relatives spend about the same amount of time having fun.

"How much time the couple stays in the wife's house, or again in the husband's house, depends on them, the families, and circumstances. If someone is sick at the wife's house, for example, they may stay to care for him.

"There is not so much fuss if it is a remarriage.

"If the bride is not a virgin, the relatives at the wife's house are shamed—they up and leave. The bride's mother and father tell her she is a naughty girl and has shamed them. At the husband's house, the relatives say the boy is unlucky, and they leave too.

"There are now official ages when the boy, maybe 19 or 21, and the girl, maybe 15 or 18, no longer need the consent of the parents for marriage. Before, they had to ask [and the procedure described above begins]."

There is a lot in this description. First, observe that from this account alone, it is impossible to tell whether the refusal by the girl's side and the subsequent pleading is being presented as part of a general pattern or is something that might arise now and then (the latter is the case). The shame for lack of virginity begins to indicate one of the things for which the husband, in "working for" his wife's family, is obligated.

Note also the sequence of events in this account from the perspective of the two families: groom's family to bride's family (the formal letter); bride's to groom's (the letter of refusal); groom's to bride's (the pleading for the marriage; the engagement announcement is obscure, but perhaps it is a combination of the two; then groom's to bride's (to make the arrangements); combination (the wedding service is understood); bride's to groom's (the first night); groom's to bride's (going to the bride's house).

Tito's account is not identical with others nor with all formal marriages I observed; but though these too vary, the back-and-forth sequencing is the same, in that no two successive steps are in the same direction (groom's family to bride's, or bride's to groom's). This point may not have seemed critical earlier because the structure seems so "natural." One can easily imagine a system, however, in which the groom's side consistently journeyed to the bride's (to ask for the marriage, to receive the answer, and so on), or vice versa.

Some aspects of the postmarital-residence problem begin to make sense as part of a ritual structure, a structure expressing a kind of balance between the two families. But if the groom "ends" at the bride's side—and not for just a short period of "groom service"—the balancing structure might seem, as it were, severely tilted. The argument thus has to be carried further.

14. July 11, 1961. In discussing naming, Ikamawa observed that the father names the eldest child, the mother names the next child, then the father again and so on. [It did not occur to me before to connect this observation with the observations on postmarital residence. But once the sequencing idea was abroad, that began to make sense too.]

15. June 29, 1964. [My friend Ikamawa, with whose family I first lived, was the island postmaster, and marriage announcements were posted on the bulletin board outside his office. I was looking at the announcements, and commented on one reporting that an old woman was to marry a middle-aged man.] Ikamawa chuckled over the ages, and I asked whether there would be a big marriage—I was hoping to actually attend one —with all the custom. He said they were living together already, and there would not. "If a girl goes and lives with a boy," he went on, "the parents would not give her the reward of a big wedding with lots of clothing and food."

This point is clear by now. The husband is obtaining from his wife's family the sexual rights to her, and if she is not a virgin those rights are no longer there to be given in the same sense.

16. July 1, 1964. [I had been doing some kin-term work with Nei Tebwebwe, and her mother, Nei Nnere, was in the house. (*Nei* is the female title, like "Miss" or "Mrs.") In a lively conversation, we were discussing many things pertaining to kinship. The point was brought up that these days a couple will go out together before the wedding, and this was a change.] Nei Nnere said that some youngsters did not marry officially because of all the expense involved in the customary procedures. "The kids may run off, and the siblings run after them and beat the boy up. If they have been living together, not listening to the parents, the parents will not give the girl wreaths and good clothes for the wedding. In the old-style Catholic weddings [Nei Nnere is a Protestant], the girl sits on cloth. If she has been 'playing outside,' there is no cloth and all can see and say that she is a bad girl." Only the girl is much cared for this way. I outlined the "double standard" in America, and Nei Tebwebwe and Nei Nnere smiled and said it was the same here.

17. July 9, 1964. [See note 9 above. Barereka's remark about residence was in response to a question of mine. He had just given, on my request, an elaborate and superb outline of the marriage sequence. There were differences with Tito's account (see note 13 above) that I cannot go into here—for example, that it starts when the boy and

girl decide that they want to get married, in which case there are some additional steps. Toward the end of Barereka's description he said that after the immediate postwedding-service festivities, the couple go to the girl's side, where people celebrate until midnight or dawn. Then they go to the man's side. The distant kinsmen leave, the near kinsmen stay. They stay at the man's side for a while, and then they are free. I then asked him about the couple's *staying* in the house of the parents of the boy, and he launched into his observations as stated in note 9.]

18. August 15, 1964. [See note 10 above. My friend Tane connected for me, as it were, the residence question and the naming pattern, which Ikamawa had briefly mentioned (see note 14). After observing how good his parents-in-law were to him, I observed that his young son spent a good deal of time with Tane's parents.] Tane said that, according to the custom, the first child is "governed" by the husband's side, the second child by the wife's, and so on. I asked if the child's sex mattered in this regard, and he answered, "No. The child stays there often when small, and goes about later." He indicated that naming is a facet of this. He and his wife, Nei Tiema, have no say in the naming. When their son Bainteiti was born, Tane's father told Tane's mother [as an act of generosity] that her family should do the naming. [Thus it may be a question of the right to give the name, and one can allow someone else to do it.] Tane's mother, her brother, and the family decided on Bainteiti. Nei Tiema's side will name the next child. Later that day I mentioned this matter of naming to Kaintong, my assistant, who said that it was a custom among some, but others do not hold to it. (I had no time to check out many actual cases of naming.)

Now let us pause briefly to consider what has occurred in this phase. One of the errors which I had committed was quite simple: taking things out of context. Observations by Eriu (notes 1 and 12) Tito (notes 2 and 13) Iotua (note 3), and Barereka (notes 9 and 17) occurred in contexts in which marriage ritual was being discussed in one fashion or another. My clinging to the category of postmarital residence as a question of concrete arrangements rather than of symbolic action (which would have immediately suggested ritual) meant that I had lifted the information about residence out of its relevant context. This seems outrageous in retrospect. My only defense (other than incomplete knowledge of other studies) is that the dictum "Thou shalt not sever from context" is more a slogan than a directive from which operational procedures can be deduced. While nodding to context, since Malinowski at least, we have not developed the concept theoretically.

At last, then, I tied the postmarital-residence statements to the balancing structure of marriage ritual. The notion of the naming pattern thus falls into place as the next part of the balancing act: with the birth of the first child, the groom's family recovers the initiative. The bride's family names the second child, and on it goes. There is, furthermore, something which can be linked at the other end of the sequence, as it were, and that is the first menstruation rite. Having made the connection between ritual and residence, this is what I wrote in an addendum to the 1965 paper:

There is no male rite functionally equivalent to the first menstruation rite *(te rara; te aoraki-n-aine).* In this, the family of the girl assemble bringing presents of coconut oil, cloth, food, and/or money. Money presents on such occasions are considered to help the parents pay for the feasting. Eating together is important here, as in other aspects of Banaban life. Coconut oil and cloth are things within the female province: making coconut oil and sewing. While the family eats, for the first two days, the girl is on a "bread and water" diet, sleeps little, and occupies herself making sennit and mats, with a few old women watching over her. She is dressed in the old form of leaf skirt, and her breasts are exposed. The big meal is on the final day, when she joins the party. Then it is over. The sequence has forms in common with many "rites-de-passage," and I will not discuss it from that point of view here. People say that before governmental restrictions, girls married sometimes when they were fourteen, one or two years after the rite.

The rite is in part a demonstration by the parents that they have successfully brought up the girl to the point where she is a woman. After this, the girl is expected more to fend for herself. Puberty and performance of adult female roles are demonstrated. In the Banaban conception, there is a complementarity between male and female roles; this is often expressed as follows: the man is the fisherman (and now, copra cutter), the woman the coconut oil- and mat-maker. This is expressed both for brothers and sisters, and husbands and wives.

The argument being made is that the first menstruation rite is a kind of announcement of the girl's availability for marriage, and thus it can be regarded as the kick-off stage for the whole business. I wrote in my addendum that the idea of the man going to live in his wife's household,

can be understood by starting with the first menstruation rite and the engagement. The argument is that the "full" marriage sequence concerns three themes: (1) the continuing solidarity of the family; (2) the recognition of claims of the other family; (3) the attaining of sexual rights over the woman. The sequence is structured in terms of the balance between the bride's side and the groom's side. The inclusion of (3) is supported by the local idea that the full sequence, including the large marriage gifts within the family, is properly operable only when the bride and groom have not already been living together, and more definitely, it is considered superfluous if they have been living together and have had children.

Actually, it would be more efficient to state for the last point that the sequence was not properly operable if the bride was known not to be a virgin.

I seem to operate with a kind of conceptual lag. Even now that I recognized a complementarity of male and female roles, I made little of it. So I had another dangler. In my doctoral dissertation, written after my third trip to Rambi, I took one further step beyond my previous written efforts. I wrote that the marriage sequence symbolizes the three things mentioned above, in more or less the same terms, but I added a fourth: the complementarity of male and female roles. I could then really begin to reduce the puzzle which the ritual argument illuminated but still did not lay to rest: why the idea of the husband's *staying* in the wife's household? It would have been perfectly consistent with the ritual argument for the couple to go off and live on their own (since the naming pattern, starting with the male side, came next). Some people had indeed said that the couple were "free." These apparently contradictory statements can be resolved by assuming that the speakers are not referring to exactly the same things. The uxorilocal statements refer, among other things, to the nature of sex roles and obligation. In saying that the couple did not necessarily live with either family, the speakers would be thinking, among other things, of concrete residential arrangements, especially as influenced by conceptions of a "modernized" way of life.

PHASE 3: SEX ROLES

It would sound tidy if I could say that connecting the first menstruation rite to postmarital residence led me to look more carefully into sex roles. I fear I was not so tidy, although I was perhaps readier for what was to come. Before I returned to the field—if I have my facts straight—I read the manuscript of David Schneider's *American Kinship* (1968), and it profoundly influenced my thinking. Things really began to fall into place, and I had new questions to ask. One of Schneider's main points was how one had to disentangle certain things on a symbolic basis, like kinship and sex roles. Consider, for example, the following from my 1965 paper, quoted above:

A male child is the worker, a female child merely a helper around the house. The male has less of a debt to repay, as he has already worked for his father. The debt of the female child is repaid by her husband.

Schneider would ask: From what cultural domains does such a statement as "A male child is the worker" flow? Is it something intrinsic to kinship, or is it really something from sex roles? The male is a worker *because he is a male,* and not specifically because he is someone's son or son-in-law. The active male parent and male sibling are also workers, because active males are workers. Hence we can look at the situation as a combination of something from kinship (for example, a definition of what a child is) and something from sex roles (for example, a stipulation that a male is a worker). The implications of this approach are tremendous, as anyone will realize who has ever read an ethnography in which kinship dyads (for example, father-son, mother-daughter) are presented, and all the things pertaining to those relations are discussed as if they all equally had to do with kinship.

To recapitulate slightly: From various observations (some of which will be recorded below), I had picked up something on Banaban sex roles, but it was really not integrated into the account. On my third trip to Rambi in the second half of 1965, however, I was looking out for this sort of thing.

19. June 30, 1965. *Riakaina* [in a general discussion of custom]: "In the Gilberts, the woman goes. In the old days she had no land of her own. The Banaban custom is good. The son-in-law works for you; he feeds the daughter and the mother. Her husband comes to help."

20. July 22, 1965. [I was with a family in which the wife's niece was living, and she was about to be married. A man from the groom's family came to discuss certain arrangements about the intervening steps which would or would not be mobilized in the sequence.] We were talking about this, and Nei Boratake said, "The man travels; it is he who decides."

21. August 21, 1965. *Nei Tina:* "[In the old days] the woman pulls the man. The man goes about. It is just the woman among them who stays. She pays off her debt for when she was small. If you just have male children, you say they are useless! If females, you are lucky. He feeds his wife and the whole family. [That's the way of] Men! [laughing]"

22. November 4, 1965. *Kauongo* [my third assistant]: "[With regard to a marriage] the male side [that is, the groom's side] goes to decide [to make the arrangements]. They come with the decision—that is the man's role." "The woman's side doesn't travel?" I asked [a purposely leading question]. "No," he replied. "The male goes about. His role is to travel. In our custom, the thing that is always with the woman is the place of marriage. The woman is the sitter." He then mentioned a marriage which was being arranged between a Catholic boy and a Methodist girl. The groom's side asked where [that is, in which church] the marriage was to take place. The girl said, "In the Methodist church," and they agreed.

23. November 5, 1965. Tororo had been discussing a marriage in which he was involved, and observed that on a number of things the two families decided together. I asked about the church in which the children would be married if they were of different religions. He said that they decide together on that, too, or maybe the two children decide themselves. In the island office, Nei Kawia [a Catholic] said to Ricky that the Methodist youngsters were being caught by the Catholics. The specific allusion she was making was to the marriage of the Methodist girl and the Catholic boy mentioned in note 22, but there were presumably other such marriages. I said [to be provocative], "Then soon there will be no more Methodists." "No," Ricky replied, "here the woman governs [hence the Catholic boys will become Methodists]."

And indeed, going back to earlier notes, things came tumbling out.

24. June 30, 1961. *Tebuke:* "In Banaban custom, girls don't walk around at night. They stay in the house. If they go around, they get a bad reputation. . . . The girl's place is in the house."

Here was one of the major answers to the puzzle, occurring in my second week of field work, only a week after Eriu's first broaching the residence matter (note 1), and four days before Tito's description (note 2), but I did not put the pieces together until *four years later!* This part of the answer is obvious: Men "travel" or "go about"; women "stay in the house." This is precisely what happens in the postmarital-residence statement. It is a statement, among other things, about men and women.

25. August 4, 1961. [See note 4 above: *"The man follows the woman.* In the Gilberts, *the woman is the traveler."*] I was not taking the language literally enough. A crucial linguistic note is in order which may partially explain why these things were more obscure to me than they might be to the reader. In many of these discussions of "custom," the Banabans speak of "the man, male" and "the woman, female" in contexts in which we would say "the husband" and "the wife" or "the bride" and "the groom." In some of my notes which I wrote in English rather than Gilbertese, I may well have written "husband" and "wife" or "boy" and "girl" when actually the words for "male" and "female" were used in the discussions. Now in one sense, the words for male and female are being used to refer to the husband and the wife. But it is not insignificant that it is the male and female terms which are used. I believe the Banabans were quite literally *telling* me much of what the system was about, but unconsciously I made a translation into English words and thus the concepts denoted by those words in English. The problem was more than one of mistranslation, however. It was one of misconception, of assuming that postmarital residence concerned only husbands and wives, and not also men and women.

26. [Probably August 12, 1961. I was working on genealogies and custom at a meeting of the members *B* and *C,* which are two Ocean Island "hamlets," that is, people descended from the founders of those hamlets. The founders putatively lived about five to seven generations ago. Three hamlets are really involved here, *B, C,* and *D.* Nei *X* was the founder of *B,* Nei *Y* was the founder of *C,* and *Z* was the founder of *D.* The three founders were siblings: Nei *X* and Nei *Y* were women, and *Z,* the last-born, a man. The meeting was of the *B* and *C* people. All the people had certain traditional rights from their ancestor many generations before, and transmitted through the father of Nei *X,* Nei *Y,* and *Z.*] The people at the meeting tried to come to an agreement over traditional rights. The pace of the discussion had gotten beyond my knowledge of Gilbertese, and my assistant Iotua relayed their information to me as follows: "The rights were given to *Z* [and therefore to his descendants] *because he was the only male issue. To his sisters* [and therefore to their descendants] *was given the hamlet's well.* His rights were 'the meetinghouse,' also called *'the speaking'* [the right of speaking first in the meetinghouse and of taking the initiative in certain ritual matters], 'games' [the right to allow the performance of certain traditional games and to perform particular roles in those games], and 'the right to greet visiting vessels.' The eldest, Nei *X,* stayed at *B. Z gave to her:* the right of preparing the playground [where traditional games were played], the right of scoring in games, and the right of distributing food among the people who participated in ritual affairs. Nei *Y* went to *B* and stayed there. She received [from her brother] the right to greet visiting vessels. Under some circumstances, the rights given to Nei *X* [the eldest] can be performed by Nei *Y* [that is, by her descendants] if Nei *X* [that is, her descendants] calls her [that is, asks the descendants of Nei *Y* to exercise those rights]."

Attend to the italicized phrases. The emphasis was supplied for this paper.

27. [Probably September 1961. See note 6. It appears from the notes that a mention of *kautabo,* "in-laws," started off another discussion of the marriage sequence. From elliptical phrases in the notes, the following can be derived.] The *kautabo* are the boy's side and the girl's side; when the two are getting married, the two groups are *kautabo*

to each other. It is hard to visit the *kautabo* [before the marriage; it is a relationship of reserve]. From one to three days before the wedding, one or two people from the girl's side go to the boy's side and ask permission for him to go with them; he goes to the girl's family. Similarly, the boy's side calls for the girl, and that is done first *(he's a man)*. And when they go to the boy's home, the girl's side come and ask for the boy —they want to have fun and enjoyment before the wedding. After, they go back to their homes. [I include this to show how confused notes sometimes are.]

On the day before marriage, each side tries to sneak in on the other side and joke around. If somebody from the other side is caught, he is taken to the house of the side which catches him, they change his clothes, give him good food to eat, they anoint him with coconut oil and give him wreaths. Then he can go home. After the ceremony there are big pranks. People from one side try to mess up people from the other side.

On the wedding night, the couple first goes to the girl's side, after the activities at the church, maybe until midnight. At 11:00 P.M., midnight, or 1:00 A.M., they go back to the boy's family. They sleep there and stay for two or three days. Then they can go back to the girl's side. When they are going back, the boy's family try to get food and lots of fish. It has to be taken to the girl's side, with beef and sacks of rice, flour, and sugar. [Perhaps on my query:] The girl's side bring nothing to the boy's side. *He feeds her. She's only a girl, and cannot cut copra and so forth.*

The emphasis is supplied here, too, after the fact.

28. October 6, 1961. [In the Tabiang village meetinghouse, talking about fishing.] *Ngaiwaka:* "When you go fishing, you only take water with perhaps a little sugar, and drink a little at a time. Before you go out [it is "understood" that we are talking about men, since only men fish from canoes], you sleep, but without women. If you break these rules, the fish will fall off the hook. When you return, you sleep first and then eat. At first Bakoa [Shark, the Lord of the Sea] is in you; he will eat too. But he goes out of you when you sleep." [On the same day, a discussion of custom with some old men.] Two of them agree that "the well" is the woman's thing, and "the word" is the man's thing. [See note 26; that is, in the descent unit, men succeed to the right of initiative and speaking first, and women succeed to the right of control over the well.] I knew of the general statement to the effect that "the word" is the right of the first-born. I asked them, "What happens when the first-born is a woman? [The understanding here is that a male relative will "speak for her."] What happens in the next generation? Do the rights go to her son [as the Maudes had said], or to the children of her brother?" One man present said that the right does not go back to her [that is, it is not passed on to her children]. Some others said that the right does go back to her children. [There is a one-word entry in my notes, "examples"; but I do not know whether I asked for examples at that point or whether they discussed examples which were beyond my Gilbertese.] The man who said that the rights do not go back said that he thought that was the case because of the well [that is, because the woman had already received her share of family rights]. But here on Rambi there is confusion because there is no well and there is no word [that is, there are no wells, and the custom of speaking in the meetinghouse is largely in abeyance, although people still worry about the rights]. If the eldest is a woman, she is still the eldest in the family. They cited a case of a woman who is the eldest in an important family, and noted that an elder male kinsman of hers

does the speaking for her. "Will 'the word' stay with her, or pass to her younger brother's children?" They did not answer the question, but the implication was, I think, that she would hold onto it.

29. October 11, 1961. [Ngaiwaka (see note 28), in some context, noted that people cannot kiss before they go out fishing either (recalling the previous conversation).] "When you are sleeping the night before you go out fishing, you cannot have either women or children with you. When you go out, the woman [your wife] must guard your sleeping mat [so that no one goes onto it] or the fish will fall off your hook."

30. June 21, 1964. [See note 8. Note the statements "The women ruled the household," and "in marriage the man is the traveler."]

31. July 9, 1964. [See notes 9 and 17. Note the statement *"In the Gilberts, the man leads the woman."* And that among the Gilbertese, the woman was the worker whereas among the Banabans, it was the man.]

32. October 2, 1964. [See note 11. Note the statement "The woman runs the house."]

33. December 13, 1964. [I started off a conversation with Nei Tina by showing her some published photographs of Ocean Island.] "The really hard thing on Ocean Island," she said, "is water. If you have no daughter, you take one [that is, adopt one] to get water. The man: he fishes."

Once I was really alerted to the sex-role question, various snippets of data could be interrelated which were not interrelated before. These snippets involved descent units, marriage, postmarital residence, ritual, religion, and fishing, among other things. Consider, for example, Ngaiwaka's observations on fishing (which were also made by many others), in notes 28 and 29. I knew that the male was considered to be the fisherman, and the arduous activities involved in fishing were sometimes phrased as the males' being "food of the rain, the dew, the sunshine." The night before fishing a man could not sleep with a woman or with a child: thus both sex and age roles are involved. The sexes had to be separate lest the fish fall off the hook. Yet at the same time, the wife had to guard the man's sleeping mat while he was away. She herself was a party to the maintenance of the separation while her husband was absent. The results of the catch, of course, would be eaten by her, too—she had her role to play to keep the system going. He was off on the sea, she was in the house standing guard, as it were. Her role is not passive, but the "stationary" aspect stressed in the postmarital-residence idea turns up here, too.

Similarly for the question of "the word" and "the well" in the discussion of hamlet or descent-unit rights. The word was the male's and in the present, at least, people speak of the word as "moving" from place to place; that is, messages are transmitted from one group of people to another. Nei Tina (note 33) stressed the role of the woman as the one who gets water from the wells and caves, water which is needed equally by men and women, as fish are needed equally by men and women. The total relationship is asymmetrical, considering the initiative and authority role of the male. But the role of the female with regard to water and the caves, among other things, gives the over-all relationship an aspect of complementarity. The male is not pictured as doing things for other males as, for example, the members of a family are pictured as doing things for one another. The female is not pictured as doing things for other females as, for example, the members of a church are pictured as doing things for one another. Neither the males nor the females constitute a group (which, in some societies, they almost do). The male is doing things for the female and for society as a whole; the female is doing things for the male and for society as a whole.

The symbolic relationship between men and women—something to which Margaret Mead drew attention long ago—is one of the few basic paradigms for the relationship of mutual but differentiated obligation. In talking about postmarital residence, then, people are in part assuming the obligation of a man to his wife's family and particularly to her father, as I observed early on. In concrete terms, there is a variety of things which a son-in-law can do for his father-in-law. The uxorilocal statement is a synecdoche for the relationship. But people are also assuming the more general obligations between men and women, and in talking about these they are talking about the nature of mutual, differentiated obligation itself. (see Lévi-Strauss, 1960).

PHASE 4: SPACE

One is fated, perhaps, to return to the things one learned in one's early encounters with another people, to one's early ideas, to one's early interests. It was only after my doctoral dissertation was completed, when I was trying to solve the problem of the place of land ownership in the definition of kinship, and the association of descent units with localities, that another development in my thinking on the postmarital-residence question emerged.

I came to the suspicious (because apparently tautological) conclusion that many aspects of Banaban culture were articulated by a relatively heavy reliance on the use of space and spatial divisions to symbolize culturally defined social distinctions and unities. This notion developed through a consideration of descent, and I then looked back at the data to see how far it could be pushed in other domains. Naturally, I scratched the irritant again. Once the general question was raised, it became obvious that the way of handling movement and nonmovement in residence had to be looked at as a subproblem of how the Banabans handle space.

In addition to being the fisherman, the male is also the coconut-toddy collector. To collect toddy from a tall tree, you have to climb it. An old myth which Maude gave me involved a woman defying the rules by climbing a pandanus tree, and a character in the myth observed, "A woman climbs no tree." Since the male is pictured as the fisherman and the female as the water-getter and since both could work on the land, a plausible case could be made that the sea was thought of as the extractive province of men. The land in itself did not carry a sex-role connotation. But it is the male who goes *above* the land in climbing trees, and the woman who goes *below* the land in collecting water. True enough, in going below the land the woman is moving, but the wells themselves are unmoving, and the symbolic statement of the male as traveler and the woman as sitter is not intended to apply to all actual male and female acts (and on Rambi there are no wells of the Ocean Island type). As in every symbolic statement, a number of things are being referred to, are being stressed, but not all things. Note that via the definition of sex roles, the postmarital-residence complex was tied in with one of the fundamental contrasts in traditional Banaban cosmology and the cosmology of many Pacific Islands peoples: the contrast between the land and the sea.

We have come a long way from the simple question of a residence rule. Symbols, ritual, sex roles, space, and cosmology, through many interrelated transformations of thinking and data, come forth as the frameworks within which the residence notion had to be interpreted. What the progression has shown is that in making such simple statements as "The man's 'true place' is the household of his wife," people are making statements which presuppose a number of things and which concern a number of things. I will pause here to consider two lessons which this progression underscores.

The first lesson is the distinction between asking about where people reside after marriage and asking about the conventional wisdom about where people reside after marriage. The second lesson is the distinction between taking that conventional wisdom as either explaining or being explained by the facts of where people reside, and trying to map the system of meanings in which that conventional wisdom inheres.

A number of implications flow from these two simple lessons. A residence (or other) "rule" may be stated for a society by a member of that society or by an anthropologist. What the rule *means* for one society may be quite different from what a superficially similar rule means for another society— "means," in terms of the frameworks of the members of the societies or the frameworks of the anthropologist (see Goodenough, 1956). Be cautious, then, of attempts to correlate, for example, a kind of postmarital residence with a kind of descent. In one place the rule may be ideal but not actual. In another place it may be actual but not ideal. It may refer to people's suppositions or expectations, which may or may not match either the ideals or the actualities of where people live. Or, as among the Banabans, such a rule may be a condensed symbolic statement.

I am not suggesting that in every culture postmarital-residence statements are primarily such highly condensed (in Freud's sense) or multivocal (in Victor Turner's sense) symbols. I concede that it could be simply a matter of who owns the gardens or who can hunt buffalo. The question of symbolic contexts might be a less powerful one to ask than the question of economy or ecology. Or both may be equally powerful—or weak. I am thus taking a relativistic view toward the potency of symbolic and concrete-functional arguments as they relate to things like residence rules. From the symbolic side, I am assuming that the "semantic load" of such a thing as residence may be radically different in different cultures and that in some cultures the category (that is, residence) itself may not be a useful one at all in the symbolic sense, while it may be very useful in the concrete-functional sense.

My use of the term *conventional wisdom* evades the problem of how within one society people can make different statements "about the same thing." I will conclude by just playing out this thread sufficiently to (I hope) interest the reader in the question.

THE NATURE OF NORMATIVE REPORTS

The reality of a kinship system as part of a social structure consists of the actual social relations of person to person as exhibited in their interactions and their behaviour in respect of one another. But the actual behaviour of two persons in a certain relationship (father and son, husband and wife, or mother's brother and sister's son) varies from one particular instance to another. *What we have to seek in the study of a kinship system are the norms. From members of the society we can obtain statements as to how two persons in a certain relationship ought to behave towards one another. A sufficient number of such statements will enable us to define the ideal or expected conduct.* Actual observations of the way persons do behave will enable us to discover the extent to which they conform to the rules and the kinds and amount of deviation. Further, we can and should observe the reactions of other persons to the conduct of a particular person or their expressions of approval or disapproval. The reaction or judgement may be that of a person who is directly or personally affected by the conduct in question or it may be the reaction or judgement of what may be called public opinion or public sentiment. The members of a community are all concerned with the observance of social usage or rules of conduct and judge with approval or disapproval the behaviour of a fellow member even when it does not affect them personally.

A kinship system thus presents to us a complex set of norms, of usages, of patterns of behaviour between kindred. Deviations from the norm have their importance. For one thing they provide a rough measure of the relative condition of equilibrium or disequilibrium in the system. Where there is a marked divergence between ideal or expected behaviour and the actual conduct of many individuals this is an indication of disequilibrium; for example, when the rule is that a son should obey his father but there are notably frequent instances of disobedience. But there may also be a lack of equilibrium *where there is marked disagreement amongst members of the society in formulating the rules of conduct or in judgement passed on the behaviour of particular persons* (Radcliffe-Brown, 1950, pp. 10–11; emphasis added).

As creatures of the post-McLuhan age, we are particularly sensitive to the fact that the "statements" of which Radcliffe-Brown speaks include nonverbal (for example, ritual) as well as verbal statements. Radcliffe-Brown himself dealt with ritual, and he may have intended "statements" to include more than the verbal. In my own work on kinship, I pay considerable attention to ritual statements and note that one's interpretation of a number of rituals is enhanced if one considers them as multimedia events. In this paper I emphasize the verbal dimension because in many ways it is the easiest to deal with.

I will not take up Radcliffe-Brown's usage of "equilibrium," but do want to go back to the problem of disagreements or at least differences among "members of the society in formulating the rules of conduct." The problem is still to account for such differences. The ways I find to do this within my data do not, of course, exhaust the possibilities.

Consider first the disagreement over whether the rights of ritual precedence within a descent unit "return" to a woman's line (that is, to her son) when that woman was genealogically senior (see note 28). As I later wrote:

In ideal circumstances, the speaker and initiator is a man. If a woman is the elder of a unit which has speaking rights [in the meetinghouse], she should call upon her nearest senior male relative in that unit "to speak for her." In one school of thought, the rights stay where they went, and thus form a rule of patri-succession. In another school of thought, the rights return to the original line in the next generation, as the Maudes indicated. There are cases supporting both points of view. It is possible that this conflict of principles formed the terms of much of the verve of the aboriginal system. Here, two cultural principles (succession by primogeniture, and male authority) bear on the same concrete circumstance, but there is no hard and fast rule for sorting them out, and thus individuals have room to maneuver and to attempt to secure positions for themselves and their own children (Silverman, 1971, Ch. 2).

In the perspective of succession by primogeniture, it makes sense to say that the rights revert to the senior line. Looked at from the perspective of sex roles, it makes sense to say that the male line holds onto the rights. The outcome in a particular case may be unpredictable unless much else is known. But note that my concern is not for the particular outcomes, but for the reasons why the contradictory statements *make sense,* or have meaning.

Turning again to postmarital residence, consider now Tito's remark, as summarized by me (note 2), that the amount of time spent by the couple at the house of the husband or the wife depends on them, the families, and circumstances. A number of contingencies exist which may be expected to have an effect on residence, on who lives where. I assume that there are expectations as to how such contingencies will affect residence, although I did not investigate them systematically (see Keesing, 1967). The idea that a norm need not be a simple statement, even if the local people make simple statements, but rather can be a complex structure of contingencies, is an idea that has not yet really been developed in the discipline.

Nei Katuroroa tried to set me straight on this when I asked her about the custom of the man following the woman:

34. July 9, 1965. *Nei Katuroroa:* "It really is not a strong thing. It is not that if you have one child he will leave. If you have several children, you will tell them to go and help [the other family]. People say that it is because a lot of Gilbertese [men] married

in." I asked, "What if you have an only child, and he marries an only child?" "They go back and forth," she said. "It is a matter of cooperation."

Nei Katuroroa was absolutely right in what she said, of course, given my question. But do we interpret this as a "weak rule"? I think not. Recall *te buraen riri,* "the strands of the skirt." It is a codified phrase, a maxim (which is capable of symbolic analysis in itself, but beyond the scope of this paper). More completely, someone said that a man "is caught in the strands of the skirt," that is, he is caught by his wife and thus his wife's family. The maxim exists, and so do the statements on the rule, or the emphasis. But what do those statements mean? Those statements are themselves like maxims. They are summations of certain symbolic relationships and, as such, are incomplete, or emphatic. They are traditionalized short-hand statements which assume and imply a whole range of contingencies and symbolism. They are one of the ways in which the people order their own culture.

At the same time, however, it should not be assumed that everybody produces the same labels, or the same exegeses on the labels.

I asked Amon, an elder, about the reasons for the custom.

35. August 6, 1965. *Amon:* "If it was the custom before, or just now, I don't know. Perhaps it is because you love the girl a lot that you go to her place. Another reason might be to help her father. Otherwise he may tell his daughter to leave you because you're no good. But if something is going on at your place [that is, at the man's family's home], you go back."

Amon mentioned love, unlike the others. Like others, however, he mentioned the relationship to the father-in-law. He did not mention the Gilbertese, which Nei Katuroroa and others had mentioned. He alluded to the possibility of change, which others had brought up too. Eriu, for example (notes 1 and 12), spoke of the rule as something which applied in the old days, but now the couple were free to live where they want. Perhaps this partially explains Barereka's report (notes 9, 17, and 31) that there is still a ritual marriage sequence to be followed, though the couple do not have to stay in one place or another. Perhaps he was interpreting the concrete realities of the situation. When I prodded him, he went into a frame of reference which assumed we were talking about "the custom," and then the uxorilocal business came up again. Looking at Banaban life from the perspective of existing realities, or even a set of modern ideals, one produces another set of conclusions.

Compare in this regard the remarks that the girl's side decides on the church in which the marriage will be held (notes 22 and 23) with the observation that the two families decide together (note 23). The first notion is an application of the customary principle to marriage; the second is looking at the situation from a more modern perspective.

Insofar as each statement describes a practice which would be generally acceptable, we can describe the situation most simply by saying that there are sets of alternate norms. But the alternates are themselves structured, both by the recognition of contingencies and by the existence of different frames of reference. A number of times "in the custom" or a similar phrase was used. In this frame of reference the range of responses is somewhat different from the range that accompanies a "these days" frame of reference. The Banaban notion of "custom" is a complex one, but we may liken it to that of tradition or heritage. Adopting this perspective, one is essentially saying, "To do such-and-such according to 'custom,' this is how it must be"—for example, living in the wife's household. One is not, however, saying, "You must do it according to custom" (see Silverman 1967, where this is explored).

Note how with this formulation the problem (to oversimplify) divides into two related questions: Why the uxorilocal pattern should be part of the "custom" frame of reference? And why the "custom" frame of reference should be part of Banaban culture, at least now? The symbolic elements which I have outlined go at least part of the way toward answering the first question. The second question has many ramifications. Part of the picture is this: The Banabans make much of the differences between themselves and the Gilbertese, and the Banabans' construct of their "custom" functions (among other things) as an identity symbol, as a way of differentiating themselves from other peoples, particularly the Gilbertese. Parts of that construct of custom can partially be understood in terms of the functions of the whole. Thus the uxorilocal pattern receives another context for its understanding. And recall that many Banabans are quite explicitly aware of the difference between the postmarital-residence pattern which they assert for their own society and the pattern which they assert for the Gilbertese.

In using the normative language of the kind I have described, people are explicitly either labeling a description or prescription to one another or attempting to formulate a description or prescription to an outsider, or both. In doing so, they can adopt different frameworks, or stress certain things rather than others which might well come up in an extended interview. The snippets from Nei Katuroroa and Amon, for example, are just that: snippets. These two Banabans are probably as aware of the complexities as is the next man or the next woman.

Yet, at the same time, some individuals might not be as aware of the complexities as others. In making such statements as "This symbolizes . . ." or "This means . . ." the anthropologist is not saying that such a response would be obtained from all or even a majority of the members of a society. Nor is he simply adding together every observation that anyone ever made on a particular topic, or trying to find the lowest common denominator. The anthropologist is trying to formulate a structure which will account for the *meaningfulness,* to the members of a society, of the things which the members of that society do or say. "In our custom, the man follows the woman" is a simple observation. Understanding even this calls for a careful investigation of each of its terms: who the "we" are, what "custom" means, what "man" and "woman" denote and connote, the area implied by "follows." And the analysis should keep a firm eye on the contexts in which such observations occur without the intervention of the anthropologist (for this reason my example of postmarital residence leaves much to be desired, since most of the spontaneous statements I had recorded are nonverbal statements). Each of the terms may lead the analyst into a different cultural domain or frame of reference. Different domains or frames of reference may be differentially emphasized by different people at different times. Each of the terms may lead the members of the community into making different statements when the anthropologist asks questions or when he turns informal conversations toward the topics which form the areas of his interest (which is what I did much of the time).

In retrospect, much of my research has been an attempt to formulate a structure of hypotheses. These hypotheses are, to repeat, about the frameworks or cultural domains which make certain aspects of Banaban behavior meaningful to the Banabans themselves. The particular aspect described here, postmarital residence, focuses on a piece of conventional wisdom, as embodied, for example, in the phrase *te buraen riri,* "the strands of the skirt." This conventional wisdom perhaps stands midway between a proverb and Lévi-Strauss' (1963) "home-made models." The building of the hypotheses "ambiguated" residence in that it attributed to it more meanings than I initially recognized. The building of the hypotheses "disambiguated" residence in that the possibilities of interpretation were narrowed, and residence was placed within a scheme of interpretation which was applied to other (here undescribed) aspects of Banaban culture. It may appear, accepting the complexities of analyzing the "residence rule" in this way, that every segment of behavior requires a treatment in such detail that no orderly analysis of the whole is possible. This is not true, I believe, because the same frameworks that are necessary for an understanding of the residence statement also structure numerous other Banaban behaviors.

In conclusion, it should be noted that in making such statements as "the strands of the skirt," members of a society are doing some of the same things which anthropologists do. As our frameworks shift, our creation and use of data shifts. As their frameworks shift, their statements change. Both we and they, for various reasons, are trying to introduce order into what we know of human behavior. In introducing order, both we and they simplify situations by stating norms as if they were simplicities rather than ranges of variation structured by contingency expectations. Both we and they stress some things at the expense of others, to make communication efficient and powerful, or because of our interests, impatience, or personal experience. It is not that every native is an anthropologist but that every anthropologist is a native.

REFERENCES

FORTES, MEYER. 1969. *Kinship and the Social Order.* Chicago: Aldine.

GOODENOUGH, W. H. 1956. "Residence Rules." *Southwestern Journal of Anthropology,* 12:22–37.

KEESING, ROGER. 1967. "Statistical Models and Decision Models of Social Structure: A Kwaio Case." *Ethnology,* 6:1–16.

KUHN, THOMAS S. 1962. *The Structure of Scientific Revolutions.* Chicago: University of Chicago Press.

LÉVI-STRAUSS, CLAUDE. 1960. "The Family." In Harry L. Shapiro, ed., *Man, Culture, and Society.* New York: Oxford University Press.

——— 1963. "Social Structure." In Claude Lévi-Strauss, *Structural Anthropology.* New York: Basic Books.

MAUDE, H. C., AND H. E. MAUDE. 1932. "The Social Organization of Banaba or Ocean Island, Central Pacific." *Journal of the Polynesian Society,* 41:262–301.

OLIVER, DOUGLAS L. 1958. "An Enthographer's Method for Formulating Descriptions of 'Social Structure.'" *American Anthropology,* 60:801–826.

RADCLIFFE-BROWN, A. R. 1950. "Introduction." In A. R. Radcliffe-Brown and Daryll Forde, eds., *African Systems of Kinship and Marriage.* London: Oxford University Press.

SCHNEIDER, DAVID M. 1965. "Some Muddles in the Models; or, How the System Really Works." *The Relevance of Models for Social Anthropology.* A. S. A. Monographs 1. London: Tavistock Publications.

——— 1968. *American Kinship.* Englewood Cliffs, N.J.: Prentice-Hall.

SILVERMAN, MARTIN G. 1967. "The Historiographic Implications of Social and Cultural Change: Some Banaban Examples." *Journal of Pacific History,* 2:137–147.

——— 1971 (in press). *Meaning and Struggle in a Resettled Community: The Banabans in Fiji.* Chicago: University of Chicago Press.

Part III / **AMBIGUITIES AND RESOLUTIONS**

16 / Musical Stones for the God of Thunder

GEORGES CONDOMINAS

Translated by NORMAN STOKLE

Avec tant de départs comment faire un retour.—*Jules Supervielle*[1]

All we know about the ethnologist is the "terrain" he has covered and the book he has written about it. Does he ever mention the dreary hours he has spent behind a desk after his return home in elaborating his book and in giving it the last touches? Everyone who writes as an essential part of his job goes through the same process. *His* "terrain," on the other hand, is not simply his research laboratory with all of its concomitant problems to resolve, surprises, suspenseful moments, and discoveries, but also—and I say this without exaggeration—his *raison d'être* here on earth. His laboratory, unique in that the subject for observation shares the actual nature of the observer, constitutes a sort of *rite de passage* from which he, the ethnologist, emerges utterly different from what he was before.

As for the book, over and above the importance any work intrinsically possesses for its author, it represents the ethnologist's justification of his "terrain," which would otherwise remain a purely personal adventure. Yet for most of us the "terrain" stands as the essential thing, as a kind of Golden Age to be recalled at every available opportunity. Sometimes even "the need to 'ethnograph' the ethnographer"[2] serves as a pretext for preserving in written form all the subjective aspects the experience contained but which had been eliminated from the scientific report. The "terrain," our private little Golden Age. . . . And yet I know that on the material level I lived in a state of even greater abjection at Săr Lŭk than at the "Hotel Mikado" (the nickname for the prisoner-of-war camp where I had been interned by the Japanese army).

I should have liked to talk here of my return, of my process of readaptation, but only a novelist can successfully render what is quite simply a long period of extrication. Again, only he would be able to convey all the charm contained in the return to family life. As the years go by, one remembers little but the difficulties. First and foremost is the ordeal of readapting to the conventions and norms of the French bourgeoisie, which are every bit as rigid as those of other societies around the world whose deeply embedded traditions are the

232

object of ethnographic study. Yet the latter are bearable, even exciting, since one has consciously run away from the former to search them out. Moreover, there is no denying they have a certain character. But what possible interest can the French bourgeoisie afford, especially to someone who has always lived on its fringes? Did I say "readaptation"? "Adaptation" would be more correct. For I never really became acquainted with that bourgeoisie until a few months before my departure, at a time when I was ready to accept as a novelty, and therefore with goodwill, anything that had to do with my marriage. In the meantime, however, I had directed all my energies toward integrating myself as completely as possible into the much more exciting environment of the "Men of the Forest" (the nickname given to the Mnong Gar of Central Vietnam by the neighboring tribes).[3] On my return home, at the very time when I had little strength left for any new adaptation, circumstances called for me to assume a respectable position in the French milieu. So far as I was concerned, this simply meant consolidating myself into an absurdity equal to that of the milieu in which I had just been living. In addition, the rules of the new milieu were imposed on me in my own home.

To complicate matters, I had to undergo a long convalescence which made me less malleable for such an effort. The initial diagnosis shortly after I regained consciousness in the hospital at Ban Mé Thuot had left me with the firm impression that my days were numbered. Since the worst could happen at any time, I had to take advantage of my every living moment to salvage all the notes I could, that is to say, to translate into French as much as possible of what I had taken down directly in Mnong since I was, at that time, the only person able to write the language. So it was imperative to avoid being caught up in a milieu of which I had no desire to be a part and from which I felt estranged. I was losing enough time already in my continual visits to the Val-de-Grâce hospital which followed upon my lengthy confinements at Ban Mé Thuot and Saigon.

At all events, when you are totally unable to conceive of an afterlife, you very quickly grow accustomed to the idea of the imminence of death; it's the greatest incentive, first, for overcoming your illness, and then for applying yourself to your work. Besides, you have to see an undertaking through to its end before you pack up your traps. By dint of living from one minute to the next, the contradictions that beset you follow one another, like time, at an accelerating rhythm: you are scarcely on your feet again before you start fuming at the prospect of a long convalescence. You want to publish a "major work" before you are thirty. (It's a fair age, and will you ever see past it?) But you have to accept the fact that it will take a long time to organize all of the material before writing a single line of your Opus No. 1. No sooner have the signs of paralysis disappeared than you contemplate returning to the site in order to fill in certain gaps before publishing whatever the piece happens to be. And so forth.

To crown it all, I work very slowly and am plagued by a concern for minutiae that borders on a mania. The tasks pile up. You realize that you have not only to acquaint yourself with all that has appeared during your absence, but also to review what you have already read, because the field work has given you a new perspective which prompts you to reread what you thought you had assimilated. To reduce the time spent on bibliographical research, I had taken but few notes during the course of my previous readings for I could then see only temporary usefulness in them. That being the case, my memory would be largely sufficient. Two decades have elapsed since then, however, and, contrary to my expectations, I often have to go back to these readings.

Any activity having no direct bearing on my ethnographical notes (which comprised forty-one school notebooks)—such as indexing, card-cataloguing, translating—seemed to me a dangerous diversion from the essential task. Even so, I was unable to refuse requests which ranged from the writing of an article for an American political-science journal to contributing to a French ethnological textbook with an accompanying bibliography. The feeling of wasting my time on this project made me lose even more time than I needed to, and my lack of writing experience only made matters worse. But I now realize that this undertaking, which I then considered secondary, was in actual fact a valuable exercise in writing.

At this point the collection of Mnong Gar objects that I had painstakingly gathered together finally arrived at the Musée de l'Homme. I had tried to assemble a sampling of the entire material culture of a village, from the spatula for churning rice to the post used in buffalo sacrifices. What now demanded my attention was not the ethnographical work, since the collection was never placed on display, but a chance discovery pertaining to archeology and musicology. Despite my previous urgency about getting to my book, I finally had to put everything else aside in order to deal with the Ndŭt Liĕng Krăk lithophone. Let me explain what this was all about.

In the village I had made a point of visiting the different homes in the evening so as to have a glimpse of their daily activities, and I had used these visits to collect a few technical details, songs, anecdotes, and so forth. The visits rarely lasted very long since the Mnongs are accustomed to retiring early unless some festivity or a jar of *rnööm*[4] (a rice beer) opened in some visitor's honor keeps them from their beds. At such times, one realizes what an asset alcohol—that bringer of joy and loosener of tongues—can be to the ethnographer.

On the evening of February 4, 1949, Baap Can had opened a jar of *rnööm* in honor of two visitors from Ndŭt Liĕng Krăk, a village upstream. They were Krae the Widower and Srae, who was the stepson of my friend Kroong the Short and our host's future son-in-law.[5] *Rnööm* was certainly right for the occasion, but even with its help our visitors were not great storytellers. They talked mainly about the tiger which, among other depredations, had killed two youths within a week—one at Dam Roong, the other at Dung Jrii. These

The Site of Ndŭt Liĕng Krăk, Where the Lithophones Were Found

incidents had greatly alarmed our visitors for these two villages were their closest neighbors on the left bank of the river.

Following a lag in the conversation, Baap Can started to denounce the Cil Bboon Jaa, who had still not paid the outstanding debt on their land rental. They were, in effect, "eating" part of the Phii Ko' forest while refusing to pay the annual levy of twelve small neckless jars. For Baap Can, who, through his wife, was the "sacred" man of Phii Ko', it was a shocking state of affairs. His protestations enabled me to question him about the regulations, both judicial and ritual (according to our compartmentalized concepts), governing the rental and sale of land.

After a while, however, when I saw that little more could be extracted from Baap Can, I left him alone. It was getting late and most of the drinking party were stretched out on the reclining platform or had slipped away. I filled a last pipe before heading back to my quarters. Only Krae the Widower and Baap Can continued talking as they passed the beer back and forth. The former gave his host news of Ndŭt, but his words floated about my ears without attracting my attention. I stretched out on the reclining platform, relaxing with my pipe. Suddenly the words *mau prum* ("Cham stones")[6] broke through my drowsiness. "What did you say?" I interrupted. Krae was startled, because he had only been chatting quietly with Baap Can about a matter that seemed to him quite ordinary. However, he related that, when they had been extending the trail serving the village as far as Dam Roong, some large Cham stones were found in the soil on the edge of the former *rngool*,[7] opposite the present site of the village. I could hardly believe my ears: Cham stones in a backwater like that! What on earth could the Chams have been doing in such an out-of-the-way place? Certainly, they had left their traces in Rhadé country, but that was in the region of a different (though related) tribe. In Srêe and Churuu territory (some of whom speak the same language as the Chams), rice-growing land is abundant. But why would they have come into the upper valley of the Krong Knô, which is separated from Dalat by a mountain chain over six thousand feet high?

Krae answered my flurry of questions as well as he could. And I managed to establish that the discovery consisted of a dozen stone "boards," that some were longer than a man's arm, and that nothing was carved on them. This description intrigued me more and more. They could not in fact be Cham stones—nor prehistoric stones for that matter. None of that size had ever been seen anywhere in the world. I was truly puzzled, but it was past midnight, and it was better to go to the location itself to determine what sort of objects these Cham stones were.

The following morning, February 5, perched on my one-eyed old horse with my feet almost touching the ground, I headed for Ndŭt Liĕng Krăk. But at Sar Lang the inhabitants invited me to attend their "Inspection of the Forest" which was about to begin. Having missed this rite in Săr Lŭk, where it had taken place at the end of December while I was away in Dalat, I stayed. I spent the whole morning with the villagers, reaching Ndŭt at 3:30 in the afternoon.

Upon my arrival, I asked to see the "Cham stones," which were stored at the house of the village chief. I can hardly describe my amazement on being confronted with the find. Reality transcended what I had dismissed as the product of Krae the Widower's imagination. I was face to face not with Cham stones but with honest-to-goodness, hewn, prehistoric stones. And what stones! They were the biggest anyone had ever seen! Just imagine how a prehistorian would feel if he accidentally discovered some Campignian pieces a meter long, that is to say, three or four times longer than the finest pieces yet furnished by that period.

Apart from one smaller, badly hewn piece of different appearance, the whole comprised ten slabs of metamorphic schist ranging in length from 65.5 to 110.7 centimeters, whose workmanship was absolutely remarkable. The largest slab, for instance, reached its maximal thicknesses of 5.1 and 6.5 centimeters respectively at each of its highly convexed extremities. It was only 3.2 centimeters thick in its central section, while it extended more than a meter in length! From the point of view of stonework, it was an astonishing achievement, especially when one considers the technical equipment of those who hewed them. Each slab must have been separated from the rock by cleavage with the help of a wooden wedge; and the slabs were probably smoothed and finished by means of a wooden chisel; cut into shape with broad, flat, chisel strokes, they reveal tiny indentations all along each of their sides, produced by percussion, while their edges have been blunted through wear. This type of workmanship links them in prehistory to the Bacsonian complex, one of the most ancient manifestations of human activity so far uncovered in Indochina. This complex corresponds to the European Neolithic, being reminiscent of Campignian material in appearance.[8]

Despite my intense curiosity aroused by the sight of these magnificent stones and by the position in which they had been found, the program of ethnographical research I had assigned myself and my poor health, which threatened to cut the work short, prevented me from undertaking immediate excavation work. One problem was that in all the enormous mass of earth removed absolutely nothing besides the stones themselves had been found. This perplexed me even more. I did attempt a very small sounding, but it produced nothing. Yet I realized that if I launched into excavation work, it could very well become a lengthy operation. The *rngool* would have furnished a copious harvest, for men have always liked to erect their houses in places where others have preceded them. I also lacked the necessary excavating equipment. I therefore postponed this research until the end of my mission when I could consider my ethnographical program as having been completed. Unfortunately, as I have indicated, my mission did not end under normal circumstances, and due to illness, I was unable to undertake the excavations vital to an understanding of this discovery. I did at the time take earth samples from the different levels of the cut produced by the hollowing out of the trail and from those levels which had been exposed by my small sounding. Most important of all, I asked permission of the Ndŭt villagers to take the stones with me.

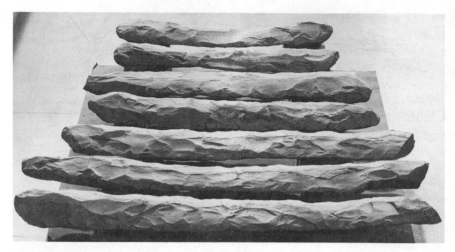

Seven of the lithophone stones as displayed on a wooden support in the ethnomusicology section of the Musée de l'Homme. (Collection Musée de l'Homme. Cliché: MH 50–24–101, 62–562–693.)

Front and back of Stone I (numbered according to placement in orchestral series—see photograph above). It is the second-longest, Stone II being 110.7 cms, with dimensions (in centimeters) as follows: length = 110.5 (axis = 98.4); width at head = 13.8 (at 8.5 from tip), central portion = 14.3 (at 47 from head), foot = 14.7 (at 3.3 from bottom) (axis); thickness (at same respective places as for width): head = 5.8, central portion = 3.1, foot = 5.1; weight = 10,440 kilograms; frequency of oscillation = 170. For a comparison with the other stones, see Condominas (1952), pp. 282–283. (Collection Musée de l'Homme. Cliché: MH 50–24–101, 51–1328–693.)

They saw no reason to object. The stones had no value for them since nobody had had a dream about them—an occurrence which could have made them into a token of alliance sent by the Spirits.

Upon my return to Săr Lŭk, Baap Can questioned me about the Cham stones. I gave him the information I had gathered at Ndŭt Liěng Krăk, and in describing the stones, pointed out that they produced a metallic sound when struck with the finger. At this the old man concluded, "Formerly made of iron, they have changed into stone."

Because of the exceptional character of the stones which, moreover, all seemed to belong together, I decided to ship them all to France, their weight and size notwithstanding, rather than taking only one or two as samples. This would obviate the risk of drawing false conclusions if, as I suspected, each piece had a value not only in itself but also in relation to the whole group.

This decision proved to be particularly fortunate. On being informed by H. Kelley and C. Lévi-Strauss that the musical stones had arrived, the musicologist André Schaeffner went over to the basement room where they had been unpacked. Intrigued by the objects, he arranged them in order of height, then in order of pitch, and perceived with utter amazement that he was dealing with an Indonesian musical instrument, or rather with elements of at least two instruments. Five of the stones produced a pentatonic scale; two others were the first notes of the octave above; and finally, the three remaining slabs (leftover pieces after completion of the instrument or, what seems more likely, parts of another instrument) were more or less in tune with those of the first group.

The scale of the lithophone is pentatonic and of Indonesian rather than Chinese type. Jaap Kunst considered it akin to the *pèlog,* while André Schaeffner regarded it as belonging to a type of scale anterior to both the *pèlog* and the *sléndro,*[9] one that has now disappeared and whose sole representative would be the prehistoric lithophone I had brought back.

The stones of Ndŭt Liěng Krăk thus constitute the sole surviving ancestor of the *gamelan,* the Javanese orchestra, that has come down to us. It is one of the very few prehistoric musical instruments ever to be discovered. Furthermore, its tone is remarkable and easily bears comparison with the *saron,* or metallophone, an important component of the Javanese orchestra which made such a profound impression on Debussy when he first heard it at the 1889 exhibition.

Given the shape and weight of the stones, the instrument must have been played like a xylophone or metallophone by placing the slabs parallel to each other on a resonant casing (which could simply have been two ordinary beams). Seen in this way, the lithophone of Ndŭt Liěng Krăk fills a gap: it is the first known working in stone of this kind of instrument. Chinese lithophones are in fact composed of jade slabs or resonant stone, most often in the form of a square suspended from a frame.

All the prehistorians who have seen these stones have been struck by their exceptional manufacture. And this quality is even more enhanced by the fact that they are parts of a musical instrument. The extraordinary skill required of the stonecutter in making slabs a meter long by about fifteen centimeters wide and several centimeters thick is already difficult enough to imagine. Yet in addition, he had to obtain a musical sound from this long, elegant slab of stone corresponding to a specific note, proving the artist's very fine appreciation of musical pitch. These tones must have been obtained through long and cautious experimentation by breaking off fine chips of stone with sharp, light taps, as I have seen it done at Săr Lŭk by a *njau cĭng* (a "healer of flat gongs"). Using a sort of metal scraper, he would remove a light shaving of metal from the bottom of every *cĭng* to be tuned, alternately striking the defective instrument and a well-tuned *cĭng*. In this way, he planed the bottom of the instrument until he had obtained the appropriate unison. But to come back to the lithophone, the tonal beauty of its slabs evokes the most delicate sonorities of the Javanese or Balinese *gamelan*.

The great majority of the prehistorians who examined the lithophone were of the opinion that it was of great age. What from the very outset prevented me from completely accepting this opinion—albeit one that enhanced the value of my discovery—was a purely subjective reaction. As it was, these stones were the largest implements of cut stone known up to that time and they were to be ranked among the finest pieces ever brought to light. That they should, in addition, constitute the most ancient known musical instrument was too much to expect. To be sure, one is under the obligation to be skeptical, whatever the circumstances; but one must be doubly cautious with regard to discoveries he has made himself for fear of exaggerating their importance. Even apart from typological considerations, another factor in establishing the date seems to support the great age of these stones: namely, the thickness of the patina, which reaches one millimeter. Nevertheless, it must be admitted that in such a climate, this affords no absolute proof. What made me more especially cautious, however, was the lack of precise stratigraphical data, a terrible hindrance in the area of prehistoric discovery. And even if I had had such data at my disposal, it could only have provided an approximation since, as we shall see later, the position in which the stones were found points to a secondary use different from the original one. On the other hand, in the study he has devoted to the lithophone, André Schaeffner rightly underscores the close relationship existing between the timbre of these stone slabs and that of gongs, bells, or metallophone slabs, all metal instruments,

a kinship that we do not find to such a degree between the Ndŭt Liĕng Krăk lithophone and various chimes of polished stone. Are we to surmise that the natural sonority of these stones led the people who handled them into transferring to them an art that was first practised with metal, and one with which they were more or less acquainted?

He goes on, however, to make the following point:

To defer the manufacture of the instrument until the Bronze Age is not to deny its antiquity. There are flawless Chinese bells dating back to the first millenium B.C. And they are too flawless not to have been preceded by a long evolution. Even if we were to date the lithophone from the beginning of the Christian era, the standard of its workmanship would still be superior to that attained by Western instruments of the period (Schaeffner, 1951, p. 16).

If it is not one of the oldest musical instruments ever discovered, it is at any rate the most ancient whose entire scale—or greatest part thereof—we know with precision. From a scientific point of view, this outweighs the empty satisfaction of possessing the oldest instrument in the world (Schaeffner, 1951, p. 2).

Another argument can be brought against the very great age of the lithophone. As I said earlier, all the prehistorians without exception admired the extraordinary technical skill of those who had fashioned it. Such mastery in stonecutting is always manifested during periods when stone enters in competition with a new material; namely, metal. And it is invariably with the advent of metal that the finest examples of lithic workmanship are to be found. Then again, in the complex mosaic of cultures presented by Southeast Asia, one frequently finds advanced civilizations on the plains coexisting with ethnic groups using archaic techniques in the mountains. It is quite possible for a group utilizing stone to live at a backward level in the forest at a time when metal is already being widely used in the lowlands. Until a thorough stratigraphy of prehistoric Indochinese soil layers has been established, no reliable date can be specified. All statements put forward concerning the probable ages of the different layers in this area of the globe are purely hypothetical.

If we cannot state with assurance that these giant cut stones date back to earliest antiquity, neither can we consider them as being of recent origin since the present inhabitants of the site, the Mnong Gar, knew nothing of their existence at the time of their discovery. We have noted how the unusual appearance of these large slabs of schist had led the Mnong Gar into thinking they were Cham stones. Had they been ten times smaller, they would have been called *suung wiik* ("nightjar hatchets"), like all prehistoric stone artifacts.[10] Had they been shaped in the form of an animal or an object, they would have been dated back to the time of the Flood. Yet in spite of their unusual appearance, they can be recognized as the product of human effort. Thus, we attribute them to man, and more specifically to a breed of men reputed for their considerable strength, men who were more skillful than the ancestors of the Mnongs: namely, the Chams, about whom the Mnongs have only the haziest notions. Moreover, the word *prum* designates both the Cham people and a distant period in their conception of time. Now it appears that the settlement of the Mnong Gar in this region, and especially on the plain, the alluvially rich part of the Daak Kroong valley, dates back several centuries.

Furthermore, there is a strong likelihood that at least one other ethnic group occupied this region at some period between the settlement of the Mnong Gar and that of the population who cut the lithophone slabs. Indeed, the position in which the stones were found leads one to suppose that the people who grouped them in such a vertical manner were unaware that they were dealing with a musical instrument. For if one assumes they were aware of their nature, one is obliged to put forward the hypothesis of a funeral gift, according to the custom among numerous tribes of Southeast Asia and particularly among those in the High Plateau country. But in that case, a number of other gifts ought to have been found at the site: weapons, tools, vases, cooking pots, jewelry, and so forth. Given the very great value the lithophone must have had, in terms of both the craftsman's skill and the time required for its manufacture, the dead man receiving such an offering would have had to be an outstandingly important person. Nowadays the offering never extends to an entire set of gongs but merely to a single component, no matter how important the person. Even assuming the dead man was so notable as to warrant an entire set, it is curious that no other object was uncovered in the entire mass of earth displaced during the cutting of the trail.

The conformation of the ground rules out any hypothesis which assumes the intentional burial of the instrument: On the basis of a substantial sampling, the soil from which these stones were exhumed is colluvial in nature.[11] Removed through erosion, the earth from the hillside accumulated around the upright stones, was compressed by rainwater, and then piled up again around the obstacle until it was entirely covered.

In the light of our present knowledge, the most plausible hypothesis is to assume that, after being abandoned by those who hewed and used them as a musical instrument, the slabs were found by an ethnic group who knew neither their manufacture nor their purpose. This tribe then reassembled them as objects of veneration in a cult. With the passage of time, the earth removed from the hillside through erosion piled up around the rocky core formed by the cluster of stones, ultimately burying them. Finally, a third ethnic group, the Mnong Gar who presently inhabit the site, discovered them. The "Spirit-stone" hypothesis stems from the connection that can be made with the behavior of the contemporary Mnong Gar in analogous circumstances. Had I not overheard that conversation in Baap Can's house when I did, and acted upon it, there can be no doubt that someone in Ndŭt would ultimately have had a dream in which these strange stones played a part, thereby demonstrating that they were a token of alliance with the Spirit of the stones.[12] The man having the dream would have vowed a cult to them, so that by the time I finally heard about them, I would not have been permitted to take even one of them, much less the whole lot. And science would have continued to know nothing about the existence of this type of lithophone. One can see that the utility of knowing the native language is not confined to ethnography!

One of the first disappointments in store for a young ethnologist is the interminable delay between the date he submits the manuscript and the date it is published. Others sometimes lose patience too. André Schaeffner and I had each given a lecture about the lithophone on June 21, 1950. But whereas his article appeared in July 1951, the edition of the *Bulletin de l'Ecole Française d'Extrême-Orient* containing mine did not come out until two years later (despite the year indicated on the journal's cover). So I was surprised to read the following remark in the *South African Journal of Science* (September 1952, p. 48), penned by Percival Kirby, the eminent and authoritative musicologist: "Unfortunately M. Condominas fell ill and died shortly after the discovery of the stones"!

At this juncture, let me recall a final anecdote concerning the lithophone. Having been subsequently appointed to serve as an expert on rural sociology for UNESCO, I was greeted at Vattay, the Vientiane airport, on October 17, 1960, by the coordinator of the United Nations team of which I was to be a part. Picture a man with the bearing of Rodin's *John the Baptist*, with magnificent white hair and white beard, and with the strong yet sensitive personality of a man who has traveled widely, read voluminously, listened well, and assimilated everything. Add to this a lively wit and the vigor of a sportsman who wants to discount the weight of his years, and you will have some idea of the impression Mr. Van der Plas made on our first meeting. Van der Plas —I'd heard the name somewhere! It sounded typically Dutch; I had no doubt heard about a namesake of his on one of my missions.

He invited me to dinner at the Settha Palace where a room had been reserved for me. He was a brilliant storyteller. The word "tape-recorder" slipped out during the conversation. "For you ethnologists," he remarked, "the tape-recorder has now become an indispensable work tool." By way of example, he told me a quite extraordinary story involving funeral rites and a "ceremony of the magical puppets" with an accompanying chant which he had witnessed on a journey into a remote corner of eastern Java. What he said caused me that slight uneasiness one feels upon hearing something one has heard somewhere before but cannot quite pinpoint.

Then suddenly he asked, "Do you know the great musicologist, Jaap Kunst?"

"Yes, of course. I had the opportunity of meeting him at the Musée de l'Homme, and even . . ." I started to reply.

"He's one of my best friends. I sent him the recordings I made of the chants and received an extremely enthusiastic letter by return mail. Do you know why?"

"Because the chants were so beautiful?"

"The chants were magnificent. But it wasn't that! I had unwittingly made it possible for him to resolve a problem. The musical scale of these contemporary chants is the only extant example of a scale furnished by a prehistoric musical instrument made of stone which was discovered in Indochina by a young French ethnologist."

"The Ndŭt Liĕng Krăk lithophone!"

At that moment, I remembered when I had heard the name Van der Plas. A year earlier, I had run into Mr. Schaeffner at the Musée de l'Homme, and he had told me of Jaap Kunst's jubilation on discovering the close relationship between the musical scale of the prehistoric lithophone and that of a contemporary Javanese chant. But Jaap Kunst had died before publishing anything whatever on the subject.

Amazed and embarrassed, I informed Mr. Van der Plas that I was the young ethnologist in question. Our astonishment, I think, was not unfounded. After all, here were a Dutchman who had discovered in an inaccessible corner of eastern Java an unknown magical chant representing the sole vestige of a musical scale and a Frenchman who had found in the Vietnamese jungle a prehistoric instrument producing the same scale. To find themselves together at the same hotel table in Vientiane during a troubled period in Laotian history was surely a fantastic coincidence. I am well aware that the paths of people who travel a great deal ultimately cross. But all the same![13]

To go back ten years: Although the preparation of my explanatory lecture on the lithophone had been very time-consuming, I had, nevertheless, managed to render what I considered the most important passages of my notes into French, enough in fact to enable someone else to translate the remainder at some future date should the need arise. This done, I began making plans for another mission to the High Plateau country in order first to check certain data and extend my investigation to the Mnong Gar as a whole, and second, to study their rice-growing neighbors: the Mnong Rlam to the north, and more especially the Lac to the east. My hope—which I confess seems absurd in retrospect—was that I would be given enough time to set up a program of study extending over several years into Jörai, the largest proto-Indochinese group whose language is Malayo-Polynesian.

As it turned out, I was not even allowed to return to the Mnong Gar country. The director of the Office of Overseas Scientific and Technical Research, the organization for which I worked, informed me I would be going to Africa.[14] It was inconceivable to me that he would hold firmly to this assignment, especially since it was simply a matter of filling a vacant post. So I hastily advised the director of the Ecole Française d'Extrême-Orient that my doctors had given me permission to return again to my "terrain." The latter's requests and the objections put forward by the Council of Human Sciences failed to deter the director from his original plan. As a botanist can readily transfer from Indochinese to African plants, so, he contended, can an ethnologist make similar transitions among the societies he studies. As I lacked the funds to repay the costs of my two-year traineeship, I had to prepare for my trip to Togo within a month, or more exactly, Togo and the Cameroons, for

I had been assigned to serve as a sociologist on a food mission to these two countries.

I was sent on ahead while my future colleagues were completing their training in Paris. I was ill-prepared not only in terms of the area's culture but even more in terms of my subject: the sociology of nutrition. This meant that I had to make a double reconversion in a ridiculously short period of time.

My state of mind upon embarking for Africa in February 1952 can well be imagined. To make matters worse, I discovered racism in a more blatant form than I had encountered in the past, racism having considerably diminished in Indochina after the Vietnamese revolution which had forced the most diehard colonialists to revise their opinions; so much does force remain the most effective argument to correct whatever is based upon it. All of this took me back to my adolescence, twelve years earlier, when I had become aware of the colonial situation of Vietnam. And even that was hardly comparable with the racism to which the blacks were subjected, a racism that was much more clear-cut and vulgar.[15] One consolation during my journey, however, was in meeting Pierre Verger on the boat and Théodore Monod upon landing at Dakar. Certainly the most inspiring non-Africans I met in Africa, both men were experts with long experience who encouraged me by their example. My debt to Verger is enormous, for it was he who revealed the riches of the Voodoo religion to me, and in that exceptionally illuminating way of one who has lived it. A feeling of genuine fondness and profound attraction had first drawn this man to the *orisha* and *voodoo* cults. He had subsequently set about studying them in order to understand them more fully.[16] Of all the gods, he manifestly preferred Shango, the God of Thunder (called So or Xevieso[17] in Fon and Mina countries), a god who very soon exercised a kind of fascination over me.

To be set down in a region for which you are unprepared is something I would not wish on anyone. Because then, the trepidation that is common to anyone at the start of any new experience turns into panic. If I was poorly prepared in professional terms, my preparation was even worse on the personal level; and that, for an ethnologist confronting his terrain, counts just as much as knowing the bibliography. The fact was that since specializing in Oceania and more specifically in the Mnong culture, I had completely forgotten about Africa, flung far beyond the Pleiades—for which I knew at least the Mnong name and legend.

Everything I saw was unexpected. On the personal level, I had been allotted an apartment over a chemical laboratory which, at that time, was certainly one of the best-equipped on the African coast. Besides the fact that this sort of comfort violated—albeit wrongly—the romantic association between the terrain and a certain asceticism, I lost that protection against the white man's world provided by the isolation in which I had lived at Sǎr Lǔk. At Lomé, I had a small apartment at my disposal which made it possible for me to live with my family (although my wife subsequently refused to join me there) and to build up my strength after each excursion. Substantial disadvantages counterbalanced these advantages. The latter involved a resumption of contact every time with the "preterrain,"[18] and there, the whites had a more colonialist attitude than those of Vietnam. Furthermore, the ones I met who had formerly been to Indochina indulged in racism by displaying nostalgia for the Far East, lauding the merits of the Vietnamese—whom I am sure most of them disdainfully ignored while living in Southeast Asia—the better to humiliate the blacks. Nevertheless, during my periodic exile in Lomé, I finally found a few likable Europeans little touched by racism. Above all, I had the luck to make firm friends with my two colleagues from the Office for Overseas Scientific and Technical Research, the pedologist and the nutritionist, both of whom had managed to detach themselves from the colonial milieu. A third friend was the agricultural engineer of Anecho whose affection for the Vietnamese was not at the expense of the Africans. Our complementary professional concerns and our friendship enabled me to enjoy his hospitality in the experimental center he directed outside of the administrative township, thereby avoiding many pointless clashes.

More often than not, the administration's attitude was remarkably stupid. Yet can we reproach them? It was simply a colonial administration in a country where an emerging local élite was demanding its due, which the authorities were refusing to grant. It was the time when, in spite of the government's electoral trickery, the Committee for Togolese Unity was proclaiming itself the most dynamic political party, to which the most distinguished persons of South Togo belonged. As circumstances would have it, my best friends belonged to this opposition party or were in sympathy with it. I have no passion for defiance and did not systematically seek out those who were at odds with the colonial power structure, yet it was among them that I discovered the most dynamic individuals with whom it was possible—despite the administrators' statements to the contrary—to have fruitful exchanges. When one is pacifist by nature, it is not very stimulating to find oneself in constant and complete disagreement with those responsible for the policy of the country to which one belongs.

Most of all, the terrain did not correspond to the idea I had of it. I always need to visualize a culture, and in spite of the books I had read—which were already outdated—Africa represented for me great forests, jungles, and wild beasts—its "dark continent" atmosphere. Instead, going inland from the Oceanian coconut groves fringing the sea, I found a veritable Beauce of manioc and maize studded with densely populated villages and townships. I had to go up to Sokode before I heard mention of a lion, and even then it was a figment of the imagination of a worthy gendarme from Limousin who had an irrational fear of the animal. Ironically, people who knew I had undertaken my early research in Indochina would recall the luster of Far Eastern civilizations in order to please me. I would surprise them without difficulty by telling them I had lived in a poor jungle village at a technical level far below that of the South Togolese. I had upset the norms: I had gone to Asia to study the "savages," and to Africa to study a civilization—namely, the Bénin.

It was common practice at that time to talk about the absence of a sense of history among the Africans. On the very first evening of my in-depth investigation of Ngoepe, I had the opportunity to be present at a confrontation between two families over their respective versions of the development of regional migrations. The voices rose very quickly, and the discussion almost turned into a pitched brawl. Far from being but a simple academic problem, history is vehemently sensed, for it represents an essential element of community life and of the entities that comprise it. And there is not a town or village whose name is not a symbolic condensation of a long historico-legendary tale familiar to the majority of the inhabitants.

But there was one domain at least in which reality exceeded my expectations, surpassing what my favorable impression of Africa, based on reading and visits to museums, had unconsciously led me to hope for—namely, the esthetic expression of the Togolese cultures. You can well imagine how attractive this factor was to someone who had had to choose between painting and ethnology. I was not of course dealing with the Ife masterpieces or with those of the Baoulé region, neither of which I had viewed in their proper setting. Yet who could remain unmoved by the expressive violence of a Legba defending a crossroads to Glidji? Besides, art is always more compelling when it gives expression to everyday life: the striking quality of cotton fabrics in vivid colors set out to dry or worn by a woman with the bearing of a goddess; the plasticity of ordinary objects; or girls of dazzling beauty wearing only a scant red triangle (pearl belt and loin-coth) which enhances their resplendent black skin.

However, I think it was the music that fascinated me most. It possessed the vitality that characterizes the plastic arts through the opposition of striking colors and lines, or masses, both curved and straight. The music consisted almost exclusively of percussion devices, with geminated bells and handclapping as well as the striking of commonplace objects such as bottles, tin cans punctured with a stick, and canned preserves. Dominating all were the orchestras of drums in varying shapes and sizes. There was a similar vehemence in the use of the voice, the most strident screechings never disrupting the harmony of the choirs. This kind of music was inseparable from its visual expression, the dance, particularly since music and dance allied to a certain dramatic form constituted the external support for religious phenomena. These phenomena together with the language—in this instance, the Mina or Gẽgbe language—seemed to me the best area of study through which to understand this culture that was so far removed from what had hitherto been familiar to me.

In South Togo, and especially in the region of Anecho that I had chosen as my field of activity, So is the form of Voodoo which counts the largest number of followers and whose prestige is the most solidly maintained. The popularity of So is due to the aura of mystery which shrouds the secret aspects of the cult and to the spectacular outward manifestations which always attract a crowd of curious people.

The Voodoo ceremonies usually last several days. They consist of secret episodes performed inside the temple to which only the Voodoo priests *(hūbono)*, the vodusi, and acolytes *(hūnovi)* have access. Anyone not belonging to the sacerdotal college found crossing the sacred enclosure, even inadvertently, would be severely punished on the spot. The greater part of the ritual takes place outside the temple and consists of a succession of sacred dances in which the elements of a more complex, more "total" spectacle (to use an expression dear to modern dramatic theorists who subscribe to the ideas of Artaud) are discernible in their embryonic state. They are a mixture of ballet, clowning, acrobatics, and sometimes even include the outline of a play. However, it should not be forgotten that this is a religious ceremony, and not a simple piece of secular entertainment.

This spectacle, to which the common people are invited, takes place on a dance square usually close to the temple. The musicians take their places around the edge, about half an hour before the start of the show, and begin to play. The orchestra is composed of different kinds of drums, calabash beaters, and geminated bells; but the principal "tom-tom" instrument playing the melody and determining the role of the others is the big bass drum.

All the dancers are Voodoo followers belonging to the *Xevieso-Agbue* cycle (the God of Thunder and his wife, the Goddess of the Sea). The spectacle consists of a danced and mimed performance by the terror-inspiring, gesticulating Voodoo, exterminator of perjurers and thieves, and by his wife, a sweet, domestic woman who constantly intervenes to calm her irascible husband's anger. Now it happens that the priest in charge of the ceremony invites the *Ananasi,* whose divinity goes back not to the Thunder cycle but to the Sky cycle, to join in. This distinction seems quite vague, however, in Togo where most people consider *Anana-Buruku* a secondary divinity of the So cycle.

The Voodoo followers of So and Agbue are subdivided into two groups each having their particular roles and characteristics. The *Avleketesi,* devotees of the goddess Avlekete (another of Agbue's names), are the clowns of these sacred performances. Dressed and adorned in the same way as the other Voodoo worshippers, they deck themselves out in grotesque emblems and headdressess, especially the latter: worn-out European hats, battered colonial-style helmets, and straw hats of unbelievable dimensions. It is they who come on stage first. During the course of the performance, they execute the same dance routines as the other Voodoo worshippers, but their main function is to amuse the gallery either by caricaturing their solemn womenfolk or by surrounding one of them and singing obscenities to try and make her laugh.

Agbue has some women initiates also in her service, with stern roles. These *Xuenusi,* or Losi, dedicated to the Crocodile, wear white headdresses and clothing. It is not uncommon to see the Crocodile "strike"—we would say

A dance by the *Avleketesi,* devotees of the goddess Avlekete (Agbue), clowns of the Voodoo ceremonies.

"possess"—one of his servants during a performance. The chosen one then dances with the violent and terrifying expression and gestures of the divinity. The movements can be so vigorous that the "possessed" one, in a state of trance, contorts herself, scrapes the earth with her fingernails, and rolls about on the ground until she is exhausted.

Even more than the Crocodile's servants, it is the *Sosi* and the *Hũsrui*—men and women Voodoo followers of the God of Thunder—who manage the dramatic part of these spectacles. All wear red parrot feathers on their foreheads and brandish the symbolic arms of the vengeful god—namely, the spear or the curved axe, which is sometimes replaced by a wooden rifle. The Husrui always look proud. Some of them are draped in multicolored togas when they come on stage, and all of them wear the warrior's breeches, over which they sometimes have a set of short corolla-style skirts reminiscent of those worn by the Greek evzones. These, however, are becoming less and less common.

A dance by the *Xuenusi,* or *Losi* (initiates of the Crocodile), women with stern roles in the Voodoo performances. This photograph shows the last woman entering in a trance and running about brandishing a knife in each hand.

Always "armed," they signal their approach by constantly shaking their small tubular bells.

The Hũsrui displays bring to mind, though on a religious level, the performances of acrobats or tragic actors. They are regarded with the greatest respect. A Hũsrui has only to signal the orchestra to play a dance, and one or two adulators immediately run up to him singing the Voodoo's praises on their geminated bells. Everything about them expresses force, violence, and fearlessness. Some charge suddenly and brutally into the crowd; others, after dancing frenziedly, fling themselves dangerously on top of a wall or roof top. The high point of the festivity occurs when, in a scene of high tragedy, two Hũsrui, after a wild chase, mime the death struggle of the god with violent and jerky movements.[19]

It was something I observed quite casually that helped me considerably in coming to grips with the Voodoo world. The first day after my arrival, I noticed a very sketchy tattoo mark representing the axe of the God of Thunder on the forearm of the laborer who was accompanying me on my rounds. The mere fact that I demonstrated an interest in such a small matter, upon disem-

The end of a *Losi* woman's trance as another woman coaxes her before she is taken to the temple.

barking from France, and commented on it politely secured me Kouassi's friendship. Not only Europeans, but fanatical African Christians were in the habit of treating all that related to "fetishism" and its practitioners with contempt when they did not pretend to ignore it (although they had certain fears of the people they associated with the satanic world). Surprised by my interest, Kouassi credited me with more knowledge about the subject than I really had, or so it seemed to me. Xevieso very quickly became the main topic of conversation on our excursions. Stimulated by my interest in the God of Thunder, our driver would also join in.

It is well known that the God of Thunder usually marks his passage—as in every other part of the world—by dispatching "stones of thunder," which are nothing more than prehistoric stones. Intrigued by my interest in Xevieso, Kouassi finally asked me the reason for it. I told him that the Voodoo gave me a very special protection since he had granted me the largest stones of thunder ever seen. And so it was that I came to talk of the Ndŭt Liĕng Krăk lithophone to a *hŭnovi* ("brother of the Voodoo") who knew nothing about prehistory or musicology. I must confess I got more pleasure out of chatting with him that day than I did with certain of my learned colleagues. Those stones, which I treasure a great deal, abandoned their secondary status as museum pieces, and as venerable witnesses to distant times came strangely back to life. They acquired a mystical charge that bound them more intimately to me than my discovery of them had done. From being an accident of my professional life, they had become a sort of component of my personality.

Some may regard my answer to Kouassi as a very cunning piece of ethnographical trickery. They would be sadly mistaken, for it was quite simply an example of that oriental form of politeness that irritates Westerners to the point where they often consider it as hypocritical or false. In point of fact, it was humanly impossible for me to let this "brother of the Voodoo" think I had been led to question him simply out of a stranger's curiosity. That would have been to lower him, almost humiliate him. On the contrary, as a participant in the same world as he, I was, in a sense, inquiring into the nature of customs similar to my own that he himself practiced. I would have been uncivil to act otherwise. But people will say to me: "Do you believe all that stuff? A fine rationalist you are, I must say!" One can be extremely vigilant in regard to those things that defy reason in his own culture (I speak of the Western); that is part of the dynamics of the group in which one lives. But if one is placed in another society impregnated with a certain type of mystical system, and he wants not only to put up with it but also to understand it and participate in its joys and sorrows, then he must let himself be carried away by it and speak its language (even if afterwards there are certain "souls,"[20] such as the rationalist and the professional, who judge him severely). Moreover, such reactions happen by themselves in a way. Furthermore, in the presence of non-Westerners, the oriental part of my education rises as if naturally to the surface. There are times, again, when it responds to Western interlocutors, and that is always disastrous; for example, I would find I had committed myself to writing an article or delivering a lecture that I had absolutely no desire to do. I would then exaggerate its importance as a means of extricating myself, and my polite refusal would be taken for modesty.

Very soon, Kouassi, an inseparable companion on my excursions, proved himself an exceptional guide. No sanctuary escaped our investigation, and I had information on all the scarifications, emblems, and ritual objects of most of the cults. But it was Xevieso that provided me with the richest harvest. Kouassi introduced me to interesting people and acted as my herald with the followers of diverse divinities. So one day, we agreed it was a logical thing for me to aspire to become a *hũnovi*. Indeed, he knew the priestess of a temple on the outskirts of Lomé who was intrigued by my story. She came to visit me, and as she could read without much difficulty, I showed her my study on the lithophone with my name on the title page and a photograph giving the scale of the stones. After meditating a long time over the document, she was convinced. The next day, laden with the necessary offerings, Kouassi and I went to the temple. The priestess consulted Fa, the God of Divination who, through the intermediary of cola nuts, expressed his approval.

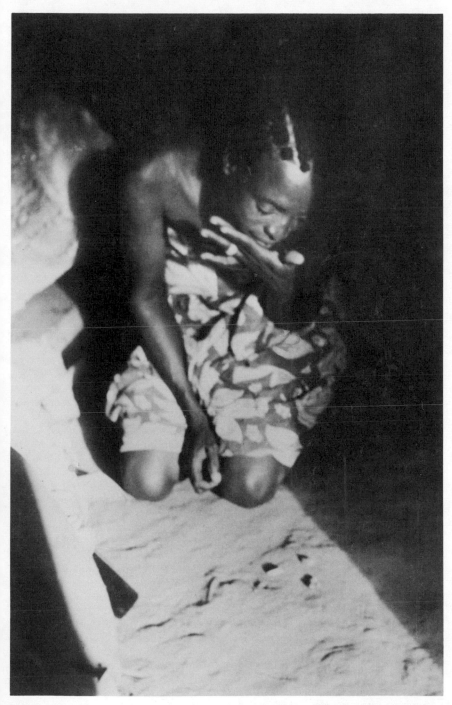

The priestess *(hūbono)* consulting with Xevieso, or Fa, by means of cola nuts to determine whether or not he approves of the new candidate (Georges Condominas), the Temple of Tokoe, April 27, 1952.

So it was that Xevieso, the God of Thunder, confirmed in Togo the confidence he had shown in me in Mnong country through the gift of the largest stones he had ever presented to any man.

NOTES

1. Literally translated: "With so many departures, how to make a return." It is taken from one of the opening poems in Supervielle's *Oublieuse mémoire* (1949), in which the poet decries the failure of memory to give a stable form to past experience. The word *retour* is used as a symbol of a desirable equilibrium. (Translator's note.)

2. Chapter 5 of Condominas (1965) bears the title "De la nécessité d'ethnographier les ethnographes." H. C. Conklin borrowed it—in French—for his paper "Ethnography" in Shils (1968).

3. The Mnong Gar are actually shifting cultivators. To use their own terminology, "We eat the forest." And as they move every year onto new land, this expression, followed by the name of the place cleared for cultivation, indicates the year to be recalled. Hence the name I gave to my 1949 chronicle about Săr Lŭk: *Nous avons mangé la forêt de la Pierre-Génie Gôo.* My article of 1966 (see References) is a partial translation of the first two chapters of that book.

4. The method of transcribing Mnong words (including proper nouns) used in this article is the one recommended by the Dalat Commission of August 1, 1949 (see Condominas, 1964). In general, a double vowel signifies a long vowel sound, and a double consonant is the preglottalized equivalent of the corresponding consonant. The circumflex indicates a closed vowel.

5. See the account of Srae's marriage to Jang, in Chapter 5 of Condominas (1957). For information on the family relationships of the people referred to here, see the "Index des noms de personnes" in Condiminas (1957 and 1965).

6. The Chams, who were "Hinduized Rhadé peoples" (to paraphrase George Coedès' expression relating to the Cambodians), played an important role in the history of eastern Indochina before it was conquered and absorbed by the Vietnamese in the fourteenth century. In their struggles against their conquerors from the north, the Chams frequently received support from their Montagnard cousins. A few fine vestiges of this once-glittering civilization can still be admired in the Vietnamese countryside or in the museum at Da Nang. Otherwise, nothing remains except one or two poverty-stricken villages in the region of Phan Ri and Phan Rang. The descendants of the Chams who sought refuge in Cambodia, however, set up prosperous Islamic communities reputed for their craftsmanship.

7. A *rngool* is a village site, recognizable in the forest by the *blaang* alignments (*Bombax malbaricum de Clerq*), former sacrificial posts which have become green again. When a village has to abandon the site it occupies (because of an epidemic or other calamity or because the land being cultivated is too far away), it is rebuilt on a *rngool* after consultation with the spirits.

8. For a detailed technical study of these stones and their site, as well as for a report on the different hypotheses that their discovery led me to formulate, see Condominas (1951). For a musicological study, see Schaeffner (1951).

9. See Helffer (1965, Vol. 1, pp. 41–42): "In the *pèlog*, or sequence of seven, which has traditionally been regarded as feminine, melancholic, the intervals are unequal. . . . The *pèlog* serves as an accompaniment to the tales of the Javanese cycle.

"In the *sléndro,* the octave is divided into five approximately equal intervals; the *sléndro* is attributed a serious and exalted masculine character and is associated with the play of the *wayang* figures, based on the Indian epics of the *Mahabarata* and the *Ramayana.*"

For more details, see Kunst (1949, Vol. 1, pp. 12ff).

10. The term *suung wiik* is given by the Mnong Gar to prehistoric tools that are regarded as "stones of thunder" not only by other proto-Indochinese groups but by the majority of peoples.

11. This conclusion is that of G. Aubert, whose laboratory analyzed the soil samples I brought back. See Condominas (1951, pp. 368–369 and picture A on p. 381).

12. This is what happened in the case of another lithophone, parts of which were seen by Jean Boulbet in the village of Maa' de Bboon Bördee on May 23, 1958. With greater insight than the Mnong Gar, the Maa' decided it was a musical instrument and played it. It was considered so valuable that only a great buffalo sacrifice (during which the various parts of the instrument are anointed with the blood of the victims) was enough to justify its removal from the sacred place in which it was housed. Concerning this important discovery, see Condominas (1965, pp. 349–351), and for more detailed information, see Condominas and Boulbet (1958). This lithophone was destroyed by American bombs, which obliterated the village of Bboon Bördee.

13. For a historical account of the mission during which the lithophone was discovered, see Condominas (1965). For more information on this particular episode, see Chapter 33 and also the note on pp. 475–476, which provides an exhaustive bibliography.

14. This was not the first time I had had to face such a radical change in orientation. After letting me spend a year preparing for Oceania, the director announced that I would be going to Africa. My professors, M. Leenhardt and P. Rivet, had managed to arrange for me to do work among other "Oceanians" (as Rivet called them)—namely, those of eastern Indochina—if I could not go to the Pacific. And so, thoroughly prepared for maritime ethnology, I was sent to study the Mnong Gar, the inhabitants of the Vietnamese mountains.

15. Eleven years later, in New York, I discovered that the racism directed against blacks in the United States far surpassed that prevalent in Africa. With each succeeding visit, however, I have been pleased to note the steady progress being made against this social scourge.

16. Verger's *Dieux d'Afrique*—which should be in the library of any man who calls himself educated—has demonstrated that photographs of high esthetic quality can be scientific documents of the first order. In any event, one cannot talk seriously about Voodooism without being familiar with Verger's complementary volume (now incorporated into the first volume): *Notes sur le culte des Orisa et Vodun*.

17. Xevioso is the most widespread form of the God of Thunder in Togo and, according to the Minas, would signify "So de Xevie" after the name of a village in Dahomey. For other etymological terms, see Verger (1957, pp. 525–537).

18. That is to say, the colonial milieu through which the ethnologist was obliged to pass in order to reach his "terrain"; see Condominas (1965, pp. 100–101). I had invented this neologism during a lecture I gave with L. Bernot to some trainee ethnologists, to put them on guard against the ethical and professional dangers that awaited them. I drew a picture of them that was published in a few dozen mimeographed copies in the *Premier Bulletin du Centre de Formation aux Recherches Ethnologiques* and distributed solely to colleagues. This action got me into trouble with the colonial administration—a factor partly explaining the intransigent attitude of the director of the Office for Overseas Scientific and Technical Research.

19. See the fifteen photographs in Condominas (1954a). For other ritual dances, such as those of the Yehue, kindred divinities to the Minas of the Anecho region, see the ten photographs in Condominas (1954b).

20. This is an allusion to the Mnong conception of multiple "souls"; see Condominas (1968).

REFERENCES

CONDOMINAS, GEORGES. 1951 (actually 1952). "Le Lithophone préhistorique de Ndŭt Liĕng Krăk." *Bulletin de l'Ecole Française d'Extrême-Orient*, 45: 359–392, plates XLI-XLV.

1954a. "Danses du Vodou de la Foudre dans le Bas-Togo." *Sciences et Nature*, 3: 19–24.

1954b. "Le Jour de l'an Mina" (a title the editor of the review preceded by "Au Dahomey" instead of "Au Togo" without consulting me). *Revue Française de l'Elite Européenne*, 52: 15–18.

1957. *Nous avons mangé la forêt.* Paris: Mercure de France.

1964. "Enquete linguistique parmi les populations montagnardes du Sud-Indochinois." *Bulletin de l'Ecole Française d'Extrême-Orient,* 46: 573–597.

1965. *L'Exotique est quotidien.* Paris: Plon.

1966. "The Primitive Life of Vietnam's Mountain People." *Natural History,* June-July, pp. 9–19.

1968. "Some Mnong Gar Religious Concepts: A World of Forms." In N. Matsumoto and T. Mabuchi, eds., *Folk Religion and the Worldview in the Southwestern Pacific.* Tokyo: Keio University.

CONDOMINAS, GEORGES, AND JEAN BOULBET. 1958. "Découverte d'un troisième lithophone préhistorique en pays Mnong-Maa' (proto-Indochinois du Vietnam Central)." *L'Anthropologie,* 62: 496–502.

HELFFER, MIREILLE. 1965. "Indonesie et Oceanie" in "Les Musiques traditionelles et ethniques," Chap. 1 of *La Musique, les hommes, les instruments, les oeuvres.* Paris: Larousse.

KUNST, JAAP. 1949. *Music in Java: Its History, Its Theory and Technique.* The Hague: Martinus Nishoff.

SCHAEFFNER, ANDRÉ. 1951. "Une importante découverte archéologique: le lithophone de Ndŭt Liĕng Krăk, Vietnam." *Revue de Musicologie,* 33: 1–19.

SHILS, E. A., ED. 1968. *Encyclopaedia of the Social Sciences.* New York: Macmillan.

VERGER, PIERRE. 1954. *Dieux d'Afrique.* Paris: Paul Hartman.

1957. *Notes sur le culte des Orisa et Vodun.* Mémoires de l'Institut Français d'Afrique Noire No. 51. IFAN-DAKAR.

17 / Tswamung: A Failed Big-Man

ANTHONY FORGE

To choose to write about a man whom I label a failure and with whom my relationship was also in many ways a failure, ending in an acrimonious parting, may seem perverse. Yet my contact with Tswamung was important, not only because he was the first informant with whom I had a relationship sufficient to provide reliable information which we could discuss and evaluate together, but also because he was the first and in some respects the only Abelam with whom I had genuine two-way communication.

If any one thing has convinced me of the virtues of the British social-structure tradition of anthropology in which I was trained, and more particularly in the analysis of political and economic relationships, it was the endorsement they received from Tswamung. We discussed Abelam social structure and the political organization of villages, the means by which big-men achieved their positions, in a way sometimes rather like a seminar, but with, on his side, the spur of past failure and the determination of future success, while on mine nothing but fear of failing my field-work novitiate to spice the academic concerns. In fact, he learned so well, he applied the principles we had discussed so earnestly, that his ultimate success was only stopped by the ultimate sanction—assassination. Our little seminars on anthropological analysis undoubtedly contributed indirectly to his death. When I returned to New Guinea three years later, I had hardly landed before I was asked to serve as an expert witness in the retrial of his alleged killers.

When we met we were both strangers in a difficult and often hostile village. He had a small garden on borrowed land but depended on two classificatory mother's brothers for sufficient food for his two wives and adopted children. He was not involved in the exchanges of the village and severed all his exchange relationships in his own village. He had no position in the place at all, any more than I did, but he at least spoke the language and with great eloquence; he was also known as a strong man throughout the area. I was imperfect even in elementary pidgin English and spoke not a word of Abelam, but my skin carried something, not prestige but a special status that conferred .

a sort of prestige on those close to me and indeed on the whole village. Whether I was a new sort of missionary, a trader, or a government man undercover was uncertain, but it was considered that any white man was bound to produce fringe benefits in cash and kind, even if he did not build an airstrip and instantly provide a deluge of European goods.

When I arrived, the first essential was to arrange for the building of a house, and it was here that Tswamung immediately stood out, although he had no status in the village, and the contract for building was negotiated with the two government hatmen,[1] the *luluai* and the *tultul,* who each organized gangs of men. Na:mei, as he was then called, was from the start the effective foreman. He was the only one who could use a saw to any effect and could work by himself without constant supervision. The house was built in a series of waves: in a burst of early-morning enthusiasm eight or nine posts would appear, be set up, and tamped home; everyone would then sit down and look admiringly at his work, ignoring the fact that two or three of the posts were too short. Na:mei would spot this at once, have them taken out, make measures of split cane to show the necessary length, and send men off to cut more while the two hatmen were just settling down to a smoke. What surprised me about his leadership was that although it had no basis in the structure of the village it was cheerfully accepted and unresented by all. His competence in this enterprise was recognized both by the hatmen, who were happy to have some of the responsibility of satisfying the strange white man's wants taken from their shoulders, and by the traditional leaders, the big-men, who played a minor part in this unaccustomed work, sitting well away from the site and making sheets of sago-frond thatch for the roof. For Na:mei himself my arrival gave him a chance to exercise, for the fortnight the house took to build, those talents and ambitions that he had had to bottle up ever since he had come to Bengragum Village. For me, he was a godsend. His presence ensured a better house built more quickly than I could have managed by myself, hampered as I was by excruciating self-consciousness and uncertainty about my position and future —desperately determined not to behave like the stereotype of the white man, cursing the stupid *kanaka* for laziness, bungling, big-headedness, and so on, but at the same time anxious to get a reasonable house built that could serve as a base for the next fifteen months. We were thus of mutual benefit in this initial phase, which also showed me Na:mei's greatest virtue, from my point of view: his freedom from *giris,* that cloying false servility with which most natives with any experience of whites treated all Europeans and which effectively blocks all communication at any but the most superficial of levels.

The Abelam,[2] whom I had come to study because I believed (with reason) that they were the last of the lowland rich cultures in the Australian half of New Guinea who practiced their traditional art for the traditional reasons, number about 30,000 and live on the southern slopes and lower foothills of the Prince Alexander Mountains in the Sepik District of the Trust Territory of New Guinea. Almost all are administered from the subdistrict office at Maprik, although some of the eastern villages came in the area of the Yangoru patrol post. When I arrived at Maprik, I was determined to find a village which was going to hold a ceremony involving art production during the year or so I had to spend. I set out on a patrol of the area, asking about prospects—a process I naively thought would provide me with reliable information on which to make a decision. Most villages assured me that they had given up the old tambaran cult and were now Christian, interested in growing rice and peanuts, at that time the two cash crops thought suitable for the area by the Department of Agriculture, Stock and Fisheries. When I pointed to the fine ceremonial houses, some with huge carved figures inside, I was told that some of the old men kept those but that there was no chance of the rest of the progressive, right-thinking villagers holding a ceremony. The missions had outlawed ceremonies, and the government thought them a waste of the time that should be spent working on the roads and growing cash crops. Only in Bengragum, a rather remote village in the southeastern part of the Abelam area, where the *luluai* was as naive as myself, did a hatman say that they intended to build a new ceremonial house and hold a tambaran ceremony that year when the yam harvest was over. To Bengragum I duly went, but the villagers did not build a new ceremonial house and held only a mockery of a tambaran ceremony with a few botched paintings, while in the dozen or so villages within five miles, fifteen new ceremonial houses were built during the season and many full-scale ceremonies were held, with months of preparation involving every known kind of artistic and other ceremonial work.

The Abelam were at that time leading a double life. When the food production had recovered from the effects of the war and the Japanese occupation, a great period of building ceremonial houses and holding ceremonies had taken place; the long-yam cult and the tambaran cult had both resumed their precontact intensity. In the early 1950's, however, mission pressure had increased as Catholic and fundamentalist Protestant missions competed for influence, until there was a pattern of alternating faiths with stations about every four miles along the government jeep roads that followed the main concentrations of population. Individual government officers, as they gradually brought the area back under full administrative control and instituted measures designed to provide improvements, had apparently manifested some hostility to the traditional cults and practices. There followed throughout most of that decade a period of standstill in the tambaran cult, although the long-yam cult continued without interruption. In Wingei village, where Tswamung and I later jointly participated at a large ceremony, two ceremonial houses whose structures were complete had been left empty and devoid of decorated facades because of mission intervention. But by 1958 the Abelam in the north and east had decided that they had lost more than they had gained by giving up the tambaran cult, the returns from cash crops had been small if not derisory, and attendance at the missions and even frequent swopping from one to the other had produced no benefits recognizable by the Abelam. Once one ritual group had decided to go ahead with a ceremony, there was a rush not to be left behind and the multitude of ceremonies put a severe strain on labor resources. The three ritual groups of Wingei village, with a total population of about six hundred, built four ceremonial houses and held three major ceremonies in the 1958–1959 season.

This conscious return to traditional ways was viewed by the Abelam as something the white man would disapprove of. They had already learned that some activities, such as the ritual cleansing by men bleeding their penes and the initiation of girls by beating and scarification, were condemned by all whites, who would launch into lectures on their evils whenever they heard of them. To avoid these tediums and minimize interference, the Abelam simply denied that they performed any of these practices; similarly the revival of tambaran activity was considered unsuitable for discussion with whites. Indeed the missionary at Wingei did not realize what was happening until he saw the ridgepole of a new ceremonial house appear above the coconut palms of the nearest ceremonial ground.

The state of withdrawal adopted by the Abelam could hardly have been more effective had it been planned and rehearsed. Virtually every adult automatically denied that any of the traditional usages that aroused the whites were still practiced or that anyone had any intention of reviving the tambaran cult. Such behavior, they implied, was unthinkable to those who had had the benefit of instruction by mission and government in the road to health, prosperity, and Christianity. Since most black-white contact took place on the stations or at any rate outside the villages, which whites very rarely penetrated, this pretense was surprisingly easy to maintain under normal conditions. It was not, however, easy to deceive a white man who not only had a house right in the middle of the village, but also went around persistently inquiring about just those sensitive areas. It must be admitted, however, that for a long time the Bengragum villagers did remarkably well in denying everything and laying false trails to lure me away from anything interesting.

During my early weeks in Bengragum, it seemed as if I would never experience other than suspicious evasiveness from the majority and an appalling blend of phony deference and false information from the sophisticates who "knew how to handle white men." As the weeks passed and I proved harmless, some friendliness started to replace the suspicion, but the evasiveness on certain key matters persisted. In this situation, my developing relationship with Na:mei was the only encouragement. He accepted early on what the majority took months to accept, and some never did: that what I wanted was information, that I did not want to change their lives in any way, to sell them anything, or to get them to work for me. But in his position as a visitor he was not prepared to reveal any Bengragum secrets, always saying he did not know, although, as I subsequently discovered, he had very full and accurate information on everything of importance that was going on. He would talk about his own village, Gwalip, several miles to the northwest, that he had left about a

year before, and thus provided me with information that I could use to discon-
cert the evaders on matters of ritual practice.

Among the treasures I had brought that whetted the appetites of the villagers was a cheap single-barreled shotgun. At first I used it myself, but was
constantly pestered by many young men, all claiming extensive experience, for
the post of *shootboi*. After trying one or two, watching them handle the gun
and blast vegetation yards from any game, I tried Na:mei, who brought back
three birds with his first two cartridges. For a while he continued to shoot for
me on an ad hoc basis, getting the occasional bird as reward but being well
satisfied with the prestige of carrying a gun, for in those days there were no
black gun-owners in the area. But as his value as an informant became clearer,
I put him on the payroll on condition that he help me with learning the
language. He tried to fulfill the condition but found me so slow and stupid—
as did all my would-be language teachers—unable to grasp some simple sentence when it was told me once, that his patience was sorely tried, and after
a time could not be found when needed. However, I found plenty of other and
more congenial tasks for him to perform and never regretted our contract.

It was soon after this that Na:mei changed his name. Name changing is a
frequent occurrence among ambitious Abelam men; any special event or having a major part in a successful and important ceremony can provide the
occasion. In this case the name he chose was significant not because it reflected
his new relationship with me (which undoubtedly spurred him to make the
change), but because the name "Tswamung" was that of a big-man and noted
warrior of a village traditionally an enemy of both Gwalip and Bengragum,
who had been killed by treachery just before pacification. The name, then, was
very definitely from the traditional system and an indication that he intended
to secure the same prestige and influence that the dead enemy had once
enjoyed.[3] A few weeks later, while we were visiting a nearby enemy village,
Tswamung behaved very aggressively toward a man who was otherwise not
taking any part in the debate. It emerged that this was the current bearer of
the name Tswamung and that Na:mei was trying to provoke him to fight so
that by beating him Na:mei would win the rights to the name. Enemy Tswamung refused to be goaded, however.

In many ways Tswamung né Na:mei had all the personal talents and quali-
ties needed to make a successful big-man; his biggest drawbacks were accidents
of nature, of which the most important was the fact that he was a second
surviving son. He was well above average in height and was in fine physical
condition with obviously powerful muscles. His face was large and square with
a massive jaw, a big mouth, and a fine, large, well-shaped nose. He could
assume a terrifying scowl, and even in repose his face suggested strength and
a difficult temper. His skin was a pleasant, dark *café au lait* color that is known
as red in the Sepik; he walked and spoke with great confidence and elegance.
He was, as far as I could tell, absolutely fearless and that was certainly his
reputation. I had seen him climb twenty feet up a large tree with the loaded

Tswamung in his role as *shootboi* with his third wife in front of Anthony Forge's house, taken at Tswamung's request.

and cocked shotgun held between his teeth. He claimed, and I heard independent accounts of the incident, that when he was working for a gold prospector in the mountains above his native village just before the war, he had given some offence and the *masta* had grabbed him by the hair and shaken him, cursing the while. Tswamung had responded in kind, and the two of them had tugged and cursed together. The prospector, never having encountered such behavior from a *boi* before, could not believe that Tswamung would not let go and resume an appropriate attitude. So they had remained, each with a firm grasp on the other's hair, locked together like fighting stags, until the *masta* apologized to the *boi,* and both withdrew their threats to take the incident to the government court. This establishment of moral equality between black and white—and equality in a very real and comprehensible Abelam way through direct, violent matching—gave Tswamung a unique standing among the younger men and returned plantation laborers. His reputation was augmented by his experiences during the war, when, having participated in the burning of Lae, he wandered back, taking a year or so to reach the Sepik. Part of the time at least he was with some semiofficial Australian units, but I suspect that some of the time he may have been working for the Japanese. Certainly, he learned to shoot and handle firearms in a most professional way. He ended the war with a Japanese rifle and grenades, but many Abelam had those. The grenades he used for fishing but the rifle he handed in just before the postwar amnesty expired.

Tswamung might have established equality, but this in itself made his relations with whites difficult and, although he was admired for his stand, his fellows knew that he was useless at getting anything out of Europeans or soothing ruffled missionaries or officials. In contrast his brother, older by about ten years, was much more successful. As a youth, he had accompanied the first government patrols into the area and when patrol posts had been established had become *luluai* for a considerable number of villages. As such, he scored great success by getting several important men jailed for sorcery in each of the villages that were traditionally enemies of Gwalip. He was also a fine orator and a big-man in the traditional system. His dominance survived the arrival of the Japanese and the return of the Australians, but in the early 1950's he retired, suffering from tuberculosis, and lived near a clinic on the coast, withdrawing totally from Abelam life.

Tswamung's relationship with his brother offered him enormous advantages. As a close kinsman of an outstanding individual, he had little difficulty in acquiring pigs, wives, and the best magic for long yams, and he was soon prominent in debate and ceremony. Furthermore, his brother's combination of firm commitment to the traditional way of life, including cults, and of adopting anything that the whites could offer that could be integrated without vital disruption exactly fitted Tswamung's own views. But, whatever he did, his brother was always preeminent. Tswamung might have more influence among the younger men but they were dependent on their elders for shell rings and magical paint—the keys to Abelam success. He tried to create his own network of obligation and support, but its natural basis in kinship and clanship was shared with his brother. The one accomplishment that his brother did not have was as an artist and Tswamung, determined to surpass him in one field, went to all the ceremonial preparations over a wide area, sitting with the sculptors, helping whenever he could, and trying to acquire the skill. But, as he ruefully admitted, he soon realized that he had no talent and that if he persisted in his efforts he would be more likely to attract mockery than praise. So Tswamung continued with his brother. Strong personalities with ambitious temperaments, who find their paths blocked in their own clan, sometimes change clan or even village, hoping to succeed a failing big-man or create a new network that they can coalesce into a group of supporters. But this course too was impossible for Tswamung; he had benefited so much from his brother, and in many ways they got on so well, that no one would accept him as a free individual.

In most patrilineal societies, the relationship between brothers is the paradigm of all relationships of mutual trust, helpfulness, support, lack of envy, and so on, but the actuality is often somewhat different. Tswamung and his brother lived in different hamlets, but often cooperated in gardening and other productive activities. They shared their inherited exchange partners, but each also had different partners within and outside the village. They had the most tremendous rows—shouting, threatening, hitting each other—several times fighting with improvised clubs and on one occasion, throwing spears at each other, while the whole village assembled to watch, until they were both wounded in the leg and, after exchanging shell rings, went off together to compensate their mother's brother for having lost blood. Despite these rows, and Tswamung's frequent threats to go away and seek work as a laborer, the two brothers continued to live in the village and, in terms of village groupings, to remain together and support each other. The diagnosis of tuberculosis in the elder brother and his consequent retirement from government office and the village should have given the younger the opportunity he had sought for so long; and indeed, he did lead the core of his brother's faction. The new *luluai* was his ceremonial exchange partner, and in general it seemed likely that he could at last become a big-man.

The followings of Abelam big-men are highly personal. They will have a core based on a clan or subclan, but that by itself is not enough. It is the personal network within and outside the village that makes a big-man. These networks die with the disappearance of their founder, but if his successor promises well they can be partially revived and augmented to form the basis of a new big-man's faction. Tswamung had reasonable hopes but, as he said himself, his temper tended to be short and in such times of peace, reconstruction, and vigorous mission activity, the virtues of the strong man, "one with bone," as Tswamung quintessentially was, were less in demand than before. The traditional Abelam rules of factional struggle had been revised as well; direct violence was on the decline, and use of the government Court of Native Affairs was on the increase. Skillfully timed and supported accusations of adultery or sorcery, instead of merely precipitating a brawl, could lead to the court and a jail sentence for the accused, especially if the accusers had the ear of the hatmen and, more importantly, the native police at Maprik station. It was inappropriate overreaction that was Tswamung's undoing.

At the time, Tswamung had three wives and two children of his own. One, a little girl, had been adopted by the *tultul* of Gwalip. Tswamung had also adopted two older children, and was as well taking responsibility for providing a wife for his father's second wife's son, in the correct manner of an ambitious man.[4] The girl was living with Tswamung and his wives, as is customary once the brideprice has been paid. She was, however, still some years away from puberty and her contacts with her future husband were very limited. The girl's father, whom Tswamung was trying to woo into his faction, but who had previously been something of an enemy, asked for the loan of a large shell ring to help with the purchase of a pig for presentation at a coming long-yam display. Tswamung was disconcerted; he had just raised six very fine rings to give the man as a brideprice and another six to make a presentation of a magnificent boar to his own exchange partner at the same yam display. His resentment of this extra demand showed as he regretted that he had nothing suitable to lend.

Within three weeks the father beat the slit gongs and denounced Tswamung for seducing his daughter. The case was heard the same day by the *luluai* and the *tultul;* the girl gave evidence, but she was confused under questioning. Tswamung denied it completely, and his wives and children supported him. The hatmen, both long associates of Tswamung, dismissed the charges, adding that since the brideprice had been paid, the injured party would, in any case, be the husband and his clan; the husband had raised no complaint and the clan was led by Tswamung. The father, urged on by others, then went to the neighboring enemy village of Ulupu, where a policeman on leave from outside the district was staying with his family. Although he had no official standing, all policemen carry with them an aura of the power of the Court of Native Affairs. The policeman came to the village, listened to the girl, and advised the father to take the whole thing to the Maprik court. He also publicly denounced Tswamung in his own village for deflowering an underage girl. Tswamung was furious, particularly since no one from his own faction spoke up in his defense. Apart from the glee of his opponents, everyone accepted this outrage by a privileged enemy in sullen silence. The policeman withdrew, and for two or three days nothing happened. The girl's father did not go to Maprik, and she continued to live in one of Tswamung's houses. Tswamung, however, refused to let the incident blow over, but went around reproaching his faction for failing to support him and for taking so tamely such an insult to the whole village.

The final episode came when the father, after again beating the slit gongs, returned the six fine rings to break the marriage. According to his own account, Tswamung was by now convinced that his faction was failing to give him adequate support on purpose and his reaction to the continued pressure of the accusation was disproportionate by Abelam standards. The rage was fine, but not if it was deeply felt; it must be abandoned and replaced by indifference the moment tactics suggested the change. The big-man must always be in complete control, first of all of himself, if he hopes for influence. The widely advertised return of the rings was well attended; the party bringing the rings contained all his opponents, and the rest of the village came too. Tswamung's own supporters were all present, but whereas at the time he was looking only for unconditional support and loyalty, he realized in retrospect that what they and everyone else was looking for was the sign of real big-man behavior from him. If he handled the situation successfully and stayed in control of himself and events, he would be a big-man, even if it meant contemptuously returning the girl and abandoning what, in any case, was a very dubious alliance. If he did not succeed, then he would remain a strong man, a dangerous man with whom one would not want to quarrel, but he would not be a real leader.

At first there was heated argument, accusation, denial, and counteraccusation, but the girl's father persisted in returning the rings. The spectators watched but did not intervene. Tswamung, as he told me, felt completely abandoned and "shamed." He seized the largest and finest ring and smashed it against a coconut palm, he broke his lime gourd and set fire to his two dwelling houses, preventing his wives from rescuing any of their possessions. When he attempted to burn down his yam house, he was prevented by force, but he was allowed to cut down some betel palms he had planted and to kill his remaining pig, which he told his first wife to pass on to her brothers for presentation to their ceremonial exchange partners. The only positive result of this display of social suicide was that he refused to give up the girl and told her father that if he persisted in his efforts to get her back a fight would ensue. The father made no further effort and she remained with a classificatory father of her "husband" for some years until their marriage was consummated after her puberty ceremonies. But the father's purpose had doubtless been served: Tswamung had shown that he was as always a strong man, but he had ceased to be a factor in the political life of Gwalip and its immediate neighbors. He left the same day, telling his wives to return to their kin, taking with him four of the remaining rings and giving the fifth to the widowed mother of the "husband" who had originally contributed it to the brideprice.

Although I was not present at any of the incidents just narrated, I have discussed them so many times with Tswamung that I feel the account to be valid, at least from his point of view. Moreover, Tswamung was by no means my only source of information. Both before and after his death I had contacts with virtually everyone involved, including his first and third widows, the only really successful interviews I have ever had with Abelam women; both were extremely shrewd observers of the political scene.

Tswamung came to Bengragum and was soon joined by his first and third wives; his second, who was lame and whom he disliked, stayed in Gwalip until he succeeded in getting a reasonable brideprice for her from a man in a village neighboring Bengragum.

I came soon after Tswamung, and already he was actively planning his return. It was going to be difficult, however, to erase the "shame" he had created by cutting himself off; he would have to give at least one pig and preferably two pigs to his ceremonial partner, who would distribute them to the whole village. He would also have to return the brideprice he had just received. All these required shell rings, but a man who is outside the exchange system has small hope of raising rings. In smashing his lime gourd, he had put a taboo on his own participation in any ceremonial activity at Gwalip—a taboo that could be removed only by the pig presentation. He needed rings and so did I, and the only rings that the Abelam will sell for money are small ones that are virtually decoration. Nowadays the Abelam may speak of their larger rings as worth ten or fifteen pounds, but they will not sell them for that or any other price. However, Tswamung knew how to change money into rings and when, after a few months, he had saved a few pounds from what I paid him and I was getting desperate because I had promised a large pig for a ceremony and found that money could only buy piglets, he went south across the Sepik plains to the Tswosh and Iatmul villages that had received a few rings in the precontact trade but that really valued only green snail shell. After about ten days he returned with some large rings, but they were stained and chipped. So he went north to the Arapesh ring makers and had them repolished. I had enough to fulfill my ceremonial obligations but he still helped me with one ring of the six needed for the pig so that we were properly associated in the ceremony and his son could be initiated into it under our joint sponsorship.

This ceremony, which was the high point of my main investigation into art, was held in Wingei about five miles north of Bengragum and on the edge of Gwalip's political sphere. Tswamung's presence and participation were the beginning of his rehabilitation. A man who has cut himself off can hope for little except being a dependent of some man in a strange village, with access to land but without any network of reciprocity to recruit labor to help him cultivate it. Tswamung could not feed his family on what he could cultivate at Bengragum. To play the role of initiate's father requires not only a large pig, but quantities of the finest yams, tobacco, and betel nut to supply the initiators both while they are preparing the ceremony and after, when the spirits wail their hunger from the enclosed ceremonial ground. Here again, Tswamung and I fitted together very well: I had money and could buy yams and coconuts, but I had no women to make them into the delicious white soup that was ceremonially required, and since I was not integrated into the kinship and clanship system in Wingei as I was in Bengragum, I did not know how to acquire cooks. Tswamung provided on one day six adult women with attendant children to prepare soup. In fact, my whole participation in the Wingei ceremony was fraught with difficulties from which Tswamung constantly rescued me.

When I first heard that Wingei was thinking of staging the largest and most important ceremony of the Abelam cycle, it had already become obvious that Bengragum was going to produce a rushed and inferior ceremony with little production of art. To encourage Wingei, therefore, I said that if they held their ceremony in the traditional way, with all the proper art work, I would present a huge pig. At that time I had not fully considered the implications of the dual organization which is the basis of all ceremony. By donating a pig, I had placed myself in the role of initiate's father and in the opposite half to the initiators who were going to prepare the ceremony and carry out all the painting. Strictly speaking, I was tabooed from entering the ceremonial enclosure where all the artistic activity was going to take place. Further, who was going to receive the pig? I had no partner and all the adult men of the initiators' half would be receiving pigs from their partners.

Before the last stage of preparation, the coming transactions are checked. Each man puts down in a line in the center of the ceremonial ground a portion of coconut husk, indicating his willingness to provide soup and other food and a pig to his partner in return for the preparation of the ceremony and the initiation of his son or younger brother. I had arranged for Tswamung to have my portion checked, and this in itself caused some comment. But it was coming to be accepted that I should be a middleman *(nyindendu)* who operated in both halves of the dual organization and that Tswamung was to have his son initiated as my representative. The problem of who should take my pig, however, remained, and as each man from the initiators' half came out and claimed the coconut husk laid down by his partner, it became embarrassingly obvious that no one was going to claim mine. Indeed, it stayed there in solitary and embarrassing prominence after all the others were gone. Tswamung was furious and wanted to take it up again, thus cutting himself, and me, out of another ritual system. I refused and various people who were debarred from taking it up themselves assured me that it would be claimed. They also hinted that it would be tactful if I left. This was just before dusk at 6:00 and I took the fuming Tswamung with me. At 11:30 the beating of slit gongs announced that all the coconuts had been taken up and within minutes I knew who my partner was, a very important man who by taking on two full-scale partners was demonstrating his preeminent status and who at the conclusion of the ceremony gave me a name of the very highest status—*Kwimbu tipma*—but which I later realized probably had reference to the incident since *Kwimbu* was the name of the ceremonial ground and *tipma* means coconut.

With his participation in the three-month-long preparations for a major ceremony assured, Tswamung started to consolidate his position. He was making important contacts in Wingei and it was agreed that if I was not around to receive the return pig at the next ceremony, he should continue to act on my behalf.[5] He organized a group from Gwalip to help with the artistic work and another from his old contacts in Tswanambu, a village between Gwalip and Wingei. He never appeared with these groups, but their presence was credited in part to him. Gwalip had never before participated in a Wingei ceremonial, and the significance of their presence was lost on nobody. Tswamung went to Gwalip from time to time but, as he said, when he went, it was secretly and while he was there he hid in the house of a classificatory brother. He was, through his association with me, acquiring the vital links outside his village that every big-man must have—and doing so very cheaply—but he was in no position to appear publicly in Gwalip yet.

Throughout all this time my field work in Bengragum and Wingei was progressing. I had many friends and informants in both villages and was involved in various social relationships that had nothing to do with Tswamung. Most of the day I did not see him but if in the evening I had no one else in, he would come and we would talk. I was usually concerned with what had happened in the village, he with his own problems. He often had special knowledge about events but was never very forthcoming about Bengragum, considering it none of his business. However, he would frequently cap some story of mine with one of his own, providing an often enlightening contrast or supplement. I got in the habit of trying on him my analyses of what was going on, and he soon started to use the same mode. We usually talked in pidgin English, which avoided the specialized meanings of the Abelam words. Time and again he would relate my speculations about Bengragum political life to his own Gwalip experiences.

Together we started to work out the criteria of success and the reasons for failure. We were both detached from the politics of our immediate environment; neither of us had any hope of becoming big-men in Bengragum. Yet our approaches were very different. I was fairly eclectic, but Tswamung operated within a set of assumptions about the nature of man as a political animal that were irreducible and typically Abelam. These were not the stated ideals of conduct—no one following those had any hope of success—but neither was the field wide open. Tswamung started to realize and then formulate a series of expectations about Abelam reactions to events that were fascinating and increasingly accurate. He then progressed to trying on me his analyses of Gwalip situations, including his own. We gradually came to appreciate the primacy of external contacts for success as a big-man and that even though he often acts overtly as a representative of his village vis-à-vis other villages, both allied and enemy, he can never hope to have any real support from the whole of his village. Once Tswamung realized that a big-man need have full support from only a faction within his village, deriving his position essentially from his relations with big-men of other villages, he knew exactly what to do in his own situation. He had acquired the understanding of how the system actually works that is the hallmark of the big-man.

To the average Abelam, the village is the war-making unit within which lies his only hope of security; all other villages, even allies, are regarded with the greatest suspicion, for at the very least they are the homes of sorcerers. Disputes within the village are to be deplored and settled, lest the enemy profit from the disunity. The big-man, however, appears to realize that factional competition is inevitable within the village and that influence comes to those who can conduct exchanges, mobilize aid, arrange truces, and so on with other villages. It is also from other villages that almost all sources of supernatural power are believed to come: paint for yam magic and paint for sorcery are both imported, and a man known to have extensive contacts in other villages is to be feared and courted. Although the scene appears to be one of independent warring miniature republics, the actual political system is in many ways a series of alliances between big-men in different villages, each competing with rivals in their home village. It is this realization and the abandonment of the "nationalism" of the village unit that big-men have and that Tswamung acquired.

Our relationship now reached a high point. Tswamung became an enthusiastic anthropologist, although always an Abelam one. On one occasion after we had been discussing the women's secret rites, he arrived in the evening with his third wife, who squatted in the corner while Tswamung proposed that he beat her until she gave the information we were lacking. This I vetoed, but four years later, when I met her after his death, she voluntarily gave me some further information on the subject. His analysis of the symbolic properties and totems of the Gwalip clans was masterly, but he was mainly and increasingly concerned with his comeback. Even while we were still in Bengragum, he started to flex his muscles. When his bitch died of snake-bite, he asked for and received three pounds as compensation from a man who had sworn at one of Tswamung's wives on a visit to Gwalip. He also settled a tangled marriage-payment dispute, making all those involved come to Bengragum for the purpose. He was building up a very extensive credit network and had a reasonable collection of rings. He frequently traveled around, picking up useful information for me about what ceremonies were due, but also making and confirming contacts. He made many visits to the plains Arapesh, particularly the villages just to the north of Gwalip and, at one time, was negotiating for another wife from there.

All this time he was watching Gwalip events very carefully. Native local-government councils had just been introduced, and Gwalip with a neighboring enemy village formed one electorate. The hatmen were retired and the office abolished. The man elected as Councillor was an enemy and a long-standing rival of Tswamung's. This linking with an enemy and the new system of local government caused great concern throughout the area. It was widely believed that the new Councillors would have dictatorial powers—some of the elected thought they had too—and the need for a strong man was felt again in Gwalip. Tswamung received some scarcely veiled invitations to return, but decided to wait until I had left, when, as he said, the Councillor would have made himself throughly unpopular.

My time was nearly up but I wanted to visit other parts of the Abelam area before leaving, intending to spend a week or so each in three different places. The move after fifteen months was awful. It took three days to cover about twelve miles, and in the middle of all this Tswamung started to complain of a pain in his left eye. For him to complain of pain was so unusual that I did my best to investigate, but could see nothing wrong. As soon as we had arrived and set up my establishment, I got him a lift to the hospital. A detached retina was diagnosed, but nothing could be done and he lost the sight of that eye. When he returned, he was downhearted. He did not know the area well, it was outside the political range of Gwalip and, although his shooting was unimpaired, he did not like the other jobs I had for him to do and became more and more discontented.

It all ended over a particularly ridiculous matter. I was very short of money and Tswamung had been having as rations mainly yams and shot game, getting rice only about twice a week when I had it. Kalabu, the village we were staying in, was within four miles of Maprik and its young men were less bushy than Bengragum's. I subsequently found that he had been teased because he was not eating exclusively rice and corned beef, considered the only fit food for those working for whites. He came one evening, when I had just got back tired and filthy from a long walk, and said that if he could not have rice and tinned meat all the time, he was going to take off. Very soon we both lost our tempers. Such arguments had happened several times before, and he had walked out twice, but had always come back. This time, however, there was no reconciliation. Our mutual usefulness had undoubtedly declined, but, of course, I would rather not think that that was the only reason. I never saw him again, but when I returned to Maprik about three weeks later, I was handed a fine, engraved cassowary-bone dagger of the type he knew I was trying to collect; it had been left for me by Tswamung. I reciprocated with a suitable present.

Three years later as I arrived in Port Moresby, I met a young lawyer who was acting for the defense in the retrial of two alleged murderers. He asked if I had any special knowledge of Gwalip. The name of the victim was Na:mei. The legal documents told me virtually nothing except that two young men from the enemy village of Aunyelim had confessed to killing him. The original trial, appeal, and retrial proceeded solely on the basis of their original confessions; they never gave evidence, nor did any other Abelam. At one stage, while waiting in jail, they had retracted their stories, saying that their confessions were a put-up job. The police made exhaustive inquiries, but Aunyelim had its story and nothing could change it. The two defendants retracted their retractions. I have no way of knowing what really happened beyond the evidence that Tswamung was found with eight spears in him beside a stream forming the boundary between Gwalip and Aunyelim. The version widely believed among the Abelam is that, having returned to Gwalip, given the necessary pigs, and reintegrated into the exchange system, he was operating very successfully as a traditional big-man, adding to his support considerably by being the leader of the opposition to the incumbent Councillor, against whom he intended to stand at the next election. He was trying to hurry things and arrange an assassination by Aunyelim of his main rival, a thoroughly traditional maneuver, but the promised secret contact was a trap and he was ambushed by a substantial force. As proof of the truth of this version, informants invariably said that the two young men who confessed would never have dared attack such a strong man, "a man with bone." It was widely assumed that I would kill at least one Aunyelim man in revenge, and this expectation rather inhibited my own inquiries there.

My relationship with Tswamung was important not so much for the information that it produced—indeed, Gwalip hardly figures in any published or projected accounts of the Abelam—but for the relationship per se. The moral equality and the friendship implied the possibility, even the probability, of quarrels. Yet the former were invaluable, not for their content alone, but because this relationship was the first that cut through all the falsities of the racial and colonial situation and convinced me not only that genuine friendship and communication were possibile but that the communication could be two-way. In New Guinea field situations, at any rate, the difference between white and black is perceived as even more extreme, simply because these societies, devoid of any idea of inherent rank, find it incredible but true that even the potentiality of equality between white men and black men is absent. It is not just that the economic systems are different and based on different premises or that a totally new form of political power has been introduced; it is the impossibility of establishing moral equivalence between white and black at any level or in any situation. Even when well-intentioned whites make conscious and continuous efforts to establish genuine relationships, the shadow of the colonial society constantly intervenes. In the field, after the first few months, I found it easy enough to be tolerated as an inquisitive spectator, slightly mad perhaps, but harmless and amiable. But for most of the Abelam all I gave was a symbol, as a tame white man, whose presence in the village or at a ceremony undoubtedly was a novelty and gave a sort of prestige, rather like having a panda in your zoo. But while this is fine and doubtless useful in itself, it does little for the anthropologist himself, living a life in which he is totally cut off from his own culture and has only the social personality allowed him by his informants and fellow villagers.

The need for two-way relationships in which the anthropologist has something to contribute of more than symbolic value can become intense. One can have many friends, and I certainly did among the Abelam, but my side of the relationship was based on my pseudo-Abelam role—my existence before I arrived in the area was irrelevant. Tswamung insisted from the start, while behaving in an interested, even friendly way, on equality between us as men, thus giving me hope in the worst of the early days, when it seemed that I should never break through the established black-white attitudes and falsity. But he also received something from me as an individual, even if primarily as an individual anthropologist, that made our relationship of the greatest value to me, not just in terms of information and insights, but in helping me balance on that tricky tightrope between cultures that is the basis of all anthropology.

NOTES

1. "Hatman" is a pidgin English term used for the two government-appointed village officials, the *luluai* and the *tultul,* who were issued caps as insignias of their office. Their powers were in theory minimal, but their position as channels of communication with the government could be exploited in skilled hands. "Big-man" and "tambaran" are pidgin English words that have acquired the status of technical terms and are used without italics throughout this article.

2. For a general account of the Abelam, see Kaberry (1940–41 and 1966). See also Forge (in press). My own field work among the Abelam was in 1958–1959 and 1962–1963. I am most grateful to the Horniman Scholarship Fund of the Royal Anthropological Institute and the Bollingen Foundation for grants which made the research possible.

3. The ownership of all Abelam names for men, women, dogs, pigs, and indeed virtually all proper names is vested in clans, with the copyright rigorously maintained. Killing a name holder is one of the few ways in which rights in a name may be transferred from one clan to another.

4. Ambitious men often adopt youths, for whom they provide wives, thus starting to build up a base of dependents and alliance before their own children are old enough to fulfill this function. They also sometimes allow the adoption of some of their own children, thus reducing the strain on their resources and establishing alliance.

5. The return pig was to be presented late in 1963 at the next major ceremony of the Wingei cycle. Unfortunately, my second field trip had to end before the ceremony was held. My Wingei partner indicated that as Tswamung was dead, the Gwalip connection was now of no interest and that he would prefer to give it to a very influential Bengragum man who was classified as my son.

REFERENCES

FORGE, ANTHONY. In press. "Prestige Influence and Sorcery: A New Guinea Example." In M. Douglas, ed., Association of Social Anthropologists Monograph No. 9.

KABERRY, P. M. 1940–41. "The Abelam Tribe, Sepik District, New Guinea: A Preliminary Report." *Oceania,* 11:233–258, 345–367.

1966. "Political Organisation among the Northern Abelam." *Anthropological Forum,* Vol. 1, Nos. 3–4.

18 / The Answer to a Prayer

HOMER G. BARNETT

One day in July of 1955, as I cautiously walked into a village in what was then Netherlands New Guinea, I was aware that I might be received as the fulfillment of a prophecy, but I hoped that I would not. During the preceding two weeks, while collecting information on the village in the nearby town of Merauke, I tried again and again to imagine what it would be like and what I would do if my appearance were given a mystical interpretation. Every role that I could think of for myself seemed childish or meddlesome or both; and as the days passed, my doubts about the wisdom and the value of a visit to the village increased. On the other hand, the principal reason for my going to that locality was to learn more about a cargo cult the leaders of which had predicted that someone like myself would one day appear to help them get rich.

In the end I decided to take the chance, but waited until the day before my scheduled departure from Merauke to undertake the one hour's walk from there to the village of Kalapa Lima. I had hoped the cult members would prove to have an image of their messiah more exalted than I could match. As it happened they didn't.

My doubts about the visit began soon after my arrival in Merauke, when I was permitted to read a set of documents kept in the office of the Dutch official in charge of that district. They had been presented to him some eighteen months earlier by a group of about twenty Muyu inhabitants of Kalapa Lima, led by their chief, a man the Dutch called Herman, and another individual whom the authorities distrusted as an agitator. The documents consisted of several typewritten pages explaining certain aspects of the cult and a series of proclamations and requests calling for action by the government. They were dated when they were written, during September 1953, not when the events they described occurred. They were rambling, disconnected, and repetitious. The contents were all the more confusing because they were written in very poor Malay by someone who had recorded the statements of other persons. Here is part of what they said, as well as they could be translated.

274

On April 27, 9:00 P.M., 1953, Kuram was in his home when the Holy Ghost entered him and told him he was to lead his people to prosperity. He was told to keep this a secret from the government until he received permission to reveal it. He was told that one day a white man would come to lead his people, the Muyu. Up until now they have been stupid and sinful. They think only of food and drink and pleasure. They are of no use to the government or to God. But now God has given them their own village, Kalapa Lima, so they must think of our FATHER and will be blessed by God Almighty.

Government must be friends with the Muyu and set a good example for them. It must give them knowledge so all can stick together and get rich. He also got the advice that God would help him open a school for those who believed him so they could teach others. Now (September 26) there are 110 teachers and they have received messages from the Holy Ghost.

September 6. We request the resident officer to arrange several matters. Take away bad things such as the Indonesians, who must go home. Also the Chinese. We natives cannot find a way to live. We want only pure Dutch here. We request that all nations gather here and bring money and God will divide it.

The Dutch government must ask all nations to bring money factories here. We want a big house here where all nations can stay and fly their flags. Everyone must bring a ton of money. We don't know for what purpose. We only follow the orders of Almighty God.

September 19, complete set of orders. All Muyu government employees must work from seven until eleven then go home. At 4:00 P.M. they must take a bath, then go to the spirit school for teachers. Orders for captains of ships. Do not bring foreigners to Merauke. Orders to shopkeepers. All prices are fixed by God as follows: rice 40¢ a kilo, long pants 2.50 guilders, shorts 1.50 guilders, sugar 15¢ a kilo . . .

September 23, explanation of a secret matter. I can see dead people. I don't understand it but it is good because it will bring change. It will make progress. The Holy Ghost says people everywhere must become one, which is written in Article 73 of the United Nations. We wish not to be deceived in matters we get with our own sweat. And there won't be a war between Russia and America because Americans are looking for all kinds of ways to keep peace. And Merauke will become a big city and much busier. I worked on this message from May 22 until June 1, and only then was it revealed at 2:00 A.M. that for the first time we would get a money factory and a money shed. Then on June 2 we would get a sun and a moon factory. On June 4 an iron factory and an iron shed. On June 8 a rice machine and a rice shed. On June 9 we will have a school with an American teacher and in three months we will know the American language. And on July 10 we will all have five hundred American wives.

September 26. On Monday night at 3:00 A.M. it was decided by God himself that New Guinea will become a part of America. We don't know how but it is God's will. He will send us a teacher.

By tradition the Muyu were an avaricious people. From childhood on, they were made to realize that success of any kind required the accumulation of material goods in the form of cowrie shells, which had to be traded to their inland country from coastal tribes, the teeth of dogs (of which animals they had none), and pigs, which were raised and even nursed by their mothers, sisters, and wives. It was impossible for a child to become a man or for a man

Muyu tribesmen on the way to a feast.

to get a wife—or better still, many wives—without a complex exchange of these objects.

Christian missionaries and Dutch officials had been in Muyu country in sufficient force since the 1930's to reduce some of the strife, magic, and cannibalism which this system provoked. They attempted to induce or compel parents to send their children to one of the mission schools in the area. They discouraged traffic in pigs, shells, teeth, and wives. Whenever possible, they confiscated ancient shells, the most treasured items in this primitive capitalism.

The result was the opposite of what was intended. The loss of some shells made the remainder more precious. The demand for payments did not cease. Brideprices went up. In fact, they became prohibitive when some fathers demanded that at least a few shells be included in the compensation for surrendering their daughters.

This development led to another that was undesirable from the standpoint of government officials. Along with their efforts to educate and Christianize, they created a yearning for the white man's riches, and since these goods came from Merauke the Muyu drifted to their source. Some men brought their families to Kalapa Lima, but most of them came alone and single or they left their families behind. The unattached and detached males created administrative problems. They were held in contempt by the coastal natives, and the feeling was mutual. Intermarriage was almost impossible between the two groups. The Muyu were accused of destroying the property of their enemies. They quarreled among themselves. They were frustrated in their quest for worldly goods. Few could find regular employment, and those who did, worked at unskilled jobs which brought only a meager income. It was barely enough to enable them to buy a few staple items. Those who worked for the government were paid one guilder (about twenty-five cents) a day with a midday meal provided. Those with families in the village received an additional three-fourths guilder a day. Their obsession with the acquisition of valuable things was not diminished by disappointment. There must be a way to get what they came for. They were all the more convinced of this because they believed they were superior to all other people except the whites. They scorned the coastal natives whom they characterized as dim-witted and unambitious, the Eurasians because they were only part white, and the Indonesians and the Chinese because they merely bought and sold the white man's goods. If these inferior people were for the time in control of the good things of life, it must be by mistake or by trickery.

It was easy to understand why Merauke attracted the Muyu in the first place and why it continued to fascinate them in 1955. Although it was a town with a population of no more than three thousand, its shops presented a dazzling array of products of our technological age. They offered cameras, typewriters, binoculars, radios, bicycles, and numerous household gadgets imported from Hong Kong, Singapore, Australia, and Holland—a feast for the eyes of a materialist and, to the Muyu, mysterious in origin and far beyond their reach. In fact, rarely did any of them have an opportunity to touch a piece of the glittering merchandise because the shopkeeper, knowing that they did not have the means to be customers, made it plain that they were not wanted on the premises. It was different with the many Chinese and Indonesian traders located in outlying villages. They stocked food and necessary but unexciting things such as needles, shovels, and fishhooks, for which they accepted coconuts in exchange.

As I thought of the difference between trading coconuts for fishhooks and the buying of bicycles with currency or coin, and as I remembered the extravagant visions on record in the district officer's files, I began to have an inkling of why divine intervention seemed to the Muyu to be the only bridge between their avarice and reality. How else could they possess the distant wonders displayed by the main-street merchants of Merauke? The gap between their world of pigs and shells and that represented by the merchant and his wares could not be spanned by their efforts alone; and yet in meaning and significance the two worlds were much alike.

A clue to their visionary solution had been in the back of my mind from the beginning of my interest in the cult. This was the belief, widespread among the natives of New Guinea, that the white man, in some strange way, is linked with their ancestors. Some of them make the connection because they think that the spirits of their dead look like ghosts—wispy, pale, and shrouded. They might appear unexpectedly at any time. Their living descendants never know whether they have come to punish them for some wrongdoing or to comfort and help them.

An early Catholic missionary in the Muyu country had an experience which brought this belief home to him. Upon arrival at one of their villages for the first time, an old woman ran to embrace him and began to weep. He was startled because Muyu women stay out of sight when strangers are around. He was alarmed because silence suddenly fell over the village when people dropped what they were doing and stared. The tension eased as other old people approached him with tears in their eyes. In the weird scene that followed he was made to understand that the woman believed that he was her dead father.

Knowing this, however, did not solve my problem. It did not answer some basic questions. Was the cult in Kalapa Lima still alive? Had the Muyu given up hope of realizing their visions? Most importantly for me, were they still expecting someone, probably an American, to bring them a message?

The authorities did not know. Kuram, the founder of the cult, was jailed for nine months in 1953, and meetings of his followers were forbidden. Upon being released, he went to the heart of the Muyu country in the interior and stirred many of the people by his revelations. When he returned to Kalapa Lima, he was jailed for another month. Police suspected that from the time of his first imprisonment, secret meetings had been held, but they decided to ignore them in the hope that the excitement would exhaust itself.

When I walked slowly into the village, it appeared to be deserted. Doors were closed and shades were drawn until I reached a house about midway down the main street. There a door opened slightly and a woman waved to me. She was smiling and obviously wanted me to come in. I thought irresistibly of the missionary's experience. As I approached, the woman called to her husband, who apparently had been lying down. He came to the door in his pajamas, bowed, and ushered me to a chair. He was Herman, short, dark, with sideburns and a goatee. I judged him to be a naturally lively and excitable person, but he was obviously shaken by my presence. His hands trembled and he laughed nervously. He could not sit or stand still. He made exaggerated gestures of humbling himself before me. He insisted upon speaking English, despite my attempts at Malay. He said he must speak English as a token of respect and as a matter of pride. He explained that he had learned what he knew of the language from an old Filipino in Merauke and from his brother, who had gone to a mission school in Australian New Guinea. His wife hovered about him, beaming as he spoke the language of this stranger from so far away. When I expressed my admiration, he asked her to show me his schoolbooks.

In an effort to quiet his agitation, I asked any question that came to mind about the books, his brother, his wife, and the village. All the while it was obvious that something else was on his mind, and it had to come out. Finally he asked how long I would be in Merauke. When I told him, he looked

stunned. He said he was sorry because he "needed" me. After staring deject-
edly at the floor for a minute, he whispered to his wife. She left the house and
shortly returned with a little old man with a pinched face and a silly smile.
I was taken aback when Herman introduced him as Kuram, the founder of
their "new religion."

From then on we spoke in whispers, following Herman's lead. From time
to time he peeked out the window, explaining that he was afraid of the police,
who were "always watching." He said he knew that I had been in Merauke
for the past two weeks. The people in the village were expecting me and he
would have gone to Merauke to get me but he had not dared for my sake and
for his—and maybe I wasn't the one after all. But here I was in their village.
The revelations they had received said that an American would come to them.
Now they were more convinced than ever that their messages came from God.

I asked about the documents on file in the government office. He said they
were messages received by many people at different times. They had been typed
by a schoolboy. Anyone could have a revelation, not only Kuram. While
Kuram had been in jail, messages continued to be received, and since his return
from his visit to their homeland many Muyu had been in spiritual contact with
their ancestors. As Herman described these and other visions, I gave up trying
to get a clear and consistent understanding of them. God, the Holy Ghost,
ancestors, and the spirits of two Americans were all mixed up as sources of
inspiration.

The two Americans dominated Kuram's revelations. He had never seen
them or their ghosts. Their names, he said, were "Nelly" and "Kamson." They
promised that when he had finished "studying," they would show themselves
to him. Such study was done in a "spirit school," which was held in homes
where people assembled to talk about their experiences and to learn a secret
writing. I could not be told any more about the meetings because they were
for the Muyu only.

Kuram was the second self-proclaimed prophet with whom I had come face
to face. The first was Ogami-sama, the prophetess of Tabuse, to whom "The
Road to the Heavenly Kingdom" was revealed at her home in the Yamaguchi
Prefecture of Japan in 1945, and who is known to her devotees as "The
Mediator" between God and man and as "The Redeemer" of the promises of
Buddah and Jesus Christ. Our meeting in Honolulu in 1952 left no doubt in
my mind about her sincerity, but it did violate my image of saints and martyrs.
Kuram profaned it even more. His colorless character was overshadowed by
Herman's lively speech and gestures. He gave no indication that he understood
what Herman and I were saying. He looked and acted simpleminded. He
giggled almost constantly. Herman did most of the talking for him. About the
only statement Kuram volunteered was that he did not care what happened
to him; he did not want to get other people in trouble and would gladly take
their sins upon himself.

At one point in the description of his revelations, Herman was overcome with emotion. He trembled so violently that I thought he was going to collapse. His eyes were closed; he gasped and grimaced as if in pain. I have often seen similar seizures at evangelistic revival meetings when converts "got religion." I remember momentarily being torn between fear and hope as Herman's agitation reached a climax. I would have liked to witness a spirit visitation but was fearful that the message it brought might call for action on my part.

Although I tried to divert it, a direct appeal for help was not long in coming. Herman put it straight: How could the Muyu make the promises of their visions come true? I stalled by asking whether God had told them that they must help each other, that they should be honest and must work hard. When I was assured that this was so, I went on to emphasize these points. I stressed work particularly, saying that Americans got money and the things the Muyu wanted so desperately only in this way. Herman listened intently, nodded, and said he knew this. Then he stared expectantly at me. This was the moment for the great message. I felt utterly stupid and helpless.

After another half-hour of absent-minded conversation, I said it was time for me to be on my way to Merauke. Herman pleaded with me, repeating over and over that he must see me again. His distress developed into another seizure. This time he became limp and sagged to his knees. His wife took one arm and I the other to help him to·a chair. He was still in a daze, his wife in tears, and Kuram was simpering in a corner when I silently slipped out the door.

As I left the house, I could see people peeking out of doorways and windows and around the corners of houses. I kept my head down, glancing sideways at them as I walked out of Kalapa Lima. I did not want to face them. No matter how I reasoned with myself, I felt that I had failed them. I had appeared as foretold, but with dull man-talk about work instead of an inspiring message. How can you explain half a miracle?

19 / Dago'om: A Man Apart

PAUL BOHANNAN

About noon one day in the middle of August, during the break in the rains that the administrative officers and missionaries call the "little dry," Dago'om danced into the compound. Onto his goatskin bag, originally dyed bright orange but now brown with use and dirt, Dago'om had hung tassels of raffia and bits of coconut shell and two small calabash-gourd bottles. Dangling among these was a monkey skull about the size of a lemon, shining like ivory with a brown patina produced by rubbing, sweat, and sun. Hanging among the tassels, the tiny skull reminded me of nothing so much as a shrunken head from Ecuador.

Like all Tiv, Dago'om danced with flexed knees. And like all Tiv, he invented gestures and steps of his own. In his most successful movement Dago'om leaned over forward, knees sprung and set far apart, and flipped his buttocks upward, throwing down his large pot belly as if it had slipped between his knees. It was funny, but not as funny as he meant it to be.

Dago'om danced forward, as if tacking into the wind, first to one diagonal and then to the other. He signaled each change of direction with his special belly-slip. He stamped and shuffled in the dust of the compound with heavily calloused feet—like the grossly enlarged extremities of a Congolese figurine, strong and tired from supporting the weight of the sleeper's head. Dago'om seemed earth-bound, each heavy step thrusting him further into the earth. But then he raised his right hand, as thick and heavy as his feet, turning a delicate movement with his wrist. This flick imparted grace to his movements. The clumsiness and heaviness were those of a clown, not a dunce. The skill of the movement even contradicted the grossness of the body. Maintaining one rhythm with his feet, he produced a counterrhythm with his hands and arms, still another with his trunk. The whole was unified and not lacking in art.

His trick of keeping his eyes almost closed drew a veil between himself and

Reprinted from "A Man Apart" by Paul Bohannan, *Natural History,* Vol. 77, No. 8 (October 1968), pp. 8ff. Edited by permission of the author.

the world, making contact difficult. But after the first few times, even our laughter had a touch of repugnance in it. Though we always laughed, I soon tried to avoid that absurd, toothy grin which from time to time spread across his face, lifted upward on his squat, sinewy neck. Undeniably Dago'om was funny, but the laughter was too much forced upon us simply because no other contact with him was possible. He did not allow any other. Without laughing, you were soon engulfed in uncharted and unpredictable confusion—including, for some odd reason, hate. Later, as I came to know something of Dago'om's life, I could understand the hate.

The words which he sang this time—for he knew but one tune—held an unrecognized prophecy. *"M gema hundu ve; m gema hundu ve; m ma msolom yum; m gema hundu ve."* "I am very drunk," Dago'om sang now. "I am very drunk. I drank a lot of beer and I am very drunk." Dago'om often did drink a lot of beer and, when drunk, would sing his song with a heavy tongue. Sober, he sang it with a burred voice that rasped forth from his throat. Yet the effect was somehow pleasantly liquid.

The words were ambiguous for *hundu* means both "drunk" and "mad." Tiv told me that drunkenness and madness are the same thing—except that drinking too much brings only the little madness which goes away after you sleep it off. Future events were to turn the ambiguity of Dago'om's song into irony as well. But that gets ahead of the story.

On September 10, Dago'om returned from a beer party in Yengev. When I heard that Dago'om was *ihundu,* I was not surprised. It took until the next day for me to realize that he was in fact mad. Recognition of his true condition forced a search of my memory (as such things seldom get into anthropologists' notes) for any symptoms or clues. One evening, he and Anwase, both a little drunk, had taken turns doing solo dances in the middle of the compound. The sun had broken through after a rain, and everyone came outside into the brilliant orange light that exists only at dusk in West Africa. Not once did Dago'om let Anwase finish a dance, but kept rushing at him, playfully "killing" him with his heavy clown's hand. Anwase, a trim, light man, moved with grace. Even as he walked across the compound he was a pleasure to watch. He danced with the sad lightness of a jester, and I remembered my disappointment each time Dago'om demanded the center of the stage and Anwase easily and smilingly allowed him to have it.

I also remembered, with a stroke or two of conscience now, that Dago'om sometimes in other ways made a nuisance of himself. I had more than once shut the door of my hut to keep him from disturbing me. His clowning had a monotony I found tedious when alone with him. With all of us there together and my hosts and servants to laugh at him, I too could find him funny. Now, I realized that, like everyone else, I avoided being alone with Dago'om. Nobody could seem to bear laughing at him except with the reinforcement of others. Alone, Dago'om made me uncomfortable. His clowning called up my pity unmixed with the wry absurdity that I obviously felt with the help of others. For his part Dago'om was always kind and thoughtful. He often brought me eggs, which were hard to buy here in the northern marshes of Tivland. I repaid him with cigarettes. Once he gave me a duck with great mock ceremony.

The night before he went to the beer drink in Yengev, he visited our compound, bringing his wife. There were a couple of small pots of beer in the compound that evening, and Dago'om came for a foretaste of what he was to drink tomorrow. He forced his frightened and overdressed but rather pretty wife to bring a calabash of beer across the compound and give it to me. She wore a brilliant orange piece of Manchester cloth, a man's undershirt of the sort the British call a vest, white knee socks, and tennis shoes. On her head was a stylishly tied cloth. Her face was smeared with face powder, imported (in Caucasian shades) from Britain. She seemed particularly subdued for a Tiv woman.

I took the beer from her with both my outstretched hands and thanked her. I tasted it and sent it into the kitchen for my servants. Dago'om stormed over, called for a chair, and insisted that she sit down opposite me. For a Tiv woman, this is a completely artificial situation. For her, it was terrifying as well as strange. I thought then that she was afraid of me, but I now think otherwise: she was afraid of him. She remained mute when I tried to talk to her. When I spoke to Dago'om or one of the other dozen people standing or sitting about, Dago'om would repeat to her in a loud voice everything I said. After about fifteen minutes of this I could stand no more and I excused myself and went into my hut. I simply couldn't take it. I did not know what he wanted; neither did he. I later learned from her friends that she became frightened when Dago'om made her dress up and go with him to beer drinks. When I talked to her in her own surroundings, myself making the adjustment to social situations familiar to her, she was not afraid.

The next morning Dago'om and his wife went on to the beer drink in Yengev. No one else from either our compound or his was present. Although I talked with her several times later, she did not disclose much about what he did there. In a tight, closed voice she told me only that Dago'om had got drunk from beer and that after he stopped drinking he became more and more *ihundu,* and it never left him.

God knows how she got him back as far as our compound. Gu, my host, helped her handle him after they appeared. Dago'om refused to continue on to Asanyi's compound where he lived. It was just nightfall, and he was ranting and shouting. When his wife tried to get him to go the rest of the way home, he screamed loud threats at her—promising to beat her or kill her if she pressed him further. She retired to the hut of Torbum's mother, one of her lineage sisters. Anwase and two younger men took charge of Dago'om and with gentleness and patience finally got him to sleep in Abum's hut. The next morning, at dawn Dago'om was unconscious. Anwase and one of his brothers stretched an old *chado* cloth on two saplings and carried him home on this litter.

I knew little about these developments at the time and thus had no insight into their true significance. I knew only that Dago'om was in the compound and that he was *ihundu,* but he avoided me. I bumped into him only once. Seeing me then, he fell to his knees and started to sing, *"M gema hundu ve* . . . ,"* but this was as far as he got. Springing up with a wild shout, he dashed off in the other direction. I concluded that the beer drink in Yengev must have been a great success. Later Anwase told me that he was asleep in Abum's hut.

When Anwase returned the next morning, he informed me by direct imitation, by reference to a madman in the next lineage area to ours, and by mention of the sprites of death which sometimes bring madness, that Dago'om was really mad, not drunk. Dago'om, I could now see, had told me this himself: *"M gema hundu ve"* means not merely "I am drunk," but "I have turned mad," and the way he had jumped into the air and run away screaming was his metaphor.

The day after Dago'om was carried home, I walked the half-mile to see him. He caught sight of me as I entered Asanyi's compound and bolted in the other direction. I talked about him with Nege and Abu. Abu claimed to have the same father as Dago'om, though a different mother. I was soon to learn that Abu's father was Dago'om's maternal grandfather and that Dago'om had no father. Nege was the son of Abu's father's brother, a sensible and patient man. He told me Dago'om had already attacked several people and had injured a girl when he started laying about him with a stick. Moreover, he had run into the bush when he saw me coming. Nege said it was unlike him because Dago'om liked me, and this proved again that he was undoubtedly mad. Abu opened wide his one eye and said that they would have to put Dago'om into stocks. Abu had a way of hovering about his listener rather than projecting his words across a space as he spoke. He got closer to my face than most Tiv. I was tempted to stand back (a feeling I associate with France, not Africa).

It was four days before I got back again to see Dago'om. Inside the compound I found him in stocks. He sat on the bare ground—a deep insult for Tiv, used in court as a symbol of a degraded and suppliant condition. One foot was stretched before him, inserted through a hole gouged in one end of a heavy log of *prosopis,* a hardwood tree related to mesquite. A second hole had been drilled at right angles to the first. After his foot had been inserted through the large hole, wooden pegs were driven into the smaller hole so that, while he could move his foot comfortably, he could not remove it from the log. The log was about eight feet long. A rope had been tied from the far end around an overhanging branch of a venerable fig tree standing in the middle of the compound. Dago'om could not reach the raised end of the log to untie the rope. Neither could he stand up to untie it from the branch, only a couple of feet above his head as he sat. The skin of his foot looked dull and dead against the glowing orange of the newly cut *prosopis* wood. His other leg had been doubled back under him.

Dago'om had the look of death. A gray film covered his smooth brown body. There is a vivid Tiv metaphor for dying: "He is sloughing his skin," using the same word as for a snake. Surprisingly, his scrotum had swollen to the size of a dinner plate. Scrotal hydroceles and scrotal elephantiasis are common among Tiv, but they do not develop suddenly. It may have been a hernia or a lymph infection, but I did not know. It is one of the many times that I wished I had had some medical training. Dago'om's eyes were wide open and staring; looking into them, it was impossible to determine where the pupil began. Even the whites of his eyes seemed to be dimmed by a thin film.

He recognized me and spoke my name twice. But that was all I could understand of what he tried earnestly to tell me. We were alone and there was nobody for me to ask. In the minutes of complete concentration I felt keenly that he was trying to get through to me, to tell me something—as hard and as unsuccessfully as I was trying to understand him.

As I walked home along the bush path, newly hoed and widened that morning, it occurred to me that Dago'om had sleeping sickness. Probably he had had it all along, and had I been trained to see it, I could perhaps have got him to a hospital and stopped the progress of the disease. I became more and more convinced in the next few days that Dago'om had sleeping sickness. It could have been avoided or halted with pentamedine injections; yet I understood how alien pentamedine was to Tiv culture. Moreover, Dago'om lived twenty-five miles from a dispensary—indeed, in the part of Tivland I had purposely chosen as farthest removed from colonial innovations. I knew that I could not have convinced Dago'om to undertake the trip to get the injections, even if I had recognized the disease early. Yet, had I myself been able to give them to him on the spot, he would have taken them. I became aware of an intense feeling of guilt—a habit among those brought up as Protestants when they look on suffering.

The Protestant reaction to guilt is to do something. The most exhausting part of Dago'om's illness and death for me, therefore, was to struggle with the fact that nobody did anything. Although I had seen many mental patients, I had never previously known one both before and after the onset of his madness. There was no change in Dago'om's personality—only his behavior. The madness had been in him all along. Dago'om got worse with his disease and his terror. I became more depressed with that most despicable of situations—pity without action.

It soon appeared to me that no one had known Dago'om well. Certainly I had not. No anthropologist ever knows more than half a dozen of his informants with anything that can correctly be called intimacy. Intimacy is difficult enough with people like oneself. Across cultural barriers it involves accepting about the other person even more things that are the negation of or at least irrelevant to what one admires. Dago'om had amused me—and I had allowed myself to be amused so that I would not have to do anything. I laughed at his poor clowning in order not to have to pity him. I believed then that I must not pity people from other cultures, a narrow and ethnocentric response. The language of mental illness can itself be used as a defense mechanism against the madness in ourselves.

During the next few days, aware that Dago'om was dying, I sought to learn all I could about him to understand better what all of his kinsmen would say at his funeral. They would surely meet to discuss who had killed him and how. I assumed that Dago'om would be given the funeral of an ordinary adult male. I had seen a number of funerals and thought I knew what would happen. All the disputes among his kinsmen would have to be aired. Then the "fault" would have to be determined. That was done by a post mortem operation in which the heart is examined for a substance called *tsav*. If the dead person's heart shows the sacs of blood in the pericardium that Tiv associate with *tsav* and all supernatural or unusual ability, then that person was guilty of his own death. If his chest is "empty," as they put it, then the killer is still at large in the community. Tiv never die from natural causes alone. To natural causes must be added an evil volition to set those causes in motion. And the volition comes only from close kinsmen.

I soon discovered that Asanyi, the head of the compound in which Dago'om lived, was gone. When I tried to find out where he had gone, I was told by one person that he had a dispute about a wife in a lineage to the northwest of us. Another told me that he had gone to Makurdi to sell some crops. Still another said there was a matter of a marriage ward—one of his half-sisters— that he had to care for in the area of her husband's lineage. Obviously, nobody knew where Asanyi was, but they created plausible explanations.

I became incensed, thinking somebody ought to summon the man so that the proper ritual could be carried out, for I knew that no ritual could be held in the absence of the compound head. It was my servant, Asema, who set me right on that. So long as Asanyi was gone the local witches could not kill Dago'om with their *tsav*. Without Asanyi's concurrence, therefore, Dago'om could not die. Everybody knew that Asanyi was a frightened man who could never hold off all the witches in the community. My own position became absurd. With no faith in the ritual they might perform for Dago'om, I was nevertheless put off that nobody did anything. It was inconsistent, and I knew it—and still I felt somebody should do something. Examining my own reactions, I soon discovered that part of my feeling of inconsistency and guilt came from the people in the community. It wasn't all a product of my Protestant upbringing: the community was guilty.

Discovering anything about Dago'om—even genealogical information of the sort that Tiv usually give freely—proved singularly difficult. I knew where he supposedly fitted into the standard genealogies. What soon became evident was that he was there by grace and not by right. Again, it was Asema who came to my aid. He told me that gossip had it—correctly, he thought—that Dago'om had been born of a "sister marriage." This is a euphemism for a recognized and approved liaison between young people of the same exogamic group but who nevertheless have no common grandparent. (Sexual relations between two grandchildren of the same individual or couple would be incestuous.) While such sexual liaisons normally occur between some members of the exogamic group (a patrilineal lineage descended agnatically from a man from five to eight generations past), marriage is strictly proscribed between them.

A young man whose name Asema never learned had come over from the MbaShija segment. He was her most distant kinsman within her exogamic group and he had paid a goat to the mother of Dago'om's mother. He thereby got her permission, as well as the girl's, to "untie the shell" that, like all Tiv girls, she wore around her neck as a symbol of sexual nonavailability. Thereafter, he had a right, recognized by the entire community, to sleep with the girl in her mother's hut until she was ready for marriage.

Dago'om's mother, then probably about fifteen, had been a fool, Asema said. When she got pregnant with Dago'om, she had refused to go to a husband. Instead she claimed that she loved this boy from MbaShija, and she was not going to take her baby someplace else to become the third wife of a repugnant old man. Her father tried to force her into such a marriage, but she fled her husband's compound and came back to her own. The father then tried to convince her to elope with a suitable young husband who came courting. Even this she refused and bore Dago'om "in her father's house." Dago'om thus became her "brother" rather than her son, and her father became his "father." Dago'om became a member, through a female link, of his own agnatic lineage. Thus, he did not have a complete set of kinsmen; the mother's lineage, which Tiv call your *igba*, protects you from the evil of selfish individuals in your own agnatic lineage. To be without a lineage to act as your *igba* is to be without protection from the witches in your own. His nickname—with which Dago'om had been taunted as a child—meant "God sent us an orphan."

I saw Dago'om five times in the next eleven days. Only once could I make any sense of what he said, although I recognized some of his words and my own name. Nege said that Dago'om talked nothing but foolishness now. Yet once when I was again alone with him, about five days before he died, he managed to break through for a minute or two. He repeated to me with great urgency that, since I was a guest in these parts and could not be harmed by the vicious people here, I must take all of his children and get them out of his compound, out of this lineage area, before they were all killed as he himself was being killed. The plea was interspersed with nonsense syllables which I recognized as the ones that Dago'om used sometimes to mutter as he danced. Again I was struck with the fact that madness does not change us but merely intensifies our idiosyncracies.

The difficulty about his request was that Dago'om had no children. Or had he? When I relayed to Asema what Dago'om had said, he told me of a rumor that Dago'om had had a love affair with one of Asanyi's junior wives some years before. Asanyi discovered it and banished Dago'om for several weeks. This woman bore a child which the entire compound thought resembled Dago'om rather than Asanyi. For the man who reported this story to Asema there was no question that the child indeed resembled Dago'om. We tried to discover which child of Asanyi's it was but did not succeed. Asema did discover, however, that Asanyi made Dago'om give him a goat in settlement of the matter and only thereafter agreed to help Dago'om get the money for a wife of his own.

The old mother of Torbum, with whom Dago'om's wife had stayed in our compound the night he went mad, subsequently told me something else. She said that her lineage sister had borne Dago'om a child about a year before, but it had died after only a few weeks. Almost surely the witches were involved in that because Dago'om "didn't have anybody."

Dago'om sat mad, babbling pitiably, losing weight, his pot belly almost disappeared, his swollen scrotum like a beach ball between his legs. Asanyi stayed away. Dago'om was an eldest child, even if not a legitimate child. Eldest children cannot be killed by the witches without the concurrence of the compound head. If Asanyi stayed away, Dago'om's death could not be laid to him. I understood this, but I still had pictures in my head of the fine moots that Tiv call "asking sessions." In such a session the kinsmen of Dago'om would be faced with his condition and asked why they had allowed it to happen, why they had not protected him from evil. I thought perhaps they would even call in MbaShija, the lineage of Dago'om's genitor. But day after day nothing at all happened.

Then one morning Asema woke me with coffee and the news that Asanyi had come back. I rushed over to see him. He was affable enough but said only that he would have to rest today. Perhaps then, tomorrow, he would do something. I asked him to let me know when he went to a diviner, so that I could go along. Asanyi replied laconically that he would, that since he had nothing to hide, he did not object to my seeing what went on.

Next day, however, Asanyi said that he had looked into his heart, and he thought the best thing to do was to forget the diviner but find a man who knew madness medicine and who would come to cure Dago'om. At the time, I concluded that Asanyi was hedging. Today, in working through all my notes and recollections, I find that I often harbored dark and evil motives to ascribe to Tiv when they did not live up to their own stated standards.

That day, when I talked to Dago'om, he had been moved into a reception hut. Nege told me that Dago'om had not eaten since the madness had descended on him. Certainly he was thin and weak, but he sat up and still seemed himself as a person.

In the evening I went back to Ukusu, in a nearby community, our base camp while we were in this area. I spent three quarters of my time at my forward camp, my wife working out of the base camp in Ukusu. Just after dawn the next morning, someone outside our hut was calling my name and I answered. It was Anwase, come to tell me Dago'om had died in the night and that they were going to bury him. Without shaving or even waiting for coffee, I rushed off with Anwase. The water was high and we had to wade through swamps up to our waists. When I entered our compound, I was told by Gu that, according to Asanyi, Dago'om had struggled with death on the ground and that death had outwitted him. It was a standard Tiv metaphor of death, to struggle "on the ground" and lose. Yet, "on the ground" has a double meaning. When applied to marriage wards, it means that they have not been assigned to guardians—that they have no one in their natal lineages to protect them. Gu and Anwase both denied that it had this meaning here, but the image nevertheless proved prophetic, whether Asanyi meant it that way or not.

The corpse had been covered with a thick layer of pink talcum powder. African corpses have a characteristic gray color and the pink powder grotesquely masks their human features. I had previously seen powdered corpses in the bush, always assuming that it was used for cosmetic reasons because it is often used that way by women. (Dago'om's wife had been powdered the night before the beer drink.) I nevertheless found it so repulsive that I could not believe that was the reason. I turned to Gu and asked him why. He replied matter-of-factly that it reduced the stink.

With no questions or recriminations about the assignment of responsibilities —an accompaniment of all other Tiv funerals I had seen—the time came to bury Dago'om. A grave had been dug out along a path, about a hundred yards from the compound. As his body was carried out, the women of the compound gathered around Dago'om's wife and wailed, but only for a minute or two and only out of kindness to her. A leprous old woman, hands almost gone, led the singing, her gritty but true voice ululating and intoning in falling intervals, "Dago'om, why have you left us?"

It is a disgrace to his community if a Tiv goes to his grave without the wailing of the wives of his compound or without the cause being determined by its men, his fathers and brothers. These women, the wives of Dago'om's brothers, were keenly conscious of their own insecurity in a lineage in which such a death and such a burial could occur. In her perfunctory and raucous dirge the old leper woman was seeing herself.

Dago'om's widow came along the path after us, approaching as close as she dared—a Tiv woman who looks into a grave becomes barren. She went toward his grave, but the forces of life held her at a respectable distance.

The black topsoil had been thrown to one side of the grave and the rust-red laterite below it piled on the other. The grave was about four feet deep, narrow at the top, with a shelf that made it wider below. The young men of the compound lifted his body into the grave while the elders looked on. They performed no ceremony although usually Tiv sacrifice a chick at this stage of the funeral, dripping blood on the chest of the corpse, sometimes on its nipples, and then throwing the sacrificed chick into the bush as a sign that the deceased is going to join the community of the dead. That ceremony is performed, however, only for men who have left living sons. Dago'om's children were— if he had any—either dead or not his own.

The two young men arranged his body—"shoved it" would be more accurate—into the shelf of the grave so that its head was to the southwest, the "top

Typical funeral scene in northern Tivland.

of the country." They covered the shelf with a few pieces of wood and clambered back up onto the surface. The opening was covered over with three logs. With a start I saw that one of the logs was the stocks in which Dago'om had been imprisoned for the last three weeks of his life. I found it fitting but melancholy: What more suitable way to get rid of it? On top of the logs they put a layer of thatching grass. Then they piled on first the topsoil and finally the red subsoil, which was smoothed into the shape of an oval mound.

Gu put it precisely: "We have put him in the ground. That's all of that." Indeed, that was all. Those who had washed him, prepared his corpse, buried him, all accepted small torches of thatching grass from the oldest lineage member present. Each stood on top of the mounded grave to swing the miniature torch around his head, his feet, and—some of them—his trunk, changing hands with the burning grass. Then dropping their torches onto the mound, they backed off. This ritual was to "gather up the dreams" so that they would not be haunted with their luck "closing up" on them.

Walking home with Atsegher and Gu, I was tense. Tiv funerals usually provide a catharsis for everybody present, including the ethnographer. We were still tense. I felt that something should have happened, that somebody ought to do something. I had an intense desire to stir them up. But I, too, did nothing.

Back in the compound, Asema asked me what had happened, for he had chosen not to attend. I told him and wondered whether the medicine that caused Dago'om his madness had been administered to him in the beer at Yengev. Asema said that he thought it unlikely because madness medicine is a very powerful substance and is usually administered by your brothers or your wife, who spread it on the thatch over the entryway to your hut. The dangling ends of the thatching grass stroke your back as you go in and out. Thus the medicine enters your body and you become mad. I tried to describe to Asema my feeling of emptiness and tension. "But did they beget him?" he asked. It was another way of saying, "He wasn't theirs."

The moral is simple. Dago'om "had nobody." He "sat alone," and there was no one to avenge him when he was dead any more than there was anyone to protect him while he was alive. He was expendable.

Tiv tell me that a lineage, in making the human sacrifice said to be necessary to keep the fetishes fertile for successful crops and babies, takes the man who "has nobody" to protect him. If the people with *tsav*—the elders of the community in their roles as mystical replenishers of fertility—make the sacrifices, there is no one to protect these people, and so they do not have to kill their own. I knew that the *mbatsav* never made human sacrifices—that the *mbatsav,* even though some elders might meet in that name, were a reference to the destructive forces in human nature and human society, not a society of witches.

Two weeks later, the rains had reached their peak. Word reached me that Dago'om's mother had arrived at Asanyi's, but the bridge over the Anu river was three feet under a rushing torrent of water. A few Tiv chose to cross it but I did not. I also heard that the mother of Dago'om's wife had come for her daughter, to take her home to Ga'ambe where she would have a better chance of forgetting Dago'om and going to another husband. I asked whether anyone at Asanyi's would inherit her. Undoubtedly somebody could go to try to collect the bridewealth that had been given for her, Anwase said, but he thought it unlikely that anyone would do so. They would forget her. He suggested that I might want to talk to Dago'om's mother about that. A few days later when the bridge was again passable I went to find her. Nobody knew where she had gone.

Nothing further happened. A man had gone mad and died. He was expendable. The Tiv were uncomfortable about it, ashamed of it, and chose to forget it quickly. It took me longer because my culture will not admit that anybody is expendable, whatever the "facts" may be and whatever our own devices for putting away from us a person who has nobody.

20 / The Lonely Anthropologist

ANTHONY FORGE

Just over 50 years ago, in May 1915, Bronislaw Malinowski invented modern anthropological fieldwork, when he set up his tent in the village of Omarakana in the Trobriand Islands, off the south east corner of New Guinea. So runs the accepted view in British social anthropology. The two principal innovations were, first, the tent, which enabled Malinowski to live actually in the village instead of visiting it after breakfast in the mission house, the accepted style of anthropological investigation until then. Secondly, and linked with the tent, was the use of the local language, and here an interesting inversion has occurred. Before Malinowski anthropologists rarely knew the language of those they studied, relying not only on interpreters but also on resident Europeans, missionaries, traders, and government officers, who often had considerable acquaintance with the language and customs. Nowadays, at least in New Guinea, the position is reversed, the anthropologists are in many areas the only Europeans who bother to learn a native language, the others relying on pidgin English. Even at the turn of the century, supposedly the heyday of imperialism, the Englishman setting off for exotic corners of the Empire expected to have to learn a foreign language: in our more democratic times it seems they can only bother to communicate properly to those who have learnt English.

Malinowski kept a diary for some of the time during his three New Guinea expeditions; it was written in Polish with bits of other European and Melanesian languages and a few passages in English. It was never intended for publication; nevertheless it has been published (*A Diary in the Strict Sense of the Term,* by Bronislaw Malinowski, Routledge & Kegan Paul, 45s). Translated and tricked out with the appearances of scholarship, what does it tell us about the birth of fieldwork or about Malinowski? In fact, very little of either;

Reprinted from "The Lonely Anthropologist" by Anthony Forge, *New Society,* August 17, 1967, pp. 221–223. With permission of *New Society,* the magazine of the social sciences, 128 Long Acre, London, W.C. 2, England. © I.P.C. Magazines Ltd.

there is only one very brief entry referring to the second and most important of Malinowski's trips during which he spent a year in Omarakana, learnt Kiriwinian and developed the fieldwork methods that are still the basic research tool of anthropology today. The first trip, to the island of Mailu, is fully covered, although most of the entries are short and the objects of his study make only very occasional appearances. The third trip, his second to the Trobriand Islands, is covered in greater detail, but the diary breaks off after nine months shortly after Malinowski heard of the death of his mother, and again there is nothing of anthropological interest.

Comparison between the two diaries, however, shows that some change has taken place. This entry from Mailu is typical, illustrating as it does the two dominant themes of the first diary: his health, and his habit of reading novels when he felt he should have been working:

"Today I sat home all day, writing my diary, dressing my finger, preparing for taking photos—this was Sunday the 20th [December 1914]. In the afternoon I had a very invigorating bathe in the sea, swam, and lay in the sun. I felt strong, healthy, and free. The good weather and the comparative coolness of Mailu also helped to cheer me up. Around 5, walked to the village and met Velavi. Ordered a stone for grinding sago and a model of a boat, for 10 sticks of tobacco. Back home—my finger hurt badly. Sat reading Gautier; Velavi, Boo, and Utata acted as my 'court.' The night was very bad; I awoke with headache—my finger was very sore all night; apparently I infected it again bathing."

From the second diary, dated 20 April 1918:

"Another day of intensive work, without tiredness or *surchauffage,* physically well and content. In the morning wrote alone and despite everything I felt a little more deserted than when the *niggers* are here.—Got up as usual. On both sides of the gray interior, green walls—on the east weeds of fresh *odila* [bush], on the west a couple of pink palms divide the upper half of the picture vertically: the road lined with . . . and in the distance *odila* jungle with cascades of vegetation. Interior: rotten sticks covered with a pile of rubbish, and patched in a few places; in the middle Samson's mat; my bed enthroned, the table, a pile of my things, . . . etc.— *Well,* I covered a great deal systematically; around 12 the *niggers* helped me finish *kaloma* and translate the texts. After lunch, Samson came back; Yaboaina, *kaloma libagwo*—I was very tired and I could not think straight. I took a walk . . . along the sandy, stony beach, then walked back. The bonfire cast flickering lights on the pastel-colored background of palms, night fell, Kitava vanished over the distant sea. Once again upsurge of joy at this open, free existence amidst a fabulous landscape, under exotic conditions (how unexotic New Guinea seems now!), a real picnic based on actual work. I also had the real joy of creative work, of overcoming obstacles, new horizons opening up; misty forms take on contours, before me I see a road going onward and upward. I had the same upsurges of joy in Omarakana— then they had been even more justified, for that was my first success and the difficulties were greater. This may have also been the cause of my joy at Nu'agasi, when suddenly *the veil was rent* and I began to collect information. —By the sea, creative ideas about *'sense of humor, manners and morals.'* I came back tired, lay down. Samson offered me his cane. I went with him and he gave me . . . information. Also *sawapu.* I came back late and slept well— oh yes, on my way back I went to the pool and delighted in the view of trees, water, and boats by moonlight. It's a pity that I may leave this forever. I want to write about all this to E.R.M. and remind her that it is just half a year ago we parted." (E.R.M. was Malinowski's fiancee and later his wife. Words not in Polish are italicised.)

This is a cheerful entry, others are made in moods of blackest depression; but in all of them there is virtually no information about the Trobriand Islanders. Many are mentioned by name but rarely do we learn anything about them. Although in his books Malinowski frequently refers to individuals as "friends," "rascals," "highly intelligent" and so on, in his diary personalities are reserved for Europeans, "scum," "a petty greengrocer blown up by his own sense of importance into a caricature of a petty sovereign" and many more friendly and complimentary comments.

The use of the word *nigger* had already fluttered the anthropological dove- cots when the publication of the diaries was known to be coming. Now it has arrived and it seems possible that it was a false alarm. Despite the fact that the editor gives a definition from *Webster's Dictionary* after the first mention of *nigger* and that the word occurs in italics throughout (which we are told means that the word is transcribed exactly as written), the facsimile of a page of the diary printed as a frontispiece twice clearly has "nigrami" where the text has *nigger;* of course it is possible, but unlikely, that these are the only two examples.

In general the editor does not inspire confidence. He is certainly not familiar either with London (not having heard of Chalk Farm) or the Western Pacific, constantly referring to "Burns Phelp" when he means the famous shipping and trading company "Burns Philp." Whether Malinowski used *nigger* or not is really irrelevant, since these diaries are not about the Trobriand Islanders and what Malinowski thought of them nor even about Malinowski. They are a partial record of the struggle that affects every anthropologist in the field: a struggle to retain a sense of his own identity as an individual and as a member of a culture.

It is frequently said that anthropologists strive for objectivity in their work, that they study societies in which they are not personally involved, in which they have no passionate investment. This is, of course, impossible. It is true that they have to avoid ethnocentricity, the belief that their own culture is "natural" or God-given, and that anything different is an aberration. But the situation in which an anthropologist finds himself during field work cannot be one of fly-on-the-wall detachment. The main problem can be summed up roughly as this: however much you participate in and understand of their culture, they can understand nothing of yours; furthermore you are not there to teach them about your culture but to learn about theirs.

It is a special kind of loneliness to be surrounded by people whom you like and who like or at any rate cheerfully tolerate you, but who have no conception of who you are, what sort of a person, what you like and dislike. Of course they know all this about you in terms of their own culture, and one is flattered by names, social position and confidence bestowed on one. But the job of an anthropologist is not to become a member of the culture he is studying but to distil its essence, to bring back the censuses, the genealogies, the descriptions and analyses of ceremonies, agriculture, birth and death from which he can abstract the social structure, the symbol systems or whatever else he needs to pursue his theoretical interests. The danger is always of over-identifying, of getting sucked in to the culture studied. When you have felt your belly contract with fury against the sorcerers of the next village who are killing all your villagers, then is the time to remind yourself that it isn't true, that you know the sorcery doesn't work and that fury interferes with your calm "objective" observation and recording of sorcery accusations.

ONE'S OWN CULTURE

In general the problems of fieldwork remain what they were for Malinowski: how to get and check information and how to stay a member of one's own culture while doing it. Perhaps Martians could give an objective account of a human society, but an anthropologist is only a man and his account must be in terms of his own culture; the very words and concepts of social anthropology are part of his culture and can never be other. In this situation one develops a longing for "civilisation" not simply in terms of Beethoven, beer and bread, although one longs for those, but as somewhere where one has a place, where one is known, not just as an individual but as a social person whose dress, behaviour and tastes are signs that other members of the culture read and understand. Furthermore this longing cannot be understood even by one's best friends among the culture one is studying.

When I was leaving the Abelam village in which I had spent 15 months, serious arguments were advanced to make me stay; it was recognised that I might want the society of my fellow whites but as they pointed out I could always go into the government station to talk, drink and listen to music. From the point of view of a unitary culture, such as the Abelam, where a group of whites were gathered together, there was the culture; not only could they not recognise a difference between Bach, *Always* and the Beatles, but they could not conceive of a culture where there was such a difference. In the end the only way of silencing them was to reel off all the many relatives I should never see again if I stayed; and even then my list was so derisory in their eyes that they took me for some sort of orphan.

Of course the civilisation for which one longs tends to be idealised, becoming a sort of fantasy to which one constantly refers. Letters when they come almost invariably disappoint on first reading, a point which emerges frequently from Malinowski's diaries. Subsequently they are integrated into the fantasy and become treasures to read and reread. In return, one cannot send accounts of all the petty frustrations and furies which would be meaningless to friends and kin, and are often incomprehensible to those who have caused them; there is only one person who can even start to understand how you feel and that is yourself. Under these circumstances a diary is an essential part of fieldwork, it is your only chance of expressing yourself, of relieving your tensions, of obtaining any sort of catharsis. No matter how friendly your informants may be, they can never understand you.

Living in a village, the only time you are really absolutely alone is in bed under the mosquito net. This cocoon in which one lies is ideal for fantasy and nostalgia, it becomes in fact the centre of your culture, as well as the natural focus of sexual frustration. His mosquito net is mentioned constantly by Malinowski in his second diary and had obviously acquired some such symbolic value. The question of sex is one that tormented Malinowski and no doubt every follower of his field methods. There is nothing laid down in one's field training, but as far as I know most anthropologists do not sleep with the local girls, although in the New Guinea situation this would be very easy and would not be taken too seriously by anyone concerned. This self-imposed celibacy is a strange phenomenon, and each anthropologist has his own rationalisation: Malinowski's was fidelity to his fiancee; the reason of most of us I suspect is again partly the need to preserve one's own identity. By directing acute sexual frustration and fantasies outside the present environment the anthropologist forges a strong and ever present link with the culture from which he came and to which he will return.

So far I have concentrated on the negative side of fieldwork simply because this is the side that predominates in the diaries—indeed, this is the function of a diary under these conditions, a place to spew up one's spleen, so that tomorrow one can start afresh. In fact fieldwork is basically enjoyable. I don't see how anyone could do anything worthwhile if they spent a year or more in misery and discontent. The joys are not only those mentioned by Malinowski in the long quotation, of the beauty and strangeness of exotic parts of the world and the satisfactions of progressing in one's work; of attaining understanding, and making the breakthrough to perceiving order and system in the confusing mass of human actions that press on you from every side all day and sometimes all night too. The only way to get good and reliable information is through genuine friendship with your informants, and it is from such friendships that one gets most of the pleasure. Such relationships take time to form, but when they do they more than repay the miseries of the first few months, when to isolation and loneliness is added the certainty that you are never going to get anything worthwhile, never learn the language, never get a straight and truthful answer to a question. If one has friends one also has enemies, those whose suspicions of your purpose in being there at all are never allayed, who are enemies of one's friends; also since the aim is to be accepted one cannot expect that immunity from public comment on one's person and actions that is the privilege and curse of the white man in colonial situations.

LOSING YOUR TEMPER

In all this it is the spectre of racialist attitudes that is so inhibiting. To lose one's temper, to curse and swear, is to behave like other Europeans and means that a lot of the culture you want to study will be closed to you; so it has to be bottled up until you can release it in your diary and retire under the mosquito net to dream of another life. The day that you can lose your temper in public without damaging your fieldwork situation is a great day. It means that you have succeeded in creating that base from which an anthropologist must work, a position that is neither that of the European, nor that of a member of the society in competition with other members for goods and status, but somewhere in between. The day it happened to me friends came round in the evening to congratulate me on behaving like a real man at last!

Fieldworkers' diaries are an essential part of their equipment and record but they are meaningless to anyone but themselves. They are the product of a sort of suspended state between two cultures, belonging to one and active in the other; they cannot give a rounded picture of either the culture or the anthropologist, being a repository of odd bits of the personality that have nowhere else to go.

It is true that the anthropologist must strive for a certain sort of objectivity but it is the objectivity that comes from analysis rather than the supercilious objectivity of the disinterested observer that must be his aim. If he is getting a real understanding of the workings of the society he is studying, he must be involved without identifying, he must participate in the exotic culture but at all times remain a member of his own.

EPILOGUE:
In Search of Intimacy

JAMES B. WATSON

A story is told of the late Ralph Linton meeting a graduate student who, some months back from a field trip, is now at work on a dissertation. "How is the writing coming?" Professor Linton asks. "Oh, it should move along quite well," replies the student, "once I get through beating the life out of my material." The selections of this book can represent some of the life that has been suppressed, the anthropologist's own experience.

The singularity of the anthropological experience does not arise from a unique preoccupation with other times, other places. Even if such were the sole concern of anthropologists, they partly share it with historians and geographers and with certain other behavioral and biological scientists. Though anthropology has had almost entirely to itself the primitives—collectively mankind's longest-lived and so far most successful cultural experiment—the few primitives who remain are disappearing one by one. If a concern with primitives were the essential distinction of the anthropological movement among the studies of man, the movement itself must now either disappear with the last of its subjects or, perhaps like the study of the classics of Mediterranean culture, become the archeology and exegesis of a virtually closed record. Small-scale, "tribal" societies, however, quite fail to define the focus of an ever larger number of anthropologists. And these students of peasants and urbanites surely share with their "tribesmen" colleagues the enterprise of anthropology. The distinguishing characteristic must lie elsewhere.

Though but a small sample, the writings of this book bear witness to some of the anthropologist's most characteristic experience. Two main points emerge. The first is the anthropologist's purpose in wanting to cross the boundary of his culture; the second, the requirements and consequences of his doing so. More of the latter than the former fills the preceding pages, no doubt, or at least it is more explicit. Understandably so, for jointly our commission has been to describe as deliberately as possible the circumstance and detail of personal involvement and direct encounter.

The circumstance and detail must of course vary as widely as the time, place, and personnel of the encounter. As some of the selections show, it would be hard to deny the purely accidental character of much that occurs. What is surely invariable and quite unaccidental in trying to cross a cultural boundary, however, is the initial lack of identity on the other side. One starts with an identity but in crossing loses some or all of it. He becomes, if not a cipher, a question mark. To speak of "building a role" sounds much too calculating, manipulative, unrealistically managerial, as if complete control were possible in constructing one's persona. Though a role is actually built, it is grossly misleading to suggest a preconceived plan, some undeviating strategy of the anthropologist in the field. What he says and does, however, what happens to him and how he responds to it progressively define his identity among the people to whom he has attached himself. The same general process ensues, to be sure, wherever an individual is in communication with others: they read him in his words and deeds; and, depending on his skill and sensitivity, he reads back in their responses what they have read of him. On the other side of a cultural boundary the difference may in theory be only one of degree; but a different setting, unfamiliar furniture, exotic meanings for speech and act give to communication and the identity process a substantial component of ambiguity. Initially the visitor not only knows far less how to say what he wants to say to his hosts, but also has less hope of perceiving in their responses what indeed—perhaps inadvertently or unwittingly—he has managed to say to them.

A party of visiting Indians accompanied by an anthropologist who had been living for some time with them were challenged at a ceremonial. "What is she doing here?" the sponsors of the ceremony demanded. A kindly older spokesman answered for her presence. "She belong here," he reassured the resident group. "She stud'ing us." Besides being delightfully literal, this statement obviously implies considerable definition. Presumably it represents extensive communication between anthropologist and Indians. Some of the episodes recounted in this book deal with more obtrusive boundaries than this or with less well-defined anthropologists.

The progress of identification more often appears episodic than gradual or smooth. Time drags by, the visited as much as the visitor uncertain of their standing, holding involvement to a tactful minimum. Then some sudden event, perhaps awkward or outrageous for one party or for both, permits a show of sympathy, a kindness, the perception of common human strength or limitations. The statement or the response convinces all the more by its very spontaneity. Boundaries appear to heighten the effect with surprise.

Identification seems inherently more fitful when shaped by unexpected events. The actors are thrown together, after all, with little or no prior notice. Though usually it is for a relatively short period, one party, within a year or two, wishes access in some sense to the entire lifetime of the other. The doubts and seeming contradictions which arise to obstruct the mutual estimation of visitor and visited are never more effectively quelled or put right than in an

incident of poignance, of clarity—a literal moment of truth. In some instan-
taneous light, questions are answered and relationships founded beyond threat
of easy erosion. The vividness of some of the incidents of this book is, then,
no artifice of writer or editor. In essence these incidents could be multiplied
many times for they largely typify life across a cultural boundary.

A recent autobiography of Hortense Powdermaker is entitled *Stranger and
Friend*—elemental social categories indeed. Apart from the variable and often
intense local coloration, it seems likely that no large number of images nor any
more complex ones are needed to suggest the extremes of the anthropological
experience. Strange:familiar; outsider:insider; sojourner:resident; transient-
:one-of-us—these antinomies epitomize well enough the gross opposites of role
within which the field man progressively knows his hosts, they their visitor.
Though drawn from a particular folk language, the words and their meanings
appear sufficiently universal.

So the anthropologist in part makes himself in the field, in part is made by
it—a combination of accident and intent. Sometimes this process is spoken of
as a kind of immersion, at other times as the technique of participant observation. "Technique" suggests self-will and direction; "immersion" implies risk-
taking and chance. There is, no doubt, some of each in the experience of any
field anthropologist, the proportions varying with differences of personality,
purpose, and situation. Whatever the mix, the emphasis is on relating to
subjects, to people. This is not conceived primarily as a test of one's humanity,
though overtones of testing are not infrequently heard. Overtly the emphasis
is justified as the means to a high degree of intimacy in the knowledge of a
group and its ways. As surely as this purpose is a hallmark of the anthropological movement in the twentieth century, so its consequences are at the heart
of the anthropological experience. The concern is the gathering of data believed to be otherwise inaccessible: to know the language as the speakers use
it, necessarily from the speakers themselves. The technical point, then, involves
the art of rapport: accepting the validity of others' feelings, the credibility of
their values, the merit of their opinions, their worth as humans. Doing this
daily for weeks and months inescapably requires an act of intense personal
commitment. Doing it well requires sensitivity, not only logic but insight. The
comparison is often made with clinical as distinct from laboratory-experimen-
tal approaches in medicine. The goal of intimate and detailed knowledge, then,
demands the particular exposure to intimacy. It involves the costs of intimacy
—the stress of ambiguity and the confusion of an altered perspective of the self
and the world. Such a quest has so frequently motivated and guided the
anthropologist in crossing the cultural boundary as to become more than
anything else perhaps the unique characteristic of his endeavor.

The emphasis on intimacy is now possibly on the wane, in a relative if not
in an absolute sense. Anthropology, though far from any disposition to belittle
the art of gathering data at first hand, is much more than in the past concerned
with methods of analyzing data. Moralists ponder the metropolitan or imperi-

alist context of anthropology and its debts to its "clients" in improving their circumstances. If it is true that, like the day with but twenty-four hours, any enterprise has room for only so much emphasis, then emphasis must be apportioned among whatever array of concerns prevails. It may follow that the place of intimacy cannot in future remain so dominant in what anthropologists attempt to do.

The selections which comprise this book were produced and collected with no thought of arriving at what any of us might view as the future anthropology. Nor was the intention, certainly, to memorialize an older style—which few of us might agree was passing. Many things are changing, including a changing emphasis on the anthropology of living peoples and cultures. The peoples and cultures themselves are changing as well as the manner in which we try to deepen our understanding of them. But while style may be modified through new emphases, it can surely be doubted whether anthropology as a movement will soon cease its peculiar and intimate concern with peoples and their cultures. Unless we are wrong, anthropologists will continue to make it their purpose, and the anthropological experience will accordingly—like nearly all of the chapters of this book—continue to reflect the crossing of cultural boundaries in search of intimacy.

Selected Bibliography

Only a few anthropologists have written of their personal experiences, and most such accounts are of relatively recent origin. For one thing, the rigid adherence to empirical reporting has precluded the reporting of individual reactions as proper subjects in a scientific study. We are now more ready to accept, however, that there is a mutual influence between a field worker and those whom he studies. Moreover, many of us also recognize the importance of understanding the impact of the cross-cultural situation on ourselves. The editors of this volume, early in their collaborative effort, began to search the literature for documents of a personal nature. The listing which follows represents the results of this search. Although the total number of items is not large, they constitute a valuable segment of the anthropological experience.

BERREMAN, GERALD D. 1962. *Behind Many Masks.* Ithaca, N.Y.: Society for Applied Anthropology, Monograph No. 4.

BOWEN, ELENORE SMITH (LAURA BOHANNAN). 1954. *Return to Laughter.* Garden City, N.Y.: Natural History Press.

CASAGRANDE, JOSEPH H. 1960. *In The Company of Man: Twenty Portraits by Anthropologists.* New York: Harper.

CHAGNON, NAPOLEON A. 1968. *Yanomamo: The Fierce People.* New York: Holt, Rinehart and Winston.

CONDOMINAS, GEORGES. 1965. *L'Exotique est quotidien.* Paris: Plon.

DIAZ, MAY N. 1966. *Tonala: Conservatism, Responsibility and Authority in a Mexican Town.* Berkeley: University of California Press.

DOUGHTY, CHARLES M. 1926. *Travels in Arabia Deserta.* New York: Boni and Liveright.

FREILICH, MORRIS. 1970. *Marginal Natives: Anthropologists at Work.* New York: Harper.

GOLDE, PEGGY, ED. 1970. *Women in the Field.* Chicago: Aldine.

HAMMOND, PHILIP E. 1964. *Sociologists at Work: Essays on the Craft of Social Research.* New York: Basic Books.

HARRISSON, TOM. 1937. *Savage Civilization.* New York: Knopf.

HELM, JUNE. 1966. *Pioneers of American Anthropology.* Seattle: University of Washington Press.

KROEBER, THEODORA. 1961. *Ishi in Two Worlds: A Biography of the Last Wild Indian in North America.* Berkeley: University of California Press.

LÉVI- STRAUSS, CLAUDE. 1963. *Tristes Tropiques.* New York: Atheneum.

LOWIE, ROBERT H. 1959. *Robert H. Lowie, Ethnologist: A Personal Record.* Berkeley: University of California Press.

MALINOWSKI, BRONISLAW. 1922. *Argonauts of the Western Pacific.* New York: Dutton.

1967. *A Diary in the Strict Sense of the Term.* New York: Harcourt Brace Jovanovich.

MARRIOTT, ALICE. 1962. *Greener Fields.* Garden City, N.Y.: Doubleday.

MAYBURY-LEWIS, DAVID. 1965. *The Savage and the Innocent.* Cleveland and New York: World Publishing Company.

1967. *Akwe-Shavante Society.* London: Oxford University Press.

MEAD, MARGARET. 1959. *An Anthropologist at Work: Writings of Ruth Benedict.* Boston: Houghton Mifflin.

POWDERMAKER, HORTENSE. 1966. *Stranger and Friend: The Way of an Anthropologist.* New York: Norton.

READ, KENNETH E. 1965. *The High Valley.* New York: Scribner's.

SPINDLER, GEORGE G. 1970. *Being an Anthropologist: Fieldwork in Eleven Cultures.* New York: Holt, Rinehart and Winston.

VIDICH, ARTHUR, JOSEPH BENSMAN, AND MAURICE STEIN. 1964. *Reflections on Community Studies.* New York: Wiley.

WAX, ROSALIE HANKEY. 1960. "Twelve Years Later: An Analysis of Field Experience." In Richard N. Adams and Jack J. Preiss, eds., *Human Organization Research.* Homewood, Ill.: Dorsey Press.

Index of Persons Cited